RACE *of* AN

Also by John Waters

JIVING AT THE CROSSROADS

RACE
of
ANGELS

THE GENESIS OF U2

John Waters

FOURTH ESTATE · London

First published in Great Britain in 1994 by
Fourth Estate Limited
289 Westbourne Grove
London W11 2QA

A catalogue record for this book is available from the
British Library

ISBN 1–85702–210–6

Typeset by York House Typographic Ltd
Printed in Great Britain by The Bath Press Ltd, Avon

for Michael Waters
and all the other angels
we never seen

Contents

The Short Version

Forgive these tangents . . . But, you see, David was the first blues singer. As well as praising, he was there shouting at God – you know: 'Where are you when we need you?' . . . 'We're surrounded!' . . . 'Your people are starving!' . . . 'Are you *deaf*?' That type of thing. He'd be wailing, this military mind, this poet-musician with enough faith to believe he had a deal with God . . . believed it enough to get angry when it looked like He wasn't coming through. A promise he heard aged eleven when the prophet Samuel came to town and anointed him, the sheep-herder's son and harp-player, to be the next King of Israel. He can't believe it, and after a while he and everyone else forgets about it, until he gets this call from the palace – not asking him to be King or anything, but to play harp for the then-King, Saul, who had a demon and music was the only thing that would still it. Makes sense to me. Anyway, you can just imagine this young Turk waltzing through the palace doors, thinking, 'Yes *please*! No more lion-wrestling! Soon all this is gonna be mine.'

And after a few weeks, it couldn't be better. He's hangin' out with the King's son, Jonathan, trainin' with the elite of the King's army. Promotion is round the corner. It's all starting to add up. Until, one day, everything turns sour. Saul twigs the fact that this bright kid is eclipsing his own son, and maybe even *him*, in the popularity stakes, and in a demonic rage tries to knock his head off with a spear. He survives, but gets banished from the kingdom and is forced to hide out in some border-town cave, where in this blackest of black holes he pens the first psalm, a song about being abandoned by God. A blues song. It's from this moment the real journey begins. It's all there in the story of David – sex, murder, faith, doubt, imagination . . . the blues.

Bono, to the author, October 1993

Mystery and Mischief

'What do you think?' The face in front shimmies and wavers through the fog of sensation. It feels like early morning, that moment of awakening from a benign dream when you try desperately to fight the encroachment of reality and return to the colour, the warmth, the story of the dream.

'Sorry?' I am conscious of trying to fake that faraway expression – somewhere, the hope is, between rudeness and stupidity – but the knowledge of its calculation warns that it is already too late. The response I want is, 'Nothing. Forget it.' Consciousness, I fool myself, has not yet set in. If he goes away now, if the crowd encroaches, if someone else happens along, I'll be able to sink back into the balm of the dream.

'What did you think?' The change to the past tense conveys a waft of foreboding, like cold air on the toes.

'Sorry, I thought . . . I think . . . Sorry . . . I was miles away . . . Yeah, it wasn't so bad.'

So now I am wide awake in Glasgow. All around the crowd is dispersing rapidly, draining away through half a dozen different exits. I try to fix on a face here and there in the flux, searching for a clue to my own feelings. Everybody looks normal, satisfied and awake, but somehow detached from the crowd noises which gradually insinuate themselves. In these moments, you wonder how your own face looks to others. The same, you suppose. The face in front has the same look. Normality. You pan the faces nearby. A few wear expressions of professional insouciance, like they've seen it before, but only, you surmise, because they have. Most of them are smiling. Nearby on the platform in front of the mixing desk, a striking young woman dressed all in black, with black hair and what for all the world seem like black eyes, is wrapped in a tight embrace with another woman. They turn and turn, holding on as though the globe had suddenly spun wildly off its axis and they had only one another for support.

You miss too much if you stop to think.

A few minutes before, we had seen the woman's husband wrapped in a similar embrace with another young woman whom he had plucked at what seemed like random from the audience of forty thousand young Scots.

Conscious of her presence, I had found myself seeking her out at that moment. She had stood watching, as engaged, engrossed as I was myself.

Once you knew that the woman was married to this man, they seemed to make a perfect couple. He too had that look of contrasts, the jet black hair and the milky white complexion, the sure look of someone who knows something ahead of the pack.

There was a song he was singing as he danced with the woman.

> A little death
> Without mourning
> No call
> And no warning
> Baby: a dangerous idea
> That almost makes sense.

The end, which came shortly afterwards, was such a little death. With only the band's guitar player remaining on stage behind him, the black-haired singer sang the first lines of 'Can't Help Falling in Love', the bit about wise men saying that only fools rush in. Spent and hobbling now, he moved finally to follow the guitar player, who had tiptoed after the drummer and bass guitarist, from the stage. The sound system moved down a gear andan even more familiar voice took up the song. Collapsing on to his knees,the singer whispered a final word to his audience: 'Elvis is still in the building.'

With that, he bowed low and walked knowingly to the steps. The banks of television screens which have sought for the past two hours to dominate and dwarf the band are quiet now. The King sings – as though alive – the song that, as the US writer Greil Marcus so memorably wrote of it, made you feel that his capacity for affection was all but superhuman.

It is a moment of strange glory, homage and humility, but its power seems to go beyond this. It is the moment that plunges you deep into the bosom of the dream from which you do not want to awake. You want this song to go on forever. Why? After all, the band you came to see have left the building. Is it because U2 have disappeared and in their place is the reason they exist? Could that possibly be right? What does it mean and why does it make you feel as it does?

Elvis is still in the building? Yes or no? Yes. You have been persuaded. That is where the magic of the moment lies.

It is a moment of surrender. I remember this black-haired singer relating in an interview a story which he'd been told by the guitarist's father, about mountain goats in the Himalayas. When the goats meet on the narrow paths on the mountain top, they risk being thrown down the mountain if they try to pass one another on the path. But instead of either reversing track or squaring up for a locking of horns, what happens is that one of the goats lies down on the ground and the other climbs over its prostrate body. Surrender, not as a gesture of defeat, but as an assertion of goathood.

This is what has happened in Glasgow, as it happened on every night of U2's 1993 Zoo TV tour of Europe. In another band or artist it might have seemed twee or presumptuous. From U2 it seems casual to the point of understatement. What has occurred in this moment is an affirmation, a possibility of redemption out of the chaos and waste of rock 'n' roll history, a yes which resonates with the inherent yesness of the U2 ethic. What has occurred is an inversion of stardom which makes possible the belief that Elvis Presley did not die in vain, that what was real about him, his capacity to touch and move, is still alive and still beyond compare.

For those who believe – and most of those present are believers by definition – this is manifestly no mere tribute. Nostalgia has nothing to do with it. It is a moment of symbolic transubstantiation. Five years after Elvis died, Sam Phillips, the man who had as good a claim as anyone to be the King's creator, told a gathering of faithful fans that the most important events in the history of the USA were the birth of Jesus and the birth of Elvis. For all that this might be dismissed as the statement of a distraught disciple riding for a blasphemy rap, only a fool would deny that in the cold clear air of the 1990s it is an increasingly plausible version of the history of both the USA and the USA in the world. Whether you are offended or intrigued depends on what you would like to believe.

'Elvis is still in the building' is not a sentimental assertion of dues or memories. It is not the jaded nod of a showbiz lag to the memory of a key inspiration: U2, when they began in 1976, were barely conscious of Elvis Presley, then with less than a year to live. It is simply a statement of the obvious. It is also, of course, a pledge to renew, to enhance, to keep the flame alive, to make it burn brighter, but always to acknowledge its source, to say that the loss of Elvis is not final, but, because of the richness of his legacy – not just what he did, sang, left, but of what he suggested – eternal.

This is no mere suspension of artistic domination: the band have left the theatre, go in peace to love one another. Neither is it the normal withdrawal of artistic dispensation which cheerfully concedes the nature of the mutual illusion which has just ended, agrees sheepishly to keep in touch and hands back to the audience the privilege of getting on with their lives. Where normally the audience is plunged back into reality, gets its hat and coat to go home with only the absence of noise ringing in its ears, here it has been invited to go home in the knowledge that what it has just experienced is only the beginning of what it is possible to know and experience; that there is a history stretching back through decades and beyond. The feeling is like being thrilled by a book and discovering that there are a thousand other books by the same writer.

The modesty of the gesture is, of course, at once both false and sincere. False because the line could have been uttered only in the secure knowledge that the show just ending has lived up to its own promise. Sincere in that it acknowledges an ancestry that is much more than a footnote. False in that it flirts with smugness, the notion that the show just ending has in its knowing progress tiptoed around the snares which dragged the King to his death. Sincere in that it concedes that what has occurred aspires without rancour or churlishness to being second best. The gesture, in a spirit of soulful kitsch, embraces Elvis and appropriates him, but ultimately admits that he cannot be upstaged.

What you have just been watching has been called the greatest rock 'n' roll show of the decade. Even if you have not seen the competition, you are ready to believe it. But something tells you that this is not the point. The scale of Zoo TV, its extravagiganticism, its pyrotechnicity, might suggest that its purpose is to provide added ingredients of zip and colour to the performance of an already passably impressive stage act. This is the Mother-of-All-Lightshows scenario. Consider the possibility that it is precisely the opposite.

Imagine for a moment that television is not a means of communication, rather a means for the refusal of communication. Think of U2, born at the beginning of the 1960s, from the first generation raised entirely in rooms with the television always on. Now, just over thirty years later, they stand on the stages of the world, dwarfed by banks of television screens and play a music which, as far as we can tell, comes almost entirely from inside themselves. What do you think it might mean? That they have invited their fans to an evening of television interspersed with a rendition of some of their more popular songs? It seems like a lot of trouble just for a singsong in front of the box.

Zoo TV, like the album *Achtung Baby* which gave it its texture, tone, mood and moral purpose, was partly inspired by the experience of the Gulf War of 1991, or rather by the television experience of it.

The pundits who nightly occupied our TV screens in those late winter nights of early 1991, discussing the war as though it were some kind of cosmic board game, bombarding the living rooms of the Western world with clinical insight into the psychology of the surgical strike, gave expression to what appeared to be a change in human nature which had crept up on us. This war defied all attempts to give it an absolute moral context, refusing to yield a bottom line or take us much beyond the realm of the pragmatic and the necessary. We knew only what we were being told or shown. For many of us, much of what we knew was what we *thought* we were seeing on television. But what we were watching was a war within a war within a war. First, the real war, then the propaganda war which attempted to distort the real war to the advantage of one side, and finally the TV war which appropriated both the real and the propaganda wars as though TV was what it had been about in the first place. Winning the battle of perception had become as important as winning the war.

'We had a problem after the Gulf War,' Bono, the dark spark at the heart of U2, told me in Milan in the summer of 1992. 'I mean U2 had a problem. It was very hard to write songs about what was going on in the world, to come at them head on. It was hard to accept seeing lives exploded by remote control. And songwriting as we had known it was no longer enough. The only way to deal with it was to follow the path of painters. Picasso stopped fleshing out people after the Second World War. He had to find humour. The humour becomes your only defence. I found the Gulf War thing completely absurd. I actually couldn't believe what I was seeing or hearing. I couldn't believe that I would change channels back and forth from watching cartoons to John Simpson describing a Cruise missile turning left on Main Street. I couldn't believe that I was part of this Pythonesque scenario, this madness. War in the comfort of your own home. Even better than the real thing. Watching one-channel satellite, one channel giving you the information. Can you believe it? I think that was a real influence. I really understood Guernica. I understood Joyce. I understood all the surrealists. They say that nervous breakdown is the sane response of people in insane situations, and I think that a sense of humour is our only protection right now.'

The first casualty in the Gulf War was not truth, but reality. Because of the scarcity of hard information, the coverage which comprised the war within the war within the war was much less of the war and much more of the coverage itself. In the rush to be 'first with the news', what emerged was not so much news as mere activity. A BBC reporter evaded a policeman to tell us that he had just evaded a policeman. A CNN reporter crouched under a table and told an agog world, 'Here I am crouching under a table.' Drama was the journalist putting on, or being unable to put on, a gas mask. The fact that a CNN reporter heard a noise overhead was circulated around the world as the latest news from the Gulf. Rumours, and rumours of rumours, were channelled, live and raw, on to the world's airwaves. Half-an-hour later, rumour had been elevated to fact. Not even the Elvis of media theorists, Marshall McLuhan, could have envisaged the medium becoming the message to this extent. For all we really knew, there might not have been a war on at all, but simply an enormous simulation of war on television.

But even if the 'real' war, with real blood and real death, was really happening, it dissolved into shadow-play in comparison with the propaganda war being fought on the TV screens of the world. In a sense, the 'real' war wasn't the real war at all. The true battle was for the hearts and minds of the Western viewers. We were the real target. If the war was a drama in which the allies were clearly the heroes, it didn't take us beyond the first ad break to figure out that the villains were the swarthy, mustachioed chaps. Saddam Hussein, smilingly denouncing the 'running dogs of imperialism' and promising 'the Mother of All Battles', fitted our notions of what a villain should look like.

After a decade or so of McLuhan's global village, experts and critics had begun warning about an impending meltdown in our emotional reactions as a result of watching too much television. The disease, they predicted, would be progressive. First, television would attack our attention spans, our concentration, even the human memory. At a more advanced stage, the mind, addled by television, would be incapable of retaining information for any significant period of time, but would function in much the same way as an electronic echo unit, constantly picking things up, regurgitating them once and wiping them forever. In the final stages we would find ourselves increasingly unable to distinguish between fiction and reality.

And here, perhaps, was the beginning of the TV apocalypse of which they spoke. The public stocked up with cans of beer for a night in front of the war. If in the past we watched appalling events on television under anaesthetic, this time we watched lobotomised. The remote control in our heads had switched to 'entertainment' and the efficient war managers arranged for this delusion to be uninterrupted by blood. The score was kept in the polite terminology of 'collateral damage'. All emotional responses were not so much stifled as disconnected from what we ought to know as reality. Not only did we not know what to think, we no longer knew what we should feel. Instead, we knew what we *thought* we felt, what we remembered as being the correct emotional responses to particular developments. The experience was vicarious, detached. We recognised the motions, we knew the words to articulate our responses, but we felt nothing: all emotional values had been extracted.

Just suppose the Gulf War was an extreme instance of something everyday: the madness of television coupling with the madness of the world in perfect synthesis – the ultimate twentieth-century experience. Suppose that the mass media, far from being a neutral conduit of communication and information, had taken the place in the world of the coloniser, which instead of subjugating us with force and insults was killing us with senselessness.

These are not new thoughts. Fears about television predated the medium itself. In his 1985 book *Amusing Ourselves to Death*, Neil Postman examines the question of whether the modern television age corresponded more closely to the nightmare vision of George Orwell's novel *1984* (published 1949) or Aldous Huxley's *Brave New World* (1932). Postman believes that Huxley got closer to the mark. 'There are two ways by which the spirit of a culture may be shrivelled,' he writes. 'In the first – the Orwellian – culture becomes a prison. In the second – the Huxleyan – culture becomes a burlesque.'

Huxley had understood, observes Postman, something Orwell had not: that a public sufficiently diverted and desensitised by technological baubles no longer has to be forced or fooled. It's no longer Us and Them, but Us and Us.

Postman, as is perhaps becoming clearer, is on the side of the apocalyptics. His argument, however, is subtly different from the orthodox pessimisms which move effortlessly towards Luddism. Big Brother does not watch us, by his choice. We watch him, by ours. What then, he asks, is to be done with a humankind happy with its zapper? 'Who,' he asks, 'is prepared to take arms against a sea of amusements?'

An old question: is it the media which induces fascination in the masses, or is it the masses which divert the media into the stream of severed images which the filmmaker Guy Debord christened 'the spectacle'? Debord fancies he has the answer: 'Often enough society's bosses declare themselves ill-served by their media employees,' he writes in his 1988 book *Comments on the Society of the Spectacle*. 'More often they blame the spectators for the common, almost bestial manner in which they indulge in the media's delights.' The 'spectacle' not merely succeeds in bringing about the subjugation it desires, but does so in a manner so ambiguous as to appear to be dominated by the choices of those who are being denied choice by virtue of being dominated.

If entertainment is the consumption of repression, television is the science of distraction. After thirty-odd years of saturation by the medium, we are only beginning to ask questions about what it does and what it is. We have tended to see television as a more refined version of earlier media, when it is something completely different. The German writer Hans Magnus Enzensberger observes in his 1988 essay 'The Zero Medium, Or, Why All Complaints about Television are Pointless' that television makes you stupid; and all current theories of the medium amount to that simple statement. Enzensberger finds such theories unsatisfying, not merely because of their high quotient of moral indignation but also because of the way they maintain a strict polarity between manipulators and manipulated. In fact, he claims, the present state of television arises precisely from an alliance between customers and suppliers, both of whom seek a sort of perfect state of 'programmelessness'. This aspiration he defines as the search for the zero medium, in which everything has finally been deprived of both content and meaning, the limits of all previous models of communication have been transcended and the 'burdens' imposed by language completely dissolved. In this medium we will have finally overcome the obsession that what is broadcast should be something rather than nothing. The zero position, he insists, is television's strength, not its weakness. The viewer switches on in order to turn off. He votes, as it were, with his on/off switch. It is akin to a form of psychic hygiene care, a method of self-brainwashing, a heroin for the mind and soul.

Another voice to advance the satanic perspectives of television is the Canadian writer and – strangely, or perhaps not – television presenter, Michael Ignatieff, who in a series of programmes, *The Three-Minute Culture*, on BBC 2 in 1989, explored the likely consequences of that culture for the human condition. Ignatieff drew a sobering picture of *homo zapiens*. But his was no stuffy impatience with the modern tendency to zap and graze gazingly in the fixed beam of the zero medium. He went on to deal with the effects of the medium on human attention spans, literacy and memory. Narrative, he recalled, is a mnemonic device, allowing us to remember meaning through time. When narrative goes, amnesia begins. It has been suggested that in the not-so-distant future we will be unable to answer the question, 'What is the human memory for?' We will have forgotten. And in this culture of amnesia, messages will be absorbed not from narrative but through repetition: pop songs, slogans, advertising, sound-bites. The result would be a society which would at most retain only a visual literacy.

In the shift from a literate to an electronic culture, the more pessimistic theories have it, a fundamental change has been unleashed in the sensibility of mankind. Part of Neil Postman's case is that television has become such an everyday aspect of our lives that we have ceased to question its ecology or symbols. Now a 'natural' phenomenon, it has become 'the background radiation of the social and intellectual universe, the all-but imperceptible residue òf the electronic big bang of a century past, so familiar and so thoroughly integrated with American culture that we no longer hear its faint hissing in the background or see the flickering grey light'.

Television, in other words, in its fragmentary treatment of information, culture and discourse, is reducing the entire world to an entertainment. 'I should go as far as to say that embedded in the surrealistic frame of a television news show is a theory of anticommunication, featuring a type of discourse that abandons logic, reason, sequence and rules of contradiction,' fumes Postman. 'In aesthetics, I believe the name given to this theory is

Dadaism; in philosophy, nihilism; in psychiatry, schizophrenia. In the parlance of the theatre it is known as vaudeville.'

Revising some of the overlooked subtleties of the work of Marshall McLuhan, Umberto Eco, in his book of essays, *Travels in Hyperreality*, reminds us that the designator of the global village was not himself an apocalyptic. McLuhan saw in the ascendancy of mass media the possibility of a new phase of history, the evolution of a New Man who would perceive the world in a different way. From here, Eco goes on to argue that since every viewer receives the message of television in a unique way, it is futile to advocate more control of the sources of television. The battle for survival, he argues, is not to be won where the communication originates, but where it arrives. This implies, he concludes, 'a guerrilla solution', which he defines as the patrol and subversion of media by other media. In the modern age, he suggests, it is the function of the 'non-industrial' forms of communication to assist in the restoration of a critical dimension where presently there is only passivity. As examples of these forms he mentions love-ins and student rallies (that particular essay was written in 1967). In another essay written sixteen years later, he didn't know how right he had been. Contemplating, a little more pessimistically, the heightened barrage of what he now calls 'the media squared', he notes despairingly: 'Power is elusive, and there is no longer any telling where the "plan" comes from. Because there is, of course, a plan, but it is no longer intentional, and therefore it can no longer be criticized with the traditional criticism of intentions.' There is no longer virtue and guilt, no longer anyone to blame – except perhaps ourselves or something inside ourselves. 'We have to start again from the beginning, asking one another what's going on.'

Somewhere between his perspicacity and his pessimism, Eco has managed to mislay the possibility he has surely glimpsed. If art, as we know it, is no longer any use, perhaps it is time we became acquainted with a new kind of art – or perhaps with an old art in a new suit. The kind of artist we are talking about would lead the subversive attack on one element of mass media from the cover of another, would be more like a guerrilla fighter, a terrorist, than a painter or poet, would explode our complacency and our weaknesses and hold the mass media to ransom while we got our senses back.

'News is the last addiction before – what?' asks Bill Gray, the lead character in *Mao II*, a novel by Don DeLillo. Gray, a novelist, is remarking on the demise of the novel as it gives way to the television-borne narrative of real-life tragedy and disaster. An apocalyptic with the ultimate in writer's block, Bill has a serious preoccupation with the usurping by terrorism and catastrophe of the role previously occupied by writers, an idea closer to the hearts of Americans than others, but rapidly becoming more plausible as the world grows to resemble a version of the USA in every possible way. Gray is obsessed with the idea that, whereas humankind's search for both narrative meaning and emotional experience was once fed by the novel, today this need is supplied by the unremitting activity being paraded across the TV screen in the form of news, to the point where 'we don't even need catastrophes, necessarily; we only need the reports and predictions and warnings'. The phenomenon Bill identifies is not so much the drift towards disaster addiction for its own sake, but the replacement, in the first instance, of fiction by reality as the principal narrative structure in the lives of human beings. Who's to say that this won't result in a sort of narrative incontinence, whereby the constant escalation of the habit will leave us immune to the meaning of human tragedy and catastrophe as anything other than entertainment and titillation? When character becomes more important than fact, current affairs becomes melodrama, and the focus of politics switches to feed the dramatic situations whereby the principal characters come alive. In the final meltdown, action is provided by those to whose murderous exploits, in order to supply the action with motivation, we ascribe a political objective.

'There's a curious knot that binds novelists and terrorists,' observes Gray. 'Years ago I used to think it was possible for a novelist to alter the inner life of a culture. Now bomb-makers and gunmen have taken that territory. They make raids on human consciousness.'

What he suggests is partly that the world has become much too serious and much too frivolous for mere novels to have the kind of impact which the intensity of their imagining deserves, but also the possibility that the human world has reached a point in its trajectory where the changes in the character of human existence now take place at a pace and in a manner exceeding the capacity of the conventional artist to imagine or represent them. The instant coverage of war and terrorism by television renders the writer breathless with wordlessness.

Moreover, the writer himself falls prey to the very forces which make him irrelevant. He becomes, for example, famous. In a world ruled by greed, lust, fear, competition, consumption, instant communication, mass marketing, hype, obsession, celebrity, commodification and – increasingly – cultural homogeneity, art and culture have been cut adrift, reduced to spectacle, diversion, entertainment. The difficulty that popular culture has always had with being taken seriously as a channel of intense experience increasingly afflicts 'real' or 'high' art, whose practitioners become increasingly indistinguishable from 'mere' entertainers. This detachment into spectacularisation of conventional art forms increasingly erodes their reliability as carriers of true impulses, so that they, too, become subject to the disconnection which characterises the leisure activities in the mass marketplace. They lose their capacity to move. The paradox of culture-as-commodity is that the more the individual needs the balm of art to lessen the pain of everyday life, the less he or she is capable of experiencing the feeling which the art is rumoured to contain. The more elevated the artistic context, the more civilised the form, the more sublime the objective possibilities of the experience, the more likely it is that the audience will have been cut off emotionally even before the curtain lifts, the first page is turned or the gallery door gives way to the pressure of the rigid hand.

The human soul disengages from the awfulness of modern life and seeks a surrogate for experience in art. But a feeling for art is impossible without a feeling for life, so what passes for appreciation is a series of controlled intellectual responses to a narrow range of off-the-peg emotional stimuli. We feel only what the context and packaging of the product inform us is appropriate. So unsure of ourselves have we become that we allow ourselves to take from the work only what is approved by popular, that is to say elitist, agreement. The chances, then, of us finding something in art that is uniquely of ourselves are diminished, just as the things which art does still allow us to feel are of diminishing use in confronting the real world.

You fight fire with fire. A world which spills into our heads its chaos, cacophony and violence in three-minute bursts of live footage cannot be adequately represented by lyric poetry or landscape painting. It can be represented only by an art which is itself chaotic, cacophonous and violent.

If Bill Gray's fears are well-founded, and the role of the conventional artist is indeed being usurped by the terrorist with instant access to the TV screen, is it not possible that art will seek in itself a metamorphosis to meet this situation? Perhaps art and terrorism were never that far apart in the first place. 'A person sits in a room and thinks a thought and bleeds it out into the world,' muses Bill. As the metaphor is drawn closer to what we call rock 'n' roll, it dissolves into pure observation.

There was a time when rock and pop stridently asserted its right to a place at the cultural table: nowadays it doesn't have to bother. Rock 'n' roll, or whatever mutation that form has now reached, no longer has to trouble with artistic aspirations, because the world is beginning to catch up with its drift. The modern rock star is, or can be, a sort of cross between the artist and the terrorist. She or he commandeers our addiction to sensation, celebrity and trivia and provides us with images of our altered condition. Madonna makes raids on our consciousness, placing parcels in our department stores. The live career of the Sex Pistols had about it the quality of the fire and movement tactic of guerrilla warfare, the band having to play unannounced so as to keep ahead of the state forces seeking to contain their attacks. Bono makes warning calls to the White House.

Zoo TV played the media at their own game. For a decade, U2 had been the victims of a media caricature: the po-faced pomp rockers who wanted to reinvent rock 'n' roll, give God the kiss of life and save the world while they were still clocked on. With Zoo TV they created a cartoon of themselves, one which both insulated them and challenged their caricaturists. Faced with someone as patently ludicrous as Mr MacPhisto, Bono's portrayal of the Last Rock 'n' Roll Star, the media had to work hard to avoid turning it into something less, rather than more, absurd. There was no way in. Zoo TV, while appearing to create a Polaroid image of the rock 'n' roll world as seen from without, was simultaneously presenting an image of the 'real' world as seen from within. In its frivolity it was deadly serious; in its seriousness it was deadly frivolous. Designed like a mini-TV station, moving around the world through 1992 and 1993, it picked up the sonic and imagistic effluent of the modern world and recycled it back through the media which had created it. The question was: would the media turn it back into sense or would it become further diluted by meaninglessness? Meanwhile, far underneath, separately and yet not, the music went on as before.

People outside its far-flung walls always make the mistake of thinking that pop can be objectified. They want to know what young people are thinking and complain because they can't make out the words. But the statement, such as it may be, cannot be siphoned off, as in other forms of communication, from the means of saying, and the very things which most annoy the uninitiated – the noise, banality, emptiness and kitsch – are, even where unintentional, entirely appropriate and therefore meaningful. The superficiality, so to speak, is always a surface thing. Rock 'n' roll is like a Chinese puzzle: the truth is always just one layer away. The truth is to be found in both the thing itself and, deeper down in its core, in the knowledge of its existence, in the thrill of the search and the glimpse of the mystery. The truth is simultaneously in the relentless noise and nonsense, what is taken by outsiders to be mere melodic consolation, and in the dark heart of the smallest box in the puzzle. And the best any song can do is hint at the strange songs all of us have going on in our heads.

Much of the debate about high art/low art has been based on the idea that the art is contained within the form. In a world changed so utterly by the presence of mass media, this is an increasingly fatuous idea. To take your cue from opera or classical music and draw a line either between artist and audience or underneath the moment when the artist leaves the auditorium, is to miss the point by a light year. The artistic statement cannot be confined to the stage any more than to the CD or video. This, almost, is where it begins. There is also the autograph, the phantom guitar and the bedroom mirror, the pin-up, the interview, the non-interview, the bluff, the disinformation, the backlash, the frivolity, the irony, the image, the review, the righteous indignation, the political correctness, the artistic snobbery, the outrage, the sour grapes, the write-off, the comeback, the slow decline, the split, the obituary, the hagiographies, the cash-in, the rumours, the necrophilia, the final amnesia and the inevitable reincarnation. What we encounter in the modern rock 'n' roll context is a form which we have been given only tiny hints about in the work of an artist like Andy Warhol.

'We use the word rock 'n' roll,' as Bono says, 'but nobody knows what it means. We just use it to cover this contemporary noise-making. But I think that it's amazing that an eighteen-, nineteen-, twenty-year-old has access to visual images – that we've moved to working with a new canvas: colour, contrast, dissolves, rhythm, beat, melody and words. And saying, "Wow! What would Salvador Dali have done, what would Joyce have done?" '

Here is just the merest hint of what we're dealing with, a hint of a form which refuses no content, a form of rock 'n' roll which doesn't recognise the word 'only'.

Attempted on a lesser scale, by a lesser intelligence, Zoo TV would have been mere ironic commentary; here it was something more. If television is, as Hans Magnus Enzensberger says it is, the refusal, rather than the acceptance of communication, what Zoo TV did was place an obstacle course between U2 and their audience which both were challenged to overcome. The uninitiated looked to the technological dimensions of the show for its hidden message and missed the point, which is that they were missing the point. Zoo TV was, actually, the Mother of All Lightshows, but this aspect existed to retard as much as enhance the essence of the experience. Culture as showbusiness, writes Umberto Eco in *Travels in Hyperreality*, 'is not inevitably a product of theatrical society; it can also be the alternative. A way of eluding organised entertainments, in order to create order for ourselves. And bearing this in mind, keep calm. We must wait and see'.

We waited and we saw. Zoo TV was both 'organised entertainment' and yet its antithesis – manipulation and also the subversion of manipulation. Like all paradoxes, this must be sensed rather than understood. It was ultimately in the very absence of control over the medium that the audience's hunger for meaning was restored and renewed. The giant banks of TV screens before which U2 performed appeared to simulate the condition of the zero medium, flicking and zapping and cutting, but for all its apparent totality the medium was rendered powerless by virtue of being out of the audience's control. If the zapper is the syringe, this was a methadone course for the mind. U2 gave their audience the fix, the antidote and finally the vaccine. What they were attempting was a triumph of feeling over fantasy, life over numbness, surprise over boredom. They sought to utilise the access which popularity provides to subvert the process of stupefaction of which the real perpetrators accused them. They posed a challenge to the assumption that it is the purpose of what we call popular culture to prevent people understanding what is happening to them. Zoo TV, at its core, was not concerned with television at all. It was about something much more profound. A close enough definition would be the word coined by Aimé Césaire as a synonym for colonisation: 'thingification'.

But we have also been colonised by our own desires, our humanity has been waylaid by the spectacle of distraction. The 'spectacle', I should by now have pointed out, was Guy Debord's description (in his classic 1968 work *The Society of the Spectacle and Other Films*) of modern society, defining the essence of what makes that society wholly different from others gone before. As an entire generation has been raised in the embrace of the mass media spectacular, our society has been forged in a new kind of totalitarianism. History having been destroyed, 'the autocratic reign of the market economy' has 'acceded to an irresponsible sovereignty'.

The drama of Zoo TV, enacted in the midst of a spectacular simulation of the modern electronic nightmare, recreated both the modern citizen's victimhood and his imagined control. And from underneath, from the dark heart of the music, there stirred the suggestion of a way of overcoming both, a roar from the belly of the machine.

The gigantic apparatus of Zoo TV – the sound system, the enormous banks of television screens, the lighting towers, the radio masts with aircraft warning lights, the vidi-walls, the digi-walls, the dangling psychedelic Trabants, the flashing, intercutting words and images, the text-bytes – all this was what it seemed – and yet not. The medium is the message, but the message is also the message. It was a metaphor and a metaphor-within-a-metaphor. It was both accuser and defendant. It pointed a finger at itself. And it was the Mother of All Lightshows. 'The true', as Debord observes, 'is a moment of the false.'

In the modern world, entertainment is the consumption of repression, not merely a source of profit, but a means of control. Culture is reduced from self-expression to product, a palliative to numb the boredom of modern industrial society. Instead of defining her- or himself by creativity or imagination, the citizen passively acquiesces in descriptions emerging from the forms of culture which she or he 'chooses' to consume. The strands of our identities become separated and commodified and sold back to their previous owners in virtually infinite combinations. This variety creates the illusion of choice; the illusion of choice creates the delusion of individuality: if what I like makes me different, then it must also describe my me-ness. The spectacle suggests that imagination and creativity exist outside of oneself. Its power depends on convincing every single human being that, lacking the gift of self-expression, you can enrich yourself only by what you can buy. In this it conformed to the most advanced and sophisticated strategies for colonisation. But, for all its possibilities, the endless choice is strangely unfulfilling, being incapable of communicating, except by random accident, the surprise which comes from recognising oneself. And this makes it boring.

This, rather than mere adolescent petulance, is the root of the rebelliousness in modern rock 'n' roll. Although rock 'n' roll may have itself been commodified, and although only the most naive would try to suggest that it is not now among the most advanced and sophisticated elements of the spectacle's armoury, it retains in its deepest unconscious what Greil Marcus calls its 'anachronistic essence': the ability to create, perhaps endlessly, the possibility of surprise. This surprise may emerge from the irrefutable originality of a moment, as with the appearance of Elvis Presley on *The Ed Sullivan Show*, or those early records of his which possibly for the rest of time will sound as though they came from another planet. When we speak of the rock 'n' roll 'greats', we are dealing with a pantheon of artists in which the true genealogical connection is the secret ethic of surprise. 'Any musicologist', writes Greil Marcus in *Lipstick Traces: A Secret History of the Twentieth Century*, 'neatly tracing the development of the music, can tell us that rock 'n' roll did not come out of nowhere. But it sounded as if it did.'

Because a society's capacity for wakefulness is vested in the young, the health of that society is predicated on the quality of surprises which serve to keep that youthful energy awake. In the 1970s, after the break-up of the Beatles, the final agony of Elvis and the decline of the Rolling Stones, pop music, under pressure from the conditions in the marketplace in which it existed, blanded out. Because it was no longer a living culture but a range of commodities, it remained invulnerable to attacks of a merely cultural complexion. It took Malcolm McLaren, an archdeacon of the marketplace, to subvert the medium in terms it both understood and had to respect. Punk was a virus in the form of a commodity, which succeeded in changing the direction of popular music in a way no mere cultural shift could have.

Because rock 'n' roll was the main carrier of culture, expression, sexuality, identity, myth, desire and, yes, entertainment, for the young, any subversion of the complacency it facilitated amounted inevitably to a subversion of the social structures which it served. As Marcus writes in *Lipstick Traces*, 'If one could show that rock 'n' roll, by the mid-1970s ideologically empowered as the ruling exception to the humdrum conduct of social life, had become simply the shiniest cog in the established order, then a demystification of rock 'n' roll might lead to a demystification of social life.' In other words, in a three-minute culture, the best hope of redemption – for both pop and the society – might lie in the possibilities of a three-minute pop song. Hence punk, a shot in the face that was both social and sonic: the Pistols setting out to destroy the world, but beginning the campaign with an assault of the tabernacles of rock 'n' roll.

And this, in a different timeframe and form, was the agenda of Zoo TV. What it attempted was a guerrilla-strike by one medium – rock 'n' roll – against another – television. Except, as we have noted, the real target was not television at all, nor even the spectacle, but the society of the spectacle, the culture of thingification. When Umberto Eco wrote in 1967 about the possibility of a communications guerrilla warfare, he seemed to glimpse only the shadow of what he was talking about. Here was both the shadow and the thing itself.

In his book *Communication as Culture* James W. Carey reminds us that there are two separate and different notions of communication: the transmission view and the ritual view. Both have their roots in religion. The transmission view of communication is the most common in modern societies. The essence of this idea of communication, Carey maintains, 'is the transmission of signals or messages over distance for the purpose of control'. All such communication is a technological extension of transportation, which remains its central metaphor. The moral meaning of both transportation and communication was the establishment and extension of God's kingdom on earth. 'The desire to escape the boundaries of Europe,' writes Carey, 'to found new communities, to carve a New Jerusalem out of the woods of Massachusetts, were primary motives behind the unprecedented movement of white European civilisation over virtually the entire globe.'

The ritual view of communication is also a religious concept, albeit a much older one. Its purpose is not the imparting of information, but the representation of common beliefs. It is no accident that the word 'common' is the root of the word 'communication'. Ritualistic communication is rooted in the idea that society is the sum of its members rather than the subject of its rulers. 'It derives', Carey elaborates, 'from a view of religion that downplays the role of the sermon, the instruction and admonition, in order to highlight the role of the prayer, the chant, and the ceremony.'

A way of seeing Zoo TV is as a duel between these two forms of communication – the transmission view, represented by the gee-whiz paraphernalia, the technological distraction; and the ritual view, represented by the music. In the middle is U2, on both sides in a sense, but not by choice. The band's heart lies with the music, but it must fight for it anew every night.

The meaning which U2 have for their fans, and the feeling which that meaning has created, are mysterious things. Truly, they are 'secrets', which belong to each individual fan, but which add up to something a little puzzling for those who are not privy to the 'secret'.

'It is the business of fiction', writes Flannery O'Connor in *The Teaching of Literature*, 'to embody mystery through manners, and mystery is a great embarrassment to the modern mind.' Rock 'n' roll, says Bono, is about 'mystery and mischief' – it must seek to embody mystery through a medium which contradicts it and denies its existence, to the great relief of that embarrassed modern mind. It is the trickiest tightrope imaginable. The mystery, writes O'Connor, is 'the mystery of our position on earth, and the manners are those conventions which, in the hands of the artist, reveal that central mystery'. The mystery is the same; the manners are no longer what they seem. In a world dominated by mischief and bad manners, we need new filters to glimpse the secret. Out of this idea grew The Fly, MacPhisto, the feint, the limbo-dancer, the sly grin that hides the true feeling but is still itself an aspect of the truth. The new orthodoxy about U2 is that they used to be po-faced and boring and always talking about God, but not, the story goes, anymore. When *Achtung Baby* came out in 1992, we critics condescended to congratulate them for putting behind them all that messianic zeal and embarrassing earnestness – it was, after all, (only) rock 'n' roll. Actually, with *Achtung Baby* U2 renewed both their *soul* and their *coat*. The casual observer saw only the change of outer garment, which is why so many of their previous calumniators remarked on the grace with which U2 now wore the sequinned cloak of showbiz. 'Lightening up', they liked to call it. But the true U2 fans knew that inside this glitzy package was the same bleeding heart. Part of the mischief ethic is the capacity to not give a toss while caring with an intensity that risks burning out your heart valves.

'I don't see it in those terms; you're right,' Bono, the chief mischief-maker in the U2 collective obliged when I sought his reassurance in the months after the release of *Achtung Baby*. 'I see a freedom there that wasn't there before. That's all. And I feel free to be *all* the people that I am. And that's one of the things we explored on the Zoo TV tour – the different personae that we all are. Because we like to cartoon our rock 'n' roll stars. You have the Bad Guy. You have your Badass. You have your Sex Machine. You've got your Mystic. You have "I like him 'cause he's that". And it's really a very childish way of looking at people. Mick Jagger's a loudmouth! Cartooning. And I realised I was being cartooned, and corralled into an idea that people had about me. And I said, well hold on a second, I have many other, even contradictory personalities to this one that's receiving so much attention. So I thought that maybe I should – as well as just write them through, which I had always been doing, and it's there in the work, it's just it was ignored, I'd better find a really strong expression – I'd better find an even bigger cartoon than the one they've sketched. So I created other characters. And one of them is a megalomaniac, an egomaniac, who works at a sort of evangelical fervour. Another is a more subterranean character, a more low-life character. Edge has this joke, "Ah yeah, Bono – he's a nice bunch of guys", and it's a little sideswipe at me, but I have no problem with that.'

Zoo TV divided naturally into three metaphysical parts: irony, soul and cabaret. This is how we will explain it afterwards. But the division suggests itself as not for its own sake, for the sake of coherence or mood, but rather the opposite. The division is superficial, being mainly at the level of transmission. The ritual is unified by the personality of the music. The Zoo TV show suggested the essence of rock 'n' roll performance, taking the various strands of the genre and winding them together, but in a manner conveying confusion rather than conclusion, further questions rather than a neat ending. The real drama was happening at a deeper level.

Zoo TV was a gigantic mobile in which the multifarious parts sought fruitful collision. At stake was neither medium nor message but the chances of meaning against both, heroic struggle between the two forms of communication: Christians versus lions.

The Zoo TV show began with the frenetic drumming of the boy Nazi from Leni Riefenstahl's long-suppressed propaganda film *Triumph of the Will*, creating the mood for the first part of the set, dominated by the black, inscrutable character of The Fly, the tart, spurned lover and ironic prophet who enacts a black parody of rock 'n' roll bluster to the music from *Achtung Baby*. At the beginning, and it seems by design, the band appeared dwarfed by the technology and at sea from one another. There were moments in the first quarter-hour when you wondered if those who had enthused about this show had been looking in the right places. The music was great, you averred, and the performance engaging, but the connection which, even in their leadenest moments, U2 have rarely lacked, was elusive and shy. Magic is a fragile thing, and technology serves to magnify both faintness and strength.

But as the ritual unfolded, the magic seeped through. The threefold division made for potent collision. The broad, earnest strides of the earlier U2 were mixed in with the strutting, mincing and knowing winks of their post-glasnost incarnation. The centrepiece of the set was the old, soulful, swaggering U2, pumping the previous decade's worth of music anew with life and soul. Under the glare of the lights and the massed banks of TV screens, Bono tripped, prowled and crawled through the wreckage of the heart he shared with his audience, like a crying child in a floodlit waterfall.

The words and images of the absurd world of alleged reality marked time and provided ironic counterpoint to the whispered screams which told of the U2 'secret' which everybody 'knew'.

A moment of breathtaking magic occurred when Bono eked out a faltering duet of Lou Reed's 'Satellite of Love' with the pre-recorded image of its author flickering on the high screen, a piece of synthetic soul that drew together the diverse ingredients of mystery and mischief, transmission and ritual, distance and intimacy, hot and cool.

This moment provided sustenance and courage for the coming satellite link up with Sarajevo, when the American DJ Bill Carter came on to give his nightly report on the situation in the besieged East European city. Carter brought a different 'guest' with him each night, sometimes a Bosnian artist, sometimes a writer, sometimes a friend. The exchanges were, invariably, taut and awkward. But, out of the fractured exchanges which teetered always between the twin minefields of slick and schlock, there rang out an ice-cold chord that sounded real and therefore was. The guest on the night I saw the band in Glasgow was a woman, a Bosnian art critic, who stated matter-of-factly that the people of Sarajevo, too, used to listen to music, but now 'all we hear is the cry of a wounded people'. Bono muttered apologetically about calling them from the midst of 'our little fantasy world' and ended, 'We are ashamed to be Europeans tonight.'

It was this part of the show that drew the band most criticism in Britain in the late summer of 1993. Some critics thought it embarrassing; others thought it awkward; a few thought it exploitative. The mistake they all made was to think rather than simply feel. There is a problem with critics – even the good ones – and U2, in that, unless by a freakish accident, they tend not to be fans of the band. That is not to say that they dislike the band (fandom is not a question of likes and dislikes). But unless you are prepared to enter into the sacred ritual in which the secret becomes visible, it is impossible to judge a U2 performance from the same perspective as a true fan. You end up, then, discussing sounds, images, arrangements, structures, in isolation from the ritual which is their sum. It is in this whole that the true music resides.

The meaning of the gesture to Sarajevo can be understood only from a position of openness and goodwill. It was a gesture of solidarity which is founded on the belief that the cries of the victims are the voice of God. To suggest that this is an inappropriate statement for a rock 'n' roll concert is to utterly misunderstand the point of what this band is about; if U2 saw it the way the critics said they ought to, there would be no U2. Bono's words across the continent were no feeble apology for the impotence of rock 'n' roll, but an insistence on limiting that impotence as much as possible.

21

The statement it makes is also part of the whole, of the assault on the exterior reality by the mystery within. Part of the dramatised struggle with the power of television is to reappropriate its devices to the service of the angels. Thus, what for the true critic is 'awkward' or 'embarrassing' is for the fan a glimpse of the mystery. And what is a bold strike against the thingification of human suffering by politics and television is perceived as exploitative by those who see only the surface, and insist on thinking beyond the point where thought can be of any use.

It was Mr MacPhisto who came on for the encore, all glitter and mischief, welcoming us to the cabaret. This was the moment of most dangerous ambiguity, which unbelievers were wont to mistake for the moment of truth, the final ironic realisation.

The cabaret is a place where the human spirit is either renewed or dissipated, a place of resolution or capitulation. It can be a place of surrender in the sense of giving up or a surrender in the sense in which U2 use the word: of bending the spirit in a wise way. In *Lipstick Traces*, Greil Marcus asks the question: 'Is the cabaret a place where the spirit of negation is born, or is it where that spirit goes to die?'

Our conventional idea of the cabaret is of a place where old lags, such as our Mr MacPhisto appears to be, retire to die. It is the place where Elvis went to be killed off by the small desires of his public. But Bono located MacPhisto in this sensory Las Vegas only to assume him into heaven. The beginning of the encore section flirted with danger and misunderstanding. MacPhisto's 'Desire' was a camped-down pretence of everything the song was meant to question. But, as though cleansed of his sins by an irrational compassion, MacPhisto dissolved after a song, a phone call and a few bad gags, and in his place was the 'new' Bono who performed that last three songs, 'Ultra Violet (Light My Way)', 'With or Without You' and 'Love is Blindness', as though it was the end of the world after all. If he were as sad and redundant as we had been led to believe, MacPhisto could as much sing a song like 'Love is Blindness' as I could play the guitar part of 'Bullet the Blue Sky': 'Love is drowning/In a deep well/All the secrets/And no one to tell.'

Bono had merged back into MacPhisto and brought mystery and mischief together under one skin. The traditional cigarette lighters peppered the arena with the light of ten thousand secrets. This was the final realisation of shared beliefs and a common faith, a moment of redemption in which the cabaret was transformed from a place in which people are thingified, laughed at, pitied and pushed out of history into a place where, as Marcus suggests, things can be said 'with more clarity and more mystery than what is said anywhere else'.

This is the meaning of the singing of 'I Can't Help (Falling in Love with You)'. Bono, aka MacPhisto, reached across the ravine to the place where the spirit was last seen alive, dragged him from the jaws of shlockiness and miscast myth and set his spirit free. U2, the only band in the world fit to kiss The King's feet, did just that. And then they lay on the ground to allow him pass along the path. It is a moment of several reconciliations: U2 with Elvis, the audience with MacPhisto, Elvis with Elvis, U2 with themselves and what they had set out to be. What else could you do, if you knew what you had witnessed, but throw your arms around the nearest human being?

CHAPTER ONE

Echo

The first U2 record to take my breath away was 'A Day Without Me', a single released in the late summer of 1980. I'd heard a few of their earlier songs on the radio – 'Stories for Boys', '11 o'clock Tick-Tock' – and thought them interesting but nothing special. Some of the songs suggested something big and interesting, but the shadow of others undermined this feeling and made it seem implausible. The music didn't appear to be consciously doing what, at another level, it hinted at. '11 O'Clock Tick-Tock' was jaggedly delicious, but its originality was in an odd way negated by 'Out of Control', which I never liked, though perhaps for the wrong reasons.

It was all either very clever or completely banal, and I denied U2 the benefit of the doubt. The trouble was that 'Out of Control' sounded indistinguishable from something that it actually was never meant to be, and was therefore sending all the wrong signals: designer revolt, amateur excess, pretence. I remember thinking it wasn't a bad sound, for an Irish band. It placed U2 in the punk camp, if a little bit on the soft, namby-pamby middle-class end. But it seemed to lack the intelligence to lead anywhere. The word 'control' was already a punk cliché, and Dublin's attempts to jump belatedly on the punk bandwagon were becoming wearisome. What we didn't need was another band suffering from a second-rate dose of the British disease. And so, for a while, U2 had an ambiguity that made them seem like their antithesis. I was missing the point. What was going on was something light years away from where I had placed it. The lack of intelligence was entirely mine. I was allowing the codes of the time to scramble the signal of the utterly new.

From the opening bars of 'A Day Without Me', the consciousness of my error hit me like a ten ton truck. Almost a decade and a half later, it has the same strange power to move and speak.

The song begins with a repeated guitar chord which contrives to sound like an echo rebounding around some unspoken chasm, multiplied and changed. And again. And again. The sound opens up a picture which, for me, is of a street backing on both sides on to mountains. Or sometimes the dark shaft of a railway tunnel suddenly lit by the frenzy of a locomotive. Better. The guitar ricochets off the smooth granite roof, the bass pads on the soft slime of the walls, and the drums shift erratically from the thud of wooden sleeper to the sharp bolt of the rail. A clean bass drum keeps the beat and holds the scene together; a scattering of drumbeats follows the guitar around. Suddenly, a rallying change in the guitar is accompanied by a sudden start in the drums, bringing a breathless expectation and at once a sense of purpose to the sound. The echo in the guitar is carried right through the song, sometimes chasing the vocal, sometimes waiting for it to catch up. The vocal, when it comes, is boyish, shrill, broken: 'Started a landslide in my ego/Look from the outside to the world I left behind.' The second line seems to come from a different place, as though itself an echo. You see the boy here, now there, now here again, talking to himself. When it gets to the punchline, the voice is in four fragments, each singing a different note for each word of the refrain: 'A. Day. Without. Me.'

I can play this song a hundred times a day without it losing a shred of its mystery. I don't know what it's 'about'. All I see is the landscape or the tunnel, which of course are not in the song at all but in my head. I've read several versions of what the song is supposed to be 'about': the effect of the suicide of a close friend, a speculation on the impact of one's own suicide. I don't dispute any of them, but somehow they are aspects of the song which I have yet to reach within the tumble and sweep of its whole. I can pluck out fragments of the lyric, but I have no idea what it is literally saying. I only know that this song represents a place, described in the reverberating guitar and the climbing bass and the tripping, tumbling drums, a place I need to go once in a while to breathe and cry. I may die not knowing what it is about, but I won't care, and not because it doesn't matter, but because it does.

Part of what the music press gives the fan is a parallel channel for understanding music, a way of talking about music without having to own up to what it means. I read an interview with The Edge in the US magazine *Musician* in which he talked about the development of the echo which began with this song and which saturated U2's first album, *Boy*. The Edge told interviewer Bill Flanagan how Bono came to a rehearsal talking about hearing 'this echo thing, like a chord repeating' in his head.

Searching for clues without wishing to learn too much, I asked Bono about it. 'I remember getting Edge an echo unit,' he said, 'and saying, "Use this, because this will get us to another place." This will get us outside of the concrete – into the abstract. I just knew that the echo unit would do that. Atmospheres – we were very interested in atmospheric music. Punk started to look incredibly limited. It seemed so . . . *rigid*, not just musically, but it started to have a rulebook and codes. And then I remember Joy Division came along, and I really related to that, because of the moods and atmosphere. And David Bowie's *Low* – that was very interesting. That's where we were. So we started to move with that thing.'

The Edge thought he might try out an echo unit and eventually found one that he could work with. The one he liked, and used on 'A Day Without Me', was a Memory Man Deluxe made by Electro-Harmonix, who made the 'cheapest and trashiest things', but always with a 'great personality', as he told Bill Flanagan. It filled out the sound, giving new life to a number of existing songs and providing an avenue into new sounds and songs. 'It gave me a whole new set of colours to use.'

This is interesting, up to a point. Music fans always like to know what techniques musicians use to achieve the sounds and shapes they make. But such information is always beside the point because the technology doesn't make the music but simply realises it. What I hear on this record is not a Memory Man Deluxe, but a magical place. As you can, if you want to, deconstruct music in terms of its genealogy, so you can break it up into its alleged technological ingredients. One of the things that makes U2 so enigmatic is that, when you attempt to deconstruct them either way, you end up with bits and pieces of knowledge, which in no way add up to the whole.

I have another explanation for 'A Day Without Me', which, though far less rational, makes at least as much sense.

Echo was a nymph, a river goddess of Greek legend, with a reputation for talkativeness. Having had her affections spurned by Narcissus, she pined away until there was nothing left but her voice, which was consigned to wander through the valleys, mountainsides and enclosed spaces of the world for the rest of time, doomed to repeat every sound that was ever made. The 'echo' is the first instance of sound being recorded and played back, a natural recording phenomenon that predates technology by almost as long as sound itself. For all I know, Electro-Harmonix, when they designed their Memory Man Deluxe echo unit, may have seen themselves as supplying a market with something cheap and trashy to make guitarists sound moderately less uninteresting. But I like to think that if only at a subconscious level, they wished to create the technological means for an obscure Greek nymph to return to life in a song.

At first, I think, I heard 'A Day Without Me' as a narcissistic cry for recognition, an indulgent fascination with the absence of the 'I' from the world. As I grow older, the song ages with me, acquiring the maturity of acceptance that comes with realising that none of us, individually, ultimately matters, but that all of us, together, must. It grows and grows. Or maybe it's me.

CHAPTER TWO

Cabaret for the Deaf

The idea of life as cabaret is embedded, consciously or otherwise, in the modern Irish mind. People around the world who have read interviews with U2 in the decade since their international breakthrough, may have occasionally been intrigued to hear one or other of the fab foursome half-jokingly shrug off the notion of fame on the grounds that to grow up in Ireland was to live with the certain knowledge that, no matter how famous you might dream of becoming, you could never be more famous than Gay Byrne.

Gay Byrne is the longest-running talkshow host in the world. On Friday nights, for eight months a year, he presents the two-hour-long *Late Late Show* on RTE television. He has been its presenter for over thirty years. But to talk about *The Late Late Show* in these terms is to invite comparisons with other talkshows and their convivial hosts.

Gay Byrne might be called the uncle of modern Ireland. He is the one to whom we run for comfort or arbitration, the one who seems as if he might have the answers to impossible questions. Of course, what he has is not the answers, but simply a knack of framing the questions in such a way as to suggest that the impossible might not be quite so impossible after all.

In an essay in the Irish journal *The Crane Bag* in 1984, Colm Tóibín explains *The Late Late Show* as well as it could possibly be explained to a visiting Martian. 'There is a war in Ireland,' he writes, 'which Gay Byrne has been dramatising for the past twenty years.' Tóibín is not talking about the war in the North of Ireland – though that, too, was part of the *Late Late Show* agenda – but what he calls the war 'between reality and the perception of reality, between de Valera's vision of Ireland and Patrick Kavanagh's *The Great Hunger* . . .'

To describe Ireland as divided between its spiritual founder Eamon de Valera's notion of a bucolic paradise, and Kavanagh's savage and tender poem depicting its sensual and spiritual famine is as precise and as vague as it is possible to get. But this is the blur in which *The Late Late* has thrived.

This, as Tóibín implies, could not be understood by the markers provided by other TV chat shows. 'It had worked in America; it had worked in England. But something different could be done in Ireland. The place was

28

changing fast. There was Vatican II, the Beatles' first LP, Edna O'Brien, the Programme for Economic Expansion, RTE, John F. Kennedy, The Bungalow. There was also a large and established set of beliefs which belonged to a large and established set of people. For the next twenty years, *The Late Late Show* would stage the drama of Irish life, the play between the established and the new, whose intensity was matched only in the emerging countries of the Third World. 'In no other country in Western Europe were the arguments about national life so heated, were the contrasts so stark. In no other country was curiosity so great about which way things were going to swing.'

The presenter was by turns Gay Byrne, the severe, solemn-faced prosecutor teasing out the delicate and provocative, and 'Gaybo', the campish cad with the quick quip and the glib grin. He was an interesting bunch of guys, and Marshall McLuhan would have called him cool. He manipulated the telephone like a mainline to the nation: 'Yes, line three,' and would nod and turn to the panel and say, 'Get out of that one!' His mood and that of the show were as one. As he, with the flick of an eyelid, changed roles, so did the angle of the *Late Late*'s penetration into the mind of the public.

As Tóibín observes, Gaybo had likes and dislikes rather than beliefs. The show did not exist to influence people or explain things to them. It was showbusiness. 'It was a drama called the Republic of Ireland, in five parts, with ads in between, relayed to every household in the country.'

Well, it was a *version* of that drama. It was the modernising discourse, a weekly enactment of the war between two versions of Ireland, both of whose protagonists took their correctness for granted. If the visiting Martian had decided to see *The Late Late* as a shop window of modern Ireland, he would not have gone far wrong. But, if he were the kind of Martian who had done his homework on the condition of post-colonial societies, he might have come to some interesting conclusions about what it all meant. When you look back now on the thirty-odd years of the *Late Late*, the moments which are said to stand out, the ones that are talked about and mentioned time and again in newspaper items about the show, are almost crushing in their banality. The most famous of these, The Bishop and the Nightie, is almost too ridiculous to mention. A woman said in the course of a light-hearted husband-and-wife quiz on the show that she had worn nothing on the night of her honeymoon. The country went mad. The Bishop of Clonfert preached a sermon in Loughrea, denouncing *The Late Late* as immoral and requesting his flock not to watch the show again. The newspapers carried the story as their lead on Sunday and Monday, complete with editorial comment. By Monday, it seemed, the incident had occasioned mass outrage in the streets, despite attracting only three calls on the night of the broadcast, two of which were complaints that the game was an idea copied from another television network. 'On Sunday,' writes Gay Byrne in his autobiography *To Whom it Concerns*, 'after the publication of the story in the newspapers, people all over the country tumbled to the fact that the programme which they had thought was all right the previous night was in fact filthy and pornographic and objectionable, presumably because they had been told so by the bishop.' Mrs Fox, the hapless woman at the centre of the 'controversy', reacted like this: 'When I was asked what kind of nightie I wore I replied "none" just to be sporting, and then added "white". It's just too ridiculous for words for anyone to find it in any way objectionable.'

If our visiting Martian had been genned-up on his Freud, perhaps the word 'repression', or the word 'psychosis', might have tripped readily to this tongue. For what he was observing was surely no less than the return of the repressed, the residue of a psychic trauma seeking to escape into the light. Perhaps our visitor might have reflected on the significance of the fact that the country he was visiting had, only a generation before, emerged from a period of trauma stretching back almost a thousand years.

This trauma, as Freud notes, 'is on watch constantly for an opportunity to make itself known and it soon comes back into consciousness, but in a disguise that makes it impossible to recognise; in other words, the repressed thought is replaced in consciousness by another that acts as its surrogate, its Ersatz, and that soon surrounds itself with all the feelings of morbidity that had been supposedly averted by the repression'.

What our Martian might find himself observing was the collective catharsis of a society caught in a deep psychosis. It is a psychosis characterised by neurosis and a violence of the heart, soul and emotions, rather than by sticks and stones and bullets. The 'war' of post-1960s Ireland was characterised by the violence of one generation seeking to jam the square pegs of the present into the round holes of the past, squeezing their own antecedents till their souls quaked. 'Every age has its prototypical violence,' writes the psychologist and social theorist Ashis Nandy in *Traditions, Tyranny and Utopias*. 'The violence of our age is based not so much on religious fanaticism or tribal blood feuds, as on secular, objective, dispassionate pursuit of personal and collective interests.' Our bookish Martian friend would find things adding up.

To be a teenager anywhere in Ireland during the late 1960s and early 1970s was a strange experience. The sixties came to Ireland just about the time they were finishing everywhere else. They also came in a different concoction. The concept of peace and love which characterised the era in other Western societies was not part of the Irish experience. Whereas elsewhere the philosophy of sixties radicalism went against the grain of industrial materialism, Ireland actually took to this concept in the same embrace as it welcomed the Beatles, Georgie Best and the miniskirt. In Ireland the sixties signified freedom, but it was the freedom to have the things that other Western societies were seeking to escape.

The Irish sixties generation was engaged in a war with that of its own parents, a dialogue of the deaf which continues to this day. For those of us born too late to take part in this revolution, there was a strong sense of being superfluous to requirements until outstanding matters had been resolved. In retrospect, of course, it is possible to see that the issues could never be resolved, because, as our Martian friend will testify, they were the wrong issues. The jump-start of the sixties has now begun to seem like a short circuit.

The Irish sixties revolution, for all the chatter it provoked, was a top-down affair. The cultural identity of Ireland – whatever that might be – was up for grabs in the verbal civil war being fought on radio and television. But, for an awful lot of younger people listening, this war had the appearance of being irrelevant to their lives, of being about people other than themselves or their neighbours and friends. And so it would transpire when, as the 1980s dawned, the shadow of emigration which the sixties were supposed to have banished forever, closed in once again. Just as the other war, the Northern conflict, was talked about all the time but hardly ever impinged, so the cultural and political war of words seemed to occur between two tribes in an adjacent place. Those who would presumably inherit the Ireland which this dialogue produced hung around waiting to be told what came next. Deep down, they already felt disinherited.

But there is always at such moments, writes Nandy, an opportunity for renewal. 'Every age also probably has a cut-off point when the self-awareness of the age catches up with the organizing principles of the age, when for the first time the public consciousness begins to own up or rediscover – often through works of art or speculative thought – what the seers or the lunatics had been saying beyond the earshot of the "sane", "normal", "rational" beings who dominate the public discourse of the time.'

Nandy instances the artistic reawakening that occurred in Europe as such a response to the mindless bloodletting of the First World War. 'As the range of human violence and the role of science in that violence began to weigh on the social conscience, a number of European intellectuals woke up at about this time to the dangerous human ability to separate ideas from feelings and to pursue ideas without being burdened by feelings.' He is talking about Dada.

Dada was an international anti-art art movement founded in neutral Zürich by a group of mainly German artists taking refuge from the Great War. Zürich at that time was, somewhat ironically, both a centre for world capitalism and a refuge for artists. The original idea, formed in Zürich's cafés during 1915 and 1916, was for an international cabaret entertainment, but it grew from this into an art movement that spread throughout Europe in the next decade. Dada was a cult of negation and anarchy, as much a rejection of the spiritual chaos of the time as an attempt to create a new style of art. It was political and yet too nihilistic to become truly engaged. It arose out of a sense of alienation from capitalist rationalisation and bourgeois social mores, but also expressed a sense of disillusion with existing art preoccupations. It raised a cry of outrage against the destruction of beauty, goodness and truth by the process of industrial capitalism, now reaching its apotheosis in a raging and bloody world war.

Dada had no formal programme, the better to develop in more directions. Being both flippant and nihilistic, it defined itself as an attempt to delineate the meaningful nothing. It rejected rules and the elites whom they served. It sought to unblock conventional channels of communication and return people to a primary state of awareness. Dada averred that art was whatever you wanted it to be, and each human being was therefore his own artist. The Dadaists, it was said, sought to become as little children, cock a snook at the Establishment and at the pomposity and solemnity of Art with a capital A, and shake off the dead-weight of tradition. The Dadaists wished to shock the bourgeoisie, on whom they blamed the war. Art was both their weapon and their battlefield. Their objective was to 'express the vortex of modern life – a life of steel, fever, pride and headlong speed', and in doing so hint at something better.

In the words of one early adherent, Max Ernst, Dada was 'like a bomb'. Dada's iconoclastic rituals constructed pictures out of junk and attempted to elevate objects like urinals to the status of art objects. Visitors to one Dada exhibition in Köln were invited to smash the exhibits. Another element of Dada was the spreading of ridiculous rumours and disinformation through leaks to the press.

The Dadaists were interested in the concept of art-as-happening, borrowing what they needed from existing forms like cubism and futurism. They mocked science and efficiency and sought to undermine all existing concepts of order, including taste, education and common sense. The title 'Dada' was coined as the result of a random search through a French-German dictionary. It translated as 'hobby horse' or 'gee-gee'. The first Dada 'entertainment', Cabaret Voltaire, was held in Zürich in February 1916 and included poems, recitals, dance and music. Dada performance artists wore what were described as 'grotesque cardboard costumes', created out of random elements to illustrate the perpetual revolt of Dada, 'the despair which refuses to lose itself in despair'.

Another of the favoured devices of Dada was a development of 'the art of noise' including elements of phonetic and nonsense poetry, or 'bruitism', developed some years earlier by the futurists. The leading theorist of bruitism was Luigi Russolo, who in 1911 built what he called a noise organ to recreate 'the distracting sounds of everyday existence'. A few years later, the Dadaists resurrected some of the ideas articulated in his manifesto of 1913, creating nonsense poems by picking the cut-up words of newspaper articles out of a hat or a bag, and 'static poems' by rearranging chairs on which words had been pinned. It was also a celebration of chance, a protest against the rigidity of rationalist thought. 'Chance creation', automatic writing and 'chatter' subverted conventional understandings and also mirrored the chaos of society. The Dadaists favoured chatter rather than discourse, because this represented a more real expression of human nature and revealed the secrets of the unconscious mind.

The Dadaists also constructed 'sound poems' which were created spontaneously out of words which did not sound like any existing word in any known language. The point, in the words of Romanian artist and Dada co-founder Tristan Tzara, was to illustrate 'the struggle of the human voice with a threatening, entangling and destroying universe whose rhythmical sequence of noise is inescapable'.

Dada had an infinite set of references. It sought to encircle everything that had gone before so as to both undermine and transform. It sought to destroy tradition by reinventing it as the now. As one 1960s critic observed, 'Dada finally cut the umbilical cord that bound us to history.'

Although Dada died out as a movement in the post-war period, its fundamental impulse survived to influence the pop art of the 1960s, which in turn influenced the pop music of the Velvet Underground, David Bowie and Brian Eno. Its ideas were part of the currency of the culture which dominated the pages of rock magazines in the second half of the 1970s. Ireland, being otherwise occupied in 1916, had not experienced Dada first time around. But in the mid-1970s, it found its outlet on the north side of Dublin.

Lypton Village, the closely knit imagined community which embraced members of both the Virgin Prunes and the embryonic U2, belonged to that generation of young Irish people which had its own experience of being isolated behind the lines of a war in which it was not involved. Like the Dadaists of half a century earlier, this community sought to define a new identity for itself, creating another locus for an imagined Ireland on the fringes of a society which seemed absurd when you walked even a short distance outside. The Dublin northside area on which the two bands converged in the fictional streets of Lypton Village was the social crucible of the new Ireland. It was at the cutting edge of a Dublin expanding in several directions. The top-down sixties revolution was pushing all before it.

CHAPTER THREE

The Children of Limbo

Finglas Village, about half a mile from Cedarwood, where Paul Hewson and Fionan Hanvey grew up, had until the early 1950s been a small village in the countryside. By the time, twenty-five years later, when they had become, respectively, Bono of U2 and Gavin Friday of the Virgin Prunes, the village would be enmeshed in a tangle of Dublin's new suburban estates. The expansion began in the late 1940s with a Church of Ireland project to build a Protestant estate. When it transpired that there were not enough Protestants willing to move to such a peripheral place, the estate was thrown open to Catholics as well.

As it expanded, the area drew in an assortment of Catholics, Protestants, working-class urban dwellers moving out from the inner city, young couples from the city's flatlands and rednecks up from the country. The result was a mishmash of worlds within worlds. You crossed the road and were in a different place, with people from a different culture and background. The novelist Dermot Bolger grew up about five hundred yards away from where Bono was born, and the area provides the backdrop for his novel *The Journey Home*. The young protagonist, Hano, observes his parents and the other displaced country folk planting trees, putting down potatoes and building henhouses in their back gardens – 'in the image of their lost homeland'. Hano lives only a few streets away from his pal Shay, the son of Dubliners moved out from the inner city. 'You'd think we would share a background,' he says. 'Yet somehow we didn't. At least not then, not till later when we found we were equally dispossessed. *The children of limbo* was how Shay called us once. We came from nowhere and found we belonged nowhere else.'

The imagery of displacement permeates what literature there is of this place. Dermot Bolger's older sister, June Considine, writing in *Invisible Dublin: A Journey through Dublin's Suburbs*, recalls that when she moved there from the city in 1948, Finglas was a quiet rural village. She moved to Finglas Park, a few hundred yards from Cedarwood. Her memories were, by the time of writing in 1991, condensed into Sunday afternoon walks down Ballygall Road, now a throbbing suburban artery. 'We would walk past Craigie's land with its herd of grazing cattle while my mother gathered bunches of overhanging hawthorn blossom. The leaves cast filigrees of sun shadow before us and each rocky wall seemed to have a river trickling quietly behind it. They shimmered in the heart of every gully.'

In the coming two decades the area would be transformed into a suburban sprawl, with regimented blocks of low density housing, pebble-dashed and plastic-cladded, concrete-block walls, shopping centres and occasional square open green spaces breaking the monotony. 'The rivers', writes June Considine in her essay 'Buried Memories', 'have been buried under glass-domed shopping centres. They run silently now, neatly channelled under rows of suburban houses. A stream-lined dual carriage-way, hot with the pulse of traffic, cuts a swathe through the memories of my childhood.' This is no poetic image; it is literally true. The houses were built on top of the rivers. 'Sometime after we settled into our new home an underground tributary which had been buried beneath our estate defied its concrete grave and surfaced in a neighbour's dining room. The excitement on the street was intense as its short-lived resurrection seeped through the new furnishings and fittings. Then it was grimly channelled back beneath the foundations of our lives.'

One of the rivers, An Fionn Glas, emerged from its underground lair to flow through the village of Finglas, to which it gave its name. The name Fionn Glas – the clear stream – was coined as a reference to a nearby holy well, the Fair Rill, once famous as a cure for eye disease. In the nineteenth century, Finglas had been a health resort and minor pilgrimage place. By the 1950s, and June Considine's girlhood, the river had sold out to the opposition. 'The devil lurked between the arches of An Fionn Glas which weaved through the centre of Finglas . . . It would tease our fears and beckon us over clumps of nettles and scutch grass until we stood on the edge of the river bank. "Can you see the Devil?" we would challenge each other and tremble as we saw him wavering beneath the tangled reeds and slime-covered stones.'

By the late 1960s, the area was a hotch-potch of private and corporation estates, side by side. There was strong mistrust between the inhabitants of corporation estates and those who lived in the 'purchased houses'. A mixture of snobbery and fear of eroding house prices caused resentments to fester between the two tribes. And yet there were not merely two tribes, two classes, but dozens. Every road was a separate entity, falling into a hierarchy of snobbery and difference. As the sixties progressed, Finglas became a dirty word. Some of the newer estates changed their addresses to Ballymun; still later on they would try to change them to Glasnevin so as to escape the spread of the effects of the revolution of modern Ireland. The strategy for survival that most people were taught, Dermot Bolger remembers, 'was to not say where you were from'. By the mid-sixties the children of those first interlopers were already into their teens, and gang warfare was part of everyday reality. People who lived a few hundred yards from one another had utterly different descriptions of where they came from. To hear some of the kids from the slightly better houses up the road talk about the Finglas he knew, says Dermot Bolger, was to hear about a foreign country.

In a curious way, the fragmentation and strangeness of the area provided a microcosmic picture of the country as a whole. In the wider Ireland, for the half-generation between the sixties lot and their children, there was a sense of being born in a place which was already halfway through a transition which had taken no account of your arrival. Nowhere was this feeling as acute as at the cutting edge of the modernising revolution, on the new suburban housing estates of Ireland's pubescent cities. These were truly to be the Children of Limbo – the stillborn, unbaptised offspring of the new Ireland, banished from the heaven of the modern Republic now being articulated on the television screens.

Taking its lead from such experiments in Britain and continental Europe, the Irish government built Ireland's first tower block apartments about a mile from Finglas, in Ballymun. The complex consisted of seven sixteen-storey blocks of low-density apartments. Each block was named after a different leader of the 1916 Rising, the fiftieth anniversary of which was being celebrated around the time the towers were being erected. This was to be a showcase for the new Ireland. In the coming decades it would emerge as perhaps its single most disastrous social mistake, since the area became a centre of high unemployment, drug trafficking, crime and frequent suicides. 'I remember running around playing cowboys and indians in the fields when the Ballymun flats were being built,' said Gavin Friday a quarter-century later. 'And thinking they were brilliant, real modern, y'know, we're going to be like America! There used to be cows in the fields, and we used to pick blackberries in a place called the Blacker, which is now a heavy place, a built-up area, called Poppintree.' Within a few years, Ballymun would be an even dirtier word than Finglas. 'Not being Ballymun,' remembers Dermot Bolger. 'That was the most important thing in your life.'

'That's true,' Bono remembers. 'We didn't know what to call it. You went into Finglas, and you might be surrounded by some skins, who'd ask you where you were from – and you didn't know! We lived in this no-man's land between, I suppose, three tribes: the posher Glasnevin, then Finglas, then Ballymun. And it would be like a roll of the dice whether you said the right name. So that meant you had to change your identity in order to negotiate your way through the mêlée. And I did.'

*

Cedarwood Road, where Bono was born, is on the faultline between Finglas and Ballymun, the two roughest areas in Dublin when he was growing up. Even today, the place is uninviting, a flat ugliness punctuated by a mixture of drab and conventional houses. Dermot Bolger observes that the flatness of the place made it unsuitable for visual depiction; there was nothing to paint or draw, only flat surfaces and slow curves. To say who you were you would have to write or sing. 'I can see seven towers,' the grown up Paul Hewson would sing on the world's stages in the late 1980s. 'But I only see one way out.'

The problem with trying to define the place that U2 came out of as 'Ireland' is to do with formulating any kind of description of that place in everyday language. You write a paragraph you fancy as a brave attempt to describe some of the peripheral reality in terms which will mean something both to those who shared the place and culture, as well as to those from outside, but you end up submerged in the confusion of meanings which contaminate the most everyday signals of communication.

And so you write a paragraph about something called the 'Lemass Era'. The trouble, or at least part of it, is that even when, as we now know, we were living in the Lemass Era, retrospectively defined by the personality of the prime minister who gave it its name, we didn't know it as such at the time, any more than we had been aware of the 'de Valera Era', defined by the personality of the previous prime minister, coming to an end. The last sighs of something as contentious as the de Valera Era, defined by the stern presence of the godfather of independent Ireland, should surely have made a trace as they were breathed, and they did not. Instead, the two eras merged seamlessly, just as the supposedly incompatible parts and peoples of the island are united, at some deeper level, by a single piece of ground.

One of the things you notice, or rather don't notice, looking back on the early interviews with both the Virgin Prunes and U2, is the number of times Ireland is mentioned. For the most part, Ireland isn't mentioned at all, other than as an incidental backdrop to an unfolding drama in which the bands were engaged. The Prunes were an angry bunch, and here and there you find a sideswipe at the Catholic Church, the Gaelic Athletic Association or some other of the favourite Aunt Sallies of the time. But you are conscious, too, that their anger is directed both deeper and higher, at both the fundamental nature of the society and at the superficial characteristics of what might be any Western-style society. It might strike you that these two bands could have come out of anywhere, or at least any Western-style society; sure, they weren't Irish at all at all! It might strike you too that something is missing from this idea.

What is missing, oddly enough, is reality. What the Irishness of both bands seems at odds with is not reality, but ideological construct. If, nearly twenty years later, you construct a landscape comprising the Lemass Era, the Catholic Church and *The Late Late Show*, you are defining a collection of ideological constructs in which, in truth, nobody at all lived. Not only did U2 and the Virgin Prunes not emerge from such a place – but neither did anybody else. People describe Ireland in these terms and are then puzzled that U2, or Dermot Bolger, or whoever, don't seem to fit in. It never seems to occur to them to stop and consider how well or badly they themselves fit into the place they have just described.

When I was a teenager, I was highly aware of some of the ideological constructs which would later be used to define the period, and less aware of others. I knew about politics, about 'Dev' and Lemass, and Lynch and Cosgrave and Haughey. We didn't have a television, but I knew who Gay Byrne was. But all this had little or nothing to do with the place in which I lived, which was defined for me by home, school, church, a couple of cafés with jukeboxes and a river we crossed several times a day on the way up and down to school. Other than that we did not connect with the place in which we lived except in a vague and fractured way. We were tuned in to the sound of the outside world, now beaming in from all directions. We listened to Radio Luxembourg and John Peel, and read the British rock papers as though they had been produced down the road.

It's a bit rich, then, to expect to find signs of Ireland in a band several years younger from a place which, on the face of it at least, was even more in thrall to the outside world.

And yet I am Irish, as U2 are Irish. The outside world did not make me less Irish; it simply altered the flow of that Irishness; in ways it may even have made me more Irish, just as the fact that two members of U2, Adam Clayton and The Edge were born outside Ireland may have made the band more, rather than less, open to the true impulses of the place in which they grew. Does that make sense? A little.

While the Ireland of the ideological constructs may have had difficulty integrating with the outside world, the reality of Ireland did not. Every day it woke up and breathed in the outside world, without thinking that what it was breathing was anything other than air.

When I read about the early days of U2, there are only two elements which cause me to stop and say: *what?* The first is the fact that members of Lypton Village became born-again Christians. The second is that Gavin Friday wore dresses. The rest of it appears now as it appeared when I was reading it for the first time: normal and everyday. These two elements require special understanding of precise circumstances; the rest of the story might have happened anywhere in Ireland to people from the same generation.

If you think of Ireland in terms of ideological constructs, it is inevitable that you will imagine that a northside Dublin working-class estate has little or nothing in common with a small town in the west of Ireland. One is in urban Ireland, the other in rural Ireland, and they are divided, are they not, by distance, fashion, ideology and the inexorable force of social change? Well, no, actually. They are as likely to be united by the songs in their heads and the stream of language through their veins. Finglas village, a few hundred yards from the sprawling estates of the new urban Ireland, is still in its space in the concrete jungle, for all the world like a small rural village.

If Gavin Friday walked down a west of Ireland street in 1980 wearing a dress, he would, let's face it, have gotten stared at. His accent, when he started to speak, would have both diluted and exacerbated that initial suspicion. But in a short time, he and the locals would have broken through to one another in such a manner as to make the strangeness of his get-up melt away.

What this implies is the paradox that what we call popular culture is both powerful and fleeting, partitioning and unifying. It is what defines for us our differing identities and allows us to make some sense of what the world has done to us. And yet, below its influences, we are united by something much deeper – by irony, humour, story, idiom and smiles. Like the weather, these things unite us deep below the foundations of the ideological constructs and stitch together the cultures that on the surface seem irreconcilable. If you describe where U2 grew up as a modern industrial streetscape, and, for example, where I grew up in the west as a rural backwater, then you will go off in different directions in drawing conclusions about the course and meaning of our different experiences. But if you search deeper down, you find things that make us harder and harder to tell apart. Every human face has a nose, a mouth, two eyes, and yet no two faces are identical. We are different in our surfaces but indistinguishable in our depths.

The Virgin Prunes were about as different as it got. 'They have arguably, by their very existence,' wrote the late Peter Owens in *Hot Press* in 1982, 'done more at a stroke for the international perception of the *range* of contributions Ireland can make [to rock 'n' roll] than all of their illustrious predecessors.' Taking their inspiration from Dada, via William Burroughs, Bowie and Warhol, the Virgin Prunes became arguably the most avant-garde act in or near rock 'n' roll in the 1980s. The Prunes were shocking, primal, devilish – the grotesque, unbelievable, bizarre and unprecedented offspring of the 'new' Ireland. Their discordant bruitish sound existed in the wasteland between music and noise. Their live performances were happenings rather than mere gigs. They were chaotically theatrical, employing elaborate sets and props – the severed head of a pig, a television, a toilet bowl, the detritus of urban living – before which they acted out the themes of alienation and disaffection. Their two frontmen, Guggi and Gavin Friday, wore dresses and simulated deviant sexual practices on stage. Mark Prendergast in his history of Irish rock describes their performance of one of their creations, 'A New Form of Beauty', as 'a vicious sliding tackle on the conservatism of Irish Catholicism, lyrically and visually pissing all over religious conditioning and its effects on sexuality and spontaneous behaviour'.

The term 'virgin prunes' was Lypton Village-speak for the psychiatric patients from the nearby 'mentlar', a psychiatric hospital off Cedarwood Road, who could daily be encountered wandering around the area. Part speculation, part caricature of the patients' wrinkled countenances, the term and its incorporation as the name of one of the Lypton Village bands were as much a statement of empathy as a joke. The toothless, shabbily dressed outcasts of modern Ireland provoked a chord of recognition in the limbo of Dublin's northside. Ireland's leading shrink, the longtime chief psychiatrist in St Brendan's, Professor Ivor Browne, always maintained that mental illness could often be defined as the failure to find a place. The area around St Brendan's, Ireland's first public mental hospital in Grangegorman, had long been one of the neglected and ignored parts of the city, as though in an attempt to pretend that the hospital did not exist. 'If we look inside at the sort of people who are deposited there,' he told the writer Aodhan Madden in a 1983 interview, 'we find that it is a human warehouse not simply for the mentally ill, but for all kinds of people who are rejected and unwanted by society.' The Prunes took from the wandering souls of modern Ireland much more than their name and their dress sense: they took also a view of themselves, which in turn resulted in a mirror image of the society which had rejected them and their generation as outcasts as well.

The Prunes were never into trying to define the precise nature of their Irish roots. Taking a leaf out of the poet Patrick Kavanagh's book, they rejected the importance of nationhood and sought to place themselves in a wider context. When they went to London, they found it like an extension of home. 'The same but bigger,' Friday told Peter Owens of *Hot Press* in an interview conducted in temporary exile in London in 1982. 'We don't really see Ireland as being separate from England,' offered Dik, the guitarist brother of The Edge who had played with the earliest incarnations of the U2 collective. 'I don't see anywhere as being separate,' added Gavin. 'Ireland is there and the people there are as important as the people in Hong Kong or Belgium. All this trip of "I'm Irish" or "I'm English", it's not important. The important thing is that we get across to people what we're saying. I don't like nationalities. All I know is in Ireland it's very fucking difficult to do anything. It's not an attitude of "Fuck Ireland!". I've seen bands sucked right down the drain. We just cut off and get away and don't get involved in that.'

Peter Owens, in that interview, seemed gently incredulous that the Prunes should be able to view their native country and the narrowness of its attitudes with such equanimity. Gavin Friday pointed out that, apart from a small area of London where he hung out and where his appearance provoked little or no reaction, he was as likely to be greeted with bemusement in London as in Dublin. If you look different, he said, you get hassle everywhere. It was, noted Owens, 'a little easy to assume that the Prunes nurture within their collective bosom feelings of martyrdom, of long-suffering self-righteousness at their misfortune in having been born Dubliners, dangerously facile to impute to them anger because they could not and cannot grow and develop in their own land, or frustration that their evolution and progress has been thwarted by incomprehension and indifference at home.'

'One thing we *never* had is an Irish hang-up,' Gavin Friday told Owens. 'Ireland for us has always been on the level of the things and people we know around us, right back to Lypton Village and before. I find it insulting that you or anyone else should think that we feel bitter about being Irish or towards Ireland. It's not that at all. I look around in Dublin and see the hang-ups, the problems. The whole thing of getting on the TV; have you seen that programme where they're all on it, "I'm on the dole" (whingeing) "I'm working in a band". I just think that's pathetic – we've never, ever felt that way.'

If the Prunes had no hang-ups about Ireland, the young U2 seemed almost unaware of its existence. Their struggle was not to escape from a place, but to gain access to a way of expression. It was as though they needed some way of describing themselves amid the flatness and slow curves of suburban Ireland. Bono, when asked to describe the culture from which he emerged, begins with a single blurt of a word:

Bland. That's what I would say it was. Very bland. The bit pieces that *were* culture were falling away. The culture of my family on my mother's side, my grandparents from Cowtown, the Dub side of things, after she died even *that* started to break up. You know, the family culture – singsongs and drinking and going down to Rush, where they had a train carriage that they lived in and the family used. That seemed interesting to me. My father painting. And he sort of stopped painting around that time as well. You know, everything just seemed to come to a standstill around the same time.

It looked pretty bleak to me. It just looked like people watching the telly and going to the pub. And I just felt, 'This is not enough for me.'

That's why I think that out of that vacuum of suburbia came this junior surrealism. And as a reaction, also, to violence. And I think that maybe I was beginning to realise that surrealism *is* a reaction to violence. And that there's nothing more *real* than violence. Super-realism; surreal-*ist*. There's *nothing* more realistic than death, violence, murder. Guernica. Nervous breakdown in the face of insane circumstances. Going to war. Eighty per cent of people involved in conflict carry major psychological bruises, or whatever. And I remember violence as part of my memory of that area to me. The place I came from was bland in terms of culture, but violent in terms of skinhead culture. I didn't call that culture. I didn't think about that as culture. I was thinking about it as the thing at the end of the street. And think about where Cedarwood Road is planted – it's very interesting. It is on the border between Ballymun and Finglas, which in the early seventies were *the* heaviest areas in Dublin. We were told we were *posh*. We lived in an ordinary house and *we were posh*? So we were out on this border, and you would be in Finglas – I can remember actually being in Finglas, coming home from the youth club . . . There was four of us. And about twenty-five bootboys, skinheads running towards us. And my friend the Cocker Spaniel put his hands into his pockets and [slurred voice] goes D'yeswanna . . . figh? And, you know . . . straight down. And I remember Guggi going down, and them kicking shit out of him. I went down. Looking around – Skello was on the thirty-four bus. He saw them coming and he'd legged it. And they started kicking us. And you know this one where they pick you up and say, 'Aryealrigh'? Aryealrigh'?' And I'd say, 'Yeah, I'm all right.' And they go, 'Okay.' WHAM!!! And then, 'Leave him alone. Leave him alone. Leave him fucking alone.' 'Naw, holdonholdonholdon. Sorry. Aryealrigh'? Aryealrigh'?' WHAM!!! The HIDIN'!! I remember Guggi was throwing up on the side of the road – it was the only thing that stopped them from killin' us. And they were askin' us where we were from. And what we were thinking was: if these boys are up from Ballymun on the warpath in this area of Finglas, and we say we're from Finglas, then we're in deep shit. If we say we're from Ballymun and they're a Finglas gang . . . So we were trying to avoid the issue . . . And . . . BAM!!! Down you go again. It's a *thing*. It's still with me. You can see it in my demeanour, in my physicality. But I'll tell you who it's with much more than it's with me, and that's Gavin. The Virgin Prunes were his revenge. In fact, he got it much worse than I did, because he was very quiet, sensitive, long hair, jeans with, you know, 'Eno' written on them or something like that. And he had a better record collection as well. They really used to kick the shit out of him! He didn't know enough about violent people to fight back in the same manner. Myself and Guggi were well able. We were pretty bad. We'd grown up fighting each other. We were getting quite good at kicking the shit out of each other and whoever else. But Gavin was never up to that. So there wasn't much company for that. And you were going to *lose*!

One of the tribal forces with which the young U2 came into contact was a punk faction called the Black Catholics, from Bono's own neighbourhood, who specialised in subversive attacks on the performances of bands they disapproved of. One night, at a gig in the Baggot Inn, these defenders of the Catholic faith against the threat of 'stuck-up Protestant bastards', threw glasses at the stage, narrowly missing The Edge's head.

'I hate violence. I hate the feelings I had,' Bono remembers. 'And yet I loved it. I had to be held. I wanted to drive Guggi's car through the front door of this fucker's house. Apache Indians – just go after them. That was the way I felt. I know it's pathetic, but I remember waiting for him outside his house, and thinking, "I'll kill you." And he *knew*. It was, like, "I'm sorry. I'm *really* sorry. It'll never happen again." Because in that moment he could see that I was capable of all the ugliness I would later give out about. Violence can be a lot of fun, you know, on a dull evening. So I'm very glad Lypton Village didn't go down that route. It was a different kind of street gang. Humour was the weapon, surrealism was the route. And music. That was what we were on about.'

Paul Hewson and Fionan Hanvey, as Bono Vox and Gavin Friday, along with a third tribesman, Maurice Seezer, wrote the theme music for the Jim Sheridan film *In the Name of the Father*, a version of the Guildford Four story, released in 1994. They wrote three songs, two of which were performed by Bono and Gavin; a third was sung by Sinéad O'Connor.

The title song begins with a wailing synth lurking in the distance, a low, moaning single note, studded with a looped bodhrán beat, building, building, building, the note swirling behind like an ache. Bono's voice, when it comes, is cajolingly gentle as a cop talking a jumper down from a ledge.

Come to me
Come lie beside me, and don't deny me
Your love
Make sense of me
Walk through my doorway
Don't hide in my hallway
Oh Love! Step over
I . . . I'll follow you down
I . . . I'll follow you down

In an instant the song is transformed by the frenetic clatter of . . . an Orange marching band. The bodhrán is still there, beating, beating, but now it is joined by the throb of a Lambeg Drum and what sounds like a hundred rattling loyalist snares.

In the Name of the Father, Bono explained to me in the spring of 1994, 'is a call away from tribalism. You have this very bizarre duet between the bodhrán and the Lambeg Drum.' Tribalism is not something Bono or Gavin simply observed in the flitting pictures of news bulletins from up the road in Belfast, but was an intimate part of their childhoods in the Limboland of Dublin. 'This thing of tribes,' as Bono says, 'doesn't seem to go away.'

CHAPTER FOUR

The Unfinished Revolution

Although the punk movement provided the core of their initial inspiration, U2 were never punks. This is exactly as contradictory as it seems. An English punk made a statement about his or her own self in relation to the society at large. It was a rejection of the otherness of the society as perceived by the dissenting individual. The nature of English punk consisted of an even more extreme version of the oppression by which the society had come to exist. An Irish punk was a contradiction in terms, partly because the nature of the Irish personality is to respond to oppression with cunning, humour and docility; but also because the only statement a colonised person can make becomes a dialogue with the other within the self. The freedom to dissent, which the coloniser enjoys, does not exist for the colonised. An Irish punk could not be a real punk, because punks had to keep a straight face. The reason Irish punks had to laugh at themselves was that they knew, deep down, that ultimately you can rebel only against yourself.

The Irish for no is yes with a wink. We say yes to outsiders and no only to ourselves, to the point where it could seriously be argued that there is no such thing as Ireland at all. 'The notion "Ireland", ' writes the Irish (ha!) intellectual Declan Kiberd, 'is largely a fiction created by the rulers of England in response to specific needs at a precise moment in British history.' What this implies is that everything we see before us which we may feel disposed to label 'Irish' is in fact the consequence of the will of the coloniser or of a defensive or neurotic reaction to it. The Irish game of hurling, though rooted in Irish mythology, contains elements of hockey, imported and amended in such a way as to disguise their derivation. The puritanism of Irish Catholicism has developed more as a response to the nature of English reformism than to anything innate in the Irish personality.

There is in the colonised mind something of the demeanour of the rape victim: a knowing insouciance, an aloof suffering, the dignified superiority of the martyr. As the coloniser perceives in his subjects the weakness which defines his own superiority, so the victim's identity is entirely composed of antithetical ingredients. As the coloniser is brutal, the victim is demure. As he is strong, the victim is mild. As he is humourless, the victim is ironic. As he is male, the victim is female. As he is promiscuous, the victim is virtuous.

The colonised is everything the coloniser is not, as well as everything he is and everything he expects. His every deed is ambiguous, seeking both to assert independence and to seek the reassurance of correction.

Let us consider the possibility that rock 'n' roll is not about rebellion at all, but about a plea for reconciliation, that its anger is directed not towards condemning but towards influencing and correcting. In other words, its thrust is reformist rather than revolutionary.

Rock 'n' roll, in its purest sense, is the voice of youth – not necessarily the 'voice of the young', but of a human condition which transcends the influence of chronological age – adultism.

In 1988, at the age of twenty-eight, the sublime Morrissey confided to the rock writer Simon Reynolds that what he does is 'something quite beyond and more complicated than "adolescence" – something that hasn't been thought out yet, but shouldn't be dismissed as "adolescent" '. He would prefer, he agreed, a phrase like 'a questioning life'. The youthful aspirations which rock 'n' roll has come, however inaccurately, lamentably or inadequately, to articulate are accessible to anyone who has refused to acquiesce in the landscaping of reality that constitutes respectable adulthood in the modern world. Rock 'n' roll at its best is the slow, contorted crouchdance of the wombwisher, a low moan of protest at the unreasonableness of an alleged reality, a defiant shrug towards the absurdity and two-facedness of a grown-up world that makes most sense to the most rigid and repressed.

But so many of the contradictions and confusions about rock 'n' roll originate from the fact that it has rarely carried expression of an outright negation. Antipathy, yes. Repugnance, yes. Revulsion, definitely. But rock 'n' roll has hardly ever expressed a genuine nihilism. It does not hate adults, nor even adulthood. It has always taken an interest in the welfare of the grown-up world. Even at its best, which is to say its most petulant, it has left the door ever so slightly ajar. It sought to influence and correct, and in doing so to be recognised as having its own integrity and maturity. It was always at some level seeking approval from the adult world it sought to excoriate. Even the Sex Pistols' 'Anarchy in the UK' was a warning rather than a verdict. It was too self-regarding to be a genuine negation and was caught once too often peeking to see what kind of effect it was having. Moreover, at a profound level it actually *cared* about the society it was excoriating. It invoked the apocalypse but secretly wished for a different world. Deep in the frenzy was a whispered 'unless'. For all the surface noise and rhetoric, it sought redemption rather than destruction, to embrace rather than spurn, to purify, cleanse, expunge, yes, but ultimately to heal. It was an attempted suicide rather than a real death wish, a cry for help and attention rather than a spurning of everything. In its heart of hearts was a nobility that hungered for a better world.

U2 made the 'unless' audible and distinct. They denied the pretence of rebellion and indifference, and openly expressed their interest in a different world. They asserted the noble aspirations of rock 'n' roll in a manner that was most embarrassing to those who thought such weakness was a secret confined to their own closets. 'Our problem,' as Bono puts it, 'was not being "conscious", but being seen to be conscious – and I suppose a bit of advertising of that fact.'

A word that cropped up frequently in descriptions of U2's demeanour and outlook was 'naive'. This naiveté derived largely from the fact that they were an Irish band, suspended between the two stools of Britain and the United States. For a British band to adopt a position and attitude like this would have been unthinkably uncool. For a US band it would have been just a little too ingenuous. The kind of things U2 said would have been regarded in Britain as simple-minded and in the US as axiomatic.

British music has always lacked a certain something – depth, maybe, and certainly soul. There are exceptions, of course, like John Lennon, who drew his inspiration directly from source (and had an Irish grandfather stashed away in his ancestral cupboard – but we move ahead of ourselves). British popular music has always suffered from a style-obsessed superficiality which came to see youth culture as some kind of tangential phenomenon, a heady cocktail of fashion, youth and – at most – a merely social change. The roots of British popular music are shifting all the time, looking for a source, for something to get to grips with, a reason to believe. The American equivalent is able to draw on a rich source of roots music. Moreover, Americans have both a proprietorial interest and a stake in making this music into a rich culture. The music, therefore, has freedoms which can seem off-limits for British bands. US bands, citing black traditions, could write songs about God. British bands, at their most engaged, would rise to writing songs about politics.

The same dichotomy is mirrored even more visibly in comedy, particularly on television. Humour is not an additional element of the Irish personality, but perhaps its most defining characteristic, the flour in the mix, not the icing on top. As the poet Brendan Kennelly has observed, Ireland's lack of a tradition of classical philosophy has made humour and storytelling an everyday necessity for understanding the world. The Irish genius for self-comprehension is through anecdote, gossip and drama. We know people by the stories about them, and the funnier the better. There is perhaps a little more to it than that – being colonised forged a cunning humorousness out of the necessary duality in our heads. It is not by accident that Irish writers like James Joyce, Samuel Beckett, Patrick Kavanagh,

Oscar Wilde, Flann O'Brien were, above all, comedians in the purest sense. And yet, although this tradition has been carried on into the work of contemporary writers like Roddy Doyle and Patrick McCabe, it has singularly failed to materialise in the more modern medium of television. This may be because we are caught in the glare of the two opposing traditions beaming in from Britain and the US. In US comedy, of the kind we see in TV series like *Cheers*, or the movies of Woody Allen, the joke is always on the humanity of the individual at the mercy of God. The humour is dark, self-deprecating, psychological. British comedy, on the other hand, from Tony Hancock to *Spitting Image*, is almost entirely class-based, the jokes drawing on the nature of the relationships between the various layers of British society. Thus, although Irish literature has a vast inbuilt comic tradition, the influence of British and American television has rendered it useless to a native TV comedy sector. Because our own sense of humour was something deep within ourselves, and was the product of forces we had to deny, we were unable to isolate and scrutinise it. Even if we were disposed to imitation – which, of course, we were – the absence of a clearly defined class structure made it impossible to follow the British route. The confusion between the two signals made it difficult for us to sort out our ideas. Our aim was always at best halfway between the British and American models and, in the rational inflexible forms which television represented, we invariably missed both marks.

This might have been true of our pop music as well, and for a time it was. Many of the early Irish attempts to create rock 'n' roll were crude and imitative, confused about whether to look to Britain or the US, unsure of what they were looking for, of what exactly this medium was supposed to be about. This copyist tendency was not confined, as revisionist history would have it, to the showband scene, but characterised also the Dublin beat scene of the mid- to late 1960s. It was only with the emergence in the late sixties of musicians like Brush Shiels and Philip Lynott that Irish rock 'n' roll would begin seeking, however tentatively, a voice of its own.

U2 were born out of punk, yes, but it would be even more true to say that U2 were born out of what happened to punk. They observed both the explosion and the implosion that followed, and absorbed both as equal parts of their outlook. The Sex Pistols were in purely musical terms a revolutionary phenomenon, but anyone who supposed that this would enable them to put their rhetoric into action was thrashing up the wrong fretboard. The Pistols attempted to imply that their rage against both the British political establishment and the music industry were synonymous and interchangeable. Touched by a demon angel, they created a music which was breathtaking in its honesty and vision, but they underestimated both the Establishment's resistance and the music industry's reactionary capacity to contain the new energy on the Establishment's behalf. The seeds of punk's undoing were actually inbuilt elements of its growth and trajectory. It could hardly have been otherwise, given that the Pistols were themselves the product of the largely commercial instinct of Malcolm McLaren. Johnny Rotten's snarls were turned into product even as they emerged from between his rotting teeth.

The Sex Pistols went to number one in the charts with 'God Save the Queen', and appeared on the despised *Top of the Pops* when they released 'Pretty Vacant'. The media's initial distaste quickly turned to mock-horror and then to avuncular indulgence. Punk became both trendy and safe, because that is how it had to be. Street credibility, that elusive quality and prerequisite for success, was largely in the gift of the industry and the media. Without the funding of the record companies and attention from the media, a movement founded on an adrenalin rush rather than a slow-burning creativity would have been extinguished in its first sparks. The inbuilt paradox of all popular culture's efforts to confront society was writ larger than ever and was exacerbated by the fundamental inconsistencies – even dishonesties – of punk. If, deep down, part of what you really want is to get rich, famous and laid, you are easy meat for those who can give you all this in return for what is left of your soul.

Once the movement was safely neutered, the major labels moved in and carved up the action. After that exhilarating initial roar, every one of punk's gains became Pyrrhic victories as they occurred. Once punk was channelled, it could go nowhere but down. One generation of clapped-out rock stars was replaced by another. It would strengthen the culture of rock 'n' roll immeasurably, yes, and a few strange and troubling voices would emerge to assuage the disappointment, but the possibilities which the movement suggested, and which its creators had hinted at, were retrospectively declared stillborn.

Yet the most 'revolutionary' aspect of punk, the liberation suggested by the idea that you could make music without being a musical virtuoso, would never be lost again. Sitting in Dublin, the young U2 were part of it all, and yet not. They were in touch with the energy of punk, and the latest intelligence about its progress, but were hidebound by neither its diktats or its limits. They could, if they wished, be *à la carte* punks, with the luxury of picking and mixing the bits they wanted. Those who do not suffer from the condition are wont to underestimate the desire of the colonised man to imitate that which he believes himself incapable of matching. There were a good few Irish bands of this period who, for all they decried the rigid imitation of the showbands, began, inevitably, copying what they could see and hear from across the Irish Sea. These would share a wake with Sid Vicious.

By its very nature rock 'n' roll is incapable of expressing absolute negation. It can articulate joy, anger, melancholy, fear, disgust, rage, but it depends for its life on an energy which is antithetical to apathy. You can paint a nihilistic painting and in doing so conceal the conviction of its art in technique. A writer can, by a prudent asceticism of language, suggest an intent in keeping with the disdain of his ethic. Both artists can, by simply staying out of the way, allow the legend of their unworldliness to gain ground even as their works accumulate value. But such luxurious disconnections between artist and art are denied to the rock 'n' roller, whose technique and statement are not so easily distinguished.

The very noise of punk denied its stated intentions. The music invites the thud of a broom-handle on the ceiling. Once you hit that chord, you indicate an interest in proceedings in the world you inhabit. You *do* care, after all. You give expression to the lament of the human soul in all its clamour for sense and peace. You express, moreover, an implicit plea for immortality. I exist, he says, therefore I matter. Listen! Look at me! Move over and let me up! In all this there is an implicit, if paradoxical, validation of all that the music's content purports to deny. It was observed at the time that by stating 'No Future', the Pistols were *creating* one. 'Deliberately masking their feelings – for fear of being pinned down, and because they were the product of a movement that denied feeling,' Jon Savage writes in *England's Dreaming*, 'the Sex Pistols offered optimism disguised as cynicism, and unleashed powerful emotions from behind a blank, sarcastic façade.'

Nihilism is not merely destructive – it is indifferent. It implies the control of knowing that nothing matters and the insouciance of not caring even if it did. It is beyond anger, contempt, hate, despair. Punk was not nihilistic. A negation, yes, but that's different. 'Negation is not nihilism,' wrote Greil Marcus in *Artforum* in 1983. 'Nihilism is the belief in nothing and the wish to become nothing. Negation is the act that would make it self-evident that the world is not as it seems.' Only when the statement is 'so implicitly complete that it leaves open the possibility that the world may be nothing' does nihilism arise.

The core idea of punk was a positive value: empowerment. It was an assertion of control over one's own existence, and of connectedness with others of like mind, anywhere, everywhere. It was a way into the world for those who had no other.

There was a profound connection, as has been pointed out by Greil Marcus, Jon Savage and others who have written about the meaning of punk, between British punk, as represented by the Sex Pistols, and the uprising by the students of Paris in May 1968. Paris represented the earliest dawning of consciousness by that first generation raised in the society of the spectacle and moulded to its laws. Punk was the consequence of the message seeping through to their younger brothers and sisters, in whom the disconnection was even more complete, and who, moreover, were caught now in the creeping seventies hangover. In a sense, punk, because it was a media revolution, was a more coherent expression than the sixties' brand of rebelliousness. Punks were the children of people who saw media as simply a modern adjunct to their previous lives – a facility, a service, a tool. Their offspring saw a different world, peopled by a new kind of human being, in which media functioned with all the intimacy of the weather, causing the debilitating numbness of an existential influenza.

There is a beautiful quote from Malcolm McLaren in Jon Savage's *England's Dreaming*, in which the Pistols' manager relates what first attracted him to the literature of the Situationists International, the radical anarchistic group which had provided much of the inspiration and rhetoric for the Paris uprising. The SI was founded in Italy in 1957 at a conference of some of Europe's leading artists, and developed a philosophy based on that of the earlier Lettrist International of the 1920s, in which art was to be rescued from the limitations of form and placed in a wider, situational context in society. He had heard about the Situationists, McLaren told Savage, from the radical milieu of the time, but when he got around to the literature, it was the colours and design that attracted him to it. 'You got these beautiful magazines with reflecting covers in various colours: gold, green, mauve. The text was in French: you tried to read it, but it was so difficult. Just when you were getting bored, there was always these wonderful pictures and they broke the whole thing up. They were what I bought them for: not the theory.'

Here we have one of the first generation of spectacular souls giving expression to the very condition which Guy Debord had diagnosed. And yet, McLaren, as we know, would be the inspirational source of the coming revolt from the very belly of that spectacularity. As though in keeping with the times, he would be inspired to do so not by the ideas of rebellion but by images, colours, textures, looks. Already the destruction of language predicted by Debord had progressed sufficiently for the ideas to be incapable of jumping the gap. But the impulse was seeking a new form, and the possibility of revolt – as resilient, perhaps, as ever – was finding another conduit, a parallel medium of communication.

Punk was only marginally about music; primarily it was about engagement with the forces of oppression, which meant with the media, with the establishment, with the murderers of language and their masters, the world's owners. Punk understood the media in a way previous generations of rebellious youth had not. It lambasted the society of the spectacle through the very channels of the spectacle itself. Punk did to the world what the world had done to the generation now answering back. It was a spectacle within the spectacle, an appalling, disorienting convex mirror image of the appalling, disorienting reality called normality. The Sex Pistols tapped into something deeply disturbed and vengeful in the English psyche. McLaren may have been the inspiration, but Johnny Rotten was the wellspring of punk's torrent of rage.

It is a moot point whether Malcolm McLaren 'found' Johnny Rotten or Johnny Rotten found Malcolm McLaren. But it was undoubtedly McLaren who functioned as both the funnel and the filter of the Sex Pistols ethic, feeding them a diet of fashion, attitude, diluted radicalism, pop context and fetishist symbolism. A reasonable description of punk would be to say that it was an attempt to recreate in the visible, external world the chaos that the external world had enacted inside the human being. It was a form of revenge, but also a cry for help. It began as an attack on rock 'n' roll and then occupied the body it had vanquished to attack the greater world. Punk fought the law, but the law won. It began as an onslaught on entertainment as the consumption of repression and ended up as a new form of entertainment. Punk did not conquer the establishment; the establishment assimilated and thereby defused it. But it was an honourable try, which enabled the compilation of new maps of the enemy's positions.

In Britain, there was a manifest connection between punk and politics. It grew like a hothouse plant in the warm, claustrophobic summer of 1976, amid the sweltering heat, recessionary paranoia, unstable government and collapsing confidence. It was as much an alienated response to a preoccupation with a disappearing past as to the uncertainty of an already bankrupted future. The movement's use of Nazi imagery in particular sought to rub the noses of the previous generation in their own smugness about the outcome of a war that had been over now for thirty years, but was still talked about as the nation's finest hour. Emerging from what was by comparison a modest decay, punk whispered a gleeful promise of the moral bankruptcy of Thatcher's Britain in the 1980s.

And yet, the Sex Pistols, being both pioneers and bridge burners, were different from anything else that travelled under the punk banner. The Pistols didn't care, then they did, then they didn't – their motivation concealed under layer upon layer of ambiguity. They led the movement and yet were almost too clever and self-regarding to be its truest expression. The dichotomy centred on both the schism between those who perceived punk as a social and political phenomenon and those who saw it as pure artistic statement, and also on the issue of caring and not caring. The Pistols were closer to nihilism than other bands – in intent if not in consequence. For all the calculation of their creation, their reality was without purpose in terms of the world in which they existed. At best it could define them as an extreme form of absurd anarchistic theatre. The Clash, on the other hand, being more overtly political, seemed like a reasonable enough bunch of guys. They were more well-meaning, more visibly connected andcommitted to the world which they condemned. Theirs was a social, almost agit-prop form of protest, but one which by its intelligence and concern about the shape of the world was almost old-fashioned in its anti-spectacularity. Both the Pistols and the Clash started out saying 'no'; but the Clash's 'no' quickly displayed itself as a 'no . . . but' – an 'unless'.

When we talk now about punk, we must concede that we are talking about something that never quite succeeded in happening on its own terms. The moment the Pistols impaled themselves on the spike of TV presenter Bill Grundy's contempt for them was the moment when the energy was short-circuited. At that point the spectacle took over. The nightmare which punk was meant to be was transformed by the tabloid culture into a manageable fantasy. The point was missed or mislaid as the energy was transmogrified into a merely grotesque precociousness. From then on it would be almost impossible to retain a coherent memory of the true impulse, now buried under the slogans and the outrage and the usurped look. Before long, punk became indistinguishable from mere bad manners. The energy was steered towards more conventional forms of protest, which had only become conventional because they had already failed. Punk was made to look like a slightly more distorted, grotesque, extreme form of youth rebelliousness, rather than as the something-completely-different it might have been. Bands which might have developed out of the punk energy were constrained by the prevailing definitions and by public expectations. Punk had been forged in the tabloid mould and could not escape from the shape it had been given. The new post-punk orthodoxies were, in their own ways, as hampering as the old. The revolution was left unfinished and, in a sense, unfinishable.

An understanding of all this is perceptible in the early U2 rejections of the precise form of rebellion that punk represented, and their admission of its critical role in their formation. Most of their early explanations for this rejection are unconvincing. U2 weren't rebellious, they said themselves, because they 'had nothing to rebel against'. So, they were nice middle-class kiddies, happy in their nappies . . . ? We know that isn't true. But we know, too, that the nature of their disenchantment was deeper and more complex than the models being articulated by British bands in the pages of the NME. They knew, or felt, that such descriptions of restlessness didn't fit with their own. Yet this did not seem to still the fury that Bono felt, which sought expression but could not find any words for itself in the incoming, surrounding rock 'n' roll culture. It was as if they were looking for a cure for something they did not know was afflicting them. They didn't know what they were looking for because they didn't know why they needed it. And the only hope of attempting an explanation was within the idiom of a culture which had few or no reference points of its own. Where the British punk initiative had been a social energy expressing itself as fashion and attitude, the U2/Virgin Prunes phenomenon seems to have been motivated by a more fundamental alienation seeking expression in music and performance.

Punk might well have liberated a new generation, but most of the possible Irish contenders shattered on the rocks of imitation before they could get afloat. U2 seemed to understand the pitfalls without being able to articulate them fully. The music they were attracted to was music that seemed to speak *for* them rather than *to* or *at* them. Coming initially from Britain, it was music they had in common with others of their generation, but they alone seemed to comprehend that, while they had been bequeathed the language, it was up to them to scramble about and search for the words and sounds. They connected to the international movement that was punk in a manner that was utterly unique to Irish circumstances.

This can be seen in early attempts of the band to place themselves in the context of post-punk British rock, and yet to emphasise their differences. 'A lot of punks reject us,' Bono, for example, was telling Chris Westwood of *Record Mirror* in 1979. 'And of course, as it is here, a lot of hippies reject us because we're new. So we have this peculiar audience, this cross section. That's why the name U2 is ambiguous; it's in between, like a tightrope we're treading.' In a late-seventies Dublin caught between the glares of different cultural headlights, the young U2 had to learn the arts of tiptoeing and limbo-dancing very early on. But they also had to rummage in the thicket of a half-alien culture for terms with which to explain a much bigger project than those terminologies were capable of articulating. This ambition implied a completion of the revolution which punk had started, though not in a form which punks would recognise.

Rock music in Dublin in the early 1970s had been even more moribund than elsewhere. A hundred bad blues bands rent the air once darkness fell. We were invited to admire the mystique, the speed, the proficiency, while feeling nothing. We could neither admit it left us cold, still less acknowledge that there was anything else it might aspire to.

'You just had to hear Wire,' says Bono, 'to know that that wasn't important. You just had to hear the Radiators from Space. You see, that is *the* moment. It happened at the right moment. Two years previous, three years previous, you'd say, "This won't work." But at that moment it was happening. It was like the carousel slowed down just enough for us to jump on.'

Even the limited ambitions of their precursors were to prove invaluable to the young U2. 'What I think really made punk happen for us in Ireland,' says Adam Clayton, 'was the fact that the Boomtown Rats had done a deal. I think that was very significant. At the time, Thin Lizzy were on the crest of a wave. The Radiators from Space had released records and had an English record deal. So suddenly it didn't seem so strange to be in Ireland. And if you look at the effects of punk as a London movement, there were very few cultures that could actually buy into that. No one in Europe could get on that particular bandwagon. And I think in Ireland we're quite lucky because we have a legitimacy of plugging into what's happening in England. We also have a legitimacy of plugging into what's happening in America, because we speak English. So we started to look to English music, and then, realising that an awful lot of those punk bands had nothing to offer, we looked into the New York scene to bands like Television and Patti Smith, which were much more of a culture, which was sort of where we were coming from to begin with anyway. Whereas with a lot of the English bands, it was just so local and so specific that it didn't really make any sense. You know – they'd be on *Top of the Pops* one week and gone after that.'

When they started to perform, U2 were a curiosity and a conundrum. There were other bands already into post-punk mode; as well as the Radiators, there were the cautiously futuristic D. C. Nein, the rhythm and fun of Rocky de Valera and the Gravediggers, the pure pop of the Lookalikes, the guitar-based rhythm and blues of the Bogey Boys. In terms of what then seemed novelty, there were near-neighbours the Atrix, purveying much the kind of theatrical post-punk rock their name suggested, and of course the Virgin Prunes. There was considerable variety, but, with the exception of a few Northern Irish bands, there was very little discretion or discernment in evidence. U2 were going against the grain of bands that might have been called their contemporaries. The sets of references in use seemed unable to understand or explain them. I remember watching an end-of-year TV pop roundup at which the Bogey Boys pipped U2 as the panel's best bet for 1980. Looking back now, it cannot be said that U2 were simply one of a collection of contenders. Only the Blades might have seemed to contain anything like the same level of intelligence, and they were eminently comprehensible as a top-quality pop band. In point of fact, U2 were as out on their own then as they are today. It is hardly surprising that every one of those other bands has since disappeared without trace.

'The Atrix were interesting' is all Bono seems able to remember. 'There were other groups that were more interesting in terms of, we'd say, "That's interesting *music* – in that sound or song that they have" – but we wouldn't think the group was *anywhere*. We just felt that ourselves and the Virgin Prunes were on a different planet to everyone else.'

CHAPTER FIVE

A Village in the Malignant Wilderness

Still, Dada and northside Dublin – you must be joking! But then again. The Irish, we keep being told, are fond of a joke. And so we are. But there is a lot more to it than that. Humour in Ireland is like a filter through which the world can be turned into something other than what it seems. It's not just about jokes, having a laugh. Humour is an integral part of everyday conversation. Irish people have a way of putting a spin on life's troubles with a joke or a one-liner, a habit they learned through a close acquaintance with trouble over several centuries.

Anyone who has seen contemporary Irish comedians like Kevin McAleer and Jimeoin will possibly have become aware of the lack of limits to their comedy. It's not just the old thing that humour is too serious to be taken lightly, but that, in a society which has for generations used humour as a defence mechanism, as protection against indignity and abuse, it is not easy to stop at the joke. Humour is an unobserved carrier of cultural values and commonality, a medium of rebellion, the evidence of the search for a less obvious kind of freedom. Irish humour is a bit like a good golf swing: it's the follow-through, which after all occurs when the ball has departed the tee (hee) that determines the scope and accuracy of the shot. Humour is part of something much bigger than light relief; it is the power source of daily life.

Tragedy, wrote Patrick Kavanagh, is simply underdeveloped comedy. 'Tragedy is really the dung that fertilises the soil of life.' For him, poetry and comedy were inseparable concepts. Kavanagh had no time for the *cognoscenti*, the self-appointed arbiters of aesthetic principles, who awarded licences for art on the basis of gravity and solemnity. 'I have lived in poverty for twenty years in the illiterate and malignant wilderness that is called Dublin,' he wrote in or about 1960. 'There I have lived among people who care nothing for the things of the spirit. They blathered about poetry and, as the fella said, they knew as much about poetry as my arse knows about snipe shooting . . . Art is a very solemn world, not a laugh in an acre of it. Of course I am not talking about ordinary coarse laughter; I am talking about the gaiety of authority and truth.' Only in so far as they can be squeezed for the comedy that is truth, he declared, are life's tragedies worth mentioning. By Kavanagh's definition, laughter is not a pressure valve but a window on the world. It allows you to see the landscape differently.

Bono read Kavanagh as a teenager: several of his poems were on the Leaving Cert course of the time. His was a voice from another place, the stony grey soil of Monaghan, what the lingo of the time called a rural backwater, more than a hundred miles from the capital. But Kavanagh had spent nearly thirty years in Dublin, railing against the smug hypocrisy of its upwardly mobile middle classes.

As the Irish rock writer Bill Graham has observed, the antecedents of Irish rock 'n' roll are much more likely to be literary than musical. 'If you are involved in American music you say: "The Ramones preceded me, or Elvis, or Blondie, Patti Smith, Dylan or whatever," ' he elaborated to Caroline van Oosten de Boer for her book about Gavin Friday. 'Since you don't have that sort of musical heritage – we have a folk heritage but no rock 'n' roll or pop heritage – you'll see Van Morrison relating himself to Yeats, you see it in Shane MacGowan also. You'll see a lot of people identifying with Flann O'Brien. You'll see it in the Radiators. Philip Chevron has all sorts of references to Joyce and O'Casey and Behan and so forth. There is that sense: if you are Irish you measure yourself a little bit against those people. You will never see an English musician taking anything from T. S. Eliot or Auden.'

These literary and comic undercurrents can be observed in the U2 story from the beginning – from Lypton Village to Zoo TV.

> Those early Dandelion [Market] concerts, those McGonagles concerts were actually quite similar to where we are now,' [said Bono in 1993,] towards the end of the Zoo TV tour. 'And that's from an Irish perspective, from a literary perspective. Surrealism via Flann O'Brien, Monty Python. Flann O'Brien and Monty Python – they're the same. In fact, Monty Python had a huge regard for Flann O'Brien – they always admitted that. Surrealism – Irish surrealism, those ideas that Zoo TV plays with, we were playing with them back then, but we never knew what we were doing. It's very interesting, this thing of not knowing what you're doing – *yet!* Getting on the nineteen bus with a stepladder and buckets, at sixteen years old, and going into Grafton Street and putting on a performance and then taking down the stepladder and going home on the bus. Put it back in the garage. And people would be looking . . . And you know we all *knew*. We were seventeen and we were into the Factory. We knew about the Factory via the Velvet Underground, through David Bowie. David Bowie, Velvet Underground, Andy Warhol. 'Let's go and see *Bad*.' I remember fighting

with Gavin outside the cinema, because I thought it was crap and he thought it was a work of genius. And out of all that, different kinds of surrealism started to break out. Looking back now, I can understand what was going on.

And you see the Sex Pistols were surrealism, Dada – the safety pin in the nose. I wore a safety pin in my nose to school, and it was all this, 'Way out!' But it's just Dada – that's all it was. And this thing of Dada and surrealism is very interesting. Teenagers are very into that. But that's not rock 'n' roll. It's very different. Rock 'n' roll is about being cool. Dada is shaving one side of your moustache off. That's where we're coming at rock 'n' roll. That was the birth of the uncool, as far as we were concerned.

Lypton Village drew both on the human impulse to express its alienation as humour and the idea of humour as a refinement of tragedy. It did not express itself in the conventional idiom of Irish humour, which had itself became oppressive in a place where the traditional solidarity of the society was at its most fragmented. Bono talks about 'finding what you might call "alcoholic" humour, or football humour as being the Enemy', as though wishing to wipe out existing forms of humour and replace them with something more in tune with the new identity they could feel forming between them. Before I forget, Bono's grandfather – his father's father – once worked as a comedian in Dublin. 'He was a morose man,' Bono said in an interview once. 'So I think this idea of laughing and then biting your tongue is something that runs in the family.'

Lypton Village was an extreme case, a revolt against banality. It was not a petulant, ideological revolt, but a weary, existential one against both the tackiness and emptiness of the lower middle class culture around them, the way in which their immediate environment seemed to embody the isolation and alienation they felt from the society as a whole, and also against the fatalistic jocularity, the Cheer Up It Might Never Happen syndrome, that lay like a damp sheet under everything.

Lypton Village also revolted against the developing anti-culture of drink and television which it encountered all around the new Ireland. Irish drinking habits are a legend, but like so many aspects of the Irish personality are profoundly misunderstood. Drinking in Ireland is much more than a pastime, it is a ritualistic alternative to reality, a spiritual placebo, a search for heaven, a longing for the pure state of return to the place whence we came. The Bachelor Drinking Group, identified by the sociologist Tom Inglis in *The Moral Monopoly*, grew organically out of a society in which marriage patterns were distorted by poverty and celibacy. Public houses were male sanctuaries, a place where men could escape from the moral supervision of women and priests. Not until the late 1970s did the sexual revolution create enough thaw to allow women to enter pubs on the same basis as men. For generations, the dark, smoky pubs of Ireland were where the cultural and social hierarchy was enacted and policed.

The young U2 did not drink. Their early pronouncements on the subject seemed, to someone on a different point of the cultural cycle, on the prudish side of killjoy. Nearly two decades on from their beginnings, Bono makes no attempt to deny it.

> One of the guys – his reaction would have been because his father an alcoholic. My reaction might have been . . . I don't know . . . It was arrogance, a real arrogance . . . it was like, if else on the street was doin' it, it must be *stupid*. That was it. And this goes back to myself and Guggi, when we were eight and and ten years old, learning to parody the mannerisms of and bootboys, learning how to smoke like Pisser Doyle, somebody, who'd be hanging out on the corner. And we'd be there, like, *ffffsscch* [sucks hard on pretend fag in a manner reminiscent of an early U2 stage routine from the Dandelion gigs]. Copying their mannerisms. This was the beginning, if you like, of mocking your enemy – the thing you were afraid of – because there was a likely chance of getting a good hiding. And we received a few. And that was part of it. It was a reaction to that. Drugs and smoke and drink became associated with the enemy. Because that's what arseholes were into. Your uncle was into drink. That fuckin' eejit the corner was into . . . the pub. Knockin' them back. Gettin' it into ya. And you just said, 'Whhggguurrgggh' [puking gesture]. So our picture then was, like, the complete opposite. We got into this *Lord of the Flies* idea of not growing up. We said, 'We won't grow up. We'll stay as we are . . . *nine!*' He pauses and smiles. 'Ahem, I guess we succeeded there! It was a little bit gauche and a little bit all over the place, but that's where it was comin' from. It was this idea of 'Let's vibe them out!' That was the phrase: 'Let's vibe them out!' Like the little boy in Volker Schlondorff's film, *The Tin Drum*. So can you imagine what it was like . . . This is an amazing moment of synchronicity for me . . . getting to London with a copy of *Boy* under your arm? And going out the first night and going along to see *The Tin Drum*. And seeing the same thing, this story of this child who refuses to grow up – in Nazi Germany – and beats out his dissent on his drum.

Back in the Zürich of 1917, Hugo Ball, the founder of Cabaret Voltaire, became disillusioned with the Dadaist movement because it had not lived up to its earlier promise to promote a spiritual rebirth. His view of Dada saw a new construction arising out of the destruction of the old, but felt that the movement had reduced itself to a blunderbuss assault on the whole human condition. 'I have examined myself carefully,' he said, 'and I could never bid chaos welcome.' He retired and became a writer.

This tension, and the emerging dichotomy, characterises most forms of anarchism. It has the minutest of echoes in the story of Lypton Village. Gavin Friday, vocalist with the Virgin Prunes, was apt to be the most iconoclastic and confrontational; from early on, you could tell that U2, and most certainly Bono, wanted something quite different. Compare their opening gambits. 'The Virgin Prunes seek both negative and positive reaction,' pronounced an early press statement. 'They are but a mirror to modern living and to you. To look or to hide from that mirror is your choice.'

U2 seemed to come from the other side of what was now a two-way mirror. 'Every teenager,' Bono said to Bill Graham in his first major interview feature in *Hot Press* in March 1979, 'does experience spiritual things.' As well as the 'normal' adolescent themes, U2 were determined to tackle bigger subjects. 'We're also dealing with spiritual questions, ones which few groups ever touch on.'

While the Dadaist connection is frequently emphasised in retellings of the Virgin Prunes story – properly acknowledged as the most innovative and subversive of post-punk entities – it is never given much weight in the case of U2. But in a particular kind of light, it is still possible to see everything that has happened since as underlining a relationship rather than a divergence between the two groups. The more you try to separate U2's artistic achievement from their merely commercial conquests, the more important Lypton Village becomes.

Through the first half of the 1980s, U2 and the Prunes might have been mirror images of one another. While the two bands remained relatively unknown, Bono was predicting that U2 would be a mainstream band while the Prunes would go 'for the oddballs and misfits'. And so it came to pass. As U2 became a powerful, benign force within mainstream rock 'n' roll, the Prunes cavorted on the margins, courting controversy and unacceptability and frequently bemusing even hardcore audiences used to the excesses of the more left-field of British punk bands. As one writer put it, the Prunes hurt while U2 healed.

In another light it is almost possible to suggest that the direction the Prunes took towards cult status, and their consequent inevitable disintegration, was as appropriate a comment on their artistic ethic as was U2's phenomenal commercial achievement on theirs. U2 exploded into the world, while the Prunes imploded into the black hole from which both bands had emerged.

If the U2 and Virgin Prunes stories are taken separately, the friendship of the two bands makes very little sense. Taken together, they suggest the twin guiding principles of Dada, destruction followed by creation – the overlooked second plank of the Dada agenda, stillborn, as Hugo Ball's disillusionment bore witness, in the first flush of Dada in the century's teenage years.

On the face of it, the Prunes did not appear to belong to Ireland at all. Their beginnings here seemed like an accident, an aberration. And yet, as Simon Carmody, a contemporary musician, would later observe of Gavin Friday, there was this almost negative symbiosis between the Prunes and their place. The entire ethos of the Virgin Prunes was rooted in their specific circumstances in the place in which they awoke. And yet that place did not comprehend its own children. Dublin looked in the mirror proffered by the Prunes and shrieked, 'I know thee not.' Gavin Friday has said more than once that he felt like an exile in his own country, and the Prunes gave expression to this very sense of alienation. And yet, as we have observed, the Prunes did not express the same flat, kneejerk rejection of Ireland and its broad shapes as, for example, Bob Geldof in the early days of the Boomtown Rats.

It is much too simple to say that there was a love/hate relationship between the Prunes and Ireland and/or Dublin. There was certainly both an indifference to places outside their own northside hinterland (Gavin was in his mid-teens before he crossed the Liffey, the river that cuts in two the city of this birth) and an antagonism towards the manner in which the values of the external Ireland had encroached on their own territory. But if there was a love/hate relationship, it was that the Prunes hated to love rather than that they loved to hate. 'Each man kills the thing he loves/The poet wisely said,' Gavin Friday would sing in 1988 in his new incarnation as a vaudevillian solo artist, putting the lyric of Oscar Wilde's poem *The Ballad of Reading Gaol* to his own melody, 'And so I know you love me not/For I am not yet dead.' Some other lines from *The Ballad*, inscribed on Wilde's gravestone in Père Lachaise, precisely frame the Lypton Village ethic: 'And alien tears will fill for him/Pity's long-broken urn,/For his mourners will be outcast men,/And outcasts always mourn.'

Wilde had long been a hero of Friday's, and a seminal influence on the work of the Virgin Prunes. What 'Each Man Kills' is saying is that when two people love, they chip away at one another until there is nothing left. And there was something of this process at work in the attitude of the Prunes to their native country in their early days. It was as if the tug-of-war resistance of their own place provided the energy of this iconoclasm. As the Prunes chipped away at the forms of the rock 'n' roll medium they invaded, so they chipped away at the weight of cultural rubble imposed upon them since birth: the smugness, narrowness and claustrophobia of the 'new' Ireland.

It may be useful to note that, whereas the four members of U2 attended the progressive Mount Temple, one of Ireland's first ecumenical comprehensive schools, the Prunes drew some of their formative influences from more orthodox educational habitats. Gavin Friday, lacking the excuse of even a single Protestant parent, went to a Roman Catholic-run Christian Brothers school in Finglas. Talking to him about it years afterwards, it was obvious that his abiding memory was of alienation. He wasn't rebellious in the normal sense, but had sublimated his isolation into a rumbling ambition. 'I wasn't, like, a *lad*. But I was rebellious in how I would look and in what I wanted to do,' he told me in a 1990 interview about his schooldays for *The Irish Times*. While at school Gavin had a liking for pop music, in particular the current glam rock of T-Rex and David Bowie, and had begun to dress in character. This interest in music would throw him together with young Paul Hewson, who lived around the corner but attended the, to Gavin, posh – if free – comprehensive, Mount Temple. Even in his pre-teen years, Gavin had long hair and wore earrings. 'I decided when I was eleven or twelve that I liked music and wanted to look like Marc Bolan. But the cost of looking like that is a kick in the face when you're going to school.' In Gavin's school, most of the guys were 'into Showaddywaddy and football and kickin' your head in. I mixed with the Mount Temple guys, with the Protestants. But I was always a Catholic in their eyes.'

Gavin Friday's experience of the Christian Brothers corresponds to that of most of his own and previous generations all around Ireland. In St Kevin's CBS, the only liberalism was in the use of the leather. Any hint of deviance was frowned upon. Friday was expelled three times because of his appearance. Each time his mother had to come down and make a case for his readmission. He was into reading and painting and music. He had no time for the alleged pioneers of the Dublin punk scene, bands like the Boomtown Rats and the Radiators from Space, regarding them as the poor relations of British punk. He identified with writers rather than musicians. He hated sport, one of the staple elements of Irish education. 'I found the constant harassment of Gaelic football huge. I'm a very unphysical person. I like walking. I like to leave it at that. I can't relate to football. I have a fear of a football. It was compulsory to play Gaelic or hurling. Every Wednesday at two o'clock you were made to get into togs. It was humiliating for me: I wouldn't know how to run after a ball. And this *hurl*! It was the strangest thing in my life. What could I do with this *stick*?'

Listening to him talk about it almost twenty years later, you had the odd sense of hearing for the first time from an inhabitant of Lypton Village a description of an experience that accorded precisely with the generality of experience in Ireland at that time. 'I don't go for the Bob Geldof "Christian Brothers were bastards!" type of rant, but I'm not going to say that it wasn't true. The humiliation of making a fifteen-year-old queue up and the brother to walk up and say, "What are you wearing those jeans for?", or "Get your hair cut!" before you went into the first class.'

The Prunes, in their statements and attitudes, were the more extreme of the two Lypton Village groups, and in a funny kind of a way this seems to have been because their experience included elements that were, in that period, more normal. The overtly sexual element of the Prunes' aesthetic seemed to be echoed in Friday's memory of the period of his own sexual awakenings. 'I think the latent homosexual thing was very dominant in the Christian Brothers. It's quite heavy when you're going for a piss when you're thirteen or fourteen and you're being watched by the brother. It's there. And the whole way sex was handled. I got no sex education at all, even from my parents. It was never, ever mentioned in school. I think that teachers should be people who understand the vulnerability of children, and I firmly believe that people who suppress their own sexuality shouldn't be allowed near young people.'

In contrast, U2 enjoyed a relatively charmed life in the culturally enlightened and, in that sense at least, privileged corridors of Mount Temple. It was an experience which makes as much sense of their journey into the mainstream as Friday's experiences seem to explain the Prunes' retreat to the fringe.

Lypton Village, with its bizarre rituals like the Village Olympics (main events were the walking-the-rice-paper contest and wall-smelling), provides the frame in which the genesis of U2 is best observed. Although the Village was centred on the relationship between Bono and the Prunes, the fantasy it provided represented a focus of refuge to which the other three members of U2 were able to relate from the margins. Adam Clayton, for example, though never a member of Lypton Village, was unfazed by its strangeness. On the contrary, although his was more a conventional English background (his family moved to Dublin when he was five), the Lypton Village fantasy made sense of the dislocation he felt from the real world in which he was required to live. 'It was a world that I found very easy to associate with, because I'd been in boarding school,' he told me in 1993. 'So I had my own private world where reality had nothing to do with the conversations I had with myself. It was a much more lonely world but there were two or three of us in the boarding school who, in a robotic way, went around the daily functions of that school, and when we had time together, we lived in a world that had nothing to do with that particular place. It was a fantasy about what one was gonna do when you grew up and left school. Those ideas that come out, those conversations that happen after somebody's read a book. So it was very easy for me to go from boarding school restriction to comprehensive restriction, which was Mount Temple, and still not have an environment. Because my home environment I didn't know, because I'd always been away from it at school. But when the Lypton Village thing happened, it was very easy for me to go, "Yeah, I can run with this. I don't have to question it." Because I didn't have any real grounding in any kind of reality.'

The possibility is inescapable that neither the Prunes nor U2 might have happened without the other. As Gavin would tell me in that 1990 interview, although Mount Temple pupils had it free and easy, that environment alone did not produce genius or freedom in anything like the truckloads which a simple prognosis might suggest. Gavin might have been amazed and envious about the fact that his friends in Mount Temple were allowed to play tapes or rehearse their own music after class, but he knew, too, that there was much more to it than that. Mount Temple, even if drawn from all strata, was broadly more middle class than the Christian Brothers, and geared towards producing doctors and businessmen rather than plumbers and electricians. But in the cosmic scheme of things the distinction didn't matter. Both were about producing fodder for the economic treadmills of post-Lemass Ireland. 'I look at certain people who went to Mount Temple,' Gavin told me, 'who are married now, settled with kids, and who are fairly well educated. But they don't read . . . They were never told to ask, any more than we were, *who are you?* They were being conditioned on another level . . . It's like, "I'm educated, but what are you gettin' *weird* for?"'

What this underlines is the possible error of looking separately at the genesis of the Virgin Prunes and U2. They provided mirrors for one another, without which neither might have found any bearings at all. It was as if each could see in the other's life a vital experience missing from its own. Gavin's knowledge of the charmed life of the Mount Temple boys provided the comparison by which the lack of sympathy in his own education could be measured, a mirror in which to observe the absurdity of his own existence. And the Mount Temple boys had in Gavin's an experience which enabled them to see how lucky they were. They saw the same absurdity, but from a more detached perspective. Each band emerged dialectically from the other. Their cross-fertilisation created the blurted refusal of the Prunes and the embrace that was U2.

CHAPTER SIX

White Skin, White Masks

We draw rough lines, in the faintest pencil, on the page. With appropriate reservations, one records that both Elvis Presley and John Lennon had strong bonds with their mothers, that Elvis made his first record as a birthday present for Gladys, that Julia bought John his first guitar and taught him his first chords, and that both men were devastated when their mothers were snatched away. The circumstances of the death of Paul Hewson's mother – from a brain haemorrhage she suffered at her own father's funeral – are deeply shocking. That she should die so suddenly and so violently when he was just fourteen, seems traumatic enough to change everything.

Paul Hewson was the product of a Catholic father and a Protestant mother, yes, but there may be more to it than that. The loss of Iris Hewson may have been all the greater for the young Bono, because she was a Protestant and had brought him up the same.

The fact that his mother was, as the terminology had it, the 'non-Catholic partner' in the marriage may have a special significance. In his book, *Moral Monopoly*, about the place and influence of the Catholic Church in Ireland, Tom Inglis writes of the special role of the Irish Catholic mother in determining the shape of Irish society. The Church and the mother entered into an unholy alliance to regulate the course of Irish family life, contributing to the emotional truncation and sexual wounding of the Irish personality. 'The [Catholic] mother maintained her power within the home in the same way as the Church did in the wider society,' observes Inglis. 'By doing everything for her sons, the mother made them dependent on her. But by limiting and controlling the physical expression of her affection, she inculcated an emotional awkwardness in her children. The denial of the physical expression of affection was a major child-rearing practice in preparation for emigration, postponed marriage and celibacy.'

Iris Hewson, being a Protestant, had been part of this culture, and yet not. She was an Irish mother, but not a Catholic Irish mother. She was, by some accounts, an exceptionally demonstrative woman, supportive of her husband and two boys. In this sense she clearly carried out the role of what Tom Inglis calls 'emotional management' in the family. She was the source of physical affection and love for all three, but particularly, because he was the youngest, for Paul.

It may mean much or it may mean nothing, but the tragedy of her death bears the echo of the experiences of others who came to mean something in the way U2 would later do. Gladys Presley, Greil Marcus quoted Stanley Booth on the King's relationship with his mother in *Mystery Train*, was 'the one, perhaps the only one, who had told him throughout his life that even though he came from poor country people, he was as good as anybody'. Julia Lennon, the errant, black-sheep mother of the saddest Beatle, was more like a big sister to John, encouraging his rebelliousness, laughing at his badness, a mad soulmate in contrast to the loving severity of her sister, Mimi, John's 'substitute mother', who had the responsibility for bringing him up.

One of the things you remark in tracing the roots of U2 is the extent of their ignorance about the past, their own and that of their place. Bono has said that the band began 'with its roots in space somewhere', and he had more in mind, I suspect, than musical genealogy. Eamon Dunphy's biography *Unforgettable Fire* makes up for its other failings by tracing, pretty much as well as is possible, the broad outlines of the U2 family trees; but the result *is* a sketch, an erratic string of historical facts, some of them more interesting than others, without much meaning for the story which is there to be told.

By his own admission, it was only in the late- 1980s, when U2 had achieved worldwide success, that Bono began to investigate the story of his own family background. For the first time, he and his father began to talk about the things which they had previously, by an unspoken contract, contrived to avoid. 'Trying to talk to my old man about the past', he remembers, 'was like trying to talk to a brick wall.' The description he gives of his family relationship is extreme and scary. He doesn't remember much about his mother. 'I forget what she looked like,' he admits. As a child he wasn't particularly close to either of his parents, and when his mother died he felt a deep resentment, because he had never been given a chance to experience the unconditional love a mother has for a child. To this day, his descriptions of the image he retains of his mother seem strange and remote: she was 'quite petite', he told one interviewer, 'really a delicate flower'.

Paul Hewson had been a difficult youngster, noisy as a baby, scatter-brained as a child and aggressively directionless as an adolescent. He would later recall how some of his extended family would refer to him, without undue irony, as 'the Antichrist'. These tendencies had created a distance between him and his old man, Bobby, a conventional Irish Catholic father, not given to overt displays of affection. Paul was almost eight years younger than his brother Norman, and their communication was mostly through the medium of argument.

The experience of losing a mother, suddenly and young, is doubly pertinent in the U2 story. It was the death, in 1978, when the band was just finding its feet, of Larry Mullen's mother, Maureen (like Julia Lennon, she died in a road accident) and the rallying-round of the rest of U2, that caused the drummer to abandon doubts about rock 'n' roll and lose himself in the U2 project.

When I ask the thirty-three-year-old Paul Hewson, by now irreversibly transmogrified into Bono, why he blundered into rock 'n' roll, he doesn't talk just about the irresistible urge to make particular kinds of musical sounds. He talks about freedom and the desire to find out who he was.

> I think it was just that it was the easiest route. It was emancipation, for sure. It's like, my head was ready to leave my body, because I was rebelling against, basically, not living in a home, living in a house with two men. Didn't like it. One of them too serious, and . . . I now realise what they were doing. I must admit I was hard work. I wouldn't help out as much as they wanted me to. I guess I was rebelling against it because . . . Nobody being in the house. Getting the pot, opening the tin of spaghetti, opening the tin of meat, putting it in the same pot, pouring the boiling water into the Smash, putting the Smash into the pot and just eating it. Not wanting to put it on a dish, because it was just . . . It was just awful. I almost *hated* the house. It wasn't a home. I loved homes. I loved the next door neighbour's house. I loved callin' round to Edge, seeing his house and his mother and so on. I loved being out. I didn't want to go back to our house.
>
> It was at that stage I developed a penchant for sleeping on the floor, which I can still do. I can sleep . . . *there*! I can sleep on the street. I can sleep in any position, anywhere. Absolutely. I *have* slept on the street. But that feeling of not having a home – was part of everything. Touring – the reason I'm so at home on the road – that started back then. I hated the house and the fighting. My brother would come home and we'd fight. We'd be thumping each other. Horrible. I hated it.

Not wanting to go home, but wanting a home to go home to, is a dark, deep undercurrent of U2's loud, sad songs. The story of the Smash and the saucepan is one of the devices Bono uses to explain his childhood. He's used it before. It provides a powerful image of displacement, although it comes, too, from someone who knows what a powerful image of displacement would sound like. But deeper down in his recollections of those teenage years after the death of his mother, there is the shape of someone trying to find a way to regain the kind of loving approval that had been lost.

There I was in school, with a peculiar kind of intelligence – is the best way to describe it – uneven. Twelve years old and, without much effort, I was playing chess at adult level. I met a guy since who I couldn't remember but he said he taught me how to play chess and that I wasn't very good. But I was playing in an adult club at twelve – maybe I wasn't the best player, but I was the youngest. I remember beating the chairman of the club at twelve, which is pretty good. So I actually *was* good at that. So I go to school and, like, I'd get all straight As for a while – easy. And the next thing I wouldn't. Then I would again. And I didn't even know why. And my dad would say, 'Oh, you're doing really well here' . . . 'Now you're not!' 'What are you doing?' I'd say, 'I dunno.' Losing interest – you know? But because of hanging out with people who were very bright, I could never do my homework. That was part of it. Because the homework was done in the house, and I never liked it there so I'd never do it. So I'd come in in the mornings, copy people's homework – copy whoever was good, correct it while I was copying it. I'd often be better than whoever it was. But eventually you can't get away with that. So my marks started dropping. I couldn't do anything about it, but I didn't like it. Didn't like that I wasn't doing well at school. And by 'doing well' I don't mean . . . yeah, you get a few honours in the Inter, but that wasn't where my head was at. My friends were getting eight honours, and nine honours. I just couldn't get organised. An untidy life. Wouldn't finish things. Wouldn't do my homework. Wouldn't study. All this stuff.

But *knowing . . . knowing . . .* that there was an expression that you had to make, and not knowing how you're going to get it. I remember going into Smart Brothers, getting the baggy trousers, platform shoes, the whole thing. A Boot Boy. Trying it out, the whole thing, in order to get off with Susan Williams, who was this girl who liked that kind of a person. Then getting rid of that batch of clothes and getting some patched jeans and a cheesecloth shirt in order to try and get off with Maeve O'Regan. It was all women-orientated. And of course chess wasn't very good in the pursuit of women, so that went! Very quickly! As soon as I realised that that didn't ingratiate you in any way. That went about fourteen! And the electric guitar followed soon behind. 'With this music I can unbuckle her belt.' That was the story. And *could*. And it was just, like, WOW! And it was, really, some kind of an emancipation.

My father, not to be too hard on him, but he definitely taught me that not much is possible. He might be hurt by this, but . . . I was definitely taught not to dream, because to dream is to end up disillusioned. And maybe that's because of his own scenario, I don't know. But he came out of, obviously, a depression era, where, you know, 'get a job in the civil service'. I found this out later – not through him but through people I've met since then – that he was a very smart man, the smartest in his class, and that the priest came around to his mother and asked her not to take him out of school at fourteen or fifteen, that he would go on to university, and probably lecture at university. He had that kind of potential. And he was taken out of school, and he did go to work, and blah blah blah. So that might explain why he always taught us, you know, 'Don't dream!' They weren't his words, but that was the vibe.

Paul Hewson's background – his mixture of middle class and working class, Catholic and Protestant, seems to speak first for the wider U2 collective and then for a generation, a time in a place. In many ways the four were an atypical bunch, and yet strangely microcosmic of a deeper level of difference that permeated the society. There was Adam, the middle-class English Protestant; Dave Evans, from a background half Presbyterian, half Welsh Baptist; Larry, the only conventional Irish Catholic, whose father had once studied for the priesthood; and Bono, the mixture who embodied the entire confusion. As he told me in 1992:

My own attempt to find a voice was made further complicated by the fact that my family crossed the two traditions in Ireland. I had a Protestant mother and a Catholic father. So that the ascendancy influence – even though they were lower-middle-class, working-class Protestants, was there. The Englishness of Tone [Theobald Wolfe Tone, the Protestant who became the founder of Irish republicanism] is something I can slip into very easily.

And in a comic way, the confusion would come to an annual head on Christmas Day, as both sides of our family fought to turn on and off the Queen's speech. It was quite funny, with my dad saying, 'Oh God! Do we really need to hear this pontificating?' And my grandmother, my mother's mother, Nanny Rankin, whose husband had been in the British army, saying, 'Shush! The English have been very good to the Irish. They gave your grandfather a pension – they looked after him better than the Irish would've.'

I'm just saying that my own attempt to find my voice was definitely further confused by these two traditions that I feel I straddle in Dublin. And growing up in Ballymun – in fact, even *that*

I have a problem with. Because here I am living in Ballymun, which is what some would see as a very heavy northside area, but I was living on the edge of it, in this sort of not very heavy street. Even *that* wasn't clear. I didn't even know whether I was working class or middle class. So I didn't know whether I was working class, middle class, Protestant, Catholic, English, American or Irish.

I grew up at points with the sense that what was Irish was a bit crap [he laughs, just a little apologetically]. That our football teams weren't as good. We supported Arsenal and Manchester United, and Gaelic football seemed so neanderthal in comparison. That was the Protestant voice that I grew up around. It was unspoken. And also, Irishness as it was touted then, which was the *fáinne nua* [a circular badge worn on the lapel, to designate an Irish speaker] and the girls who went to – what was the school up the road? – Coláiste Mhuire. It was everything that was crap. And it was very uncool. I just knew that much. It was *very* uncool. Now if you speak to Liam O Maonlai, the singer in the Hot House Flowers, you'll get a very different story. He came from middle-class parents, and embraced Irishness and things Irish, and went to the Gaeltacht. And it was very cool, in fact, where he was coming from. It was Yer Culture and it was your roots, and it was something to embrace, and he did. He's an Irish speaker and he can play the tin whistle. But not where I was coming from – it was not cool. And that wasn't *just* the Protestant influence in my family – even on our street it wasn't really cool. Thunderbirds were go!

In a funny kind of way, perhaps the most potent image which the U2 story offers to the place where they came from is that the story reflects Ireland's dislocation, its loss of history, its amnesia, its rupture with at least the surface layers of the past. Although Irish people have a reputation for long memories, the truth is that we have hardly any memories at all. The trauma that lies at the heart of our past is too tender to be other than lightly brushed with a soft and myth-soaked swab.

A conversation with Bono in the spring of 1994 didn't add much flesh to the skeleton of his family background, except that he was able to tell me that his comedian grandfather had suffered from tuberculosis.

He was a very morose man. Quite dour. Because he *had* very bad health. His chest. He died of TB. I didn't know him. My father never talked about him. My father is verbal about everything that isn't important. He loves to talk about the big subjects, as long as it's not his thoughts. He likes to debate rather than own up. That kind of not talking. In every other respect he's full of guff, and great fun.

He's a crank. No, he *plays* at being a crank. It's just that I thought he was serious all those years. If he was sitting here in my house he'd point to something and say, 'Did you pay for that?' Or he'd say, [points to sideboard] 'They saw you coming. I wouldn't keep rabbits in that!' He's a wind-up. I get on very well with him now, and it's a really great place to be at. He did his very best trying to be father, mother and policeman, and it must have been very, very difficult. There's obviously strong feelings down there that I have to come to terms with.

I had a little amnesia about my mother. I had a problem visually trying to get back. I had a sort of a late fall-out from it when I reached sixteen. Definitely I hit some kind of a wall. I did well, if you look at my school results, up to that point. But I guess they must have declined just after my mother died. I always say in interviews that I basically just discovered girls and that was that. But there may have been something else. This thing about memory, about forgetting things, not being able to take things in, as a result of trauma. And I definitely went through that, in that period. Not being able to take on board stuff. My schoolwork went to pieces and I didn't associate that with what had happened, but looking back now, maybe it had more to do with that than just discovering girls. It wasn't that I was a dull student, just not taking it in.

Sorting through the U2 story, you become intrigued at the way it begins to accumulate baggage which seems to equip it to make statements about Irish society from a position of knowingness. The death of one of the band's mothers in tragic circumstances would have been unfortunate, the death of a second seems almost perversely fortuitous. 'That's obviously one of the things that means we have a sympatico with one another,' says Bono. 'It's funny, seeing Larry now. He's one of the clearest people I know. When we're sitting around in politburo mode, he's a guy I always look to. "What's goin' on here? Are we goin' too far off the point?" He's incredibly clear, whereas I'm the opposite. So in that sense we have absolutely nothing in common, as personalities. But we have this moment we share.'

'In Europe,' writes Franz Fanon in his 1952 book *Black Skin, White Masks*, 'and in every country characterised as civilised or civilising, the family is a miniature of the nation . . . an institution that prefigures a broader institution: the social or the national group. Both turn on the same axes.' By this I think he means that the family is the place in which the child is taught to make sense of the world, to perceive the present in terms of the past. If the society is abnormal, the family will be abnormal as well, and will

72

moreover return its offspring to the society with these abnormalities entrenched in their souls. Fanon is talking about black society – the young black at home among his own colonised people, and away amongst the white coloniser. In a colonised society, by Fanon's analysis, the relationship between the family and society is reversed: 'A normal negro child, having grown up with a normal family, will become abnormal on the slightest contact with the white world.'

Ireland, of course, is not a black society; but it is a colonised society, the conditions resembling those in a colonised black society, but in a more complex and all but invisible way. There are no black skins, but plenty of white masks. The difference is that the faces they obscure are also white. Colonisation has left a different mark in almost every head, but the heads look more or less the same. It is almost impossible to tell, just by looking, the faces of the native ascendancy who took the reins from the departing coloniser, from those of the colonised subjects. But colonisation has always two types of victim – the colonised, who sees himself only in the aspiration to be like the coloniser, and the coloniser, who knows himself only through his superiority to the colonised. This ensures that the virus of the conquest festers invisibly beneath the surface long after freedom has ostensibly been granted. To make it even worse, the conditions of colonised and coloniser often seem to exist in the same skull, tearing the individual in opposite directions.

It's an interesting aspect of the U2 collective that it incorporates four discrete personalities who together seem to make explicit that which bubbles below the surface of Irish society: the tall, well-spoken Englishman, the diffident and good-natured Irishman, the ragamuffin Celt whose family come from South Wales, and the description-defying frontman who makes all the other diversities as minimal as he makes them superfluous.

The sense of seeking different kinds of freedom from the society around them is discernible in different ways in the four stories. Adam, for example, the comfortably-off west Brit with the posh accent who attended prep school in Dublin before moving to Mount Temple, displays in his descriptions of middle-class discontent a longing for freedom as real as anything felt by the most deprived of the Republic's Children of Limbo.

> I think freedom, the concept of freedom, has to be a very big part of what we were looking for in U2. We grew up with those obvious limitations. Parents always rowing about money. 'Can I have a new pair of shoes?' 'No.' 'Can I light a fire?' 'No.' 'I'm cold, I want more heat.' Whatever. 'No you can't.' I guess everyone grew up with those economic restrictions. And then there were the restrictions of discipline – what was drummed into you at school. You must do

well at school, otherwise all these avenues of whatever are closed down to you. And I think it was just a disbelief that that was the way one had to live, a disbelief that as a human being you could be brought down to these very, very narrow forms of experience in life. And I'm sure it's something that a lot of teenagers react to. I think every generation says, 'No. Sorry. I don't want that.' And it's only the very strong – or the very stupid – of any generation that actually says, 'I'm gonna close the door on that, and this is where I'm going and I'm not coming back.' And I think that's what it was for us. It was: these are real friendships that we believe in. They offer us the fantasy and the escapism to go anywhere. And they give us a means of expression through lifestyle, instruments, conversation. Whatever environment we were in we made our own. And I guess we never wanted to give that up. We kept following that.

U2's quest for escape from the place they woke up in didn't just cause them to dump that place for the refuge of music. No sooner were they aboard the good ship rock 'n' roll, than they were organising a mutiny there as well. They grew as a kind of alien presence both within their own culture and subsequently in rock 'n' roll. They remained outsiders, even on the inside, allowing us to see more clearly the ways in which the two cultures are similar and how they are not. The particular nature of their existential rebellion could only have happened through the particular defiance U2 had – a defiance they picked up from their own place, and the negative relationship they had with it. And since they were as much a reaction against where they came from as a creation of it, this perversity, when applied within rock 'n' roll, was what would drive them against the grain of the time.

CHAPTER SEVEN

A Race of Angels

When we were children and teenagers, growing up in the west of Ireland in the 1960s and 1970s, music was something that was present but misunderstood. An awful lot of humbug attached itself to the notion of music, which made it difficult to perceive its having any purpose in expressing how people felt in their hearts and souls. This, in fact, was a mildly ridiculous idea. Music was perceived as requiring to be useful first, and beautiful only as a bonus.

There was plenty of music in my background, as there was in most people's. My grandfather on my mother's side had been a traditional fiddle player, and my father's brother, my Uncle Michael, had played both fiddle and accordion, both at home in Co. Sligo and later on when he went to New York. He worked as a street musician, a busker, and was found lying on the street on a winter's day in 1961 with injuries from which he subsequently died. When I say that music was present but misunderstood, I mean partly that whatever musical tradition had existed in our area had died or been repressed long before I arrived. Music had died in both the community and within our family. This death had begun with the Famine of the 1840s and continued ever since. 'Poetry, music and dancing stopped' when the Famine started, an old woman had said to the President of the Gaelic League, Douglas Hyde, a native of my home town. 'Sport and pastimes disappeared. And when times improved these things never returned as they had been.' It was almost as though music signifying joy could never again be played until some unspecified aspiration had been achieved.

So I walked, or crawled, into a decimated musical culture. Some would suggest it wasn't a culture at all, but then culture is a pretty fluid concept. By 'culture' I don't mean just values or activities or forms of expression which are mummified or kept on ice and maintained as a sort of defiant self-assertion in the face of an unfriendly outside world. I mean culture in the sense of things people do when they don't have to do anything – the ways in which they choose to express themselves without thinking that they are 'expressing' themselves, the things they do when they are 'merely' having fun. What I find interesting about it now is that the culture in our area was so broad and varied, and yet nothing of it was what might be called

75

indigenous; everything was borrowed or imported. In fact, our confidence in what this culture bespoke was very much related to the fact that it was *not* of ourselves. In this sense my experience was emblematic of Irish culture in general around this time. Not everywhere, of course, because there were exceptional pockets of indigenous cultural activity, some of it healthy, some of it not. Irish music was strong in counties like Clare and Donegal. In other places it was kept alive on an artificial respirator. But in most places, what culture was occurring spontaneously rather than in a premeditated and self-conscious way, was the culture we drew from outside.

The mass media came to Ireland with the opening of the first national radio station, 2RN, in 1926, when the Free State was just a few years old. There was then, it seems, little awareness of the epistemology of mass media, or even that such a concept might exist. The *Official Handbook of the Irish Free State*, published in 1932, while dealing comprehensively with every other imaginable aspect of culture and public affairs, has not a single mention of the national radio station. The notion that the magics of speech and writing were in the process of being supplanted by the magic of electronics had not occurred to those charged with teaching the fledgling state to fly.

This was not surprising, seeing that much of the grace, intelligence and inspiration of the liberation movement had been lost in the final push to independence. Republican leaders like Padraic Pearse and James Connolly, who had nurtured visions of a free Ireland based on a profound sense of sovereignty and spirituality, had been executed after the Rising of 1916. Today, the ideas of these men have been caricatured out of recognition, but to re-read them is to catch a glimpse of the extent of the loss the new Ireland suffered even before it began. Pearse was a poet, a visionary and a teacher – the most obvious modern comparison is Václav Havel in the Czechoslovakia of 1989. In the years before the Rising Pearse had written about the freedom project and what it would mean. 'Vivifying the whole,' he writes, 'we need the divine breath that moves through free peoples.' True political independence, he elaborates in an essay, 'The Spiritual Nation', 'requires spiritual and intellectual independence as its basis, or it tends to become unstable, a thing resting merely on interests which change with time and circumstances'. This consciousness died when he did, and the newly liberated Ireland was inherited by lesser men with smaller minds. Interests ruled, and instability beckoned. The word 'spiritual' was interpreted in its narrowest possible connotation.

It was perhaps inevitable that the initial years of independence would be characterised by a cultural protectionism, a backlash to everything considered 'alien'. The Gaelic Revival, which had begun in the final decade of the nineteenth century, became the inspiration for the new state. But, unleavened by the wisdom and perspective which people like Pearse might have brought, it became fanatical and insular. Pearse, in his essay on the British system of education 'The Murder Machine', articulates a positive cultural and educational project: 'To "foster" the elements of character native to a soul, to help to bring these to their full perfection rather than to implant exotic excellences.' Interpreted by those who lacked his learning and subtlety, such dicta became the basis of an official policy of cultural xenophobia, which then proceeded as a rhetorical parallel to reality.

What I encountered, when I came to cultural consciousness towards the end of the 1960s, was the product of fifty years of this approach. Raidió Éireann, the successor to 2RN, played everything from Céilí bands to the Beatles, *sean-nós* (old-style traditional singing) to showbands, light classical to ragtime, 'come-all-ye's to light opera, and without any sense that what they were purveying was a culture of any kind. For all the official rhetoric about the revival of the all but extinct spirit of cultural nationalism, radio had been the true cultural formulator. Even the form of 'traditional' music most frequently heard on the wireless was Céilí, a strange, mechanical form of Irish music incorporating drums and saxophones, which invariably began with three taps on a wooden block, proceeded as a blast of collective energy that would make the Ramones blush, and ended as suddenly as it had started. Céilí, devised to serve the needs of radio programming and dances, was a classical example of the unmonitored effect of mass media on traditional forms. The official rhetoric of the time, which described the media as a neutral instrument of cultural revival, was now addressing itself to a nation in which the central metaphor of communication had been utterly transformed by the arrival of mass media. Douglas Hyde, a leading light of the Gaelic Revival, had talked about the necessity for 'de-anglicising Ireland'; but, even leaving aside the desirability or feasibility of such a project in the previous reality, the *new* reality was turning it into a nonsense.

We didn't have a radio in our house until I was seventeen. The only reason I knew what was on the radio was that we used to go on holiday to our aunt's house in the country every summer, where the wireless setting alternated between Raidió Éireann and the BBC Light Programme. I was in my late teens before I got to listen to Radio Luxemburg. In a sense, the way I discovered music was a slightly exaggerated version of the way the generality of Irish people encountered it. There were, obviously, pockets of the country where the tradition of Irish music had been preserved, in varying degrees of health. But where I came from, which was definitely not one of these places, was more typical of Ireland as a whole.

When I say that we encountered music by accident, I mean we heard music on the radio, and decided, 'Yes, that is music.' We thought very little more about it. We rarely stopped to ask, 'Whose music?', or 'Where does this music come from?', or 'In what way is this music about my life?' The idea that music could, or should be 'about our lives' would itself have seemed a little strange. Music was for dancing to, or cheering yourself up, or having a bit of a singsong. It would be broadly true to say that most of us who grew up in Ireland after the mid-1940s simply encountered particular forms of music almost at random and tried to adapt them to our needs as human beings. Because there was so little of the sense that what we were listening to was an accurate representation of what we were, we became a little like what we listened to. And because what we were listening to was neither the expression of an organic culture nor the result of the stated desire for a revival of an earlier identity, but rather the product of a particular set of media metaphors, we had simply, in this area at least, replaced one form of colonialism with another.

What is often forgotten in post-colonial situations, writes Franz Fanon in his classic book about post-colonial societies, *The Wretched of the Earth*, is that the forms which culture feeds on, 'together with modern techniques of information, language and dress have dialectically reorganised the people's intelligence and that the constant principles which acted as safeguards during the colonial period are now undergoing extremely radical changes'.

If this is not recognised, what happens is that it is the colonial mentality, rather than a true cultural identity, which transmutes itself in the allegedly free post-colonial society. This is something that can be clearly observed in the Irish experience. Largely as a result of the way music was taught, for example, there emerged in the society a profound disjunction between the acts of listening to music – of consuming music – and of singing or playing an instrument, of performing, entertaining, producing or creating music. One of the ways in which the virus of colonialism has been handed down to this day was through the educational system, which was adopted without amendment from the British system which Pearse characterised as 'the Murder Machine'. Pearse is most specific that, in order for real freedom to be achieved, this system would have to go. The Murder Machine, he writes, was there to teach Irish people 'not to be strong and proud and valiant, but to be sleek, to be obsequious, to be dexterous: the object was not to make them good men, but to make them good slaves . . . A soulless thing cannot teach; but it can destroy. A machine cannot make men; but it can break men.'

With Pearse gone, there were only his interpreters left. The education system of the new state, like the system of government itself, was simply a continuation of the old system, based, as Pearse had observed, around the manufacture of jailers and slaves. Until the 1980s, the Irish education system continued to be based on a marriage of hierarchy and violence.

We learned music in much the same way as we learned everything else. You learned *or else*. As with the teaching of the Irish language, we acquired music by rote, by being forced to play particular things in a particular way, with no mention or thought of how we might seek to make it relate to our everyday lives. I had a single-row button accordion, in the key of C. It's now thirty years old. I played it for three or four years as a child, and then put it aside. Only in the past year or so have I taken it out and started to play it again.

I was never any good. I don't mean that I couldn't play. I actually had a wide range of pieces in my repertoire, which I performed competently, but without ever having the feeling that I was actually playing. I don't have even the slightest memory of being able to play anything that moved me. I assumed, as did others, that the reason I was never any good was that I didn't have any natural aptitude for music, that I had no ear, no sense of natural rhythm. Some slave! This puzzled me, on account of my grandfather and my uncle. It seemed to me that something should surely have come through to me.

But I did have an ear for music. I could sing. For several years, I was one of a hand-picked choir which sang the High Masses in Latin whenever someone died, which was not half often enough because you got off school for two hours every time. But I can't sing now, and I know why. I remember the moment I lost my voice. It was when I was twelve, doing the exam at the end of primary school. One of the exams was in singing. I know now that when your voice is breaking you're not supposed to sing. But the brother insisted that I sing anyway, and we didn't argue with brothers in those days. I sang 'The Minstrel Boy', which in retrospect seems pretty appropriate. I can still recall the torture, the agony of that song, on a bright early summer's day, which caused irreversible damage to my vocal chords. A few weeks later I had a voice like Sylvester Stallone and I never sang in public again.

It was a similar story with the button accordion. We were conditioned with the idea that the purpose of musicianship was to impress, to be able to go through your paces, that music was to do with technical dexterity and skill. There was no sense that you were working out of a tradition, or feeding off a culture, or seeking to enrich that culture. There were set pieces, traditional arrangements, songs like 'The Minstrel Boy', 'The Rose of Arranmore', 'A Nation Once Again', 'The Irish Rover', 'The Dawning of the Day'.

'The Dawning of the Day', or 'Fáinne Geal an Lae', was the first tune we learned to play. An old Irish melody, it provides a good example of what we were taught in the guise of music. The first thing we learned was the notes: *Doh ray mee mee mee, ray mee so so lah, so mee doh ray doh doh doh* . . .

We played it as a military march. It had this strained, regimented rhythm which drained all the life out of the tune. I grew up hating it. Then one day, on the radio, I heard Luke Kelly's version of the same tune played by the Dubliners. It was called 'On Raglan Road', with words by Patrick Kavanagh:

> On Raglan Road on an autumn day I met her first and knew
> That her dark hair would weave a snare that I might one day rue
> I saw the danger, yet I walked along the enchanted way,
> And I said, let grief be a fallen leaf at the dawning of the day.

I cried that first time I heard Kelly sing this song. Not just because of the magic of Kavanagh's words, or the power of Kelly's voice. It was the way Kelly held and moved the melody like a dancing partner, this way and that, to accommodate Kavanagh's lyric. The Irish poet Paul Durcan, writing about Van Morrison in the current affairs magazine, *Magill*, some years later, sketched an unseen connection between Morrison and Patrick Kavanagh, a song that Van himself recorded later on. Durcan writes that 'the only new development in recent Irish poetry was Kavanagh's introduction of the jazz line, and Morrison's continuation of it'. Durcan is talking about the improvisational dimension of the relationship of Kavanagh's lyrics to the tune, taking the same basic melody on a journey through a maze of words, thoughts and daydreams. 'Kavanagh', Durcan writes, 'was a great tenor sax who was content to blow his horn in the sunlit angles of Dublin street corners in the 1950s.'

All that, I suppose, was part of what I felt when I heard Luke Kelly's version of this presumed dead tune. But more than that, it was the realisation of how I had been cheated, of how *we* had been cheated. Because here was Kelly administering artificial respiration to an air that I had always regarded as not just dead but fossilised, and the song was getting up and walking away with him into the sunset. This was the melody that we had been taught to play as a march, and yet was nothing like one. It had sex, soul, passion. It had an intoxicating quality which I had never dreamt of in that tune before. It had *meaning*.

> On a quiet street where old ghosts meet I see her walking now
> Away from me so hurriedly my reason must allow
> That I had loved not as I should a creature made of clay –
> When the angel woos the clay he'd lose his wings at the dawn of day.

It was a new song and yet an old song. It told me so much about what had happened to me as a would-be musician, and the reasons why so much Irish music had failed to express so much of what I felt inside. In the last few months I've started to play that tune again – the same notes, but in a different way. And I've begun to see as though for the first time that this music is more than notes or form or structure – that it is the transmission of feeling.

In his book *The Third Ear*, Joachim-Ernst Berendt writes about a survey of composers and professional musicians involved in western concert music. In most of the people examined, he observes, their musicality had moved to the left side of the brain, which programmes what we do with the right hand as well as our sense of form and design. 'Musicality is thus, as it were, deprived of its natural feedback from the heart and feeling side, and transferred to the realm of logic and functionality which are usually in the left side of the brain.' As a result, the music that is made is inhabited not by inspiration and sensation, but by space, form, functionality, logic and purposefulness.

'I believe it,' says Bono when I tell him this in 1994. 'I could tell you that anyway, just from working with them. Because a lot of them have suspended imagination. I think it starts at school, the way music is taught – we teach the children how not to be creative. You are taught to be imitative, not creative. You are taught to copy other people's styles by watching the marks that they have made. And so, after a while, you suspend imagination. It's mechanical. That's obvious to me. A lot of these people seem to have lost the fun and the playfulness and the creativity, because they're lost in doing the best possible imitation. The people who are in charge of it are not creative, and that's a problem. I mean, our school was progressive, but if you couldn't play an instrument or read music, it was assumed you were unmusical. But I could hear songs in my head all the time. I knew what the music teacher was talking about, but I had no way to express it. I couldn't play in that mechanical way . . . I couldn't play *at all*!'

We don't talk about the war that kills the music within our heads. Colonisation is not a word you will hear in the public discourse of modern Ireland. It wouldn't be polite. But its effects are as real today as they were the day before our notional independence.

The coloniser, as Franz Fanon says in *The Wretched of the Earth*, seeks to 'plant deep in the minds of the native population the idea that before the advent of colonialism their history was one which was dominated by barbarism'. This idea was driven into the Irish mind like a nail. Today, when there is talk at all about the past, it is in terms of the occupation of our territory and the abuse of our ancestors. But this, we lead ourselves to believe, is all behind us now. The English are no longer our enemies. But what if, when the English left, we became our own enemies? What then?

Colonisation is an insidious and double-edged process. The people both believe that they are savages and yet, at another level, refuse to believe it. We believe that we are not savages – we tell ourselves that we are the inheritors of an ancient civilisation – but yet we recognise ourselves in the descriptions of the coloniser. We wish, deep in our souls, to be like the one we fear and despise. We are doomed to imitate without identifying. We are thrown into confusion. What if the coloniser is right? And when the coloniser leaves, unless there is a coherent project for the restoration of national consciousness, the suddenly liberated colony simply internalises the colonial condition in invisible ways, in both the country at large and in the heads of its inhabitants.

Ireland suffers still from the schizophrenia which is the principal hallmark of colonised peoples. This is both metaphorically and literally true: Ireland has the highest incidence of schizophrenia in the world. Today, after more than seventy years of alleged freedom, we are stricken with the disease which afflicts colonised peoples elsewhere, and yet appear to have none of their excuses. The freedom we achieved was a freedom in name only, and its occurrence simply served to drive the true nature of the colonial heritage underground where it could not be observed.

The classic pattern was followed. We developed our own native ascendancy class, who took over the administrative, political and cultural roles of the coloniser. The mentality continued to be as before. The Irish mind, though now 'free', but perhaps because of the nature of that 'freedom', repressed those aspects of itself which it had been taught to despise. It lost sight of the true meaning of culture as an expression of some inner compulsion, and either surrendered to the wash of culture from outside or adopted a version of culture which perceived it as a badge of defiance, a tight-arsed defensive roar in the face of the contempt which had been showered upon it. It undervalued its indigenous culture, or in some instances sought perversely to defend a superficial version of that culture in a manner which was bound to destroy it anyway.

'The native artist who wishes at whatever cost to create a national work of art shuts himself up in a stereotyped reproduction of details,' warns Fanon. And again: 'That extremely obvious objectivity which seems to characterise a people is in fact only the inert, already forsaken result of frequent, and not always very coherent, adaptations of a much more fundamental substance which itself is continually being renewed . . . Culture has never the translucidity of custom; it abhors all simplification. In its essence it is opposed to custom, for custom is always the deterioration of culture.'

This is what happened to 'Fáinne Geal an Lae'. We sought to revive it as culture in a form which was already inert. From the best of intentions, but out of a deep and basic insecurity, we began to think that if we were to preserve our cultural heritage we needed to keep it sterilised in clinical conditions. If it was to survive at all it should not be allowed to mix. This idea was based on a profoundly pessimistic view of the quality of Irish culture – in fact, on the coloniser's view of that culture. This idea was itself a product of colonial indoctrination. Ignorant of the dialectical nature of the relationship between culture and the post-colonial condition, the powers that be perceived themselves to be confronted by an opening up of the cultural pores characterised by a one-way process of cultural transformation. Misled by their own rhetoric, they saw a direct relationship between freedom and cultural nationalism. Moreover, they perceived the restoration of national values as an end in itself, overlooking the fact that the purpose of national cultural realisation is to enable a people to influence, permeate and interrelate with other cultures. Because they believed the people wanted what *they* had told them they should want, they imagined that all they had to do was provide the channels for the rendezvous of Ireland and the Irish mind. When it wasn't happening as they imagined it would, they panicked and reverted to an even more fanatical fundamentalism.

A brief glimpse into the mindset involved is afforded by this extract from a pamphlet entitled 'The Imported Press', written by an Irish Jesuit, Revd R. S. Devane SJ, in 1950.

'The final stage of the long struggle between Ireland and England is now drawing to a close,' he begins. 'In recent times, success on the Irish political and economic fronts has been encouraging; on the Irish cultural front there has been very heavy loss. Political freedom and economic freedom are, in themselves, valuable national assets. But if they do not, at the same time, connote the freedom of the Irish mind they must be seriously discounted . . . The process of anglicisation, about which so much was heard at the beginning of this century, has rapidly, though unconsciously, gone on, and in such proportions that the freedom of the Irish mind has been lost.'

The subject of the pamphlet was the influence of the British press in Ireland, but this it placed, reasonably enough, in a broader cultural context.

Where the analysis is seriously flawed is in the unwritten assumption that what is 'Irish' had, by definition, to exclude things which were 'not Irish', in the sense that they were the creation of other cultures. In this sense, Fr Devane's analysis is typical of much similar thinking by Irish nationalist intellectuals over the period from independence onwards. He continued:

> A factor of deep significance in the recent evolution of our country has been the establishment of the Gaelic League in 1893. Only those of the older generation can adequately appreciate the dynamic influence of that movement during the first decade of this century.

The soul of the nation was then deeply stirred by it. A mystic idealism spread throughout the land. A national messianism, the feeling that the nation had a sacred mission, took possession of the people. Ireland was on the point of realising the long-dreamt hope of being 'a nation once again'. The widespread revival of Irish music, song and dance, and the language revival, gave ample proof of the dawning of a new day. The nation was one in ideal and in action.

It is now sad to look back on those halcyon days, and to see the blight of the Civil War and the fratricidal strife that followed in its wake. Gone is the idealism; gone the mysticism; gone the messianism. They have been replaced by cynicism, fatalism and pessimism. Native music and song have given way to jazz, crooning and the dances of African primitives.

Given his view of their culture, Fr Devane might not thank me for lumping him in with the intellectuals of post-colonial Africa, but I think he shows signs of a condition which Fanon identified in that particular strand of post-colonial syndrome. In Africa, he notes in *The Wretched of the Earth*, 'the unconditional affirmation of African culture has succeeded the unconditional affirmation of European culture. On the whole, the poets of Negro-ism oppose the idea of an old Europe to a young Africa, tiresome reasoning to lyricism, oppressive logic to high-stepping nature, and on the one side stiffness, ceremony, etiquette and scepticism, while on the other frankness, liveliness, liberty and – why not? – luxuriance; but also irresponsibility.' The result of this process, he implies, is an excessive and uncritical insularity about the native culture of the newly liberated. He elaborates:

It is true that the attitude of the native intellectual sometimes takes on the aspect of a cult or of a religion. But if we really wish to analyse this attitude correctly we will come to see that it is symptomatic of the intellectual's realisation of the danger that he is running of cutting his last moorings and of breaking adrift from his people. This stated belief in a national culture is in fact an ardent, despairing turning towards anything that will afford him secure anchorage. In order to ensure his salvation and to escape from the supremacy of the white man's culture the native feels the need to turn backwards towards his unknown roots and to lose himself at whatever cost in his own barbarous people. Because he feels he is becoming estranged, that is to say that because he feels he is the living haunt of contradictions that run the risk of becoming insurmountable, the native tears himself away from the swamp that may suck him down

84

and accepts everything, decides to take all for granted and confirms everything even though he may lose body and soul.

In other words, there is at this point a danger of compounding the original wrong done by colonialism. The colonial mentality required a denial of the validity of certain aspects of the native personality which in our case would have been called Irish – and had to whatever extent supplanted them with elements which might be called, perhaps, English or British; now, we were being asked to make a further denial, to deny those elements which, for all they had been forced upon us, were inescapably now part of what we were. Paul Durcan, writing about Van Morrison, has referred to the Englishness which is an essential ingredient of the Irishness of Morrison's music. His song 'Summertime in England' is, writes Durcan, 'an Irishman's Hymn to the Englishness that is in us all if we care to look inside ourselves, which of course so many of us don't'.

The dialectic rears its interesting head. We should not be too critical of those who, out of excessive zeal or grief, sought to extinguish all those elements which they regarded as being alien to themselves. Neither is Fanon. There is a need for 'tearing away', but this could not, in the Irish case, refer to a tearing away from England and all she stood for, but rather from the slavish imitation of all she stood for while hating her all the while. The 'tearing away' would occur in the mind of the colonised; in negating the inferiority which the native felt towards his own culture – it would, paradoxically, enable him to re-enter the world and embrace his former master as a full human being. This tearing away, writes Fanon, painful and difficult though it may be, cannot be escaped. 'If it is not accomplished there will be serious psycho-affective injuries and the result will be individuals without an anchor, without a horizon, colourless, stateless, rootless – a race of angels.'

What Fanon was saying is that there is a sense in which you have to choose between the culture of the coloniser and the culture of your own past. You cannot have both together at once, because one has threatened to extinguish the other. But you must proceed in a manner so as not to negate that which you have chosen. The point is to understand the complexity of the choices to be made. They are not clear-cut. The mistake made in the pubescent years of the Irish state lay in thinking that we were completely free to reject everything English – forgetting that this rejection would involve a denial of part of what we were now. This error was compounded by a panic protectionist response to the fact that things were not working out as expected, the notion that, to preserve our own culture we had to reject *everything* from outside.

The Fr Devane approach in targeting jazz and African dancing in the course of a legitimate critique about the intrusion of the British media into Ireland is a graphic example of this response. It denies the very essence of all culture – that it is constantly alive, that it feeds off interaction with other cultures. You cannot mollycoddle a culture; you must interrogate it constantly. You must push it out the door into the rain. To serve your own culture you must in a sense betray it. But such subtleties were beyond the ken or interest of the Irish state apparatus. Having appropriated the rhetoric of the Gaelic Revival, it proceeded to internalise the colonial condition in its own policy. It spouted the rhetoric of cultural nationalism, but in practice made any such revival impossible. By, for example, insisting that broadcasting had to be self-financing, it made inevitable that indigenous cultural expression would come under severe pressure from imported product. The government's response to the unavoidable consequences of its actions was to increase the rhetorical quotient and try to ban jazz, crooning and primitive dancing from the airwaves. The unsustainability of this response led to the gradual abandonment of the Revival in all but rhetoric. As the 1960s were ushered in, the native elite was turning away from cultural nationalism and seeking its civilisation in the higher forms of imported culture. The Plain People of Ireland, meanwhile, were left to the tender mercies of the strange new metaphors beginning to envelop their lives.

In a 1988 essay, 'From Megalith to Megastore: Broadcasting and Irish Culture', Luke Gibbons makes the obvious observation that 'one does not counteract the one-way flow of cultural imperialism by closing ports and placing an embargo on all imported products'. This is a lesson Ireland has never learned. Instead of enabling the dialectical transformation of our own culture through contact with the world, we have largely seen ourselves only in the arrested, traumatised, mummified scraps of culture which the colonisers could not destroy. And despite decades of exposure to the incoming tide, we have yet to fully acknowledge ourselves in the offspring of the marriage between the 'indigenous' and the 'alien'. Each piece of Irish culture is therefore categorised as either natural or an aberrancy – part of what we are, or the consequence of what we were made to become. It is not difficult to work out why we have trouble knowing who we are.

'The strength of an indigenous culture', writes Gibbons, 'does not lie in its ability to avoid contact with the dominant forces in the culture industry, but in the manner in which it appropriates the forms and products of the metropolitan centre for its own ends.' The lack of commitment by successive Irish governments, he argues, had prevented Irish culture from making 'a sustained, creative engagement with popular culture'.

It seems like a contradiction, after all that, to say that where indigenous Irish culture was healthy it was *very* healthy. Some of the traditional music of the period was staggering in its power and inspiration. Some places, and some individual musicians, seemed to possess an immunity to the general condition.

In the 1970s in Ireland we underwent a whole cultural search to locate some kind of musical Irish Holy Grail. As Seán ÓRiada was beginning to cater to the higher-minded sections, the 'waiting for our Dvořák' school, by opening up traditional music to jazz and classical influences, the success of the Clancy Brothers in the US led to a folk revival which, for a brief moment of flowering, suggested that we had found what Fanon called 'the seething pot' out of which the future would emerge. (To be true to our colonial mindset, we waited until the Clancys came home announcing that the Americans liked them before we allowed the revival to begin.) A succession of bands and artists attempted various forms of fusion between the indigenous and the incoming in an effort to create a music which would be true to its place and yet not attempt to deny the irrefutable cultural torrent from outside. Much of it was highly inspirational, emblematic, fun. But much of it fell short of absolute truth, because it was less than entirely plausible.

Forgetting that the disease of the colonised mind is a progressive one that moves as we sleep, it attempted to go back to the source of the disease and take up from the last point of pure expression. It was an interventionist cultural expression rather than an organic one, which resulted sometimes in an uncomfortable – occasionally grotesque – mixing of the traditional and the modern. But these bands and artists did serve the very useful purpose of focusing our minds on the issue, which was that the choice to be made was not between our 'native' culture and that of outsiders, but between a way of expressing ourselves which was true to ourselves, whatever we were and whatever we felt, or being content to parrot the sounds and signals which the torrent of invading cultures told us were appropriate means of expression.

What was missing was spontaneity, self-confidence, and the ability not to care. We were obsessed with 'Irishness' – either with utterly embracing it or utterly rejecting it. Neither way left us with a truly spontaneous method of expression.

Most places in Ireland suffered from this constant war between the invading and the indigenous culture, and either the invading culture won or there emerged some bizarre hybrid which nobody could have imagined or created. There is a strong connection between the bland, fixed smile of the country and Irish showbands of the sixties and seventies and the militaristic marches we learned in school. Both were a denial of real feeling, and in that sense came from the same place. Both were expressions of inferiority, fatalism and self-hatred, defensive self-assertions in the face of cultural supremacy which damned us with low expectations. They were the pale imitations of those too half-hearted to find a true echo of themselves in what was raining down upon them. All this contributed to a culture that was sprawled on the ground unable to move, unable to interact except at the lowest possible levels of imagination.

Even at the most mawkish and banal levels of the makeshift culture, we could at least have managed to believe in it and struggled on to higher ground. Brian Eno, who has produced several of U2's albums, has expressed an interesting perspective on culture as compost. If you let the refuse pile up, and open yourself to its possibilities, it will eventually be transformed into something worthwhile. If you think of it as rubbish, that's how it will remain. But we were too inhibited, too lacking in self-confidence, to trust the evidence of our own senses. If we'd had the sense not to care, we would have pulled ourselves clear. We were trapped inside our own shared prejudices about one another, about the invading culture and about the seeming certainty of our inability to make our own culture come alive.

Then, one day in 1984, I turned on the radio and heard a young London Irish band called The Pogues, playing with accordions and tin whistles, and a singer with the voice of a rootless angel. This might have been the music which, had we the confidence to believe in it, we could have made for ourselves, had we not been numbed by the heavy hand of the Murder Machine. It then struck me that what made a culture was not the instruments or the tunes, or the style even, but the feelings that went into the playing, the source of the inspiration. There was nothing self-conscious about the way The Pogues played; they weren't trying to avoid any references, or emphasise any, either. They weren't trying to create fusions of hybrids, but were simply giving voice to the kind of music which made sense to them. Shane McGowan spoke in interviews about growing up in Co. Tipperary as a child, surrounded by Irish songs and music. The Pogues were not afraid to admit that they had been influenced by Big Tom and Philomena Begley, whom they heard on the jukeboxes of London Irish pubs in their teenage years. No straightforwardly Irish band could have made such admissions, but The Pogues didn't know enough to care.

It struck me that one possibility for Irish culture, repressed in the womb of post-colonial Ireland, had escaped in, of all places, London. This is not to suggest that the kind of music The Pogues made was the kind we should have been making all along. Well, maybe for a brief moment I *did* think this was the great missed music of modern Ireland. Then it occurred to me that I was making the same mistake as those who had set themselves up as the custodians of our national culture: I was perceiving in The Pogues a narrow Irishness, rather than the exhilaration and spontaneity which was its most interesting aspect.

CHAPTER EIGHT

Lead into Gold

When U2's fifth album *The Joshua Tree* was released in the spring of 1987, I, as editor of *In Dublin* magazine, asked one Billy Brown to review it. Brown was not a journalist, although I knew he could write, but an ex-showband star in his forties who had once been as famous in Ireland as Bono is today. I didn't know what to expect. Many of the showband heads deeply resented U2 and their success, usually parroting the old mantra 'They can't play' to conceal envy behind purism. Brown, as it happened, knew very little about U2. His interest in contemporary music had waned after his retirement from showbusiness some five years or so before. Having forged a new career as a landscape and wildlife painter, he didn't listen any more to pop or rock 'n' roll.

The piece he wrote is short – about five hundred words – enigmatic and strangely moving. Mostly it is about Brown's own childhood. 'When I was a boy,' he begins, 'if you wanted to be in a band, you had to be a musician.' It sounds ominous, but it is just a bald statement of fact. Brown had grown up in Larne, a Protestant town in the North of Ireland. He came from a musical family, his father and uncle playing in a band. He remembered going with them in the taxi to their gigs – 'they called it an "engagement"'. He recalled the big bass drum tied to the roof of the taxi, with the bass fiddle and the fold-up plywood music stands which he had helped his father to paint with the name of the band and the big G-clef in real gold leaf, and the drums with their layers of oil-painted scenes of Hawaiian sunsets and Alabama moons keeping out the rain. 'In the body of the vehicle, I'd sit with the horns piled on and around me, listening to the conversations of these sensitive men. I can still hear the leather and cardboard cases creak and smell the stale saliva from the saxes and the anguished shrieks of "Hell roast ye, Tommy", when the driver went over a bump and threatened to damage the delicate system of levers a saxophone depends on.'

The men would talk about Count Basie and Duke Ellington, Glen Miller and Benny Goodman, Charlie Parker and the new-wave be-bop. The musicians had GI haircuts, wore gold-rimmed glasses, 'and some had pork-pie hats and shades, which was as near as they could get to being black. They pulled all the best women and were looked up to by their peers and achieved a bit of local fame, but when they played they never made the hair prickle on my neck the way it did when I listened to some of the records they talked so much about.'

Brown goes on to describe briefly his own initiation into music. 'If you wanted to be part of it you had to learn to read the little dots of music and that excluded many.' He relates the advice he'd been given by his betters: 'Don't compose, sonny. Just read what's written, eh?' But, writes Billy Brown, 'I was saved by rock and roll.' After that came the explosion – first skiffle groups in the North, then showbands all over. 'There's a simple natural law at work of course,' he writes. 'A trout lays a million eggs but only one or two ever amount to anything. Van Morrison was notable from that batch.'

He is into his last one hundred words when he gets around to U2. 'Larry Mullen mentioned a few bands the other night on the wireless. He picked the ones that I liked. I think I would get on with young Larry.' The final paragraph ends with the following assessment of *The Joshua Tree*: 'I'm not sure what the words mean, and really I find it hard to get worked up about Salvador or the Yorkshire Miners or Ronald Reagan or the Spirit. But I love it when the hair on my neck tingles and the tears come in my eyes.'

In that short piece is contained not merely thirty years' worth of potted history of Irish popular music, but also a sense of perspective culminating in a sort of elder-brotherly dispensation, an acknowledgement of the U2 achievement that is both generous and proud. Billy Brown was not a man to sit on fences or to damn the young pretenders with faint praise. He knew and loved rock 'n' roll, and knew when it was good.

Latter-day music historians writing about the culture from which U2 emerged tend to dismiss the showband era beside which they grew up with a paragraph as angry as it is superficial. I say 'beside' rather than 'in' for a reason. U2 owe little or no direct dues to that culture, but it was nevertheless a central element of the culture that created them. The tendency up until now has been to paint Irish rock music since the 1970s as a new culture starting from scratch with Skid Row, Taste and Them and making a frenzied sprint via the Boomtown Rats to *The Joshua Tree*. The truth is far more complicated.

The sixties in Ireland were the creation of Seán Lemass, the revolutionary-turned-politician who had been involved in the Rising of 1916 and in 1926 became a founder member of Fianna Fáil, the party that would dominate Irish politics right up to the present. When Fianna Fáil went into government for the first time in 1932, Lemass became Minister for Industry and Commerce. Over the coming four decades he would have an unequalled impact on Irish economic affairs. He was a practical, energetic man whose aims were to make Ireland prosperous and peaceful and allow it to take its place in the twentieth century.

'We are not prepared,' he wrote early in his career, 'to watch calmly the de-population and impoverishment of our country . . . Unless we are prepared to see the scattering of our people over the face of the world and the destruction of our nation, we must take steps to preserve and develop here the industries which mean employment for our people in their own country.' In 1959, at the age of sixty, he became Taoiseach, and for the next six years – known today as the Lemass Era – would lead the most energetic government the Irish state had ever seen. His two Programmes for Economic Expansion are regarded as the most significant economic achievement by an Irish government. In any event, Lemass succeeded in reversing the centuries-long trend of out-migration from Ireland. As a consequence of the development of the Irish economy in the Lemass years, the seventies became the single decade in recent Irish history in which there was a net inflow of population rather than the reverse, with an average of more than a thousand people returning every month of that decade. Lemass had a favourite line – 'a rising tide lifts all boats'. But the rising tide of sixties Ireland was a highly selective one – economically and socially, and, ultimately, culturally as well. What in retrospect reveals itself as a top-down revolution had the effect of concentrating population on the east coast, where much of the discourse about the nature of change was then focused. The idea of modernisation was twinned with that of industrialisation, which henceforth became the mantra of progressiveness. This was the agenda dramatised week to week in the cabaret of *The Late Late Show*.

In the brief and fragile flowering initiated by the Lemass Era, Ireland acquired for a time the semblance of normality. The dramatic economic turnaround was accompanied by a revolution in popular culture, of which the showbands were part. It is almost impossible today to obtain objective descriptions of the kind of culture Ireland is – never mind of the kind of culture U2 emerged from. Usually what you get is a particular prejudice about an aspect of that culture, or even worse, a reaction to such a prejudice from someone who has been wounded by it.

Irish culture, in other words, remains tribal. We see only what corresponds with our idea of what we are, or conversely, the image of something which we definitively are not. The possibility of a dialectical understanding has not yet surfaced.

Kitsch, wrote Milan Kundera in *The Art of the Novel*, is more than simply a work in poor taste. There is a kitsch attitude, he insisted, kitsch behaviour, 'the kitsch-man's need for kitsch'.

Those generations which emerged from the Ireland of the past half-century, whose contact with art was limited to weekend dancing to showbands in the local ballroom will, in applying Kundera's words to their own experience, divide more or less equally in terms of their response. Half will be convinced that the other half are 'kitsch-men', and the 'kitsch-men' will regard the others as snobs. But the more you think about it, the more likely it appears that, because of our hidden post-colonial psychosis, we are all of us kitsch-men, incapable of distilling from the experience anything other than superficial delusions. All of us see culture where there is simply arrested development. Half of us want to rehabilitate the past, to tart it up as an icon for the present, the others to burn it at the stake. Both responses are kitsch, because neither is the truth.

This is a pity, really, because an objective enquiry into the state of recent Irish popular culture might end up yielding far more than a story of song and dance. We might, for example, see in the showband culture an image of our own colonised consciousness. 'It is imitation when the child holds the newspaper like his father,' says the psychoanalyst Annie Reich. 'It is identification when the child learns to read.' Franz Fanon argues that it is one of the hallmarks of colonised people that they can imitate but never identify. The showband culture was at once an unconscious expression of the post-independence failure to reconstruct an indigenous culture on solid footing, and a valiant attempt to create an instant culture with a big bang.

In the ebb and flow of this culture through the sixties, seventies and eighties can be seen the shadow of the social dynamic of the times. During the boom years of the late sixties and seventies, the showband culture was a dolly-mixtured range of music and styles, from the simple strains of the sub-country mutant known as Country 'n' Irish to the progressive rock of bands like the Platterman, whose singer was Rob Strong, father of Andrew who in the early 1990s would sing the songs he learned from his old man in the hit movie *The Commitments*. I grew up in the west of Ireland, allegedly the most conservative part of the country; and yet, in the early 1970s, I was conscious of belonging to a society which, for all its outward appearances of backwardness, was intensely 'modern' in its cultural aspirations. There wasn't much pop on the national station, RTE, but we listened to Radio Luxemburg and John Peel and Bob Harris on the BBC. Some people could even get BBC television, and would talk smugly about something called *Top of the Pops*. To grow up almost anywhere in Ireland in that time was truly to believe yourself at the centre of the world. But as the economic winds chilled with the 1970s oil crises and a mounting national debt, the thinning out of the more 'progressive' musical voices signalled the recommencement of emigration.

Country 'n' Irish has been the surrogate folk music of many parts of Ireland since the 1960s. Developing around the 'Galway Wallop', the rock 'n' roll offbeat applied to old-time waltzes and Irish standards, it was emblematic of the fears, conservatism and longings of the time. There is even a theory that it was a reaction to the mid-sixties shift from US to British pop, that Irish audiences, or at least those outside the cities, responded badly to the change in the beat which resulted from the emergence of the Beatles and Stones, which did not suit the strange ritualistic dance known as the jive. Country music, in any event, had been the product of the transmuted idioms of Irish narrative singing carried in the minds of the emigrants to America in the eighteenth century. Now it came home, a new mutant.

In 1992, when the controversial Fianna Fáil leader Charles Haughey was replaced as Taoiseach by Albert Reynolds, a former ballroom owner from the midlands, the Dublin intelligentsia unleashed a torrent of bile in the direction of the new prime minister on the grounds that he was a purveyor of 'country and western values' and therefore not a fit person to run the Irish state. On one level, it was pure snobbery, the old hillbilly taunt. On another, it was the expression of other, mirror-image fears, conservatism and longings, nurtured by a different section of 1990s Irish society.

After almost a decade of renewed emigration, that society had plenty to be insecure about, but these insecurities did not emerge in the rhetoric of 'the sound economic fundamentals' much in favour at the time. While it was pretty difficult at the time to work up any great enthusiasm for or against Albert Reynolds, I found myself rowing into the fray on his behalf in my column in the *Irish Times*. What bothered me most about the 'country and western' smear was its utter disregard for the facts of Irish popular music history. Albert Reynolds had little or nothing to do with cultural values, one way or the other. He was a businessman who had made his money in the entertainment business, who had never shown any evidence of interest in the music he facilitated. There was, *is* a debate to be had about pop versus country, but this wasn't it. It was an attempt to smear not just Reynolds, but also the three-quarters of the population who grew up listening and dancing and courting to showbands. As I wrote at the time, I felt stupid having to write in the *Irish Times* that there was nothing intrinsically backward or sinister about showbands, that there were good showbands and bad showbands, just as there are good writers and bad writers, and this is as much a matter of personal prejudice as objective aesthetic considerations.

The Irish rock orthodoxy about showbands is identical in essence to the snob-response to Albert Reynold's leadership ambitions. This view describes a hegemonic stranglehold by the talentless and derivative, a plagiaristic miasma of country and western and bad pop. This is accurate only up to a point. But moreover, the moral invective which invariably accompanies the charge betrays the extent to which the argument is off the point. What is being articulated is an ideological aversion, rather than the anger of the deprived.

In the first place, the showband scene did not consist merely of bad country and western copyists. There were actually some *good* country and western copyists as well, and one or two grotesque originals thrown in for good measure. Big Tom may not have been everyone's cup of tea, but he could not have been accused of sounding like anyone else. For all the sense of a slumbering sentimentality about him, his hulking, unsmiling presence bespoke a strangeness as real as anything in Samuel Beckett. All his material was cover-versions and much of it was sickly-sweet, kitsch-and-make-do songs like 'Gentle Mother', 'Flowers for Mama', 'Tears on a Bridal Bouquet', which were every bit as bad as their titles predicted. But neither was he incapable of mysterious empathy with the songs he sung. As you listen to his version of Merle Haggard's 'Sing Me Back Home', you cannot escape the sense that what you are hearing is not entertainment but drama. Big Tom's voice is hoarse and almost tuneless, but its ordinariness seems to match perfectly the mood of this one song. It is, moreover, his *own* voice, a husky Monaghan accent which makes no attempt at Americanisation. The storyline is both nostalgic and sentimental, but the guitar contains a strand of magic that rescues the lyric from the grip of self-pity. The song has in one verse more soul and meaning than a thousand guitar solos ringing around the bars of Dublin at the time. 'Sing Me Back Home' may be the one egg in a million that amounted to anything, but it gives the lie to at least some of the misdirected prejudice of rock myth about country showbands. They may not have achieved it often, but a lot of showband musicians knew what they were after. And the people who went to hear them went not because they knew no better but because they wanted something that they sometimes found, in short sharp flashes in the night.

There was also a mass of pop bands, literally hundreds, who played cover versions of US and British hits on the ballroom circuit. The Freshmen, Billy Brown's band, was one of these. It is almost impossible to convey to today's pop kids how much of a star Billy Brown was. He and his co-frontman, Derek Dean, were the target of hysterical mobs of young women wherever they went. Brown cut a particularly startling figure, with his long blond hair, dark beard and flower-power dress sense. He looked like a hippy but sang like an angel. He would walk on stage, take the cigarette out of his mouth and begin:

Apa-pa-pa-pa-pa-pa apapa oom mau mau/A papa ooom mau mau.
The funniest sound I've ever heard
A papa ooom mau mau/A papa ooom mau mau.
And I can't understand a single word

A papa ooom mau mau/A papa ooom mau mau.

It was impossible to hear this and avoid the urge to do something. It spoke to you at a level that bypassed your ears and your brain, and struck some dark corner of your psyche. It was strange, disturbing and made you want to throw yourself around.

Greil Marcus, writing about the original of 'Papa Oom Mow Mow' by the US band the Rivingtons, puts his finger on the song's secret: it made you sit up and say, WHAT? *What*? 'I know,' he writes, 'it's "Oom Mow Mow", but "Mau Mau" is what the Rivingtons meant.' Well, 'Mau Mau' is what the Freshmen *sang*. For anyone who was there, it was the funniest song they had ever heard. This was no pallid, diluted version of the original, but a blurted shock of the new from a band who knew exactly what they were doing. If rock 'n' roll is about strangeness – and, among other things, it is – then no one who was there would try to say that Ireland in the sixties was denied a rock 'n' roll initiation. The Freshmen were mainly a covers band – though Brown did write a number of fine songs – and they were best known in the early days for their covers of Beach Boys numbers. I remember the guitarist Rory Gallagher telling me many years later about going to a Beach Boys concert in Belfast at which the Freshmen played support and seeing the local band blow the headliners off the stage with their own songs. *Of course* the showbands stifled creativity, but many of them brought a new spark and an original touch to the music they covered. There were enough of such moments (the Royal Showband's 'The Hucklebuck' was a blistering three minutes as good as anything since) to convey to those who were attuned to the strangeness of the new sounds that there was a world out there unlike anything they had dreamed of.

The point, I suppose, is that while the showband scene was undoubtedly infected with mediocrity, predictability, sterility and reductionism, it was not completely lacking in variety or opportunity. The scene developed as a business rather than a culture – neither organic nor spontaneous. But in spite of – perhaps *because of* – the artificiality of its origins, it provided a distillation of the options of modern pop music and gave the emerging generation a glimpse of the possibilities that they might not otherwise have been given for another decade. If you want to talk about Irish popular culture in this period, it is the showbands and the folk revival that you must deal with. There was a beat scene in the pubs and clubs of the bigger cities, but it was small and no more original than the showband fare. Moreover, it did not percolate to the radio, which both the folk groups and showbands monopolised between them.

And then came Horslips. I can remember the first time I saw them on television, on one of the intermittent pop shows which RTE transmitted to us in one-channel land in the early 1970s. It was about teatime, probably on a midweek evening and I was watching television in a friend's house. I had vaguely heard of Horslips, but thought of them as some kind of variation on the orthodox 'progressive' sound, which did nothing for me.

The television presenter announced that the band had come into the studio to perform 'An Bratach Bán', a track from their debut album. The rest is a blur of sensation. I was conscious of the opening notes, three notes repeated on the bass guitar – *bbuuuumbbd bhed dumh! bbuum-duh-dum/ bbuuuumbbd bhed dumh! bbuum-duh-dum* . . . Then the organ came in, introducing a layer of something low and promising underneath. Then a hi-hat began to stake out the beat, a light ska that gave back to the tune in rhythm everything it took from it in reverence. And finally the electric fiddle: mocking, yet totally on top of its craft.

This is a lame attempt to describe the music in words. At the time I heard it not as the output of specific instruments but as a statement of intent. Even today, though I know what's coming, it has that same capacity to surprise. 'An Bratach Bán' was a traditional song in Irish, and this was the most shocking part of all. The five musicians all had long hair and wore glitter costumes and platform shoes. It seemed both sacrilegious and revolutionary, funny and serious, but above all . . . *right*.

The voice came in. Jim Lockhart, standing behind the electric organ, sang into the microphone, holding his hair away from his face. '*Vickheil yun un bradack banya/Vickheil yun on bradack banya/Vickheil yun un bradack banya . . . Cumyon mein thu lun hard salya* . . . It is impossible to convey today how deeply shocking this was to those of us who had been raised in an atmosphere of reverence for both Irish music and the Irish language. What Horslips were doing wasn't utterly unique to them – there were other bands like Planxty, in Ireland, and Fairport Convention, in Britain, but these seemed to be more interested in developing the tradition on the terms on which they had encountered it. Horslips seemed not to care. This was not merely a rocked-up version of a traditional tune, but a reinvention of the medium for a different version of history. It was as though we were being given a glimpse of what the radio might have sounded like if the past eight hundred years had happened differently. It was as though the underground stream of Irish music culture – the way it might have been – had suddenly erupted through the ground into the living rooms of early-seventies Ireland. Horslips changed the history of Irish popular music, and possibly much more besides. They acknowledged a hunger for an Irish music that would respect the permanent and yet be new, that would transcend all tradition and yet be real, everyday, spontaneous and true.

For a decade, Horslips tried to break out of Ireland, and ultimately they failed. But while they lasted they blew the cosy nexus of Irish culture wide open.

Horslips were the first genuine Irish rock band. They put Irish tunes to a rock beat and wrote songs based on the folk tales of Irish mythology. In retrospect, they seemed to have understood completely the dialectical nature of cultural growth. Refusing the diktats of both trad purists and rock snobs, they sang rock songs in Irish and folk songs in English. They used Ireland as their home, their inspiration and their source. Unlike contemporaries like Rory Gallagher and Thin Lizzy, who focused on London, they were based in Dublin and saw the ballroom circuit as the principal live market. They went away to Britain and the US and were written up in the music magazines, which allowed us to measure our own perceptions against the possibilities of the outside world. Then they came back and brought their increased quotient of prestige and credibility to the hall down the road. Their comings and goings, recreated in their music, provided a dramatised version of the culture which they now promised to bring to life.

Horslips were at once both a product of the showband culture and a reaction to it. They appropriated its slipstream, and ultimately made it bearable. They showed us its limits and its possibilities. They lasted a decade, until, caught between the conflicting demands of an idiom born someplace else and another as yet unable to free itself from the limitations of post-colonial babytalk, Horslips found their chances of growing shattered on the rocks of cultural incomprehension. Their early music was too rooted in Ireland to travel well to Britain and the US, and when they tried to develop it to appease the US market they found themselves losing the spark which had made them appealing at home. After a time, the Irish market was not enough for them, and the band split on the question of how to approach a definitive assault on the US market. When they broke up in the early 1980s, Irish rock again directed its gaze, through the prism of Dublin, to London and the US.

Horslips are the most plausible fragment of ancestry to be found in recent Irish popular culture for U2. In the smallest sense first: their experience provided a map by which U2 manager Paul McGuinness could plan his baby band's assault on the world from Ireland, for which there were few other guides. More importantly, they provided a cultural model by which their putative offspring might seek truthful ways of self-expression out of their own experience. It is not a coincidence that the Horslips bass player, Barry Devlin, produced some of U2's earliest recordings.

But there is an even more interesting way of seeing it. There are, according to Franz Fanon's analysis, three cultural stages in the trajectory of a colonised people towards freedom. Fanon wrote only about the role of literature, but let us, for the fun of it, spread the net a little wider. In the first phase there is unqualified assimilation: for which read showbands. In the second phase there is an attempt to remember, a going back to the past: 'old legends will be reinterpreted in the light of a borrowed asceticism and of a conception of the world which was discovered under other skies'. Let us see this as a reference to Horslips.

And the third phase? 'During this phase a great many men and women who up till then would never have thought of producing a literary work . . . feel the need to speak to their nation, to compose the sentence which expresses the heart of the people and to become the mouthpiece of a new reality in action.' What if, for 'literary work' and 'sentence', you were to substitute the word 'song'? And what if the third phase of Irish cultural reawakening had dawned in the form of . . .

But we move ahead of ourselves. It will be enough for the moment to say that U2 came not so much out of a place as out of a time. They emerged from a chink in Irish popular culture, a freak accident which in retrospect the entire culture seems to have conspired to create, a spectacular one-off now perhaps impossible either to better or repeat.

U2, having themselves been born with the sixties, belong to the first generation to grow up in Ireland in the post-Lemass era. The point about the sixties in Ireland is that while, yes, there was a revolution in attitudes, this revolution was fought mainly by the generation then in its twenties and thirties. Every Saturday night on *The Late Late Show*, they debated the shape of the society, slagged off the Catholic bishops and the outmoded notions of their parents' generation and demanded a form of freedom defined by the issues of contraception, divorce and abortion. They were obsessed with their society, but more with their needs from it than with their perceptions of *its* needs. And yes, they did succeed in changing that society, though not necessarily in the ways they had planned or imagined. One of the things they *failed* to do was hook up the younger generation, the one between themselves and their own putative offspring, to their wagon of concerns.

The Irish sixties revolution – being neurotic rather than political, and ideological rather than practical – provoked a very odd response in the young. In leaving them and their concerns to one side, it both limited its own development and created a generation which did not answer to any of the descriptions which its elders framed. To this day, for example, foreign journalists come to Ireland expecting to find a priest-ridden island where contraceptives are either forbidden or at least only to be obtained in highly controlled circumstances. In fact, for well over twenty years, contraceptives have been available to practically anyone who wants them. Condoms, for example, were common currency in schoolyards since the late sixties. What has been missing, however, is the legal framework which would acknowledge and guarantee this freedom, and it was the battle to establish such a framework, rather than the practical realities of the sought for freedoms, that preoccupied so much public debate.

This provides a perfect example of how the younger generations born from the mid-fifties onwards and who grew up in Ireland in the post-Lemass era, might reasonably have been described as living in a confused, almost schizophrenic state. In this state the descriptions they heard of their society were often as much in conflict with its reality as the sixties version of society itself differed from the certitudes of the era before. While the sixties' kids were fighting their parents about access to contraception, the younger generation was getting on with using condoms to full effect: while the 'rebels' fought a war against a reactionary Catholic Church, the younger generation made its own arrangements, reacting with a puzzled indifference towards both sides.

This was an odd phenomenon of a post-modern generation in an essentially pre-modern, sub-modern or half-modern, context. The sixties generation was already intent upon liberating itself, and succeeded to the extent of ensuring that its children would be brought up in a totally new place. But this other generation, halfway between the sixties generation and its own offspring, had to make do as best it could with the unfinished state of affairs.

It was noticeable, for example, that the effects of sixties liberation had not yet trickled down to provide cultural outlets for the attitudes of the generation perhaps ten to twenty years younger, and yet those attitudes themselves had moved on of their own accord. Other than one music magazine and a couple of half-hour pop shows on radio and TV, there was nothing to even acknowledge that young people existed, never mind give them an outlet for their creative energies and viewpoints. This generation was thus in a peculiar state of half-liberation and half-imprisonment within the moribund broader culture. While they were being bombarded with the language of liberation, they had to find images for their own feelings outside the society which for them was characterised by two conflicting forms of reaction: the old and the older still.

These forces are part of the chemical reaction that unleashed U2. Such subtleties of Irish pop culture were touched on by Simon Carmody, a contemporary of U2 and the Virgin Prunes, in an interview with Caroline van Oosten de Boer, for her book about Gavin Friday, *The Light and Dark*. 'If you want to understand anything about Gavin,' he told her, 'you got to understand he is coming from Dublin . . . The way he had to deal with things, you have to deal with that with humour and heaviness. You should suss out the scene he grew up with, the scene of the *Late Late Show* being the big thing. And Joe Dolan and the Wolfe Tones, Gay Byrne and Maxi, Dick and Twink [bands from the ballad and showband scenes] – and all that kind of thing coming in and being in Dublin. I was the same on another level when I was a kid, growing up and getting turned on to American rock 'n' roll and punk rock and not knowing anybody else who was into it. And having to deal with it within an Irish context. And that gives you a certain unique perspective on things, as opposed to an American kid who grew up on rock and roll, or a German kid who grew up listening to Lotte Lenya and being aware of the whole Brecht/Weill scene. It's not like that here, the culture didn't exist for that. You don't deny your own culture, you transmute your own culture. Which is why Gavin is still in Ireland, that's why I'm still in Ireland, involved in a process of transmutation of this culture. Not necessarily consciously, but that's what's happening. We're not in London or in New York, where we'd fit in. We are trying to turn lead into gold here.'

Gavin Friday himself, quoted by the same writer, was in agreement: 'The words come from me, how I see things, the world according to me. One of my main influences in life is the Catholic Church . . . football, bootboys, racism, macho-ism, you know, all the things that hurt you and mess you up when you're a kid.'

The post-Lemass era might be said to have peaked in cultural terms around the start of the 1980s – oddly enough, just as Britain was in the throes of a deep decline. Only then, and for the briefest time, did Irish society begin to have the appearance of what might be called a 'modern' society, with outlets of expression available across the generations. When finally it came, the new pop culture boom was a concoction unique to Irish circumstances, a reaction to what had gone before and yet an affirmation of a particular youth voice.

By 1977, there was a booming pirate radio sector in most of the bigger cities and towns. Dublin had a number of thriving pirates, including Big D, which featured a chaotic late-night rock show presented by Dave Fanning and Smiley Bolger, on which you might as easily tune into four hours of Tom Waits as an all-Irish rock night. Around the same time, there began a number of alternative periodicals dealing with arts, culture and politics. Three such magazines, *In Dublin*, *Hot Press* and *Magill*, started up in a fifteen-month period between 1976 and 1977. The principal drawback of the showband culture had been the absence of any instruments of discernment or discrimination. The scene was served by one music magazine, *Spotlight*, later *New Spotlight* and, later still, *Starlight*. In its various forms, this publication provided the public with a weekly diet of features, charts, gossip and news. It carried 'interviews' with international celebrities, many of which were cobbled together from foreign publications, and gave equal billing to interviews with local showbands. There was virtually nothing in the way of serious criticism, and showbands, beat groups and traditional bands were dealt with in a similar bland fashion.

When *Hot Press* began in 1977 it was a purely music paper, a shambolic cross between *Rolling Stone* and the *NME*. At this time, *In Dublin* was still in its infancy, a postcard-sized guide to entertainment in Dublin. The two publications maintained a healthy rivalry which caused them to spark off one another to mutual benefit. By 1980, *In Dublin* had grown into something indescribable. Over the coming decade, *Hot Press* would branch out into politics and social affairs, although largely in response to an ethic forged in the consciousness of the music that was its staple ingredient. In their different ways, both publications threw themselves into their times. I entered journalism through *Hot Press* and, a few years later, ended up editing *In Dublin*.

Hot Press brought, for the very first time, a vigorous and discerning critical view to Irish pop music. It was well written, though in a conventional and somewhat derivative way. *In Dublin* espoused a completely different approach to the business of journalism. It seemed more concerned with stylistic development, approaching language in a different way, using formal tricks which come from the novel rather than from journalism – intros, conclusions, narrative structure. It was a strange hybrid that derived mostly from US journalism, from magazines like *Esquire*, *Rolling Stone* and *The Village Voice*, but didn't look to any British model. *In Dublin* had sharp, vigorous criticism but, much more than that, it was about attempting to expose the world in all its irony and difficulty.

Although the magazines grew from different sources, they fused in themselves the cultural influences coming in from outside, not unlike the way country and western music had developed a decade before. The interaction between the two strands would create a peculiarly Irish hybrid which would seep into practically every crevice of Irish journalism over the coming decade. The connection between *Hot Press*, *In Dublin*, and the current affairs magazine *Magill* was less to do with content or objectives than with attitude and style. But together they amounted to an Irish counterculture. This was the first time there had been general interest feature magazines in Ireland, in which you could write about anything, from wrestling to politics to country and western music, all in the same way. *Magill* was concerned with the government, with electoral politics, while *In Dublin* looked to what was going on outside of that – women's issues, the inner city, media and general cultural issues, while *Hot Press*, in the early days at least, concentrated on rock 'n' roll and other forms of contemporary music culture.

These magazines helped in a manner utterly disproportionate to their circulation to change the way Irish society saw itself, particularly the post-sixties generation. Whether they were exploring pop music or police brutality, the magazines brought, for the first time to Irish journalism, a thing called *attitude*. You read them less to find out something that no one had known before, as to be shown something everyday in a way that nobody had *thought* about it before. As Irish society became increasingly complex, and these complexities could not be dealt with in relatively short newspaper pieces, a new generation of writers began to deal with issues in ways that defied the journalistic handbooks.

The people who wrote for the new magazines were the contemporaries of U2. In many ways it was a manifestation in print of the same energy of a generation lost between the aspirations of the sixties crowd and the new Ireland which they had only half-delivered. Most of those involved in alternative media were not professional journalists, and didn't particularly want to be. Like the would-be musicians, they were just hanging around. The seventies generation, in a sense, had to conduct not one but two rebellions: against the orthodoxy of the Ireland into which they had been born, and against the orthodoxies of those who could see only one direction in which it could go. There is a minor irony in the fact that these acts of rebellion came out of Ireland's only recent period of relative stability. The generation involved had been the first to grow up in Ireland believing that they would stay and live their lives in Ireland. It wasn't that they believed this to be their right, but that, for the first time since the Famine, they grew up without having to consider another option. For five or six years Ireland had this extraordinary climate of confidence and questioning. And then it went away.

Adam Clayton recalls that when U2 began, 'there were still showbands and there were still bootboys. And we existed somewhere between the two.' U2 grew up in a context that was not merely external to the cultural entity that was Ireland, but external to the Dublin of the time as well. You might say that they developed as a reaction to both.

Music doesn't emerge in a culture in a manner lending itself to glib footnotes and easily decipherable strands. It is not possible to explain a flowering such as U2 represent by reference to rock 'n' roll culture alone. Brian Eno once elaborated his humus theory to an interviewer: if you think about music as compost, 'it makes it much easier to accept that there might be lots of things that you might not want to hear again. They happen and they pass and they become the compost for something else to grow from.' For all its limitations the showband scene created a context in which some form of pop music could thrive – the compost heap of Irish pop culture through the sixties reawakening.

The U2 generation, while drawing on its indigenous culture at a deeper level, drew most of its motivational inspiration from outside. 'The *NME* was our initial education into the way that the whole thing worked,' Adam Clayton remembers. 'And the way we built the career of the band was by contacting journalists that we thought would be sympathetic to where we were coming from, and encouraging them to come and check us out. I remember one of our demo tapes – and this was a big thing – was in the *Sounds* chart, which their journalists did each week of music that they were listening to, and our demo tape was number one for a couple of weeks. And that was amazing. That was like, "We exist!" '

CHAPTER NINE

Water into Air

'One Tree Hill', from *The Joshua Tree*, was written for Greg Carroll, a U2 employee and friend who was killed in a motorcycle accident in Dublin in 1986.

This was the second time for Bono. 'I've already had it once, with my mother, and now I've had it twice,' he told one interviewer. Carroll had been a friend and an inspiration. They met in Auckland, New Zealand, when the band played there for the first time. That first night, Greg Carroll had taken Bono to One Tree Hill, one of Auckland's five volcanic islands. The images of the place would haunt him through the second half of 1986 and the recording of *The Joshua Tree*. Carroll was buried with full Maori honours after the wake lasting three days and three nights. 'One Tree Hill' is about that funeral. The song is the unspoken centrepiece of *The Joshua Tree*, the most intense articulation of its central metaphor of loss and rebirth, death and renewal. It's the saddest and yet most hopeful of songs.

The first time I heard *The Joshua Tree* right through, I had to write an article about U2, and that morning, as I sat down to listen and write, I heard that a close friend had died. Without having been told what 'One Tree Hill' was about, and long before I began to hear or think about the words, it was the song that lodged in my heart. 'I was thirsty and you wet my lips,' goes a line in 'A Trip Through Your Wires', the song that precedes it on *The Joshua Tree*. 'I was callin' out, I was callin' out.' The final bars seem to contain the threat or the promise of the song to come. This is true of all albums that you listen to a lot, but in this case the echo of the first guitar fragment of 'One Tree Hill' has somehow buried itself like a deep dread in the last phrases of 'A Trip Through Your Wires', maybe in that tight little drum roll with which Larry winds things up.

The Edge begins with a splintered guitar fragment, like the arid tapping of the first drops of rain on a galvanised asbestos roof. Larry shuffles about with a few brushes or sticks on dry stone or wood. The guitar softens as The Edge deftly smooths the figure into a rippling refrain which you can almost hear just before he plays it. He takes a bar or two to find his bearings. Like so many U2 songs, it sounds like it is being played for the first time. But somehow, no matter how often you hear it, it both surprises you and allows you to anticipate it. You know what it is, and then it becomes it. The bass drum abruptly descends on an offbeat, forcing its logic on the guitar, bringing sense and life to the almost desultory beginning. The guitar figure does a sudden chucka-chucka-chucka and is forced into the song. Then Bono. His voice is desiccated, but sweet rather than croaking.

> You turn away to face the cold enduring chill
> As the day begs the night for mercy, love.
> The sun so bright it leaves no shadows
> Only scars carved into stone on the face of it
> The moon is up over One Tree Hill
> We see the sun go down in your eyes
> You run like a riv-er
> Ooon to the sea
> You run like a riiii-ver
> runs to the sea.

The stream of sound has begun to course now through a channel which opens up before it. The vocals almost slow it down, dam up its gathering power. The highlife guitar ripples along, hardly seeming to touch the backing as it sketches in a light ringing figure. You see the sunlight shimmer off the surface of the water as it flows, shallow and unhurried, down a slight incline, gathering speed as it tumbles over the small rocks that litter the riverbed.

> He runs like a riv-er
> Runs to the sea.
> He runs like a rive-e-e-e-r
> To the sea.

You can hear the river come into its own. A low keyboard soars up from the depths, and at the same moment a cloud passes over the sun. You see the river broaden its sweep through the overhanging branches light as drumsticks. Majestic and relentless, it gathers speed. You step back; afraid. You see it shimmer in the guitar, but feel its energy in the driving force of the drums. The rocks are bigger now, the flow more insistent. Adam Clayton's bass drives the current on. The keyboards soar and swell underneath a surface that still glimmers in the sun; but there is a menace there now that sends a chill of dread and knowing through your bones.

Bono comes back in. The vocals, which previously fought the music, slowed it down, are now caught up in its swell.

> I'll see you again
> When the stars fall from the sky
> And the moon has turned red

> Over One Tree Hill
> We run like a river . . .

The water is too fast and too deep. The lines come out as low screams.

'And when it's raiiiinnning . . . They returnnnnnaah . . . That's when the rain will . . . break my heart-arrgh . . . Rainnnning.' At the moment of hope he sounds his most desperate. 'Raining. Raining. Raining in your hea-rt.' The voice is at full stretch now, the brittle roar of a deep-felt fear. The backing tears along, rapidly disintegrating in coherence, though not in power. The instruments blur into one, distorting and obscuring one another in a wash of sound. The guitar retains only the memory of a melody as it disintegrates into a thousand droplets. Only the bass remains strong and clear, steering the music into the mouth of its resolution. Then the band stops, as though in confusion, having scattered itself over the rocks into oblivion. Only the voice remains over the drone of a lone keyboard.

> Oh Great Ocean
> Oh great sea-e-ahh
> Ru-u-u-u-un to the oceaaannn
> Run to the-uh sea

The voice is calm now, accepting. Already the band has moved into the next song. It is called 'Exit'. It, too, seems to begin around the knot of an echo of its predecessor.

Aware that everyone who listens to a piece of music hears a different thing, I ask The Edge if he is conscious of 'One Tree Hill' in the way I have described it. Yes and no is, I think, the answer. 'I can see what you mean in pure sonic terms, yeah,' he says. 'That guitar sound and that guitar part. Yeah, there's something . . .'

He goes back to the beginning. 'I'd just got this new guitar, and I was seeing what it could do, and this part came out. It was just a jam. We were jamming with Brian [Eno]. He was playing keyboards, I was playing guitar, he was playing bass, and we just got this groove going, and this part began to come through. It's almost highlife, although it's not African at all. It has something of the highlife African guitar feeling about it. And the solo was then, like, I was playing with my toys . . . and the sound was for me at that time a very elaborate one. I would never have dreamt of using a sound like that before then, but it just felt right, and I went with it.'

Bono, who came to the song when it was half-realised as a sound, had not been conscious of the water connection until I asked him about it.

I didn't hear that. But that's a very interesting example of songwriting. Because those verses were written on paper, but the chorus was written in the moment. So it is likely that I picked that up. And rather than the song echoing the lyric . . . i.e. 'I have this song with this idea of the river, let's construct it around a river', it becomes the opposite. It becomes that I put down the language which is hinted at by the structure and the song. And that is the classic U2 scenario. Me having to put voice on the music, having to give voice to the music.

Sometimes, afterwards, you can see it. But at the time you just know that you've hit on something. You know: 'Yeah. I like this!' Or: 'Where are we going to bring this one?' So it's much less conscious. I think sometimes you start thinking about it and you actually put your hands on it, and I find that the trick is to actually keep your hands off it until it's done. Then you can start examining what you have. Things tend to get overworked and tired-sounding if you're too conscious and analytical as you record and as you write.

'I think that that's an interesting thing about Bono as a lyricist,' observes Edge when I relay him Bono's recollections of the song's genesis. 'He's often trying to express ideas that don't easily fall into pure vocabulary, pure words. And sometimes in the past, particularly when he hasn't really been as concerned with the pure meaning of the words as what they *tell* you – kind of below and above their pure meaning: what they tell you as a result of their context in the music – he used to write a lot of words by improvising on microphone. When we'd have finished the music, Bono would start applying a stream-of-consciousness vocal. In fact, we released one of these, "Elvis Presley and America", and that's exactly what he's doing. He doesn't do it much now, but back in those days – *The Unforgettable Fire* in that case, *The Joshua Tree* to an extent, although he was really getting much more, I guess, disciplined in his lyric writing on that record – but back in those days, sometimes the meaning, if you took it out of context, would not hold up. For us it was the meaning created by the context of the words in the music. "The Unforgettable Fire", the title track, is I suppose a good example. If you take the words out, they have a meaning, but nothing like as significant a meaning as they did in the context of the music. It's a very hard one to explain, because words are finite, but I guess music is not. There is no lid on music, in that sense. The possibilities go on and on. I guess Bono as a lyricist was touching on something in his writing which attempts to transcend pure meaning of the words, almost like a mantra, where the meanings would be separate to the importance of the utterance itself.'

*

From early Celtic times, the lament has been one of the standard forms of Irish balladic tradition. One of the chief functions of the poet in medieval Ireland was to write verses singing the praises of his master when he was alive, and to raise a keen for him when he died. Waters, the river, the raging sea, the tide, were constant motifs in such poetry as signifiers of life and death.

The Irish musician and composer Mícheál Ó Súilleabháin has spoken many times of the idea of music as rivers of sound, of the healing power of music deriving from its capacity to connect man with his true home. I saw him on television one night as I was writing this very chapter, talking about life as 'being somewhere you should not be . . . The place you should be is somewhere else', and music as the language by which we keep in contact with that place. He spoke of music as being like water, which begins at some point of resurgence, 'starting out somewhere', goes through life and finally enters the home of the ocean. To tell of this knowledge, he said, you must go into yourself, 'to find the dearest and deepest words'. And then? 'And then you go further, and you find music.'

'But you know,' says Bono in the same spring of 1994, 'rock 'n' roll was always made around rivers. Think about the Beatles, the Mersey sound. Think about Belfast. Think about the widest of them all – the Blues, Gospel, Jazz, all came out of the mud of Mississippi. Think of just the few towns around the Mississippi – there's more music in that hundred square miles than in the whole of America. So it does seem to be.'

And as he said to me a couple of years before, U2 are knee-deep in the mud of their own local rivers. 'It's Liffey mud, not Mississippi mud. But it is the same mud that the bluesmen wrote about. It's just the mud of everyday life and its contradictions and how you sell yourself out, and how you put the gun to the head of your innocence. You cock back the hammer, and one day you fire.'

Or you magic this thing out of air.

'Gone from air to water. And maybe back to air again.'

CHAPTER TEN

The Star Trap

We don't want our stars to be themselves. We want them to be what we want them to be. We want them to be idealised versions of *our*selves. In a sense, the relationship between fan and star is the missing part of the fan's relationship with himself. We look to the stars to act out our fantasies, and pay them well, we fancy, for the privilege. We give them everything we ever wanted, and they discover – too late! – that it wasn't what they wanted. They come to think of their stardom as belonging to themselves, and we flatter this presumption as much as is necessary. But we know that what we have given we can take away. We have tried to write the scripts of their lives in accordance with the pilot plot we prepared earlier for ourselves, but which is now gathering dust in the innermost crevices of our fantasy world. They are the living manifestation of our innermost identity, the escape of our uninhibited selves. They feed us with images of what we long to have become, and we in turn feed them valuables and hamburgers and cocaine through the guitar-shaped railings that keep us apart.

They begin with a look that is the marriage of themselves and an aspiration they have plucked from either the ether or the clothes rack of the time. They give it to us and we say, yes, yes, yes, but maybe . . . what if? And they change, and we change, and they change. And before they know it they have ceased to resemble the person they started out to be. They belong not to themselves but to us. We gather at the gate to take a look at our property, at the creations of our human craving. We strain to catch a glimpse of what might have been, of what we would have had happen to ourselves. We walk away uplifted and self-satisfied. Glad to have touched or glimpsed the garments of what might have been ourselves, but glad, too, that it isn't us on the inside of that gate. We are filled with a mixture of envy and relief. We have it both ways. The sour grapes turn sweet on our smug tongues.

The difficulty is when the cause of the stardom is perceived differently – as invariably it is – by the human being inside the body of the star. To become a true star, the human being must surrender his or her own identity to the greater public need. This is, usually, the only deal on offer.

The relationship between the star and the fan reminds me of the character in the Flann O'Brien novel *The Third Policeman*, who is gradually absorbing the characteristics of his bicycle, which in turn is coming more and more to resemble its rider. We 'invent' our stars in the image of our ideal selves, but they end up as fat, drug-addled, dependent, fucked-up, crushed and/or broken as we are able to make them. Except that their collapse is multiplied a millionfold. Our disintegration is but the square root of theirs, minus their bank balance divided by the number of their Grammies or gold discs. We start out believing that we want to be like them and end up knowing that we want them to be like us. Part of what we pay them for is the feeling we get from knowing that we, at least, haven't choked on our own vomit. We give them everything we ever wanted so as to prove to ourselves that it isn't worth it, and so vindicate our own ordinariness.

U2 have fought not to be drawn into this vortex of abuse and manipulation. The band, and Bono in particular, have become icons of the late twentieth century, after a journey which was for them creative, but which for us is a mixture of the creative and something else, something cobbled from the debris of the society of the spectacle. They fight this battle all the time, but they cannot, of course, completely succeed. They still live behind high walls and security cameras. There is no electric guitar in the railings of Bono's front gate, because there are no railings. It is made of iron bars backed by solid wood, almost ten feet high, behind which an imitation of normality reigns.

It is difficult not to see these men as stars, to remain uninhibited by the ubiquitousness of their faces. You see the human being but have to fight the idea that he is an interloper in the body of the icon. But determinedly, through the mists of illusion, their humanness seeks to peep through: Bono eating a mixed grill for breakfast in the Killiney Court Hotel in Dublin; Adam poking the fire of his Rathfarnham house; Edge arriving late because he's been delayed at the funeral of a friend's father; Larry sitting talking over a meal backstage among the technicians and road crew.

Because it is impossible for a fan to talk to a star on common ground, it is unwise to generalise about how the relationship is seen from inside the glass cage of stardom. But a few things can be said in reasonable certainty. Firstly, there is almost always a certain ambiguity in the mind of the young man or woman embarking on the road to stardom. To begin with, the star is a wanna-be like the rest of us. Celebrity comes, by and large, to those who want it. And this desire can be detected in even the most vehement and heartfelt protests against the invasion which ensues.

U2 sought to subvert the process of stardom, not by running away from it, but by walking into its jaws. From an early stage they seemed to understand that, in the modern world, celebrity is not something which occurs as a by-product of creativity, but is an organic element of it. In other words, nothing tells us as much about ourselves as our need to create celebrities, and those who supply that need become the statements which best describe our condition. No such artist remains a star for long without understanding this condition implicitly and completely. It is arguable that any artist who does not have to grapple with this situation is not an artist at all, at least not in the sense of engaging with the condition of his species at this moment of evolution or disintegration. And yet, as we have seen so often, the procees itself extinguishes the creative spark in the unwary or the unwise.

U2's unique odyssey has, fortuitously or by dint of a benign instinct, allowed them to confront this condition as nobody has ever quite done before. Their lopsided development, which caused them to write songs about God before they wrote songs about love, has also allowed them to become anti-stars at the moment of their greatest celebrity. Not entirely, of course, but in essence at least.

U2 came of age as human beings during the period when the world lost, within forty months of one another, the two greatest stars of the modern world. Elvis Presley was dehumanised by becoming the embodiment of our longings, John Lennon tried to buck the system by walking away. Bono remains himself by turning the lessons inside out. U2 had just enough time to think it through before stardom was thrust upon them. By the time we turned our appetites on them, this Fab Four were ready for us. Almost. There was a moment or two of hesitation, during which they struggled in our determined hold. We tried to turn Bono into God, so we could mock him and crown him with thorns, but he had seen the movie. We wanted him to be important so we could accuse him of self-importance. Be vocal and caring, we said, so we can laugh at your earnestness. This, said Bono, is not a good deal. The Fly was born, a sort of postmodern Judas who knew both the value and the price, who could laugh at us laughing at Bono and so short-circuit our attempts to destroy him with his own pomposity. Instead of offering himself up as a blank canvas for our fantasies, Bono created for us a star as empty and one-dimensional as anything we were capable of inventing. So now we ride the U2 celebrity bicycle, but little or nothing rubs off. Our attention is directed, willy nilly, towards the music which travels, snug as a bug in a rug, inside the Trojan horse with the star on its brow.

Popular culture is centred on glamour and stardom, and anyone who fails to recognise this had better look for a means of expression someplace else. Hand in hand with the glamour factor goes an earning capacity unmatched by other forms. This interrelationship is partly the reason why rock 'n' roll and related forms are never taken seriously by cultural establishments. Because glamour and money *can* corrupt, the assumption is made that they always do. Because stardom is a necessary part of the journey and the statement, it is assumed that everything exists to serve the alleged drive towards fame and wealth. Nothing else is perceived, or at best is perceived only as a meretricious attempt to achieve wealth and celebrity. Rock 'n' roll songwriters and performers are credited with intelligence, but only the kind that can calculate the means to the objective of stardom. Their work is admired, yes, but only as artefact – the cunning creation of a mind in search of fame and money. Into this thinking is built the inversion of normal critical criteria. The greater the work, the argument goes, the higher the order of cunning.

Rock 'n' roll artists cannot avoid this trap. They must handle it as though they were already behind the wheel of their coffee-coloured Cadillac and the vehicle taken into a bad skid. They must steer *into* it, not, as their creative instinct whispers them to do, *away*. This is why they sometimes make self-conscious jokes about their wealth and success, like Larry Mullen's gag about 'The Money Tree' – so as to anticipate the prejudice with which they expect to be greeted.

But there is another difficulty, which arises not from the malign intentions of the industry or external world, but from the aspirations of the people at whom rock 'n' roll is addressed. The fan looks to the artist for something he or she cannot get anywhere else, and thereby contributes to the process of making the artist into a star. The artist needs the fan, and in this sense needs stardom as an intrinsic element of the apparatus of his developing creativity. But it is in the essence of fandom that the relationship is to some extent an exclusive club, embracing only like minds in a conspiracy to which outsiders are not privy. Thus, an artist who begins to perceive stardom as something in and of itself is immediately in direct conflict with the aspirations of the true fan. By definition, artists or bands who become too popular become, by the same process, suspect in the eyes of their truest fans. Before long, the star is at the mercy of those who see only the star on his brow.

Fame, in other words, starts out being a part of what you want and ends up being a pain in the arse. 'It is a complete contradiction,' says Adam Clayton, who is in a position to know. 'You think that by being given the platform you can express yourself to other people. And you think that fame gives you that – that you can actually go on a one-to-one with the whole world, and they know who you are, and what your problems are and what you're feeling. But that's not actually what it's about. That's not what the people want. They want to give you this fame, but they want you to pretend to be the person they think you are. They don't really want to know who you are. And that's what trips up everyone who comes across it young – you suddenly realise that you're completely exposed, and you don't have any tools or devices to cover your ass. So you *do* go out there waiting to be crucified – for want of a better word. And you're prepared to lose your temper in public and shout at photographers and hope that next time they'll not do that. But, of course, they'll do it even more, to get that reaction from you. So it's a strange thing, but I think we probably *are* gettin' the hang of it.

'I think that when Bono decided to redefine himself as the Fly, as a public persona, I think he already knew that he'd already been crucified for wearing the cowboy hat, and become a caricature. So, rather than expose himself to that extent, he said, "Well, okay, let's give the media something that I don't particularly care about, that allows me to do certain other things but isn't me." And I think that's what happened with Zoo TV, and the Fly character and MacPhisto. I think the real Bono is kinda harder to find now.'

CHAPTER ELEVEN

The Absent Presence

On 18 May 1987, U2 were the guests of the Taoiseach at a special state function to mark the launch of *The Joshua Tree* which had been released some weeks earlier to virtually unprecedented worldwide acclaim. For some reasons that I am unable to recall, I cut out some photographs of the occasion from the newspapers of the time. I can't remember then being conscious of what they signified, though now I have the beginnings of a glimmer of understanding.

One of the photographs is from the front page of the *Irish Independent*. It shows The Edge shaking hands with the Taoiseach, Charles Haughey. The photograph was taken on the steps of Iveagh House, the headquarters of the Department of Foreign Affairs, in Dublin. The U2 guitarist is as soberly turned-out as ever I've seen him, but he still isn't what you'd call respectable. He's wearing what is obviously his best jacket, a dark sports coat with a light check. His shirt is buttoned up to the neck, but he is tieless. On his head is the then familiar wide-brimmed hat. He is clean-shaven, and his long hair is tied in a ponytail. The Taoiseach is wearing a pin-striped suit – *blue*, the newspaper article informs us – and a shirt and tie.

If you allow yourself to see from inside the bubble of conventional thought from which we have gawped at U2 and what they signify, you look at the photograph and think: *there's a picture of The Edge shaking hands with the Taoiseach.* But if you emerge from the bubble, the image becomes utterly fascinating on a number of levels. The Edge's face is a picture of openness. He is smiling pleasantly and looking directly into the face of the Taoiseach. Charles Haughey, on the other hand, is looking downwards, in the direction of The Edge's midriff. In the background is a bearded man, possibly a civil servant, and a member of the Garda Síochána. Both of them are looking at Charles Haughey, not looking at The Edge.

I'm not trying to suggest that, throughout the two-hour lunch, the Taoiseach avoided eye contact with his guests. He couldn't and wouldn't. I'm more interested in the awkwardness which this photograph suggests invested the initial meeting between these two men. Charles Haughey was not given to shyness; through the seventies and eighties he was the most vain and flamboyant of Irish politicians. During a couple of brief periods as

Taoiseach in those years, he met and entertained many of the leading world statesmen of the period, and remained unfazed. But this photograph suggests that he was more than a little out of his depth with U2: he did not know what to make of The Edge.

There is, too, an ambiguity in the photograph as to who is meeting whom. Is the occasion supposed to honour this world-beating rock band, or to massage the ego of the prime minister? A good question, but not as interesting as the one that lies bubbling underneath Charles Haughey's fixed smile: who the hell are you and what are we supposed to talk about? The Edge's demeanour suggests that he is quite happy to meet the Taoiseach and shake his hand. Dave Evans is a well brought up boy. He is here because he has been invited. He is here, he may reasonably presume, to be honoured for the music he has created, and which has now insinuated itself into the soul of the modern world.

The lunch was the Taoiseach's own idea. The report informed us that he thought it would be a fitting tribute to the band's 'magnificent achievements internationally'. Just three months back in office at the head of a minority government, Mr Haughey was working hard to cultivate his public image so as to pursue the overall majority that had evaded him in the past. But the occasion was not necessarily a cynical gesture designed to court favour with the young (it may well have been, but that is beside the point). What you realise, looking at the photograph is that Charles Haughey thought he was meeting a *pop star*, and he didn't know what you're supposed to say to pop stars.

Charles Haughey, in or out of power, was not an easy man to encounter. He resented competition and sought always to gain the upper hand. But this photograph betrays none of his normal poise and arrogance. He is genuinely awkward about the encounter. He is awkward because he does not understand the first thing about U2. For two decades, Charles Haughey had talked about the heritage and vision of our proud nation, and here he is shaking hands with one of its greatest modern exponents, and he doesn't know where to look. A year before, Haughey published a volume of thirty years' worth of his own speeches, a gigantic doorstop of a book comprising 1216 pages of pure ego. He called it *The Spirit of the Nation*; here, now, is that very spirit staring him in the face and he cannot look it in the eye. All he can see is this pop star with a ponytail and a funny hat. The photograph is entitled: 'Getting The Edge on Charlie'.

Of course, this is only one photograph, one fractured image caught in the click of a single instant. Maybe. On page nine of the same newspaper, there is a group shot of the Taoiseach and U2 inside Iveagh House. Charles Haughey is standing in the middle, looking to his left at Bono, who stands between the Taoiseach and Adam Clayton. To Mr Haughey's right stand

The Edge and Larry Mullen. None of the four members of U2 is looking at their host. Bono is obviously giving out a line of chat, and the Taoiseach is looking smilingly on. His smile appears forced to the point of strain. Bono is looking at the camera. His hands are coming up in a gesture of some kind, but he looks uncomfortable, in spite of his smile. Larry Mullen and The Edge look evenly across Charles Haughey to Bono. They appear relaxed, if not quite at home. Adam Clayton looks disinterestedly towards the camera. The headline on the photograph is: 'It's only rock 'n' roll . . . but he likes it'.

He doesn't particularly. Although Charles Haughey liked the folk music of the Dubliners and the Furey Brothers, rock 'n' roll was as much a mystery to him as to most other Irish politicians. 'He had been in the same class at school as Larry Mullen's father,' the newspaper report confided, 'so he knew "a bit about them", he boasted. And, oh yes, he knew their music.' As for the band themselves, they were 'lovely' – 'simple, straightforward North Dubliners'. The Lord Mayor of Dublin, Mr Bertie Ahern, who would later become Minister for Finance, was also present and was, we were assured, 'immensely impressed by their up-to-the-minute knowledge and strong opinions on a wide range of topics'. 'They're not rock 'n' roll full-stop men,' he 'quipped'.

I am reminded, for some reason, of a piece of writing by the Irish journalist and critic Fintan O'Toole, first published in *The Irish Times* in 1989 and reprinted in his collection *A Mass for Jesse James: A Journey Through 1980s Ireland*. Entitled 'Strangers in Their Own Country', it deals with the renewal of emigration from Ireland in the late 1980s. O'Toole is a fine writer, a Dubliner, and, by a happy coincidence, almost a contemporary of the four U2s. 'I keep coming back to emigration,' he writes, 'and I know why. I and people of my generation belong to a quirk in Irish history, a flaw in the otherwise perfect pattern. We are the only generation since the Famine which has not emigrated in large numbers.'

O'Toole then addresses the question of why it is that emigration, which for him, as for me, was virtually unthinkable, 'had become for people only three or four years younger something that you didn't have to think twice about'. The basic – he might have said the banal – answer is economics: not enough jobs. But there are, he decides, many other factors. 'And more and more, I find it hard to dismiss the idea that one of these particular things is the sense of internal exile, the sense that Irish people feel less and less at home in Ireland, that Ireland has become somehow unreal, unrecognisable.'

This is one of the things I saw in the *Irish Independent* photograph. Charles Haughey did not recognise The Edge, although Dave Evans *did* recognise Charles Haughey. They came from the same side of the Liffey but from different parts of the Irish mind. As O'Toole dryly observed, there are no statistics on the state of unreality. 'Ireland has become so multi-layered, so much a matter of one set of images superimposed on another, that it's hard to tell what's in the picture in front of us.'

Another book that comes to mind on seeing that photograph again is *Dead Elvis*, a collection of pieces by Greil Marcus about the iconography, meaning and memory of the life of Elvis Presley and his relationship with America. 'American culture,' writes Marcus in a response to Albert Goldman's posthumous assassination of Elvis, 'has never permitted itself to be exemplified by Elvis Presley, and it never will. But certain Americans – and of course people from all over the world – have recognised themselves, and selves they would not have otherwise known, in Elvis Presley: Americans whose culture had taken shape long before Elvis Presley appeared, and those whose culture would have had no shape, would have been in no way theirs, had Elvis Presley been willing to keep the place allotted to him.

'He wasn't willing to keep his place, and now he is being returned to it. It is altogether fitting and proper that this be so, because as a redneck, as a hillbilly, as a white boy who sang like a nigger, Elvis Presley was never permitted to join the culture that has never permitted itself to be exemplified by what he made of it.'

Together, these two observations can be rearranged to capture the essence of the relationship between Irish society and U2. Ireland is incapable of recognising U2 for what they are, because they belong to a place which has never been admitted into any of the official descriptions of what the society is like. They make no sense, other than as celebrities, stars, rich young men who somehow felt it appropriate to begin their assault on the charts and minds of the world from a place called Ireland. Given the descriptions we have had to work within, U2 are an aberration of Irish cultural historiography. The fact that they are perhaps the most up-to-date representation of Irish culture available has been rendered invisible. Just as the US never permitted itself to acknowledge the self-description that Elvis Presley gave it, Ireland has never shown the slightest sign of allowing itself to be exemplified by U2. That is what was to be seen in that photograph of Charles Haughey meeting The Edge.

What are 'rock 'n' roll full-stop men'? This is the statement of someone who has never hurried home to put on yet again the record that has been in his head since he first played it a week before, and which has dominated his existence since then like a new infatuation that makes the 'real' world seem trivial and unlucky. To somebody who has grown up with a part of this music, for whom it can mean everything as well as suggesting a million things that have never been thought of, the phrase has no meaning and yet is full of significance. It is not merely a slamming-door denial of everything the music makes possible, but a steel bolt driven home against the recognition of the denial itself. Anybody who has taken the trouble to listen to even the smallest part of U2's music would not be in the slightest bit surprised to find that its creators had 'up-to-the-minute knowledge and strong opinions on a wide range of topics'. 'They're not rock 'n' roll full-stop men', is just another way of saying 'They weren't as empty-headed as I had expected.'

U2, apart from all their other achievements or impacts, have also been responsible for pioneering a new development in Irish popular culture. 'They have acquired,' wrote Eamonn McCann in *In Dublin* in 1987, 'the credibility of both Seamus Heaney and Barry McGuigan.' Nobody had ever done this before. The problem is that, in attempting to make sense of what U2 has achieved, we in Ireland tend to look more to the McGuigan end and leave the rest of the world to work out the precise nature of the relationship between U2 and Seamus Heaney. We have always felt proud of U2, and yet have failed to understand what they've done in a way which is true to what has actually happened. Their achievement is therefore liable to be of limited use in making sense of where we now live.

'Somewhere along the way,' says Adam Clayton, 'we became synonymous in Ireland with the football team, with any other successful Irish sports star. And that's always been something that I think the band has wrestled with. I mean it's always flattering when you come back to your country and someone wants to hold a state lunch for you, and you go along with it, because, you know, it's a little bit like the Beatles getting the OBE or something. Although it's not a part of your culture you feel it's churlish to cut these people off from being involved in your success. In actual fact, most of that side of it is they're really looking after their own end – they couldn't give a damn about what you do, except somebody's told them that you've been good for the country. But at the end of the day they're not really that interested in understanding – they just want the association.'

The problem, says Bono, is in confusing statement with achievement and meaning with phenomenon.

> At first we used to just love it – I thought, 'Wow, this band, we might be one of the first artists in Ireland that actually Ireland doesn't turn on.' Because we have a history of revering, and then eating, our artists. And I thought, 'Well, it's not gonna happen,' because everyone was so into us winning that I thought, 'This will be very interesting, because this really breaks new ground for Ireland.' So we went along for a period with the idea of, yes, if you like, carrying the torch, the flag, whatever. And then you start to realise that people are into you without even knowing, or having any understanding of, your music. It's like supporting a football team and you don't even know who's playing on the team, or what

the strategy is, or what competition you're even in. You just know it's a team. And that's started to frighten us, and we started to be a little wary of that. And also the thing that went with that, which is that stance that most artists take, which is just to the left of the mainstream, or just on the fringe of whatever is going on, is taken away from you. You find yourself centre-stage in the spotlight, standing there like rabbits in the headlights.

The issue is not of retaining a state of disestablishment. There is no danger of U2 or any other rock band getting too close to the government or the centre of power. The problem is that, in embracing one aspect of the band's achievement, the Irish establishment pulled up the ladder on their wider meaning.

It isn't that U2 are not admired in Ireland, but that they are admired for the wrong reasons. 'The number one rock band in the world,' we tell ourselves, without asking what it means. We count the record sales and tour receipts, or measure coverage in the international media. We are well pleased with their success and what we think it tells us about ourselves. The *Band of the Eighties*, no less! There is hope for us all yet, we tell ourselves happily. This kind of recognition, however generous or well-intentioned, is ultimately a short circuit. U2 woke up in an Ireland which isn't in the official version, although it answered to the name of Ireland. And in trying to assert, define or even address this place, they find that approving noises are coming in their direction, implying that their version has been accepted. 'Yes, yes, yes,' people say. 'Sure we *love* the U2! Sure the U2 are great!' The problem is that the speakers almost invariably want U2 to join the official version on *their* terms. But they neither know nor care where this band came from or what it is they've been trying to say.

The idea that what makes U2 special is the way they have entered the imagination of the modern world, extending that imagination by means of the senses rather than the intellect, evoking feelings and perceptions which transcend the medium of rock 'n' roll (yes, Bertie Ahern was right about that!), is an almost impossible idea to communicate in the country which begat them. The idea that U2 are one of a small elite of bands and artists who have sought to transcend the role of entertaining is something we have little capacity to grasp. The notion that their music is actually 'about' something causes a furrowing of brows which is not in the least abated by the announcement that what it is about may actually be *ourselves*. The idea that U2 are attempting to give a voice to the feeling of being alive at this point in history is simply too much. Lighten up, John! It's only rock 'n' roll (but he likes it).

How do you begin to explain? To say that the story of U2 is one of the most interesting and exciting in modern culture? *Oh yeah?* That it is the story of four nobodies who, through the discovery of their own creativity, defied their own destinies. *So?* So here were four ordinary young men, from a nondescript part of a run-down capital city, who believed sufficiently in their own capabilities to imagine their own escape. *And?* And unearthed their own creativity from the debris of unhope. *Yeah?* In a land where dreaming was all but illegal, Paul Hewson dreamed out of himself a capacity to sing that might have made us look at one another with different eyes. The Edge, Dave Evans, because he couldn't play the guitar the way other guitarists did, learned to play in a way that nobody had ever played before. *So what?* So the sound U2 made together seemed to give voice and flesh to all the dreams and hopes of a generation which had momentarily glimpsed the same possibilities for itself. *Get up the yard, there's a smell of Benjy off ya.*

U2 came to hold a mirror up to their own generation because in many ways their experience was a kind of topsy-turvy version of the generality of that generation's experience. They represented a mix of backgrounds and sensibilities which belies the conventional insistence that we are all the same. These Children of Limbo, born in the blank space between a thousand different versions of their country, grew up with a need to express dissent from everything we had taken for granted.

If you lived in the Ireland of the past thirty-odd years, and were intimately attuned to the ideological conversations being conducted when U2 were making their first tentative steps and sounds, it was almost impossible to understand the band without undergoing a serious wrench. Their success made them noticeable, by making their existence irrefutable. But it did not make them understood, because that would have fatally undermined what we perceived as reality.

U2 are an Irish band. I don't mean simply that they are a band which happened to begin performing and making records in Ireland, which is not a matter of widespread controversy. I mean that they have emerged from a place and a time – Ireland in the 1970s – which was the product of a historical and evolutionary process, and that they are as faithful a representation of that place and time as it is possible to conceive of. Moreover, I contend, this very fact is not an incidental, but a vital part of the reason for U2's appeal and success.

The hardest place in the world to communicate this idea is Ireland. It is not so much that we have wilfully decided to deny U2 their proper place in our culture; rather that circumstances have conspired to lock us out of an understanding of what they mean. It is not that our culture has not allowed itself to be exemplified by what U2 make of it, but that this culture has never been given the slightest acknowledgement in the mainstream. It is an invisible culture, as invisible as angels. It receives no affirmation other than by virtue of misunderstanding. We pay tribute to what we imagine is the substance – the money, gold discs, column inches – and ignore the shadow which tries to tell us everything.

In the Irish newspapers, for example, there are essentially three types of mention which U2 receive. Most of all, and increasingly, they are the subject of celebrity gossip: Adam's love-life, Larry's motorbike, The Edge's marriage, Bono saying 'fuck' at the Grammy awards. Then again, there is the inevitable, 'Who the hell do they think they are?' stuff – particularly in evidence in the Zoo TV period. But most interesting of all is the 'It's only rock 'n' roll' faction, who pay glowing tribute to U2's 'achievement', wealth, fame, popularity and charm, but intercept every attempt to treat the band seriously with sneering rejoinders aimed not at the band but at those who try to write about them as either culture, or – Heaven forbid! – *art*. The only place serious criticism or analysis is permitted is in the pages of *Hot Press*, which is therefore the only place where it is remotely possible to gain an understanding of what U2 mean. But because *Hot Press* is a rock paper, the thrust of the coverage there tends to put the music in the context of rock 'n' roll culture, rather than of mainstream or Irish culture.

In the early days, U2 were protected in Ireland, cherished by the love of their more dedicated fans. In a sense they were over-protected, treated as delicate flowers against whom not a word of criticism could be uttered. But, in a manner uncannily emblematic of the drifting away of their protectors on the rising tide of renewed emigration, the band have become increasingly exposed to a new kind of scrutiny. Adam Clayton, through his involvement with the supermodel Naomi Campbell, has been able to observe the changes at close quarters.

> I now have to think a lot more carefully about where I go, and just accept that there will be press there, there will be people watching. Ireland was always beyond that – it never came into Irish life. It is now beginning to be part of it. Every little itty-bitty story that comes out of here gets wired out and ends up in the British press and then it gets to New York. And we can all sit around and laugh at some story about Larry's girlfriend leaving him and going to live in Paris – because *we* know the *truth* – but when that story is running across Europe and into America, it's a bit more serious. In the past few years in Ireland, there's been this, 'Hey, we can all get on the gravy train. We've got *celebrities*! We can take a picture of them going in or out of the National Concert Hall and make a bit of money. And perhaps U2 have become natural prey.

A sufficiently banal example of how grotesque things have become is afforded by the public response in Ireland to the opening early in 1994 of the newly renovated Clarence Hotel along Dublin's quays, a staid relic of a bygone era which U2 bought and refurbished as a gesture of participation and respect in the direction of their native city. In the basement of the hotel is a state-of-the-art nightclub, The Kitchen, for which the band had ambitious plans. It was, of course, misunderstood. The impulse and sentiments behind the project were swamped in the rush of the media celebrity hunt of the opening night. There were none, so the press carried a raft of articles complaining about the absence of celebrities.

'The whole idea of having a club', The Edge explained to me, 'is it gives us a chance to develop a place to connect with Dublin culture and music directly. Somewhere that is your own, that you feel comfortable in. We've talked about having a club for years. I have this idea that I'm loosely calling ClubNet, linking up some audio-visual ideas. So you'd have people dancing in a club in Dublin to a DJ in another club in London. And each crowd could see the other on monitors, and maybe there'd be a telephone by the monitor . . .'

The point, as Bono says, was to do with what U2 have to do with.

> There's no going back. For me where it's at has gotta be in the new processes and technologies. Dance music is happening. But the problem with dance music is it has no personality. It has the personality of a Toyota commercial. They're using sounds that are quickly used up. Each synthesiser comes with its own set of sounds and everyone quickly uses them and every record sounds the same. But the ideas of rhythm, the ideas of that bottom end that we have now through these sound systems in clubs, that's something I'm interested in.
>
> Sonically, it's fucking up the hotel, but that basement is amazing. If you look at the design of the Kitchen, it's like a heart of the hotel. It's shaped like a heart. And you have this big bass: bdoom! bdoom! bdoom! It's like this pulse going up through the hotel.
>
> I had very pretentious ideas about the hotel. I have this idea that there is no indigenous architecture for hotels in Ireland. That's curious. When you go to Santa Fe, you'll find Santa Fe-type hotels. But not in Dublin. The Dublin hotels are defined by the Ascendancy. They're all English. There's nothing different from the Shelbourne and what you'll find in London. And I was thinking, there must be something that defines Ireland in hotel-style architecture. And I got quite excited about the Clarence Hotel, because it is peculiarly Irish. Why? It's a Mackintosh-influenced building but they couldn't

afford the flair of Mackintosh. It's a poor man's Mackintosh. But it ends up more modern. It has this humility about its design that I really like. Simple wood panelling, terazzo flooring, which to me is always associated with institutions like hospitals and schools. And so I had this idea to take all these things that were associated with bad memories and turn them into good memories. I wanted the hotel's rooms to be quite small, very spare. None of that made-to-measure furniture. Just one single table. Hi-tech. TVs and everything that works, but just a simple wooden bed. And in another sense, when we're doing something like the club or the restaurant, we can be nineties. When we were kids, myself and Gavin, we'd be sitting around thinking, 'Dublin's crap! It'd be great to make it brilliant.' Even when we were sixteen we were talking about starting a Dada Café. Recently I thought it would be great to have this Dublin hotel, with this thing of trying to point in a very quiet way to surrealism as an Irish position. Going back to Flann O'Brien. And it's like you grew up in Dublin and there was nuthin' doing, and you want to make it so it's cool. And I love these projects, and I get really into them. The problem is that I get bored, *and* there's a new thing: they could get grotesque.

The question is: can U2 continue to relate to Ireland in a 'normal' way?

I don't know. Everybody's really rocked on that question at the moment. It's very difficult now. A group like us in New York wouldn't be such a big deal. We'd get all the same kind of interest but we'd carry less baggage. I think that's what it is. It's a bit messy right now. I think we have to ride it out.

It's almost as though, as time goes on, Ireland is doomed to suffer all the worst aspects of the modern world while being denied its compensations. We have the modern tide without the youth to swim in it. We have a tabloid culture, which grows like an ingrown toenail, but nothing sharp and questioning to expose it for the empty clatter it is.

Fame makes your world grow smaller and smaller, until in the end you have to invent your own world in order to live at all. Perhaps U2's experience of a shrinking Ireland provides a graphic image of what has really happened to the country since the 1960s. It gets smaller and smaller, in its possibilities and its imaginings, until finally it will no longer exist.

Media attention focuses on U2 elsewhere, of course, as well. U2 are world superstars, attracting the glare of publicity wherever they go. Tough, you may say, plausibly enough: they have to take the rough with the smooth. But this is only a small part of the point. In a sense, it is possible not to care

less about whether or how Adam Clayton gets to live his life, and yet be
bothered by the fact that U2 are treated only as this star commodity. You
worry not for U2's sake, but for the sake of the culture from which they
emerged and which they still represent. As long as we are fed only the
images of their celebrity and indulgence, we are denied the knowledge of the
band's true meaning.

'At the end of the day,' says Adam Clayton, 'it must stimulate people to
question their situation. Because you can't solve their problems – all you
can do is give them an ideology that denies everything that's been beaten
into them previous to that. And I think that that's what we mean in this
country. There is the assumption, just because U2 have been successful, that
everybody else who is making records is on the same road – and they're not.
I think most people out there, they don't really have much of an idea of how
we've done what we've done. And why it is the way it is. They just see the
effects of it. It either fits into their view of the State of the Nation, or it
doesn't.'

Other western societies in which U2 have at least as much influence as
they do in Ireland, have, of course, the kind of cultural/critical infrastruc-
ture which Ireland lacks. But they don't have either the reason or the
wherewithal to make sense of where U2 came from. There is no reason
why the relationship between Ireland and U2 should be a pressing issue
anywhere else. The problem is that, because of Ireland's watchful imitation
of other cultures, we depend for our understanding on *our own* popular
music, upon what outsiders make of it. We cared little for the Clancy
Brothers until they came back to tell us that the Americans liked them. The
most recent example of this tendency was Limerick band the Cranberries,
who were virtually ignored in Ireland until word trickled through that their
debut album had sold over a million copies in the United States. Within a
week, the Irish newspapers were telling us that, begorrah, the Cranberries
were now 'bigger than U2'.

This is complicated. It's not simply a question of poor self-confidence
or the perennial national inferiority complex. The problem is that this
complex has been ingrained in Irish society by the tangible consequences of
its earlier incarnations. It is a self-perpetuating condition. Emigration is
both the chicken and the egg. The consequences of the haemorrhaging of
population have not simply been the net loss of energies and enthusiasms,
but the institutionalisation of old images. For over a hundred years until the
1960s, and again for the past ten years, Ireland has been running to stand
still.

It seems that nothing changes and everything is changing all the time.
Things change, people leave, and it's like they've taken the changes away
with them. In fact, they leave the shadow of the change behind. Every fallen

angel leaves a blessed spirit in its wake, an invisible shadow which seems to exude the change that their presence here meant. In the immaculate existence of the race of angels, the changes in Irish culture and sensibility are registered beat by beat; but in the 'real' Ireland, they are registered at best in fits and starts, a sort of catching-up process that occurs every ten years or so, when we decide to have a referendum to change some article or other of the Constitution. For the rest of the time, we live with the most recent stab at a definition. The actual experience of the changes which we provoke and undergo is enacted someplace else out of our sight. The reason we do not recognise ourselves is that we cannot see what we look like. It is like someone suddenly uninvented the mirror which would give us an image of our soul.

The U2 story is a clinical swab of this process. I remember in the summer of 1987, walking back towards O'Connell Street in Dublin after seeing U2 perform in Croke Park. Having conquered the world, the band had just played to their home-town audience. I remember clearly the sense of excitement I felt walking back down the street. It was growing dark on a latish summer evening. The U2 fans were everywhere, young people between their early teens and mid-thirties. Most of them were wearing U2 T-shirts, headbands, scarves, some of them seemed to be dressed completely in U2 gear. Everyone was talking, laughing, shouting out, singing lines of U2 songs. 'And I sti-lllllll haven't found . . .' There was an openness about the fans that ran into one. It was tribalism, yes, but a benign tribalism, a moment of sheer joy and release, a little death in one another's arms. I felt as if I could talk to anyone and we would know what to say about anything. We would *recognise* one another. There was a sense for that moment of being in the Ireland we had grown up expecting to inhabit. For that brief walk through Dublin, I felt as if I almost couldn't wait to grow old to see what it would be like.

Six years later, I went to see Zoo TV at the RDS in Dublin. There was nothing of that feeling there. There was the band and there was the audience. Many people seemed to be there out of curiosity, because they had heard so much about the show and wanted to see for themselves, to be able to say they'd been there. There was no sense of unity to be felt about the crowd. The spread of ages had widened in both directions, but the mutuality had disappeared. What you encountered was a crowd of individual punters. As you looked from face to face, you noticed something missing: the rapture of belonging.

The difference, it might be argued, was to do with the nature of the show: all this sudden irony and spectacularity was bound to create a barrier between the band and its audience. I don't think so. I had seen Zoo TV around Europe and the United Kingdom several times in the previous months, and had felt a connection of varying strengths which was much closer to the feeling of Croke Park 1987 than to the RDS in 1993. And what this seems to suggest is, yes, that the relationship betwen U2 and their home fans has altered – and not for the better – over the past few years.

It doesn't take a genius to work out that the relationship between U2 and their Irish fans has not deteriorated at all. It is simply that their fans keep changing all the time. Irish people are born, grow up, do the things that young people do all over the western world, and then *leave*. The chances are that many of the people who were in Croke Park during the *Joshua Tree* tour were part of the audiences U2 played to in Europe and America in 1993. About 200,000 young Irish people left Ireland between 1987 and 1993, and while there are no statistical breakdowns available for emigration among rock fans, it seems plausible, given the popularity of U2 in Ireland, that the people who leave are more likely to be U2 fans than not. So, in a real and graphic way, the feeling I have about U2 and their following in Ireland captures the shifting reality of the society in general. The U2 fans are the angels who depart, leaving just their blessed spirit behind. That spirit is what is captured in the music, in every breathing beat of it. It is the voice of modern Ireland, but the Ireland it represents cannot be found in Ireland. It can be felt there, by its absences or its ghostly presence, but it can be located only outside.

'I'm beginning to feel that very strongly,' says Adam Clayton. 'And I hope it's not just personal. I'm beginning to feel more in common with those people out there who are exiles, who can't come back. I'm beginning to feel that when I'm here I live in my house, and I go to work every day – and that's about as much as I see of Ireland. Maybe that'll change – maybe I'll get to spend more time here – but – Eamon Dunphy, funnily enough, said it when we did *Unforgettable Fire*. And I don't agree with him, but it has stuck in my mind. He said, 'Oh yeah, it's all very well you staying in Ireland, and supporting Ireland and so on, but eventually they'll drive you out. And I hate that to be prophetic, but it does feel that . . . anytime you open a newspaper, there's some ridiculous story about you. And after a while it just gets to you that you can't live a normal life.

'You're even questioning how important your role in domestic Ireland is. Or whether there is a wider world out there you can contribute to. In a sense, one's self-esteem and identity is no longer related to toeing the party line. It's all to do with: why should I put up with all this bullshit?'

CHAPTER TWELVE

Remember the Future

'How does the music of U2 relate to our being Irish?'

The first serious attempt by someone in U2 to address this question was in an article entitled 'The White Nigger', based on a conversation between Bono and the Irish philosopher Richard Kearney, published in a book of essays on Irish identity, *Across the Frontiers: Ireland in the 1990s*.

'I come to this question', said the singer of loud, sad songs, 'as someone who does not know who he is. There are people out there who know who they are . . . I like to meet these people . . . But I am not one of them.'

This was in 1988, in the post-*Joshua Tree*, pre-*Rattle and Hum* period, when U2 engaged in a rummage for roots in the oldest cultures of the new world. When Bono and I talked about this, four, five and six years later, we did so in the knowledge that U2, and everyone in it, had changed a bit since that time. I wondered if he had figured out who he was in the meantime.

> Maybe it's just that I feel a bit more comfortable about *not* knowing who I am. I've always felt, if I can be so pretentious, that art is an attempt to identify yourself. That if you're sure of yourself you build bridges and steam engines. That it is the very loss of our identity that actually drives us to create literature or music or whatever. And that our revenge on . . . I suppose, *England*, for seven hundred years of oppression, for the colonising of both our geography and our consciousness, was to abuse and to reinvent their language. And this was where Joyce was coming from in *Ulysses*. And I suppose any Irish writer, even in a medium like rock 'n' roll, which isn't purely literate, is coming from that kind of perspective. And you're trying to first of all find your own voice against these very strong foreign voices. And of course the UK, Great Britain, has been replaced by America in this colonising of our unconscious. And so you attempt to find your own voice in the din of these other very strong voices.

One of the problems is that the word 'modern' has painted us into a corner. The word, as we have come to understand it, implies a rejection of the past. But the past stays alive within us, and insists on not being left behind. It's not just that we need to finish the previous chapters before we begin another, but that the image of the future is contained within the vestiges of the past which we carry through the present. We need to perceive anew in the artefacts of the past the meaning they might have had at the time.

> That's what William Burroughs' cut-up method is all about. You cut up the past to find the future. As I said, Joyce taking revenge by messing up the English language. And rock 'n' roll is the sound of revenge – if unconsciously so. Revenge against *what*? You don't know – whether it's your dad, your past . . . you just don't know what it is. But that seems to be one of its energies.
>
> That period around the *Joshua Tree* was about roots. It was almost like, 'We better *find* some!' I think now we know that we can take them or leave them, that just because you use the tin whistle does not make you Irish, that just because you play the pipes – 'Oh, that's an *Irish* tune!' We're way beyond that now. I'm still interested in instrumentation – like the uilleann pipes, for instance, which is an Indian instrument. And I love the ballad thing. But we're not hung up about it.

While instinctively rejecting the standard models of Irishness on offer, U2 had to go right round the world to find what was Irish in themselves. Up until then Bono hadn't given it a moment's thought.

> I think it's fair to say that I found out I was Irish when I went to America, and had people throwing money at us when Bobby Sands was on hunger strike back in the early eighties. America had quite a distorted idea, a romantic idea, of what the IRA were on about. And they tried to imbue us with this kind of street-fighting Irish credibility. And I had to start asking myself the question: how *do* I feel about this? What *is* it to be Irish exactly? And my own discoveries led to the idea that there *is* something to it, that there is *something* which you might call Irish, but it's not a surface thing. It's not either petrol bomb identity, or Aran sweater identity, 'The Fisherman' by W. B. Yeats, or Behan or Wilde. It goes deeper. And I found a connection to the African-American, and I started to see that what in America they called 'soul', that we had something of this. And I think what it was was a spirit of abandonment that lay at the heart of our music, of our literature, and of our lifestyle, actually, in one sense. And that it was against the grain of Anglo-Saxon behaviour, northern European behaviour – if you wanted

to see it from some sort of anthropological view. And I still see that.

In his conversation with Richard Kearney, Bono had restated the orthodox analysis of U2 and their 'Irish thing'. U2, he noted, is perceived as an Irish band. But hardly anybody goes beyond the obvious in considering what it means. If you look at the surface level of the music and its content, there is nothing about it that strikes you as quintessentially Irish. It seems to come, as Bono observed, 'From a suburban blank generation culture where I grew up watching cartoons on TV, *Thunderbirds* and Hanna Barbera and designer violence. That was the real world: concrete, grey, kicking footballs and admiring English football stars. That's the culture that I came from, and that's what our music reflects, on the surface at least. It is very "un-Irish" in the accepted sense.'

U2 are Irish. Some of the more surface details appear to contradict even this simple statement. The fact that U2 comprises two Irishmen, one Englishman and a Welshman supports the orthodoxy that the background of the band was incidental to a typically untypical post-modern phenomenon. This is the view that sees modern Ireland as an outpost of Coca-Cola culture, conquered once again. There is some truth in this, but it is a superficial truth. I prefer to see the mixture of U2 as a symbol of what modern Ireland is – a mixture of things which have perhaps been inadequately labelled or understood. Think of it like the Irish soccer team, the odd mix of nationalities or backgrounds which is actually an accurate representation of the reality of the Irish race in the past couple of centuries. The resident population on the island itself has been just the tip of the iceberg of a vast, seventy million-strong diaspora spread through the world. In a sense, *any* team, band or group purporting to be Irish would not be an accurate representation of Ireland *unless* it contained people who were born somewhere else.

'I think,' says Bono, 'it is amusing that we have Larry Mullen on one hand, and Adam Clayton, Edge – there's so many traditions, whether they be middle-class, English, Irish, working-class – it really is *mixed-up*. And in a way that *is* where Ireland is. And I think that's probably the most interesting aspect of U2, sociologically speaking, that in fact it's kind of the way it is. That there *is* no pure Irishness anymore, and that there *shouldn't* be. And that it has to be allowed to mutate and cross-breed, and that what you get is a *new* kind of Irishness that comes out of it. I'm really wary of people putting too much importance on the past. You go to America and you get these awful – really awful – Irish people that come up to you, and they're using all the old terms and they're talking to you in such clichés about an Ireland that just doesn't exist. It's an Ireland of their imagination. It's *way* out of date. And we're not quite sure what the *new* Ireland is, but there are certain things we don't want in it. And it might be interesting, you know, to take orders of what we don't want in it!'

And then there is the more profound dimension of this displacement, which, for all we may deny it, has wedded us to cultures around the world. A modern Irishness will by definition contain not just elements which are recognisable as Irish, but also elements which are not.

Maybe this was floating around in the back of Irish poet Patrick Kavanagh's head when he observed that 'Irishness is a form of anti-art'. Kavanagh said he had 'no belief in the virtue of a place'. Art or culture could flourish only where there is openness and connection between peoples. But we should perhaps distinguish between the form of Irishness celebrated in Kavanagh's lifetime in post-independence Ireland – a narrow, provincial, insular protectionism – and the qualities which emanate uniquely from a particular people because of their experience, or qualities which they share with other marginal peoples because of the experience they hold in common. The choice, as Franz Fanon observed, is between 'a concentration on the hard core of culture which is becoming more and more shrivelled up, inert and empty', or a genuine attempt to 'describe, justify and praise' the action through which a people has created itself and kept itself in existence.

When the time comes to re-evaluate the culture of late-twentieth-century Ireland, in perhaps a hundred years from now, the discussion will return again and again to this band called U2. The point of trying to define a way in which U2 might be seen as an Irish band – as opposed to a British band, or an American band, or a European band, or a world music band – is not academic. Nor is it a question of presenting an elaborate mathematical proof, topped off with a glib 'Eureka!' or 'QED'. It must be an attempt to understand whether this band and their phenomenal success around the world represent any kind of image of the country they come from.

There is a tendency in Ireland to perceive U2 as an aberration. We celebrate and wonder at their success, but we place rigid limitations on how we allow ourselves to enter into and share in that success. There is a sense in which we accord to U2 the kind of recognition we bestow on the more successful Irish businessmen, television or sports personalities who have done well in exile. We celebrate the fact that U2 are world famous, as though this was the principal meaning of their achievement. We celebrate their wealth, their gold records, their sell-out concerts in far-flung parts of the globe, the U2 phenomenon, their celebrity. The one thing missing from all this is a celebration of the statement they make in their music. The fact that this might tell us far more about ourselves than all the extraneous matter put together is something we can't yet glimpse. In effect, we celebrate U2 as an aberration. The subtext of our attitude to them is that they are great, yes, but they are great at doing something which other people respect, which other people relate to, and which is therefore, we seem to assume, a consequence of the communion between these four young men and the world outside Ireland. It's fabulous, we tell ourselves, that U2 are regarded as the best rock 'n' roll band in the world. We marvel at that fact, and even more so at the fact that they are this *in spite of* being Irish. *Wow!* we say, can you believe that people are saying these things about an *Irish* band?

What if the success of U2 is not something that happens in spite of their being Irish? What if their Irishness is not merely an incidental aspect of their worldwide success? What if they became the biggest band in the world precisely *because* they were Irish, if the elements in their music which gave them their worldwide appeal were elements which they derived from the place and culture they came from?

'I used to think,' said Bono, 'U2 came out of a void, a black hole; we seemed completely rootless. Though we had many influences, our version of rock 'n' roll didn't sound like anyone else's in the present or in the past . . . we didn't belong to any tradition, it was like we were lost in space, floating over many traditions but not belonging to any one of them. It then struck us that there was a journey to be undertaken. There was something to be discovered.'

There is an echo of resonance between what Bono is saying here and Franz Fanon's warning about the fate of a post-colonial people who become 'individuals without an anchor, without a horizon, colourless, stateless, rootless – a race of angels'. To begin with, U2 were, as Bono said, 'a band with its roots in space someplace'. The most interesting aspect of the U2 journey is the way, as though in defiance of the grain of the time, they travelled from noplace to someplace. Their music has, from those rootless beginnings, attempted to envisage a place in which to live in the present. The source of U2's triumph and appeal has been in their search and discovery of a modern means to express a primitive fund of feeling and knowledge, which they have come to respect precisely because they grew up with the possibility that it could not be taken for granted. They are products of a colonised collective personality who, for that very reason, are better able to survive in the colonised marketplace of modern popular culture. They have broken through the psychological barriers which might have frozen the very thoughts on their lips or fingers. They have tapped into the well of expression, of music and language, that runs in all of us. They have stumbled upon their own latent musicality, and in doing so have been liberated from the constraint of description. They have realised that being Irish gives them the ultimate freedom to be *anything*. There are no rules, no codes, by which they have to live. They are uncool and they don't care. They are Paddies with Attitude. They go against the grain of cynicism and pessimism which has characterised Western art and politics and culture through the history of Western imperialism. They have suggested to us, the Irish, ways of liberating ourselves from stereotyped ideas of what we are or what it was possible for us to become. They give voice to what it is to be Irish in the modern world. They *are* what it is to be Irish in the modern world. You might even remark, remembering our Jesuit friend, Fr Devane's concern about the loss of qualities of 'mystic idealism' and 'messianism', that these are among the qualities that U2 are most frequently accused of bringing to the modern medium they inhabit.

U2, like many of the recent generations of Irish people, came to be interested in their Irishness through trying to escape it. Having been force-fed the clichés, they threw them up. Suddenly they felt hungry. 'I'm not a bitter person in any way, but I'm almost bitter about some aspects of being Irish,' says Bono.

And as they went against the grain of their place, they went against that of the culture in which they sought refuge. From the beginning, U2 had a different agenda. Bono says:

Again, making this attempt to identify ourselves even more difficult was the fact that, say, comparing us to Van Morrison, he started out writing songs about girls and ended up writing about God; our story is the other way around. We were supposedly a punk band, coming out of 1976/77; but I also felt that the sort of pseudo-violence of punk music was such a sham – I suppose in the light of having very real violence fifty miles up the road, or, you know, around the corner on the street. Pretend violence, middle-class kids with safety pins in their noses – of which I was one, for a minute – it just didn't ring true. And the whole idea of rebellion, of what rebellion is, was up for grabs at that moment. And I started to feel that at that moment in time the most rebellious thing I could do was in some ways believe, in some ways follow this instinct I had that – this is a bit heavy, but – the archaic, anarchic idea that *there's a God and that he might be interested in us*. But it was just . . . you know. You *can't*! . . . You just *can't* do that. *No way! Rock 'n' roll?* You can write about cars, cocks, revolution, marriage, S&M, nihilism, but you can't write about *that*. And at first we felt completely like fish out of water. And then you start to realise, you know, *hold on a second* – that's *precisely* what Bob Marley's been doing, and Marvin Gaye, and Dylan and Van Morrison. So we started to realise that that was part of it. And again, because we as a nation, because Irish people have been spiritually abused, most people have had just enough religion to inoculate them against it – this seemed like very rich territory. Because everyone else was afraid of it. And so we went down that road.

Faith – which is the opposite to fear – is an incredible thing. And I think that, above all in U2, we have this faith in ourselves and in that spark that happened when we played. But there was nothing else there. We couldn't play very well, and the songs weren't good, and I didn't even know what a couplet was. And we certainly hadn't got our *walk* right. We hadn't got the *haircuts* right. We were a very uncool band at the bottom of the heap. But we knew one thing – at least we *sensed* one thing – that any artist is as interesting or as important as the new colours he finds. I see a yellow in Van Gogh's paintings that I never saw before. It's *his* yellow. He *owns* that. And certain artists, there's an emotion that you've felt but have never heard expressed before. So we started out to find unique territory, because then it wouldn't be as obvious how inexpert we were. That was, kind of, our strategy.

Around the time of the release of *Achtung Baby*, Brian Eno remarked on what he described as the emotional depth of that record, and took a stab at saying why it had been achieved. It was, he observed, an album of musical oxymorons, of feelings that shouldn't exist together but are somehow credible when placed within the U2 frame. After a decade of cynicism, Eno was pleased to welcome the world to the warm nineties. This warmth, he averred, was a critical element of the U2 ethic; its antithesis – 'Cool', the definitive eighties compliment – was everything that U2 were not. U2 were positive where cool is negative, engaged where it is detached, open where it is evasive and recklessly passionate where it is cautiously remote. This warmth he connected unambiguously to their Irish context – a racial capacity of passionate concern – born, he hinted, out of a resistance to the cultural disdain which characterised our nearest neighbours. Temperamentally, Irish people were not disposed to remain spectators to received ideas about how things were. Being storytellers, pattern makers and inspired fantasists, the Irish were in the habit of remaking their own history several times a day, by the simple expedient of uttering it anew. And this reckless capacity for invention and involvement, Eno declared, made the Irish terminally uncool.

'Cool' became the sour aftertaste of sixties optimism. In a sense it was the response of a disappointed generation to a stinging slap in the face to its expectations, a sullen defence adopted by erstwhile idealists in the wake of the death of the sixties dream of peace and freedom. After the murders of the Kennedy brothers and Martin Luther King, the break-up of the Beatles and the death of the spirit of 1968, there was no refuge for survivors but the comforting embrace of indifference. Those who had hoped, now just doped; those who had rocked the system, now merely rocked. The murder of John Lennon at the beginning of the eighties was the symbolic act that finally sealed the fate of sixties optimism. Scepticism became a cult. Even the most ardent dreamers now denied their earlier idealism as the aberrant and naive pursuit of an empty illusion. And the reactionary cocks crowed and crowed.

By the late eighties, when the Thatcherite cock had crowed for the third time in a decade, 'cool' had become both a lifestyle trend and an industry to serve it. The eighties belonged to the postmodern sulk-realists, who thought indifference the peak of chic. Nothing mattered, and what if it did? Pop music became increasingly soulless and dehumanised, television trite and disposable, politics were for the socially freeze-dried. This process had a complicated effect on the Irish. We had our own, indigenous disappointments: the end of the Lemass era, the death of pioneering education minister Donogh O'Malley, the departing tide that beached many a boat. It was hardly surprising that apathy and cynicism would put down healthy roots. From the loins of the semi-detached generation of the disillusioned Lemass children there emerged a generation totally detached. Even those of the younger generations who resisted the pull of the cultural vacuum that told them that life was elsewhere, remained in Ireland but became increasingly removed from their surroundings, dancing to a different drum which beat insistently from afar. Those who investigated the beat found nothing but a hollow skin without sinew or flesh.

'I remember the first time we went to London,' says Bono. 'I remember feeling uncool before I was smart enough to see through cool. The style fascism and musical elitism, which to me is antagonistic to what rock 'n' roll is. And that has much more to do with a snobbery that is a hundred years old, an actual class thing. And I'm amazed that the media don't see that in themselves. When you see in some English music paper some band flogged, that they don't see fagging there, that they don't see that they're part of something that has more to do with the public school than it has with art. I see this as a cultural thing, and I feel it stronger because I'm Irish and we feel it in other ways. I'm talking about a vein, the stiff upper lip, which is by definition completely uncool, and which goes beyond England – it's a northern European problem – of being *very white* . . . and I *sympathise*. Let's just say, some cultures need drugs more than others. If it wasn't for E, we'd still be force-fed punk rock. Nihilism sits so much better.'

There are three ways of seeing it. It could be that the Irish reaction against cool is yet another example of our tendency to define ourselves as what the English are not. On the other hand, it could be something that goes way back to before we had anything to compare it against. Or it could be a mixture of the two. But what Brian Eno perceived in U2's demeanour was not an ideological position, a badge of difference, but something coterminous with the essentials of U2's music.

The meaning of U2's uncoolness went beyond their look and their shoes. 'We were up there,' as Bono told Richard Kearney, 'soaked in sweat, unpoised – not concealing but revealing ourselves, what was on our minds and in our hearts. I began to realise how alien this was to the white, stiff upper lip syndrome which I still find in UK music criticism. They seemed to find any kind of passion hard to take, they prefer a mask of cool – unless you're black. Which is interesting because, though this passion is to me an Irish characteristic, in American blacks it's called *soul*. I was called a 'White Nigger' once by a black musician, and I took it as he meant it, as a compliment. The Irish, like the blacks, feel like outsiders. There's a feeling of being homeless, migrant, but I suppose that's what all art is – a search for identity.

'The images of our songs are confused, classical, biblical, American, Irish, English, but not in a negative sense. The fight, the struggle for a synthesis, is what's interesting about them. The idea of an incomplete, questioning, even abandoned identity is very attractive to me.'

And yet, there is – is there not? – a need for some defining self-knowledge, some kind of core idea of who you are.

'Yeah,' Bono nods agreement. 'I think there are some valuable – some *real* valuable – aspects to knowing where you come from, even in some vague way. This is what's happening in black America, this drive to know where you've come from. Roots, man. To know you can't go forward unless you know where you've come from. I agree with that – just don't be *bogus* about it. To not be afraid of the new – which is where we're at, musically speaking as well, using the new technology that's available, not being afraid of computers, computer programs, sequencers, samplers. The technology that's available right now means that rock 'n' roll is reinventing itself every minute. It's even mutating into an audio-visual artform. And I'm not afraid of that. There's people going, again, you know, "Rock 'n' roll is about being in a garage with bass, drums and guitar." Well it *can* be, but it can also be a lot more.'

After *The Unforgettable Fire* in the mid-1980s, U2 made their journey of discovery through American roots music – blues, gospel, people like Robert Johnson and John Lee Hooker – the old songs of fear and faith. And this journey led them to see in their own music what was Irish about it, its 'Irish thing'. American music became their passport home.

'When we first started the band,' Bono had said to Richard Kearney, 'we felt like outsiders to rock music, but these themes were very much inside U2. They are also very Irish, so even though there isn't an obvious Irishness in a song like "Bullet the Blue Sky", there *is* something Irish about the subject of oppression, and also, I think, about the language I used to paint the picture: "In the howling wind comes a stinging pain/See them driving nails into souls on the tree of pain/You plant a demon seed, you raise a flower of fire/ See them burning crosses/See the flames higher and higher."'

'I now realise that beneath the surface there are certain characteristics to the music – even the choice of words. Eno said that he thought I was a better poet than a songwriter – what I think he meant was that the sound, rhythm and colour of the words seem as important at times as the meaning. The love of language for its own sake and not just as a vehicle to comment on or describe events, seems to me to be very Irish.'

A contemporary Irish writer, John Banville, has spoken about this quality as one of the distinguishing marks of Irish writing – of the language as being like a stained-glass window, a filter which allows the reader to see what is being described, but through the contours and distortions of the language, which hold the eye as much as, perhaps more than, that which is described. The glass is as important as the landscape on the other side. The 'revenge' of Irish artists for the theft of their own language was to entrap the unwary eye of the world in a version of English which distorts and subverts the reality which, with a smug clarity, conventional language would seek to rationalise.

Bono gives as an example of this 'revenge' tendency in his own writing, the song 'A Sort of Homecoming', from *The Unforgettable Fire*: 'The wind will crack in wintertime/This bomb-blast lightning waltz/No spoken words . . . just a scream/Tonight we'll build a bridge across the sea and land/See the sky, the burning rain/She will die and live again/Tonight.' This, as he says, is not American folk or blues. 'The words are much more influenced by poets like Heaney or Kavanagh than, say, Woody Guthrie.'

But it is not merely revenge. It is also defiance becoming self-assertion becoming self-knowledge. It is an attempt to define yourself within space, time, place. It is a way of saying, 'This is who I am and where I live.'

The most important cultural and economic questions facing the human race as we enter the twenty-first century will not be to do with ideology but with place. The more fluid the world becomes, the more the human being will desire, metaphysically, to realise a loyalty to a place he or she can call home. *Where* is home? How is 'our' place to be described? For most of the present century we have been drawn in the direction of the assumption that loyalty to small entities was inherently negative and loyalty to bigger entities inherently better, that in the drift towards a single world we would lose our hankering for security and bearings. But, perhaps because we are of the earth, we reassert our need to know the location of our source. As the twenty-first century beckons, the emerging issue is between the global and the local, between the external and the internal, between the heart and the mind, between the system and the soul. This need is increasingly denied by modern politics, which comes more and more to be concerned with the development of stable global finance systems. In the future we are drifting towards, there will be at most two or three competing units in the world economy. National boundaries and local cultural integrities will become increasingly useless in the face of the planetary forces bearing down upon us. Over the past couple of decades, the western citizen has been subjected to a relentless campaign designed to soften up his hold on concepts of nationhood, community and home. Our innate tendency towards communality has been manipulated in the creation of the kind of global economic climate which will make the world's owners even more fabulously wealthy than before.

Any manifestation of difference – geographical, environmental, cultural, psychological or developmental – becomes a negative asset in the drive towards efficiency and productivity. A belief in the human need for a voice that speaks of uniqueness and difference is regarded as sentimental and backward-looking. The loyalty, for example, that is required of us as 'Europeans' is not to a culture or a history or a society, but to a consumer superstate in which the worth of the citizen is measured in purchasing power. And yet this European project is posited as a progression from the cultural condition of nationalism. European union is not about culture – even European culture. It is not even about Europe. Within this economic superstate, the only philosophy on offer is the law of the naked market.

The Irish have perhaps been the easiest to persuade. Because we have had to make our home away from home, and because we have yet to experience true freedom in a place we could *call* home, the supremacy of the external is to us the most natural thing in the world. Politics in Ireland has developed not as a means of achieving freedom, but as a means without end, dividing people without purpose other than division itself. Our politics has detached Irish people from one another, and the society from a clear connection with its own nature and means. Because we have never succeeded in integrating our own cultural experience with politics, we are unable to perceive the shifting patterns which conspire to deny us permanently what we have lacked for so long. One form of colonialism is replaced by another, but because the language used to describe the process by which this occurs is constructed in such a manner as to obscure this reality, we are unable to see its true shape. We are told that it is small-minded and insular to believe in the idea of a place, and yet we are required to transfer that belief on to another – bigger – place. This is *now* our culture and our new home. But only for a while. Soon they will want us to move to a bigger home, and transfer and adjust our loyalties accordingly. In the end we will all belong to the same entity, but it will no longer be a culture, a home or even a place. The choice we are being asked to make is not between small places and big places but between *any* kind of place and a *non*-place, between home and homelessness. The unaccountable free market strives to make us strangers to one another, but by using the language of unity and togetherness, it bombards our sense of identity with images of a placeless belonging, images forged in the shape of coins and notes and bottles and boxes.

This drift is difficult to combat, or even identify, without sounding fearful and backward. Even to articulate the process is to be placed among the ranks of the Luddites and apocalyptics.

Language is central. 'What a weird fate', observed Václav Havel, 'can befall certain words!' In the modern world, it is difficult to communicate essential truths because the language of communication has been stolen by economic and political interests. Every phrase has been colonised, its poetry denied and removed. Words have been contaminated, made dirty or merely useful. Thought becomes platitude. Inspiration becomes cliché. The word made flesh turns back to dust in the mouth. To even perceive where we are, we must all the time renew the language in which that locus might be imagined. In a world with no other fixed points, language, for all its limitations, becomes our only true hope of perceiving. The possibility arises that our home may exist not as a place, but as a *phrase*, or even the *sound* of a phrase – that the identity we seek is not one we can hope to describe in sentences, but one we create in a form of language developed with this in mind. The world made word. This is the project in which U2 is engaged, which unites them in purpose with the other great modern Irish artists.

It may, in other words, be the journey itself that we are seeking to perceive. In an article on the poetry of Seamus Heaney in the three hundredth edition of the Irish Jesuit journal *Studies*, Richard Kearney observes that Heaney's poetry is less about place than about 'transitions from one place to another'. Kearney is making the case for Heaney as modernist rather than traditionalist. As with so many writers and artists who attempt to grapple with the contradictions of modern Ireland, Heaney has sometimes found himself caught in the ideological traps that lie all around. One of these traps disposes of anyone attempting to deal with the past as a seeker of nostalgic comforts rather than evacuated truths. Because such explorations must necessarily deal with the same bank of material, these two objectives are easily confused, and when mixed with disingenuousness, this confusion is fatal to discovery. In the false dichotomy erected between a pious, authentic past and the filthy modern tide, artists must either make a straight choice or risk misunderstanding and marginalisation. An example of this has been the tendency to place Seamus Heaney on the side of the angels, as custodian of the traditional province of homeland. This, Kearney argues, since Heaney's exploration is not a quest for place, but for images of transition, is unhelpful. Yes, he agrees, the poet has a duty to seek that sense of belonging to a shared ancestry of culture and experience, but this is a linguistic project rather than a poetic creation of a tribal mythology and identity.

'One of the central reasons for Heaney's preference for journey over sojourn, for exodus over abode, is, I suggest, a fidelity to the nature of *language* itself,' Richard Kearney elaborates. 'Far from subscribing to the traditional view that language is a transparent means of representing some *identity* which pre-exists language – call it self, nation, home or whatever – Heaney's poetry embraces the modernist view that it is language which perpetually constructs and deconstructs our given notion of identity. As such, poetic language is always on the move, vacillating between opposing viewpoints, looking in at least two directions at once.'

Words, writes Martin Heidegger in *What is Called Thinking?*, 'are not like buckets and kegs from which we scoop a content that is there. Words are wellsprings that are found and dug up in the telling, wellsprings that must be found and dug up again and again, that easily cave in, but that at times also well up when least expected.' Seamus Heaney in his book of essays *Preoccupations*, writes about his belief in the idea of poetry as a point of access to or exit from the buried life of feelings. 'Words themselves are doors; Janus is to a certain extent their deity, looking back to a ramification of roots and associations and forward to a clarification of sense and meaning.' This is not to say that the poet is concerned with language for its own sake; rather, it is, as Richard Kearney underlines, a recognition that reality as we perceive it is always profoundly informed by the words we use to describe it, that a multiplicity of realities arises from the very ambiguity of language – 'an endless creation of new worlds'. Homecoming, then, is not a search for an idealised place, but 'a linguistic search for an historical identity'. 'Home' exists not as a place or a set of ideas, but as a metaphysical preoccupation. There is no home, except in the imagining and speaking of it. Home for the Irish is an oasis that moves ahead of us, step for step.

The buried theme of much modern Irish writing and art, of home as a journey rather than a fixed destination, is explicit in the work of another present-day Irish writer, the playwright Brian Friel. In his 1980 play *Translations*, set in a hedge-school in Co. Donegal in 1833, he deals with language as the site of a dig for lost identity. A squad of Royal Engineers comes into an Irish-speaking community to translate the local placenames into English. The schoolmaster, Hugh, replying to an enquiry from one of the officers about whether the Gaelic language is as enormously rich and ornate as reputed, combines confirmation with irony: 'A rich language. A rich literature. You'll find, sir, that certain cultures expend on their vocabularies and syntax acquisitive energies and ostentations entirely lacking in their material lives.'

'Yes,' he elaborates, 'it is a rich language, Lieutenant, full of the mythologies of fantasy and hope and self-deception – a syntax opulent with tomorrows. It is our response to mud cabins and a diet of potatoes; our only method of replying to . . . inevitabilities.'

'But remember', he cautions moments later, 'that words are signals, counters. They are not immortal. And it can happen – to use an image you'll understand – it can happen that a civilisation can be imprisoned in a linguistic contour which no longer matches the landscape of . . . fact.'

Translations deals in a complex and intimate way with the violence done to a culture when its language is taken from it. The idea is beautifully encapsulated in the issue of placenames, which are not merely Irish versions of English words, as the coloniser would have it, but precise linguistic representations of the places they name. Lis na Muc will never exist again from the moment it is renamed as Swinefort, even though this is the literal English equivalent. Once language is destroyed, *a place itself* is destroyed, and its people consigned to the perpetual journey in search of a home that cannot ever be found.

'We must learn those new names,' Hugh says later, his irony erased by pragmatism in the presence of family and friends, as he recommends to them the book of placenames newly coined in English. 'We must learn where we live. We must learn to make them our own. We must make them our new home.' Why? Because 'it is not the literal past, the "facts" of history, that shape us, but images of the past embodied in language . . . we must never cease renewing those images; because once we do, we fossilise'. There is no point in going back, because the past does not exist. We need to construct a new future, based on present realities. 'Homecoming,' as Richard Kearney advises, 'becomes a dialectical search for some forfeited or forbidden presence in and through the awareness of its absence.' We must live not *by* language, but *in* it. It is our only home.

In his keynote address to the annual conference of the Ireland Fund in 1988, Seamus Heaney himself made a stab at defining the shifting common ground underneath all Irish feet. Ireland, he said, is a place where 'doubleness' is easy, 'the doubleness we are capable of as inhabitants of time and place'. Irish people have a capacity – unique? Perhaps not, but then again – 'to live in two places at the one time and in two times at the one place'. We have it both ways. 'The Republic may indeed be a country of conference hotels, computer printouts, fax and fish kills, property deals and stereophonic discos; but it is also, to a greater or lesser extent, the locus of an imagined Ireland, a mythologically grounded and emotionally con-toured island that belongs in art time, in story time, in the continuous present of a common, unthinking memory life.'

This doubleness, he went on, is characterised by a split-level language, 'a kind of unconscious bilingualism, an evolved verbal amphibiousness'. In other words, we have one language for the modern world and another for who we really are. Both are knitted together in what we call everyday speech. Heaney told a story about a Cork schoolmaster who asked his class of young boys to write an essay under the title 'The Swallow'. One of the boys wrote what Heaney described as 'a two-sentence history of Anglo-Irish literature': *The swallow is a migratory bird. He have a roundy head.*

'First,' said Heaney, 'comes the correct, stilted, schoolbook English, a kind of zombie speech which walks shakily out of the evacuated larynx where Irish once exercised itself with instinctive freedom. *The swallow is a migratory bird.*

'Then into this undead English there arrives the resurrected afterlife of the Irish and vigour is retrieved. The personality has found access to all its old reservoirs of sureness and impulse. Grammar goes wonky, vocabulary goes local, and an intelligence which had been out of its element in the first sentence gets right back into it in the second.'

Irish people are said to have long memories, to remember old grudges long after such recollections are either reasonable or polite. But the truth is that we have conscious memories like sieves and unconscious memories like magpies' nests. We remember nothing and yet, at a deeper level, we remember everything. We forget that we have remembered, but the things we have forgotten are remembered *in* us. We recognise ourselves, not in ourselves, but in each other. We know who we are because we see ourselves in the street every day. We hear ourselves in the hairdresser's or on the radio.

And so while the loss of our native language is remembered as a fact, it is forgotten as a reality. But then, deeper and deeper into our souls, it is not forgotten at all, but nursed like a bleeding wound that we cannot see. And the possibility arises that not only is the memory of the loss still there, but the language itself is maybe still alive within us, to slip out in ways that we are ourselves not even conscious of. He have a roundy head, we say, in moments of truth or desperation.

Look at this for a sentence, again from Seamus Heaney's talk, taking up the lesson of the roundy-headed swallow. 'I cite this as another example of the Irish psyche flitting like a capable bat between the light of a practical idiom and the twilight of a remembered previous place, alert as any linguistic philosopher both to the arbitrariness of signs and the ache of the unspoken.' The same thing is there again, side by side in every phrase and clause.

Heaney traced the root of the split to the rift in twelfth-century Irish consciousness resulting from colonisation. The symbiotic relationship between the ancient pagan culture of Ireland, and the mother tongue, Irish, was seriously traumatised by the arrival, first, of Christianity and the formal, pedantic influence of Latin, and later with the shift from Irish to English as the main language of everyday communication. Irish culture had been myth-based – meaning carried through stories, which bore through the ages fantastic truths and historical narrative. Subsequent influences drove this culture underground, into the unconscious of the race, and the virtual extinction of Irish made it an underground stream without a mouth.

The dichotomy which the issue of language renders visible also characterises recent Irish culture and social history, and, as Seamus Heaney observed, 'matches very intriguingly the modern clash between an international style of commerce and culture and the more indigenous conservatism of Irish life generally. Corresponding to the Old Irish immersion in the phantasmagoria of myth, we have the demure, frugal, admirably visionary if intellectually obscurantist world of de Valera's Ireland – pastoral, pure and Papist; and corresponding to the organisational, ecclesiastical, administrative Latin culture, we have the rational, international, pragmatic spirit of Seán Lemass, Dr Ken Whitaker and the First Economic Plan. Need I go on? Of course I need not.'

This is an example of the both/and rather than the either/or of which Richard Kearney writes in *The Irish Mind*. We have it both ways. It suggests, of course, a paradox, a logical impossibility: identity as a flux rather than a fixture, or more puzzling still, a fluid fixture. But we are not talking about logic, and perhaps the failure to realise any concept of Irish identity has to do with being imprisoned in a new linguistic contour which places too much emphasis on facts and not enough on feelings. We have then developed a cunning middle voice which allows us to express this fluidity. But only those on the inside can recognise and absorb its two-faced contradictions. To outsiders our two-facedness is a flaw in our character; to us it is a prerequisite of survival.

The shapes of ourselves which make us different are deep within us, emerging through language, gesture, humour, the way we walk. Heaney's talk was so sharp and sure-footed that it slipped through the ideological constructs and arrived at a forgotten place. Just as the fire, the hearth, has been replaced by the central heating system, he said, so our psychic consciousnesses have been supplanted by modernity, 'the cancellation of wonder'.

> Your being is insulated from the physical and metaphysical life of flame. Your space has been made abstract by the imposed grid of pipe and radiator. You have comfort but also have something inside you that is out of alignment. In a dumb old part of yourself you have left the world of roundy heads and entered the world of migratory birds. You are stumbling about in the international Latin and suppressing the hearth Irish. You are a secular, modern citizen of the world, with a sort of lacuna in your midriff. You are capable, comfortable and a little displaced. You are vaguely in exile from somewhere inside or outside yourself, but you don't quite know how or why. You are probably a professional, urban, Irish eighties success story. You may even be London Irish, or American Irish, Canadian Irish, but whoever you are, you feel this vestigial capacity to focus around an old field of force that is neither marked on the map nor written into the schedule.

In all of us, said Heaney, there is a supply of dammed-up energy to be released. There is a trigger somewhere that, if we could find and pull it, would release the floodgates. He told of one such experience he himself had, a visit to an old house, lifting a latch for the first time in years, feeling the cold of the metal on his hand and the harsh slap of the latch mechanism. 'My body awakened in its very capillaries to innumerable and unnameable rivulets of affection and energy.' In other words, he said, 'a connection is possible between your present self and your intuited previousness, between your inchoate dailiness and your imagined identity. Your Irishness, to put it in yet another way, constitutes a big unconscious voltage and all it needs is some transformer to make it current in a new and significant and renovative way.'

But Heaney knew, too, the pitfall he was heading for. In modern Ireland, to talk of a slap of a latch with such feeling and conviction is to invite irritation and dismissiveness. The thirst for modernity contaminates everything old or past with a coating of sentiment, which, like rust, has no neutral existence. Between prejudice and nostalgia there is no middle way. We reject the mention of the old as we mistrust the sentiment in ourselves. It is difficult to find reference points to which any two people will attach the same meaning. Most of us cannot see beneath the patina of the illustration to the meaning below. The task, as Heaney said, is to find *new* things, to create new points of recognition, on which to consruct a meaning for ourselves.

We are already doing this, although frequently our efforts are all but futile on account of being mistaken for something else. Such a phenomenon is the music of U2. Their music is the expresion of that unconscious voltage, the transformer that makes the meaning of one existence current in a renovative way. They are in the business of creating shapes to fill that lacuna in our midriff.

Earlier I have used the image of the U2 entity being like a set of boxes in a Chinese puzzle, one reality inside the other, contained by its outer appearance and yet with its own separate integrity. I know that this is a condition forced on U2 by the modern world, by the medium they inhabit, the industry they work within and the category they are filed under. And yet I have this sense that the separations are a positive assertion of the fact that there are several different things going on, that these things make limited sense to one another, and yet must be contained in some kind of entity. The boxes change their shape as time goes on. But, if you pay close attention, the shape of the outside box always contains an image of the innermost, and no matter how the outside box changes, the innermost remains the same. The integrity of the boxes is retained even as the visible exterior goes through a rapid series of contortions. Another phrase of Seamus Heaney rings and rings: 'testing the ground by throwing shapes'.

Brian Eno, seeking a way of illustrating the nature of the U2 exploration, wrote about U2's language 'of praise and criticism', the words which enable to band to mark out new territory for themselves as they advance. The way he chose to describe what connected U2 when they were making *Achtung Baby* with their past identity was to isolate the words which informed the making of that record. Those words created bridges to future possibilities as they dismantled the bridges by which U2 had reached their present place. The positive buzzwords during the recording, he recalled, were 'trashy', 'throwaway', 'dark', 'sexy' and 'industrial'. The negative words, the ones which represented the reservations of the past, were 'earnest', 'polite', 'sweet', 'righteous', 'rockist' and 'linear'.

The channel of discovery is language, or rather languages. Because the U2 language includes music as well as poetry, the words are merely codes for the deeper language that they provide access to. The gaps between language and reality are filled by the sound of a guitar and a bass drum. Everyday language has been abused by its application to technocracy, so we must search, or someone must search on our behalf, for those deepest and dearest sounds that might make sense of who we are. U2 do our dirty work in both the belly of the technology and in the democracy of themselves.

But music is, so to speak, an invisible language. It speaks to us while appearing to be doing something else. A reel played on a fiddle may well be speaking to us at some primordial level about the nature of our identity and existence, but we experience this communication as both message and commodity. All we are conscious of is that it makes us feel better, like a pint of stout or a cigarette. Nobody would suggest that a pint of stout is either a language or a culture, for all that to be seen drinking it may be a statement about oneself. Thus, music, popular music in particular, needs to be 'outed' for what it may be: a landsape in which we can place ourselves.

U2's journey through the modern world has from the beginning been a quest for a compatible landscape. Each of their half-dozen hit albums of the past decade could, in retrospect, be perceived as the identification of a location. Other bands make records that reflect them and where they come from. U2 make records that reflect their lack of a place to call home. Before you listen, take a look at the photographs on the covers, invariably by the photographic artist Anton Corbijn. The photographs are not merely of U2, but of U2 in a place, which, as often as not, makes the band less significant than the place.

The U2 journey is not a mission, but an odyssey. It does not derive its purpose from the images of a remembered past, but from a recognition that imagination is the true essence of remembering. The music is both the journey to the future and the articulation of the present. The past is only useful as a model of perception. The future will be exactly as we remember it. In this, the character of the music is marked, defined by the band's membership of the race of angels. But its destinations are of interest to a world in which homelessness is rapidly becoming the norm.

'Maybe,' Bono surmised to Richard Kearney, 'we Irish are misfits, travellers, never really at home, but always talking about it. I met a fisherman who told me we were like salmon: it's up river all the time against the odds, the river doesn't want us . . . yet we want a way home . . . but there is no home. Religious minds tell us "exile is what having eaten the apple means", that "home" is a spiritual condition. We in Ireland already know this.'

CHAPTER THIRTEEN

It is October over all Our Lives

The first time I heard U2's 'Gloria', I was sitting in a corner of Miss Ellie's nightclub in Roscommon. I heard the DJ mumble something about U2 over the PA and, more hopeful than expectant, pricked up my ears in a casual way. The words and sound blurred into a whole, in which they still remain. Even now, contemplating how to begin talking about the song in mere words, I find it difficult to separate the pieces and parts that I hear. I had the vaguest sense of what the song was about, but what it said seemed to be much bigger than at least my idea of what that was.

Better to talk about the backing whirring around under the feet of the vocal, chasing it, being chased by it. The song seems to begin out of nowhere. The voice fading in at the start might be that of Sting, a high-pitched yodelling backed by a desultory drumbeat. Then the guitar spins into a dizzy circle of sound that draws the drums and bass with it, as though away from the voice, which then frantically tries to catch up. The first lines I could make out are:

> I try to speak up
> But only in you I'm complete.
> Gloria, in eo domine
> Gloria exulto day-ee.

The ending of the song is stunning. An instrumental break moves from The Edge's circling guitar to a question-and-answer session between Adam's elastic-slap bass and Larry's methodical pottering on an array of jamjars, biscuit tins and piled-up dinner plates. Then The Edge slices the air with a chord as sharp and jagged as a broken slate and draws the confusion to an end. The drums wind up into a parcel of tightness and determination and the song gathers itself for the final stretch, achieving a synthesis and resolution that resonates back to the beginning. Bono's voice, layered upon itself a thousand times, sings into the distance:

> Gloria, in eo domine
> Gloria Gloria.

I wanted to dance but I didn't know why, so I didn't. The song had an unaccountable joyfulness about it, which because of the content made me uneasy. With hindsight it was my own positive response to it, in the knowledge of what it was, that made me uneasy. There were plenty of other pop songs with that title, but this was the least ambiguous. 'You probably wanted it to be about a waitress,' Bono joked to me a dozen years later. What I wanted was the song to be about what the song was about, but to be able to pretend I thought it was about a waitress. When the record had finished playing, I said to a girl sitting beside me that this band was going to be the biggest in the world. Don't ask me to explain why.

'Gloria' is the opening track on *October*, U2's second album, released in the late autumn of 1981. Reviewing the album in *Hot Press*, Neil McCormick, a school friend of the band, observes that U2 had at last openly embraced in their music the faith that had been running 'in more subtle forms' through earlier songs. McCormick's review echoes my own feeling about *October* pretty exactly:

> It is a Christian LP that avoids all the pedantic puritanism associated with much Christian rock, avoids the old world emotional fascism of organised religion and the crusading preaching of someone like a born-again Bob Dylan. It is fortunate that the main spiritual issues dealt with can be related to in a wider frame of reference than Christianity: man's struggle to know and control himself and his own nature is something that comes to everyone in some guise . . . U2 can touch and involve as the best art should do, but I cannot relate to all their words because often they respond to the basic problems of life and youth with the catch-all of having a saviour . . . I can only relate to what U2 sing in a broad rather than a specific sense.

His conclusion would have found a resonance with many young Irish people, of the time and since, who grew up in the shadow of a joyless, puritanical Catholicism which denied the very flesh they inhabited and taught them that there was a choice to be made, for a start, between chapel and nightclub.

'I actually really like that lyric,' said Bono in March 1994. 'It was written really quickly. I think it expresses – the thing of language again. This thing of speaking in tongues. Looking for a way out of language. "I try to sing this song . . . I try to stand up but I can't find my feet . . ." And taking this Latin thing, this hymn thing. It's so outrageous at the end going in to the full Latin whack. That still makes me smile. It's so wonderfully mad, and epic and operatic. And of course "Gloria" *is* about a woman in the Van Morrison sense. Being an Irish band, you're conscious of that. And I think that what happened at that moment was very interesting: people saw that you could actually write about a woman in the spiritual sense and that you could write about God in the sexual sense. And that was a moment. Because before that there had been a line. That you can actually sing to God, but it might be a woman? *Now*, you can pretend it's about God, but not a woman!'

People refer to 'traditional Irish Catholicism', intending to signify that joyless version of the faith that has been imposed on the country, in living memory and before. But this form of Catholicism is anything but 'traditional' to Ireland; like a lot of what we regard as reflecting some innate ethos, it is an imported product. Far from the present model of Irish Catholicism being intrinsic to the Irish character, it was part of the means by which the end of colonisation was furthered, the primary instrument in the process of softening us up for the industrialisation that would finally arrive in the 1960s. It is an example of the contradictory and complex nature of colonisation, being both part of it and reaction to it.

The freedom of Irish sexual mores – the fact that concubinage was tolerated, for example – came as a profound shock to some of the early invaders, in particular the Normans. A degree of sexual licence 'quite out of character with the more conventional restraints of English and Western society at large', was still prevalent well into nineteenth-century Ireland, notes L. M. Cullen in his 1981 book *The Emergence of Modern Ireland*. 'Not only were the morals somewhat freer than the conventionally stricter Anglo-Irish ones, but there was generally an element of license or libertinage, at times involving the use of force. With the church disorganized into the eighteenth century, a whole range of misdemeanors which were uncommon in Western Europe existed, ranging from irregular marriages to libertine conduct in which sexual favors were sought at a lower social level.' In his study of the subject, *Moral Monopoly*, Tom Inglis describes the period of the sixth and seventh centuries, in which Ireland was an early centre of the Christian movement, sending out missionaries to rescue Europe from the grip of savagery and magic, and notes that the exported product bore only a passing resemblance of the one consumed at home. This export model contained strong elements of penitentialism. Sexual appetites were curbed and restrained through fasting, praying and kneeling, and celibacy was regarded as an elevated state. But, according to Inglis, attitudes at home took on a more relaxed character, with elements of the penitential rites being incorporated into more traditional pagan practices to produce a heady mix of magic, mystery and masochism. This, if anything, was the 'tradition' of Irish Christianity, and survived until well into the nineteenth century, when it was arrested by the mass deaths of the Great Famine in the 1840s. From that time, the Catholic Church took in hand the task of curbing the uncivilised habits of Irish citizens by close supervision of gatherings like wakes and May Day festivals, of which sexual symbolism had been a vital ingredient and which frequently involved submission to passion in the form of sex, drinking and/or fighting. 'In nineteenth-century Ireland,' writes Inglis, 'sexual ribaldry was reduced from the physical to a verbal level. Sex became a serious subject and the Church developed a monopoly of knowledge about it. Shame and guilt about sexual practices were instilled in every individual, privately, in a hushed manner, in the dark, isolated space of the confessional.'

Thus, the innate, primitive nature of Irish Christianity – joyful, playful, magical and sensual – was diligently suppressed by Irish priests and nuns. There is an odd paradox in this, in that the suppression was carried out with the stated intention of defining Irishness against the alleged decadence and immorality of the coloniser, but it also had the effect of facilitating the coloniser's purpose: the civilisation of Ireland. In the absence of the opportunity to possess economic and political power, identity and social prestige became centred on the practice and expression of moral virtue. The Church, according to Inglis, developed a virtual monopoly of Irish morality, which allowed it to exercise both civil and physical control. Under English domination, the politics of morality allowed the Church to become the moral government. After independence, Church and state became effectively one. The question of whether or not this relationship was appropriate, and the belief of the modernising elements of Irish society that it was not, have been at the core of the moral civil war that has dominated Irish public discourse to this day.

A useful way of explaining might be to present the Church's role as the surrogate for the coloniser's, in post-independence Ireland. Without the kind of spiritual and cultural reawakening which the 1916 leaders had called for, what occurred was simply an internalisation of the forces of colonialism in the Irish mind. The Church took on the mantle of authoritarianism to satisfy the people's needs for an external power on which to project its dependency habit. In a sense, the virus of colonialism was carried invisibly into the late twentieth century, with the Catholic Church as one of its chief agents. The sixties generation, seeking to liberate itself from the constraints of an excessively moralistic and confessional Church, were actually engaged, unbeknown to themselves, in an increasingly neurotic struggle against the forces of colonialism itself. The virus was being handed down in unseen, unconscious forms.

But, while the sixties revolutionary generation strove to wipe out the influence of the Catholic Church and usher in a new, liberal, progressive and secular state, where the pleasures of the flesh might presumably get a better shake, the members of the lost half-generation of the 1970s were moving on to a question that had not yet been posed: 'What then?' Theirs was not an overt revolt against an oppressive Church, more a washing of hands, a walking away from all the available alternatives – a plague on all your houses. There was no struggle, just a sudden absence.

Throughout the 1970s, the domination of Irish Catholicism came under what for a time appeared to be a significant threat from Christian revivalism. Groups like World Vision and Campus Crusade for Christ began to actively evangelise in the streets and campuses of Irish cities. Many of these groups were actively hostile to Catholicism, a feature which appealed to many young Irish people disillusioned with the authoritarianism and joylessness of the Irish Church. In an article on the phenomenon in the Catholic intellectual journal *The Furrow* in December 1981, Fr Jack Finnegan observed that many young Irish people had lost faith in the Church's ability 'to offer an acceptable framework for life and worship . . . where teaching is sought and needed but not forthcoming, then others listening to different music will come in and sing a different song'.

In his 1985 book *The Church and New Religious Groups*, Fr Martin Tierney observes:

> There is a deep desire in many young hearts to know the Lord. The basic goodness of their lives is evidenced by their concern for the deprived and for the third world issues of poverty, justice and peace. The essential goodwill towards the Church is often manifested by a continuous respect of clergy and religious. However, the point of alienation arrives through the Church's inability to deliver with power the message of the gospel of salvation. Evangelisation today, that is bringing young people into a personal relationship with Jesus Christ, is often hindered by the Church not through the laziness of Christians but through the busyness of Christians in the wrong area. There is disillusionment with the presentation of what ought to be at heart a very exciting message. On the other hand there is conviction, power and an effective pastoral strategy among many of the new evangelical groups which have recently arrived in Ireland. I am surprised that they have not managed to attract more disaffected young people.

There was something in the air. Maybe literally. In the summer of 1977, the Charismatic Renewal Movement, an emerging evangelical movement within the Catholic Church itself, hosted a major four-day conference at the Royal Dublin Society. Some seventeen thousand delegates from eighty countries came to hear the promise of a New Pentecost. Fr Martin Tierney was present and spoke critically of the failures of the institutionalised Church, which had 'relied on power, influence, position, money, censures, interdicts' – all 'unworthy instruments of evangelisation'.

As in so many things in Ireland at this time, there were countless little pendulums swinging this way and that, clanging into one another, swinging too far or not far enough, arresting one another's course or sending it spinning in a different direction. Many young Irish people in this period turned away from issues of faith and religion; others went in search of a more meaningful sense of connection. For the first, read Neil McCormick's *Hot Press* review; for the second, listen to U2's *October*, the album he was writing about.

It was the experience of Lypton Village, with its iconoclastic rituals and Dadaist dilettantism, that had bonded U2 and their friends to the extent that they would plunge themselves into the waters of the Shalom Christian community. The *Hot Press* journalist, Bill Graham, the first to write about the fledgling U2, recalled years later that, in the first interview conducted in the spring of 1979, he had actually played down this aspect of the Lypton Village sensibility, in order, as he saw it, to protect the band from themselves and the forces which they might unleash against their own chances of survival. In a 1989 book on U2's early days, *Another Time, Another Place*, Graham recalls that, in that first interview, Bono had volunteered: 'One other thing you should know about the Village – we're all Christians.'

In 1993 Bono remembered:

> We were on our performance art missions in 1977, when we met our first preacher, in McDonald's in Grafton Street. This guy called Dennis Sheedy. *Phew!* He was as hard as nails. And he was goin', 'You're mad, aren't ye? Yese are into music. *Look* at yese! The way yese are *dressed*! Ye're *mad*! And yese don't drink? And ye don't do acid?' And he starts talking and he starts touching off things that I heard as a kid, via Guggi's [of the Virgin Prunes] family. They were like an Old Testament family – across the road. There must have been several hundred of them living in the house. There were thirteen kids. And Robbie Rowan was an unbelievable Prod. They were just *out there*. And when he used to talk I just knew – 'there's something goin' on here'. I loved the way he talked about this. I had gone to a few evangelical meetings in Merrion Hall when I was younger. And I didn't like it. I picked up bigotry. I didn't like that. I remember being dropped home and this, obviously, Protestant bigot saying to me in the car as a kid, 'What's your name? Paul? That's a very, very famous name. What is the most famous person of that name?' And I go, 'Paul McCartney.' And the guy goes,

'No!!! I'm talking about religious figures!' And I say, 'Oh, I'm sorry. Pope Paul!' [Long intake of breath, and whispers viciously] 'The *Apostle Paul*.' He was *not* into Catholics, and my dad was a Catholic, so I didn't like that. So I backed out.

So we thought this guy, Dennis Sheedy, was off the wall – one of us! He was goin' on about God – fair enough! Welcome in! Have a cup of coffee! Then we started to learn from him. We got into that. What had happened was that, in '77, this movement of the spirit had happened. And a very rigid Catholic Church started to suddenly loosen. Suddenly there was the sort of sexiness that you got in American gospel churches – people singing and dancing. And it was very easy to point at people jumping for Jesus in the RDS and dismiss it totally. But it takes a lot to get hard-boiled Catholics to jump and carry on in that sort of drugged-out fashion. It was like a rave for the God-squad. That's what was happening. They were just out of their minds. But, instead of E, it was the Holy Spirit.

This was interesting. It just *got* very fervent, and heavy things happened. I can look back now. I can see. Wow! I meet people from different places who were burned by the same fire. They'll say, 'Yeah, I went through that. You start to realise this wasn't a sporadic thing. This was a *thing* that happened, which *happens* every so often.'

The Pentecostalists have this idea that a spirit falls and they can trace its movements. There was one that fell around 1917, 1918, and a number of things came out of that. These are movements of the spirit. They fall and they stay somewhere. And there was one around that time. And out of it came such various anomalies as charismatic movements – who'd ever have heard of Catholics singing those hymns? You know, that was a *mad* concept, people jumping for Jesus in the RDS – insane! But something happened. I just know that.

Like punk 'happened'?
'That's right.'
Before? After? Simultaneously?
'Maybe sometime quite similar.'

In the Ireland of the 1970s it was almost impossible to be young and be other than superficially interested in any idea of God and escape the suspicion of the majority of your peers. What may have made U2 somewhat immune to this phenomenon was the odd mix of religious backgrounds they represented. Larry was the only Catholic. The other three were Prods of varying kinds. 'I'm half Protestant too,' says the country's leading

153

psychiatrist, Ivor Browne. 'The fact of feeling yourself not part of the culture gives you a seeing eye into the culture that you don't have if you're simply brought up in it. I had no choice but to look at it, because I knew I was different. Whereas typical Irish Catholics never reached any consciousness about what they were. They didn't have to.'

Bono, for example, having a Catholic father and a Protestant mother, could mix and match his beliefs pretty much as he pleased. Brought up a Protestant, he had no axe to grind with the Catholic Church. This afforded him an unseen freedom from the collective neurosis of the society.

> I didn't have it in my face. My father drove me to the little Church of Ireland church in Finglas with my mother. We got out. We walked in. He went off to mass. And he picked us up afterwards. Occasionally I'd go to mass. I never thought there was any big deal. In that sense I had the most ecumenical background possible in this country.

Did you always, I asked him, believe?

> No. I *knew*. In a very powerful way, I knew that there was something to this. And I didn't believe then, instinctively, the line that I was being sold in school and in the intelligentsia – which is the God is Dead line. I always remember in school, written on the wall 'God is dead – Nietzsche' and written underneath it, 'Nietzsche's dead – God'. A classic graffiti line. I just knew that there was something there.

Something outsiders find hard to figure about born-again Christianity is the concept of a personal relationship with Jesus. Catholics, in particular, have difficulty grasping this.

> I suppose it's the idea . . . Judeo-Christianity is about the idea that *God is interested in you* – as opposed to *A God* is interested in you – if you've got a money problem you go to the money god. This was a radical thought: that God, who created the universe, might be interested in me. And this is the stuff that got them into so much trouble in the Middle East. I mean, if you come in from working the land, smelling of sheepshit, and you stand in front of Pharaoh and tell him that you are equal in God's eyes. You know? It's like, 'FUCK OFF!' Seriously! It's *MAD*! It's an incredible thought. And it is the thought on which democracy is founded, and anyone who thinks it was a Greek idea is up their arse. The Greeks *never* lived by democracy. There was an elitism. The *people*? No chance! We're not equal with the *people* – we're equal with *each other*. So it is the most

extraordinary thought. But if you follow it through to its conclusion, which is that if God is interested in you . . . and what are we
told to base this relationship on? The relationship to begin with is
Father, then Christ, who's the Son of the Father. So it's not the
Father who's there; it's the Son of the Father.

Mates. That's the relationship. That's the idea of Christ, I
suppose. And it is at the root of megalomania also, I imagine,
because if you think that God is available to you, it's got to change
your world view.

Maybe the difficulty we experience is a product of our all-too-human
imagination. We cannot comprehend with intellect, but we have to *try*. We
create images, pictures of God. We can think of God only in terms of Jesus –
God become man. The suspicion is around that this may be a mere fable,
a way of explaining things which our human intellects are otherwise
incapable of grasping.

When I get to this position, and this is a bit of a wall for me, I say,
okay, we know Christ existed as a person. It's all in the history
books and there's not a shadow of a doubt but that this person
existed at that moment of time and went around the place saying
that he was the son of God. My problem is: he either was who he
said he was, or he was a complete maniac. This idea of The Prophet,
this idea of 'Good Teacher' – funnily enough, Christ hated this.
Whenever somebody would come up to him and say, 'Good
Teacher', he always sorted them out. Somebody would come up and
say, 'Good Teacher, I would like to follow you, but my father is
dead and I have to go and bury him.' And he'd say, 'Let the dead
bury the dead.' And I used to think, 'What a *horrible* thing to say.
The guy wants to bury his dad!' I remember goin' up to somebody
who knew about these things and saying, 'This is terrible. I don't
understand. He's tellin' him to fuck off. He just wants to bury his
dad! That's a bit much!' And, as I recall, the guy said to me, 'He
called him Good Teacher – that's the first clue. Which means he
didn't recognise what was going on.' The most popular thought
within our world, the West, is the idea of *Christ: Good Person* –
someone who came up with good ideas about how you should live
your life. Well, that is a load of bollocks. I mean, if that is true, this is
a fucking looper of Charles Manson proportions. You know? This
guy went to the cross, was crucified. King of the Jews! *Here I am!*
We're talking *psychopath*! And it strikes me that it would be one of
the great ironies of human exsistence that the entire globe has been
shaped by a lunatic. 'Cause there's plenty of lunatics in this world –

and there's been a lot more colourful than that. And I ask myself, 'How could an entire globe be shaped by a lunatic such as this? How could we live by a calendar that's post-lunatic? I mean, it's *too much*! Now if my own beliefs were based purely on that, that would be nothing. But mine are based on feelings, senses, instinct, music. I'm a musician. And music is all about faith. You step from one note to the other, believing it will be there when you put your foot down. You're walking on water – all the time. And faith is about that. I don't have it all figured out or anything, but I *know* that there's something to this. And I *feel* more than I know.

Does this mean it's a blind faith? You don't know where you're going. 'Yeaaahhh,' (doubtfully), 'I don't know where I'm going, but . . .'
Is that the point, then, that it *does* keep you going?

No. You see I don't think it's that simple. That's almost like the crutch, isn't it? If it works, use it. But I don't think it works like that. We're at an extraordinary moment at the minute. It's like, never in the history of human civilisation has there been a people who did not believe in the idea of their spirit, in the idea of God. *And we're living it.* This is it. It's never happened before. Ever, ever, *ever*. People worshipped the stars, and the moon. We worship money. It's an incredible thing. And religion is a shell. But what I think is that if God is dead, if God is a myth, it's a very hard myth to shake off, because we've had a hundred years at it now. And it's still there; in communist Russia, where they even took it from the schoolbooks, from everything. It's a very deep thing in us. And even if you don't believe that God exists *out* there, you must believe that the concept of Gods exists *in* there. So you have to deal with it. But how come *nobody* is dealing with it? How come that so few artists are dealing with it, so few writers are dealing with it? This is *the* thing. This is what Milan Kundera, in a way, is having a go at in *Immortality*. People like Wim Wenders are getting into it with things like *Wings of Desire* and *Faraway so Close*. That's what U2 are at, Patti Smith, Bob Dylan. People are trying to find out: what is that place and how come it won't go away? What is it? And how can we get to working our way through it? Is it *the same as* the music? Is it coming from the same *place* as the music? Is it *our language* that we speak to God – is *that* what music is? There are *so many questions*. And it's so rich.

The faith on which the music was founded is a continuous strain in U2's music right up to the present. But the caricatures of U2 which emerged in the wake of *October* have remained as well: the image of joylessness and self-righteousness born out of what can only be a complete ignorance of the music and its content. It's as though U2 had been forged in the public mind as the Mother Teresa of rock 'n' roll bands. This paradox provided a pressure which was as enriching as it was enraging. Bono says:

It never was self-righteous. What people would see as self-righteousness is defensiveness really. The tautness of the *War* album came out of defensiveness. The defensiveness came out of the fact that our idea of God, which was so big, was becoming smaller. People around us were closing in, trying to change and shape us. Gavin wore dresses and boots, and that was fine at first. The next thing it was, like 'Could'ya quit the dresses?' People started dressing plainly. We used to have the sexiest women around, with beautiful bodies. They would cover themselves up. And we didn't like that. There was a closing in, by people who didn't have the freedom that we did. This period just kind of came in, and that was the driest time. They didn't understand our freedom. And they started to look towards the lifestyle. And you can't do that. You mustn't do that. It's invisible. Lifestyle is nothing to do with it. There are alcoholics who are believers. There are drug addicts who are believers.

I don't belong to any church. But if there was one church that I'd be a member of, and go every Sunday, I'd go to the Glide Memorial in San Francisco. If you ever get a chance to go there, you'll have your mind blown. It is extraordinary. It's in the Tenderloin in San Francisco. There's a fella there called Cecil Williams – the Reverend Cecil Williams – he comes out in an electric blue kaftan, with 'Love Power!' and, y'know, 'Pow!' written upon really bad slide projections upon the wall. They've a choir of street angels – people with crash helmets, gay guys, hookers, people who are clean, people who are not clean, and skinheads, singing. It's packed every Sunday. There's a queue round the block at Easter to get in. It's the only church I know where you can get an HIV test during the service. He's funny, he's a completely irreverent Reverend, this guy. No subject is out of bounds. I've seen him do a sermon on orgasms, how the best ones you have to [preacher's voice] . . . 'WAIT FOR! YOU KNOW THAT LADIES! YOU SEE, THE LADIES KNOW THIS! MAN, YOU'RE SO SELFISH!' And the choir – you have this incredible singing. You see cops in tears in this place. It's an incredible place! And this guy, he says, 'You're all welcome. You're welcome here if you're heterosexual, if you're homosexual, if you're tri-sexual – we don't care. If you're a user, if you've been used. You are all welcome here.' It's an incredible sense of freedom. He's not saying to the hooker, 'Have you stopped? Okay, if you've stopped, come on in.' He doesn't get into that. 'You're all welcome here.' That's my version of religion. Freedom. When people start to close in on that freedom, I get very nervous.

But doesn't the fundamentalism which large reams of the Bible suggest set limits on the freedoms that you desire? Saint Paul, for example, was not exactly a buttery liberal.

It can look that way. There are things that are hard to swallow. I think it's very important to separate the gospels. He was like a hitman, Paul. He was sent in to sort it out. Because it was kind of getting the name of a crackpot religion, because religion had always been so strict. Judaism was so strict, and all the other things of the time were so strict. Islam was so strict. And suddenly here was this *freedom* from the law, which was what Christ was preaching. And people were goin' mad. And Paul was sent in as this kind of repairman, to sort it out. 'Don't do that! Oh God, don't do that! Will ye quit that! Women! Stop speaking in the churches! Will you stop wearing that! You have to wear a headband when you come into the church!' It was sort of local and set in that time. And that isn't as important as the central idea . . .

Which is?

Well, you know, when Christ was asked to cut to the chase, in the soundbite sense, he said, 'Okay, love God and love your neighbour as you love yourself. That's it.' Jesus's vibe was – if pushed – 'What are you all about?' – 'That's what I'm about! That's my Greatest Hits!' Now each of those has huge implications. But it's the third idea that's completely ignored by religion. Religion teaches love your neighbour, the love of God, but leaves out the love of the self. And so you have this imbalance. People might look at me and the way I live. I don't live an ascetic life anymore. I'm not as disciplined as I'd like to be. And at times I'm sure I'm, sort of, AWOL, and at times I'm more centred. But I actually have a love of the self – of myself, which in a way gives me the freedom to make those mistakes. They are part of the discovery, and getting to know yourself is part of that.

The Mother Teresa idea is one with which Irish Catholics are swamped from birth. Goodness means a bowed head. This is one of the things that, consciously or otherwise, what I may be forgiven for calling the U2 ethic has set itself against. If they were true to the caricature versions, they would sound like Chris de Burgh. Their seemingly innate consciousness about what would be wrong with this route is what makes the band sound the way they do, what makes The Edge play the guitar in the way he does, what makes sense of the seeming contradictions which swamp the music in its escalating blur. I saw a clip of Bono on a TV programme about Joy Division in the autumn of 1993, talking about that band's singer, the late and great Ian Curtis. He talked about 'the holy voice of Ian Curtis'. Addressed to the lumpen simplicities of conventional society, this is a shocking, almost blasphemous, statement. To rock 'n' rollers it is an example of the foolish piety that we have come to expect from U2. But for anyone for whom Curtis's memory still means something, and who is honest about what they have gleaned from his dark-angel voice, it may be just a modest assertion of the simplest truth.

A useful way of seeing things is to say that, over the past dozen years or so, U2 neither remade themselves nor the world, but held a mirror up to the world as it was remaking itself without knowing. They began in clarity – simple ideas which were strange only because of how much the world had forgotten. The music of the young U2, growing from boys to men, as well as the format of guitar, bass, drums and voice, was emblematic of the passionate simplicities it contained. As the band grew and the world changed, the music was as though driven into what crevices and cracks of space it could find to carry its core spirit as far as possible towards the threshold of the twenty-first century. As the band's view of the world became necessarily more complex, the sounds and textures they created became more intricate and ambiguous.

There is a view that, with the release of *Achtung Baby*, U2 cast off the naivetés that made them different and threw themselves with gusto into making a soundtrack for damnation. Nothing could be further from the truth. The sound they made and the musical heights they achieved with that album may have placed them at the business end of the devil's medium, but they remained on the side of the angels. They recolonised the devil's language, the dirty, distorted, sleazy rumble of reality, and nestled within it a dozen songs which sought to bask the world in the same heavenly light.

'Until the End of the World', for example, is a song about a conversation between Jesus and Judas. More than ten years had passed since the recording of 'Gloria', but the song had the same exuberance, the same redemptive insistence. When you delve in, you find that, instead of dividing its listeners between those who want to believe and those who do not, it attempts to reconcile them at the heart of the differences that divide them. In its doubt, it is liberating. In its confusion, it is reassuring. In its ambiguity, it seeks resolution:

In waves of regret, waves of joy
I reached out for the one I tried to destroy.
You, you said you'd wait until the end of the world.

There are striking resonances between aspects of U2 and the work of the poet Brendan Kennelly, who has consistently attempted to draw out and exorcise the difficult demons of the Irish personality. He did it with a long poem about Cromwell, one of the unholy spectres of Irish nationalistic victimology, attempting not so much to rehabilitate as to rehumanise him. He did it again with *The Book of Judas*, a collection of poems around a single theme, which was published coincidentally with the release of *Achtung Baby*. An Irish newspaper, *The Sunday Press*, had the bright idea of getting Bono and Kennelly to review one another's work. Bono picked up immediately on the themes in Kennelly's book with which he had himself become preoccupied. 'Religion as antagonist, that ould crutch of Irish writing, is not enough for someone as smart as Brendan Kennelly,' he wrote. 'As a rebel his five smooth stones are kept for much less obvious Goliaths than Catholic guilt or political gridlock. He knows that with less than ten years to go, the twentieth century has left Judas/Kennelly with no one to blame . . . but himself that is . . . If not exactly stained glass windows, he has found in Christianity a parade of colours, a vat of symbolism, ceremonies and rituals that takes on new meaning when juxtaposed with the cruel mundaneness of the real world . . . There is light here, bright white light, but if you do find Jesus, you know Judas is just 'round the corner and he knows . . . it's got to *be-e-e* perfect!'

The infatuation was reciprocated entirely. 'What I like most about U2 is the style with which they have survived their own popularity,' wrote Kennelly. 'This record goes further than merely rejecting cynicism. It praises in a joyous yet sometimes quite ironic way the fragile but enduring power of love in a world whose values seem to denigrate that power.'

In the ducking and diving that has characterised the U2 attempt to make music that would connect with its times is an image of those times, a shroud of Turin etched in sleaze and noise but still recognisable after all these years. And I have this thought that maybe the reason the music succeeded in making that connection was that its central idea had to be implicit rather than overt, and so allowed a generation which couldn't admit to its need to meet that need without having to own up.

'Sex and music', said Bono in 1992, 'are in many ways the only mystic acts left. Because religion amongst people has gone cold. I really feel that people know that they're three-dimensional. But, for a hundred years now, the intelligentsia has told us that we aren't. And we live in this two-dimensional world, but we're three-dimensional beings. And we have no expression for this. And if you can't deal with the contradictions of organised religion, which I personally find hard to take, but if you at the same time still know that there's a part of you that isn't being touched by politics – it *might* be touched by art . . . In music . . . there seems to be something there. For most people who don't go to art galleries and get slain in the spirit in front of a Rothko, it's just sex and music.

'As a form, rock 'n' roll is one of the few areas where you get to work out this thing of the flesh and the spirit. Like, Jerry Lee Lewis walking into the studio in Memphis and saying, 'This is the Devil's music.' And there's his cousin, Jimmy Swaggart, who is this preacher, but they are one and the same. And it's Elvis reading Corinthians XIII, and shooting his television set that same evening. This thing, the choice that religion has made us make, between the flesh and the spirit, when to be whole we have to be both. And the music that draws me in always has both. And even if that's kicking against, railing against God, like Robert Johnson and "Me and the Devil Blues", it's still an acknowledgement of the spirit. And I worked out a while ago that the music that kept my interest for the longest was music running away from or toward the spirit.'

But let's be honest about it, for all that the medium they set their sights on was rooted in forms like gospel and soul, the U2 Christian-fix was as bizarre an idea, to begin with, as is possible to imagine. You can say what you like, but please don't tell me you *believe*. According to The Edge, at least, the band members themselves were conscious of the aura of weirdness with which the then perceptions of such beliefs inevitably surrounded them. In the beginning, there was no room for irony. What had to be said had to be said straight and simple. Only in growth could the ambiguities be entered into. They were fighting prejudices from both sides: from those who said leave it out and those who told them to get it 'right'. To one side their statement appeared bland; to the other, irreverent. U2 merely said as much as they needed to say for a start. This, they seemed to say, is 1981 – whatever it is that that implies – but if Christ was here now he wouldn't be the guy with the crewcut and the lemon cardigan playing 'Streets of London' on an out-of-tune guitar.

'We just didn't buy that image at all,' says The Edge. 'We felt very uncomfortable about people hearing the music and listening to it with this idea in their head – that this was a band of Christians. Christian soldiers. We really did not want that to be the first thing on their minds. Because we didn't see that, ultimately, that information was relevant. We've always hated clichés and stereotypes. There was the most awful stereotype of what the good Christian was supposed to be like. It was so dull, more than anything. We just did not want that label. It wasn't gonna affect the way people perceived the music, so why should we fly that particular flag?

We *were* telling people what we believed – it's just we weren't telling them in interviews. We didn't want it to be on the album sleeve.'

Bono sometimes uses the world 'glasnost' to describe the period in the mid-eighties when the band began to acknowledge that there was maybe something unnecessary about their imprisonment in other people's ideas about what they were saying.

What it was was that our instinctive ideas about freedom of the spirit were being challenged by people who didn't have that kind of freedom, and had a very rigid idea. And I suppose we withdrew from that, and I suppose there was a period of some doubting as to whether it was right to withdraw from that, or whether we were wrong. So there was an uncomfortable period there.

Religion is the enemy of God, as far as I'm concerned. It can be very dangerous. I have this phrase – it's one of my clichés – 'Never trust a righteous man who looks like one.' I have a sort of wariness of the clothes of morality, which might explain why on the Zoo TV thing we took off those clothes. In fact, we dressed in the clothes of *im*morality – black leather, shades . . . Because people look for righteousness in the wrong houses. I think the status quo can be the enemy. The statement of the status quo is that everything is okay. 'This is it. You got your car. You got your television. You got your holiday in the sun. Everything is okay!!' Well, everything *isn't* okay. And in that sense you feel that you're on the same wavelength as the rebel, 'cause he's saying that too. His ideas as to what the problem is are very different from yours – he might think, or she might think, that it's structures. I don't. I don't think it's that simple. I don't judge people by discipline. I admire disciplined people, but I don't think they're any better. There's a line in scripture – you see it on the bus stops, I love it – 'For all have fallen short of the glory of God' – or something. Everyone, basically, is in the same shit. Just some people are in better suits, some people look like they don't need. There's that classic line from Leonard Cohen – what is it? – 'Only drowning men know they need to be saved', or something like that.

Fundamentalism really frightens me, because it's this old idea that one's works will get you into the kingdom of heaven. If I live a very good life, and get up early in the morning, and take a cold shower and I beat myself twice a day, and I help the old person across the road – this will get me into heaven. And that is absolutely bollocks. And I just don't believe that the God who created a universe as complex as this would think like that. I'm into this idea that it's *free*. That's what I connect with in all these people – the born-againers or whoever – this idea that it's free. And what worries me about *religion* is that it's *expensive*.

Even our most 'sophisticated' ideas about God and what God wants from us are still only human. How, as human beings, can we see past that wall?

I think you *feel* past it. You innately know, you sense, what God is. And you know that it's not this, but you're taught by religion that it is. That's what I mean by 'free' and 'expensive' – you *have* to do this, you *have* to do that. But I think it's *more* expensive, and at the same time free. All you have to do is give *everything*. Surrender. And that's a position of the heart, of the soul. It is not a political position or a social position or a 'right' position. It's the heart, I think, that God is after. It seems to me that religion is preoccupied with the details, which is like the story of the two sisters and Christ goes around to see them. And one of them breaks open the oil. You only use this oil once in your life. And she breaks it open over His head. And the other one is going, 'That's ridiculous! You're making a big fuss.' And she's going in to wash the dishes. And He says something like, 'You're *so* preoccupied with all the unimportant things.' And I always think, you know, that's religion – washing the dishes, getting the table clean for the priest to come in. And it's completely unimportant. And maybe we know that. And maybe that's why our lifestyles get very confusing.

The band are the first to admit to confusion about what the modern world has opened up for them. It's a long way, as Bono says, from fasting for Christ in a caravan on Portrane beach to riding around Beverly Hills on a Harley Davidson wearing nothing but underpants and warpaint. U2 made that journey in a few years, without making it seem like a U-turn. The U2 perestroika was an organic element of their creative growth. Not only was the manoeuvre documented in the music, but the purpose was explicit as well.

The trip has not been without its moments of doubt. Bono remembers that the very first time he and his wife Alison slept in the house backing on to Killiney Beach, south of Dublin, where they now live, they woke in the night freaked out by the size of the place. Next morning, following a frantic call from Bono, a close friend who was more used to this kind of problem had to come round and persuade him not to put the For Sale signs up right away. The issue was finally dealt with on the basis of a saying of Bono's father, Bobby: 'The problem of wealth. Now that's a great problem!'

The high life thing had started in LA around *Rattle and Hum*, and continued right through. But I suppose that I'm impossible in that I need to have a reason – in my head at least – for why I would be giving in to this. So, my attitude is, '*This* is interesting! Let's see what we can make of this!' I mean I'm perfectly relaxed, and have gone through the questions of wealth and responsibility and all that. Well, I'll never be completely relaxed, but at least I know where I stand.

Wholeness is the thing. I think that God wants from us to be whole: body, spirit, soul. Trashy, transcendent, human. That's what we're trying to get at. That's why there are no contradictions, because they're all the same. These characters, the Mirrorball Man, the Fly, MacPhisto – if it was just irony, it wouldn't be as interesting as saying, 'No, no! I'm not messing. This is actually a side of your personality. I may have exaggerated it, blown it out of proportion. But to try and exist all at the same time' – that's what I'm trying to get to with the group. I demand . . . [country accent] I absolutely fucken demand!!! . . . to be sacred and profane in the same breath. To own up to all that. Media is about caricatures, cartoons. So with this disinformation . . . but it's not just as simple as disinformation. It's, how can you be this *and* that? How can you feel like *that* and live there? Freedom again! People can't stand to see you have your cake and eat it. And as much as we've got it in the neck in the eighties for being lopsided, we'll get it more for the balance. That's a thing that I'm starting to figure out. I didn't think that would happen. But actually it drives people mad. 'YOU MEAN THAT YOU WANT *ALL* THIS?'

It can scarcely be overemphasised that, rather than being some kind of peripheral and slightly embarrassing distraction from the music, the Christian ethos is what guides U2. It is the reason the music exists. (Up to a point, but we'll get to that later.)

'Life is faith,' says The Edge. 'Anyone who's creative has to admit that you're tuned into things that are at times beyond your own understanding. We would certainly make connections between our spiritual beliefs and our creativity. Definitely. There's a sense, a spiritual . . . call it *presence* . . . just a *spirit*. It is full of a spirit that is connected and wrapped up in U2 as a band. Quite where it comes from I'm not sure.'

'There are aspects of U2 that are very unusual,' Bono elaborated to me in 1992. 'We spent, really, from 1981 to, say, 1983/84 caught up in discovering our spiritual lives and paying attention to that. And, at that moment, it was like we grew in a distorted way, we learnt things a lot of people don't learn until way later in their lives. While other people were getting *just* the right shoes, and *just* the right haircut, we were reading books, talking with people about very abstract things, and we were completely wrapped up in it. So, by the time we got to 1984/85 – which we now call glasnost – we were advanced in some ways, but *so* lopsided. In some ways – socially – and I speak for myself – I was *retarded*. Not quite knowing how to talk, so pretending you did! Being around rock 'n' roll, but not really *in* rock 'n' roll. We'd been travelling in the blue bus across America and Europe, playing rock 'n' roll concerts, but then just going back to our rooms. And it was an incredible period of growth, mentally and spiritually. But in terms of just hanging out, and in terms of just pickin' up on what rock 'n' roll is, we were way down the road. So, by 1985, we thawed out a bit and realised that this was not right, that we were out of balance. And that's really when we started to become a rock 'n' roll band.'

The course the band has taken in carrying its flame through the vicissitudes of the late twentieth century has had them shot at by both sides: by the secularists as goody-goody-two-shoes, by the Christians as counterfeits. 'We probably, at this point, have deeply disappointed a lot of Christians,' agrees The Edge, 'because what I perceive as freedom, they would perceive as complete decadence and self-indulgence.'

The nub of the issue is language in its widest sense. The sounds and images which U2 produce are deeply shocking to those who think about Christianity in fossilised images and words. Elements of righteousness and rebellion are sprinkled through the U2 story and statement, but not in the places you might expect to find them. The more time passes, the more U2 seem to fit into place in the external world. But the perspective of the external world can perceive in the changes in U2 and their music only a dilution or an abandonment of their earlier beliefs. There is an alternative explanation: that the world is moving along a course of reconciliation which will create new images of the things which it needs to believe – and that U2 have been ahead of their times.

The Edge insists in the spring of 1994:

> I don't think we've changed our beliefs. I would say that, myself, I'm probably relying on faith even more. The more you are around, the idea that there's any kind of grace out there becomes increasingly difficult to hold on to. So you need a different logic to resist the logicswhich are coming at you all the time. I went to see *All Things Bright and Beautiful*, Barry Devlin's movie, and it's a really beautiful story about a little kid. I think it's probably very wrapped up in Barry's own experience. It's really about, I suppose, the death of innocence – or, if not the death of innocence, the attempt to hold on to that childlike way of looking at the world in the face of everything

else that's around, which is just constantly eroding all your faith and your beliefs. What I'm saying is I need my faith even *more* now. And it's much more of a challenge to have faith than it was ten years ago. I suppose it's just the way that, when you're around a few more years, you just see a lot more of what goes on. There's so much more negativity. So it's much more of a challenge to hang on to it. Because faith is another form of this naive creativity. It's something out of the imagination, to an extent. It's an assertion – that you're not going to give in, you're going to hold on to a conviction that is beyond logic, beyond adult attitudes.

Or is it that U2 are struggling more with the contradictions in their own position? How much of the change has been for external reasons, how much for internal?

I think it's external and internal, because I think the world and society . . . [working-class Dub accent] '*I blem suss-i-itee*' . . . it conspires as you get older to make you feel more and more isolated in your own life. So that obviously makes it more of a challenge to get outside of yourself, to believe in things that are external. And then in viewing the world – just, the badness out there is so overpowering that sometimes it's just a struggle to hold on to beliefs that are so, I dunno . . . *simple*, in the face of such sophisticated *evil*. It is really. It's *terrible*.

It was the faith issue which, in the wake of *October*, had come closer than anything to breaking up the band before it had rightly begun. It was a moment of knife-edge precariousness, but its resolution created a bond which became all-but unbreakable. 'Within maybe two years of that time,' recalls The Edge, 'I came to realise how the whole idea of there being a prohibition on any form of creativity on the grounds that it was morally unsavoury was just completely stupid and ridiculous. So I've never really given it a second thought after that point.'

Nevertheless, the uncertainties of the three Christian members had been real and profound, and the divisions they created between them and Adam Clayton equally so. Another of the U2 caricatures is of a band comprising three-plus-one. Because there was so little understanding of what exactly the three stood for, there was even less about the relationship between the three and the one. As Adam remembers it, the real source of the tension which developed within the band was never centred on issues of faith, but on the division which this issue created. He says:

In fact it had nothing to do with religion. It had more to do with my being on the outside and not wanting to give up that position, but feeling very pushed out. It was a crucial period for the band. We'd made our first record, we'd gone on tour, and suddenly the influence of the meetings was disrupting the progress of the band. Myself and Paul [McGuinness] were plotting and scheming. It was, you know, whatever you had to do to stay in business. You'd be on tour somewhere, and the bus would be about to leave, and the other three would be in a meeting. So there was this situation. I didn't have a problem *at all* with spirituality, and identity. I just had a problem with the disruptiveness that it brought to the band's activities. And then later, as we got into the *October* album, and the others were considering whether rock 'n' roll was the right form of expression – I never wanted to go to those meetings. I didn't like the tone of what was going on. It was another band. It was an exclusivity that I didn't buy into. I felt that one could have a spirituality that was one's own. I mean, I regret now that I never went through it, because they have a spiritual strength that I don't think I'll ever have. And they have a knowledge that I'll never have. And I think they were very right at the time. But I was really getting over my own kind of religious stigmas that had come from the boarding-school approach to religion. I felt them being more drawn towards the meeting group, and less drawn towards dealing with the problems of the band. And less tolerant. And all the paranoias that that produces. And Paul and myself very much ended up, after a gig, going out to the local clubs, meeting the record company people ourselves, staying up all night doing those rock 'n' roll things. And that made me very insecure, because I was making commitments that, yes this band was going to go all the way, and I wasn't actually sure whether I had the guys behind me. And musically I wasn't as accomplished as them, so I knew if they wanted to not back me up, there was an opportunity to not support my playing, but to expose it.

I certainly went along with the spirituality. I didn't have a problem with admitting to that. It was just at the time, the *charismaticness* of the charismatic meetings was something I couldn't feel comfortable with. I knew the guys in a different way, so it could never be so po-faced with me. I'd known them since '76, so the relationship I had with them was pretty straightforward. And we spent time in business meetings and artistic meetings together. So I knew the people behind some of the pronouncements.

Adam agrees that, yes, it might be said that there was a narrowness in the language which U2 used to get across what they were on about. But he also sees that the journey of the past ten years has seen the language expand in a way that's brought the four of them closer together.

> I suppose there was an absence then of the rock 'n' roll spirit, which was staying up late, going to clubs, drinking – whatever. Meeting people. Which I embarked on from the early years through to – probably *The Joshua Tree*. I kinda had enough of that by then. And by then everyone else was beginning to go to clubs and seek out different things. And I was less driven, I felt like I'd done that. I'd been in enough bars and clubs all over America, and not really found – with the exception of some in New York – anything all that exciting.

The Edge goes a little further, to the heart of the U2 paradox. You might say that the seeds of the later music were contained in the make-up of the band from the beginning. The U2 mix of personalities ensured that nothing was given, nothing could be taken for granted or accepted at face value. The band's range of identities always made them question *everything*. Adam's rock 'n' roll agnosticism kept the others as safe from fossilising as their faith kept him from complete unbelief. The two forces worked in a creative symbiosis which ended up as the gritty spirit of *Achtung Baby*. If they had been four straight Irishmen, they might have ended up as a rhythm 'n' blues quartet; if four Christians, as Cliff Richard's backing band. Their differences made them whole.

'That's a very good theory,' enthuses The Edge. 'Yeah, I'm sure. I mean it was critical that Adam did *not* believe the same things that we did. So that the paths that we took were . . . It's *true*. I've never thought about that. I would agree.'

That *Achtung Baby* might never have happened if there had been four Christians instead of three?

'Yeah. Probably it would never have happened.'

U2 began with their roots in space – in the heavens, if you prefer – and then grew to earth. They confronted the demons that stalked that earth in a way that promised to either reclaim the Devil's music for God or damn them as well. (How would we know which of these had occurred? Perhaps we couldn't.) In attempting to fill in their own lives what Salman Rushdie called the 'God-shaped hole', they had tried to express in their music a faith based on the radical if ancient idea of love, but to clothe this meaning in the texture of the times. They have sought to redefine the humanly desirable in a manner that would be both fearless and plausible, and in this they have both betrayed and embraced their times. The question they have asked is this: is it possible to live in the twentieth century in all the ways that the twentieth century seems to demand, and still believe in something that the times appear to deny? U2 began with a fear of the world and ended up looking like they loved it too much for their own good. But deeper down there was something else going on. In this sense, their story may provide one of the most powerful parables of the century.

'Mock the Devil and he will flee from thee.' Bono smiles and affects his best preacher voice. 'I remember hearing a story once, I think it was a missionary in Haiti. There were all sorts of demons that would mock him while he preached his sermon. People would go into trances and give him abuse. So he'd bring in exorcists from all over every week, and they'd try to exorcise the people and the church. And this went on for weeks and weeks and weeks, until finally he brought in the Pope of Exorcists, the Big Shot, and he spoke to the demons and he said, "*Why* are you here?" And the demons spoke back: "Because we get so much attention!"'

'We saw success like a big bad wolf. It was like this thing we had to keep at bay. And now I genuinely find it funny. Four jerks in a police escort – that's funny. Being a rock 'n' roll band and taking the same hotel suite that normally industrialists and presidents take – that's funny. And it's actually fuel for our fire.

'Eunice Shriver came to one of our shows. People said she was the smartest Kennedy – that she would have been President in a different time. She'd seen us a few times. She's very *au fait* with Irish poets and writers, and she sees rock 'n' roll as part of that and wants to know what's happening. And one night after the gig she said, "Ahh, I see you had a few more devils on stage tonight." And I said, "Oh yeah?" And she said. "Still angels. Still angels. More angels and more devils. But I like it better this way. It's a fairer fight."'

CHAPTER FOURTEEN

The Life of the Building

And the doors shall be shut in the streets,
when the sound of the grinding is low,
and he shall rise up at the voice of the bird,
and all the daughters of musick shall be brought low;
Ecclesiastes 12:4

The important element of U2's music that is Irish, Bono told the makers of the television programme *Bringing It All Back Home*, broadcast in 1991, is what it contains of the Irish tradition of the storyteller. This, he felt, lay in that 'romantic spirit' of the words he writes and in the way The Edge plays the guitar. 'Irish music reminds us of the humanity that we're losing,' he said, 'of a past we all share . . . You tend to put a glass case around folk music, but I think U2 are a folk group, an out-and-out folk band. We're the loudest folk band you'll ever hear.'

Bono suggested that his primary access to this tradition might have been via Bob Dylan, who was himself influenced by Irish ballad groups like the Clancy Brothers and the McPeakes. 'That blew my mind when he told me that because I never thought of him in that way.'

There was a moment, embarrassing but strangely touching, a few years before, when Bono interviewed Bob Dylan and Van Morrison together for *Hot Press*, and it emerged that Bono had never heard of the McPeake family. Embarrassing for the obvious reason, touching because Bono made no attempt to conceal his ignorance.

Such ignorance was not unusual for Irish people of his generation: the famous northern ballad-family the McPeakes were seldom heard on primetime radio. The fact that they had influenced Bob Dylan but not the young Irish pretenders was another consequence of the distorted cultural channels in sixties and seventies Ireland.

'The Irish are less uptight about what's inside them,' said Bono on *Bringing It All Back Home*. 'They let it out easier and it comes out in a raw way and that's very like the spirit of black music and gospel music. The confusion over my own identity and the group's identity is part of the reason why I'm digging into Irish folk music and the ballad form.' Because he had rebelled against Irish music at school, Bono had few conscious memories of being influenced by Irish music as a child. He remembered liking Luke Kelly. He remembered being introduced to the music of Seán Ó Riada. And he remembered 'Whiskey in the Jar' – before the Thin Lizzy version – as one of the first songs his brother Norman taught him to play on the guitar.

To talk about the Irish ballad form may seem vague and unfocused, but Bono was referring here to something specific and distinctive in Irish cultural history. The ballad form is not something which began with the Clancy Brothers or the McPeakes – it is a form with a long and complex genealogy going back well over a thousand years. It has its roots in the bardic tradition of poetry in the Irish language.

In his amazing book *The Hidden Ireland*, Daniel Corkery unearths a treasure trove of Irish culture and learning which had been buried alive under eight hundred years of abuse and self-hatred. Up to the point when the book was published – 1924 – histories of Ireland had confined their minute attentions to Dublin and the life of the Ascendancy there. In such books, with one or two honourable exceptions, the life of the rest of the country was either ignored or dismissed with a sociological sweep of the quill. In a sense, Corkery tries to do for Irish culture in the 1920s what Greil Marcus was to do for rock 'n' roll in the 1990s, constructing an alternative skeleton of antecedents and raising a whole new set of questions about matters believed to have been settled beyond controversy. *The Hidden Ireland* contains something of the humility which Bono expressed in his frank admissions of ignorance to Bob Dylan and Van Morrison; for example, Corkery predicts in his introduction that those who sought errors would find many in his book. But, he adds, 'the propulsive course of epics is not to be hindered by even shoals of errors'. *The Hidden Ireland* is a thrilling book, made even more so by its hints of what it has been unable to discover or what it has had to leave out. It prostrates itself before the enormity of its subject and all but admits defeat. But in doing so it manages to *suggest* far more than it *says*. 'The best that history has to give us', writes Corkery, quoting Goethe, 'is the enthusiasm which it arouses.'

The Hidden Ireland takes us through the forgotten poetic tradition of the southern province of Munster from the early centuries up to the 1700s. Corkery takes us back to the bardic schools which littered the southernmost province of Ireland through much of this period, bringing them alive with his love and his pen. The bardic schools pre-dated Christianity in Ireland, and, therefore, also the monastic schools set up under Christianity's aegis. In a country which has come to regard the terms 'Catholic' and 'national' as all but synonymous, it is strange and exhilarating to learn that these schools provided in Ireland the only secular intellectual system in Europe during the Middle Ages. The later mixing with the monastic tradition brought forth a heady cocktail of spirit and imagination which conquered the soul of Europe in the Middle Ages. 'Who shall fathom,' asks Corkery, 'its various promptings and achievements on its native soil?'

The bardic schools taught through two mediums: poetry and the Irish language. The literary tradition which centred on these schools had, writes Corkery, 'not been so much misunderstood or underestimated as entirely omitted' by previous writers of Irish history, and indeed novelists as well. The very existence of the tradition had been buried under the myth of the savage Irish, in the words of one historian 'a paralytic body where one half of it is dead or just dragged about by the other'.

A masterly and passionate work, *The Hidden Ireland* traces the literary voice of Ireland from the early poetic forms through to ballads like the *aisling*, an eighteenth-century poetic form which told of the darkness in which the Irish mind was then enveloped, and the *amhrán*, or song, which developed side by side with the literary story. The bardic culture went back far before colonisation, before Christianity. This was, as one collector, Professor Gerard Murphy, would pronounce, 'the earliest voice from the dawn of West European civilisation'. In those early centuries, the poetic tradition was an attempt to achieve in language what the monastic illuminators of the time achieved in works like the *Book of Kells*.

Only a meagre part of the poetry and music of this period survives. Of the poetry, just fragments remain. This is mainly because it was largely an oral tradition, but also because most manuscripts of the period have either been lost or reduced to dust by time and the elements. During the period of colonisation, the culture of Ireland was confined to the intimate arts of poetry and music. Quoting Romain Rolland, Daniel Corkery reminds his readers that, 'the plastic arts in general have need of luxury and leisure, or refined society and of a certain equilibrium in civilisation in order to develop themselves fully. But when material conditions are harder, when life is bitter, starved and harassed with care, when the opportunity of outside development is withheld, then the spirit is forced back on itself, and its external need of happiness drives it to other outlets: its expression of beauty is changed, and it takes a less external character.' In the poetry and music of the colonised period was contained, as Corkery puts it, 'the life of the building', the stifled cry of a buried civilisation, a refuge in passion which provides a story without equal in the history of literature. This was a literature rooted in the rhythms of nature and the land, infected with the beat of Celtic and Latin rhythms, fertilised by almost continuous trafficking with continental Europe and finally bottled and corked by the colonial assault. It is a tradition steeped in spirituality and primal consciousness, looking not at the mud and slime at its feet but always at the stars over and in its head. It was, writes Corkery, 'a network of song laid over the land'.

Corkery does not claim to have rediscovered the tradition; his entire book is peppered with caveat and regret at the limits of his excavations. He can only hint, he says, at what has been lost, the tradition which 'the historians scanted'. But history, he writes, has belied the historians. 'For that people, if they were a mob, had died, and their nationality died with them: instead of which that nationality is vigorous today, not only at home, but in many lands abroad – "translated, passed from the grave".'

Reading Corkery's book makes Bono's tentative identification with the Irish ballad tradition come suddenly alive with meaning and possibility. What if it has been 'passed from the grave', perhaps from grave to grave to grave to grave, right up to the present day, hidden in the folds of language, its strength ebbing and flowing, transmuting and metamorphosing, the spark jumping when the gap was exactly right, but retaining its essence to some extent all the while? What then? Or perhaps the proper question is: *why not?* For, as Corkery says, if nothing of this has survived, then the entire civilisation was but 'an expense of spirit in a waste of shame'.

What then? Well, in the musty, crumbling manuscripts reproduced in Corkery's book might be located the ancestors of a music which has taken the twentieth century by storm. Or perhaps a hint of the dust of that ancestry. The hardest thing is to prevent yourself being carried away with the enthusiasm which the gift of true history arouses.

An idle flick through the pages of *The Hidden Ireland* might bring you to a fragment of a poem by Andrias Mac Craith, said to have been the wildest of all the bards of the eighteenth century. 'There is,' writes Corkery, 'a strength and ease in everything we have of his; but in his most famous poem there is more: there is fine feeling; two at least of the stanzas are priceless: he has been driven from Croom of the Merriment into loneliness [Corkery quotes in Irish and translates into English these two priceless verses from that most famous poem]:

> "*Is fánach faon mé is fraochmhar fuar . . .*"

> "A wanderer and languid am I, furious and cold
> Weak, prostrate, disease-smitten,
> Wretched on the mountain-top, with none, alas
> To befriend me – except heather and the north wind!

> When as a bird in its questing I enter the village,
> There's no welcome for me, they are cold to my jesting
> And the women, gathered together, question one another:
> "Who is he? Where is he from? Where is he going?"'

The words, written in Irish, could be rendered into English only in a dim and shadowy mime of the original. And yet, even in this crude translation there is something strange and expectant about the sketch which is drawn. As Corkery says, 'the heart stirs to it'. And even as the heart stirs, the hand of the modern searcher for connections reaches to the rack for a CD of the most recent U2 album, *Zooropa*, and lines up the final track, 'The Wanderer', written by Bono for Johnny Cash, who sings it on the record. If Corkery searched for the most ancient traces of the ballad tradition, here, in the industrial pop of the latest U2 album, is perhaps its most up-to-date expression.

> I went out walking through streets paved with gold
> Lifted some stones
> Saw the skin and bones
> Of a city without a soul
> I went out walking under an atomic sky
> Where the ground won't turn
> And the rain it burns
> Like the tears when I said goodbye

'The Wanderer' seems to capture perfectly the duality of the U2 ethic and yet to walk a little distance from its implications. It contains the contradictions of the limbo dance and the dialectic of the story from the beginning. It is serious, then laughable, then even more serious. It brings the diverse strands of the journey together in one stretch and yet widens the vista to embrace the broadest imaginable horizons. But then perhaps not, because the ambiguity is both denied and enhanced by the fact that it is Johnny Cash, not Bono, who sings the song.

'I couldn't sing it,' Bono insists. 'For whatever reason, it didn't sit well. But it *is* a complete cop-out. And Brian Eno worked very hard to try to get me to sing that song. But I wanted Johnny Cash to sing it. It was his voice that I heard in my head. So I didn't argue with my own instincts.'

'The Wanderer', according to the man who wrote it, is inspired by readings of the Book of Ecclesiastes, but the influence is not directly traceable in the words. You have to sift very carefully through the pages of Ecclesiastes to find echoes of the song. What it draws on is the mood, light, rhythms, sense of moral isolation and sense of humour.

> And so I saw the wicked buried, who had come and gone from the place of the holy, and they were forgotten in the city where they had so done: this is also vanity.
>
> Ecclesiastes 8:10

Bono says:

It starts in that kind of Psalmist song type of thing, 'I have climbed
. . .' all that stuff. It sets out in very similar terrain. But it develops
into something else. It's a sort of postmodern postmortem. It heads
off. Ecclesiastes is quite funny, quite wry, in a way. This idea of this
guy who sets out on this epic journey and experiments on himself on
every level – knowledge, sex, gold, whatever is going he's taking it.
On one level it looks like straightforward existentialism, except that
there is another dimension . . . He's a preacher. I wanted to call
it 'The Preacher', but somebody talked me into calling it 'The
Wanderer'. But it also holds with the idea: 'Never trust a righteous
man that looks like one.' The strangest folk can be signposts. You
turn on the television set in Texas and there's this complete lunatic
and he's making sense to you. I'm very influenced by Flannery
O'Connor in that. She had it. Humour – but with love, not cynicism
– she had love for these characters, love for their do-it-yourself
religion. She was a Catholic, but she had this sympathy for these
people, and she saw that there was something in what they were
saying. And with a kind of smile, rather than a smirk, she drew
them. And I suppose, in our picture, I want to have that kind of
crackpot in there who's off to save the world and, at the same time,
he's just up for the ride.

If it was a novel, you'd cut your throat at the end of it. At the end
of Ecclesiastes he goes, 'I've tried everything and I've decided that
the most important thing for a man is to enjoy his work and . . . get
on with it' . . . *WHAT???!!!* Run that by me again!! That's why I
love that line, which Johnny finds very hard to sing, this thing about
'I went out for the papers'. He says to me [Johnny Cash voice],
'Bono,' he says, 'you know I'm singin' this in concert now. And I'm
down there and we got these young ladies with purple hair comin' ta
see me now. And they're down there and they're jes lookin' up at me
and I'm diggin' it. And then I get to the thing about goin' out ta get
the papers . . . but maan, y'know, the rest a them poeple in there –
they can follow it, all the way to that moment . . .'

I still haven't figured it out. It's a very Zen place indeed. It blew
me out.

The wanderer in Bono's song is adrift in the city, but his wanderlust and
sense of alienation are the same as Mac Craith's outcast on the mountain-
top more than two centuries before. In both songs, the elements are the
wanderer's only companion: for Mac Craith's, the wind and brambles
scratching at his limbs and skin; for Bono's the burning rain. For Mac
Craith's wayfarer, the overweening sense of doom is given expression by his

own senses – he is cold, weak, wretched – projected through the elements; for Bono's the sense of foreboding is expressed in the image of an atomic sky. Each speaks from the soul of its own time.

The thought, breathtaking but plausible, occurs: Andrias Mac Craith was in the habit of reading Ecclesiastes as well . . .

> He that observeth the wind shall not sow;
> and he that regardeth the clouds shall not reap
> > Ecclesiastes 11:4

The leading characters in both songs are outcasts but also, one senses, by choice. They have stepped outside because they do not like the way things are within. Both men, too, come upon the settlements of alleged civilisation. Mac Craith's wanderer enters a village 'as a bird in its questing', but finds no welcome.

Bono's hero feels a similar coldness:

> I went drifing through the capitals of tin
> Where men can't walk
> Or freely talk
> And sons turn their father in
> I stopped outside a church house
> Where the citizens like to sit
> They say they want the kingdom
> But they don't want God in it.

Both songs are about the loneliness of the high moral ground, the isolation of someone who, believing in his own forebodings, is unable to interest the rest of humanity in his visions.

With a what-if countenance you read Corkery's account of the life of Andrew McGrath, the Merry Pedlar, a schoolmaster by profession, who plied his art in the Cork-Limerick area in the eighteenth century. But soft. Mac Craith was a Catholic who, having 'abjured the errors of Rome' and turned Protestant, later became disillusioned with both religions, to become 'a wanderer, neither Protestant nor Papist'.

The modern pop song lyric being infinitely more condensed than the ancient bardic tradition, it is in the music of U2's 'The Wanderer' that we find the details shaded in. The guitar, bass and drums are as much a part of the format as the words or the voice. Johnny Cash tells us the outline of the story, but U2 steals our brains away.

It is as though the band has shifted its identity away from itself so as to see itself more clearly. 'The Wanderer' seems, at first, a light year away from the rest of *Zooropa* – as one critic put it, 'a different movie in a different cinema'. But this is only true if you are paying attention only to the point the album has taken U2 to on the rock 'n' roll mantelpiece. The sound and mood of 'The Wanderer' are different from the album's other songs, but then again, these songs are equally distant from one another. Just as sonic unity was one of the more obvious themes of *Achtung Baby*, *Zooropa* is characterised by its sonic disunity. Here, the concept of U2 has finally transcended the limitations of form; has rendered itself capable of anything. 'The Wanderer' both underlines this and in a strange way denies it. In a certain light, it is the album's most conservative track; in another it is its most adventurous. Ultimately it embraces both the album and every single one of its predecessors, linking them in a single statement. 'The Wanderer' tells the essentials of the U2 story in four and three-quarter minutes. But it tells much more besides. It is the story of the Boy who thought the world could go far if it listened to what he said, walking now amid the debris of the city in which he grew up, seeking to understand what has happened to it and to him, and trying to summon up the Pretender who will set things back to rights, and laughing at his own earnestness and two-facedness.

The paradoxical connection between the 'The Wanderer' and the song of Andrias Mac Craith is that each, from its own time, describes a different landscape to tell broadly the same story of insecurity, of fear, of frittering identity in a changing world; but also that each flirts with the freedom of unknowing, the certainty that comes of uncertainty, the peace that follows the abandonment of the search for self-knowledge.

This theme is held in common by all the best rock 'n' roll artists of the era of commerical pop: Elvis, Bob Dylan, the Beatles, Jimi Hendrix, The Rolling Stones, The Smiths, The Pogues, Talking Heads, Bruce Springsteen, Van Morrison, U2. The greatest popular music of this period has told the story of a generation of fallen angels caught on the doomed journey from the farmlands to the city, but with neither the motivation nor the inclination to turn back. Modern rock 'n' roll is the sound of the city, both from afar and in its heart. It is the music of mankind gradually losing sight of his means, but too contented, too cool to care. Its story is that of a generation of Western civilisation smart enough to know where it was headed, but too pampered and intelligent to be other than slightly fascinated by the clatter and babble up ahead.

'The Wanderer' opens with a rustling brush upon a tensed-up snare, and a plodding, walking bass padding about underneath a high-pitched keening whistle which follows the song through its whole journey. It might be Brian Eno playing some newfangled gadget, or it might be the north wind such as accompanied Mac Craith's wanderer from Croom of the Merriment into loneliness. The bass is awkward and heavy-hearted, almost tripping self-consciously over the riff. Soon the sound gives way to a thin veil of voices,

177

building and receding. *Ahh-uhhhh*. Immediately it acquires echoes of things from the vast chatter of pop music, but you will never be able to say what. Thin Lizzy? T Rex? Bob Dylan? Your stab is as good as mine.

Johnny Cash's voice is . . . what? Is Johnny Cash's voice. He is here not as guest star, but interpreter. This is not *his* song, although it has been written with his voice in mind. U2 started out to write songs because they couldn't sing other people's; now they need other people to sing the songs they write which have outgrown them. Cash seems to understand that he is not there as himself, but as part of the U2 thing. His performance sounds like a rehearsal, as though he is coming to the song for the first time. That is not to say that he sings it badly; rather that he doesn't so much sing the song as read it out, almost as background to the music. His function is to provide distance. As though reworking an old motif to a new situation, he recites the song as though he is simply helping the band to get their sound right, and in doing so he succeeds in objectifying it and so making it more urgently real. His voice moves through the song with as little inflexion or modulation as it is possible to imagine. This is the story, it seems to say; take it or leave it.

The dynamic of the song is carried almost entirely in the music, with the lyric providing an insouciant counterpoint and a rough map. The first few times you hear the song you are caught by the shock of hearing Johnny Cash's voice on a U2 track. Then your ear moves from the voice to the story underneath. Finally, the superficial details of the story having registered, the voice is absorbed into the music and you hear for the first time the subtle, irresistible witchcraft of the whole.

The song begins in doubt, alienation and loneliness, travels through chaos and confusion and emerges wryly in the light of some kind of strength and knowledge. The music builds and builds through those first three verses, as though gradually coming nearer to some sort of resolve. The bass grows a little steadier and the brushes on the snare a trifle more insistent, accompanying Johnny down that old eight-lane, searching on a thousand signs for his own name. But they emerge on to this bypass as though still unconvinced, and trudge manfully into the middle eight:

> I went out there
> In search of experience
> To taste and to touch
> And to feel as much
> As a man can
> Before he repents

Suddenly the song lifts out of its despondency as a note of irony enters. Here, the device is a mocking reprise of a thousand bad country and western ditties, a spoken homily of self-pitying fundamentalism. Bono plays guitar, a twanging, knowing parody of an Edge parody of Johnny Cash, mocking but yet with a hesitancy in strange sympathy with the singer's deadpan delivery: *Dang-dang-da-da-dang-da-da-dang-dang-dang! Der-nang da-dang!* The chanting voices build and build into a mosaic of humour and pathos and sentiment and, yes, rapture.

As Johnny Cash continues:

> I went out searching, looking for one good man
> A spirit who would not bend or break
> Who would sit at His Father's right hand

the eye strays to a passage in Daniel Corkery's description of the *aisling*:

> And from this the poet's words pass into the form of a prayer to the Only-Begotten Son, Who, whilst yet young, trod this earth in humanity, in divinity, to banish the tyrants, the perverse 'sprats' of falsehood – to blow them beyond the waves without feasting, without wind, without estates, without the crown . . . There! the lines fall, as is ever happening in these poems, into the bitterness of earnestness as soon as the one root-sorrow of all the tribe is reached – the Gael in bondage, his land in the grip of the alien.

And Johnny sings:

> I went out walking with a Bible and a gun
> The word of God lay heavy on my heart
> I was sure I was the one.
> Now, Jesus, don't you wait up,
> Jesus, I'll be home soon . . .

The backing has by now gathered to it an assurance and confidence that seems to trot ahead of the lyric. The bass has started to skip and frolic a little as Adam gets to like the riff, and Larry Mullen is beginning to sound almost animated. The drum-machine snare has metamorphosed into a full drum kit, albeit one which, a cymbal or two excepted, has yet to be taken out of its wrapping paper. In the background there is what might be the vague shuffle of an acoustic guitar, indicating that The Edge has arrived in the building. Cash takes the curve into the final chorus but has yet to break into a sweat.

> Yeah I left with nothing
> Nothing but the thought of you
> I went wandering

The story of the song, in as much as this is vested in the words, has been told. But the lyric's ending is inconclusive, leaving us more puzzled than enlightened. Is he going home now? Is he any the wiser? Is he any happier than when he started out? Who, if anybody, is going to be waiting at home? What conclusions does he bear with him?

Johnny, I'm afraid, is unable to be of much use. He's walking away to an early shower, leaving the song half-finished. Then a voice which can only be Bono's rises from the ashes of the song,

Uuuuuuuuuuhhhhhhhoooooooooooooo
aahhhhhh-uuuuuuuuuuuuuuuuuuuuuu.

In this final keening is contained the resolution of the song, the hint of a connection going back into the previous millennium and into the sensibility of this band, and maybe also their race of angels, as they turn the corner into the next. This, if ever such was heard, is a refuge in passion in the face of chaos and meaninglessness. In this awakening alarm-cry is the life of the building. The song lightens and lets go. And Adam Clayton's bass goes skipping off into the distance.

The connection with the ancient poetry of Gaelic Ireland is both real and unreal, tangible and ridiculous. It is too strange to be really true. And yet the comparisons are there: the same spirit seems to inhabit both U2's 'The Wanderer' and the opening of Mac Craith's poem of two centuries before. There is no doubt that what remains of the folk music of the Gaelic period has its roots in the poetry that preceded it. The bridge between the literary and folk traditions appears to have been the *aisling*, the vision poem, originally a literary form with a musical stressed-metre rhythm. With these sometimes erotic, sometimes patriotic poems, usually rendered to the accompaniment of harp music, a connection was made between the higher form of poetry and what Daniel Corkery describes as 'the local singers of the hidden countryside'. These 'anonymous poets wrote folk-poetry, with, it is true, the influence of the schools showing clearly through it'. With the decline of the bardic schools in the mid-seventeenth century, the two forms blurred into one. Undoubtedly that is the route by which we have received what songs remain.

Perhaps the spirit of those times has been transported to the present day in songs like 'Whiskey in the Jar' or 'Róisín Dubh', or in transmuted form in the music of Bob Dylan and the legion of modern artists who have, directly or indirectly, come under his influence. Perhaps. We are what we eat as well as what we have thrown up. U2 would not be the same band if the Clancy Brothers, Bob Dylan or Thin Lizzy had not existed – any more than they would be the same band if Bono had not read *Wise Blood*, the novel by Flannery O'Connor about Hazel Motes who grew up, as did the fledgling U2, seeing Jesus move from tree to tree in the back of his mind, the wild, ragged figure motioning them to turn around and come off into the dark where they would not be sure of their footing, where they might be walking on the water and not know it and then suddenly know it and drown. All this and more is part of the lineage of 'The Wanderer'.

But perhaps we should allow ourselves the merest whisper of an indulgent fantasy that there is the shadow of something more, some strange and authentic chord which conspired to resonate across the centuries from Andrias Mac Craith to U2. The Dylan or Lizzy connections alone do not seem to fill in the whole picture. If you listen to 'Whiskey in the Jar', you find that while the form is similar, the spirit is not there. It is, as its name suggests, a drinking song, perhaps derived from an early erotic *aisling*, a story celebrating villainy, mischief, sex and excess. It is diverting and intoxicating, and yet, delivered in a full-throated roar by a ballad group, or condensed to a film of irony by Thin Lizzy, it contains nothing of the soul of its hero. Philip Lynott played him with a bravado and élan that nobody else could bring to the song. He breathed the song full of sex and mockery which is captured utterly in his singing of the refrain: 'Musha ring-dom-a-do-dom-a-da/Whack foll ma daddy-o.' The wandering highwayman laments his wrongdoing, but not really. He outlines his predicament and makes little of it. The lyric is full of pretend self-pity, which Lynott realised to perfection: 'Here I am in prison/Here I am with a ball-an'-chain-yeah!' What Bono brings to the writing of 'The Wanderer' is in no way explained by songs like that. 'The Wanderer' and 'Whiskey in the Jar' bear a superficial resemblance to one another, but that is all.

A paragraph jumps out from Corkery's book, about the existence of inexplicable levels of erudition and literary gifts in some eighteenth-century poets who had neither been abroad or given tuition at home. 'But such culture as these poets gathered and set store on,' decides Corkery, 'was in the air of certain localities; they hardly knew themselves when or how they had come by it.'

Part of what U2 represent at the fag-end of the twentieth century is a role which, in their different ways, Philip Lynott and Andrias Mac Craith fulfilled in their own times. While Lynott's connection with Irish folk music is frequently the cause of vague discussion, the point is nearly always missed that Lynott was not attempting to recreate a tradition, but *to carry it on in a modern form*. Because 'Whiskey in the Jar' is a traditional folk song, we tend to make the obvious connection, but miss what it suggests. The most interesting point of contact Lynott had with the folk tradition was not how he interpreted old folk songs, but how *he created new ones*. It was as though he did this one cover version to lay down a marker, and then went about writing songs which, on the surface at least, had no connection with the tradition. 'One of the things we used to do,' he told Philip Chevron in a 1981 *Hot Press* interview, 'was to write modern Irish songs. Like "Shades of a Blue Orphanage" was a modern Irish song. If people wanna know what it was like in the late '60s when we used to hang around St Stephen's Green and just pull chicks and drink bottles of wine, it's there in that song.'

This, we tend to forget, is what balladeers and folk singers used to do, before we got all hung up about tradition. That *is* the tradition. Irish verse of the seventeenth and eighteenth centuries, while greatly changed in some respects from that of the early centuries, had retained that primary function of providing self-description in a society with no other forms of communication. The Gaelic poet was a bit like the journalist in modern society. He functioned as essayist, chronicler and satirist, though always in verse form. Many of the earlier bardic poems were encomia to the Gaelic chieftains on whom the poets depended for a living, often consisting of descriptions of the rooms and houses in which they lived.

How might such a fund of knowing be preserved? Sometimes, the melodies Bono hears in his head consist of sounds, with only the vague shape of words inside them. To find words to sing requires a process of sorting, as with a jigsaw puzzle. Sometimes he finds that the words he senses there are not English words at all. One such song is 'Elvis Presley and America', on *The Unforgettable Fire*, which moves from clear lines in English to thick-tongued mumbling that could be anything from Irish to Apache. A possible explanation, he believes, is the fact that, although, like many of his generation, he resisted the learning of Irish at school, he was also attracted by the poeticism of the language, especially when one particular teacher would sing unaccompanied songs in Irish in class. The hairs, he remembers, would stand on the back of his neck.

> Peadar Mac Colmcoille. That was his name. He came in and sang, and I was interested. And he talked about poetry, and I was interested. He got into the sound. He was the only Irish teacher who could pronounce the language. I grew up hearing people speaking Irish who couldn't pronounce it. It was like hearing an English person talking French. So why would I like the language? Suddenly, Peadar Mac Colmcoille came and he could actually speak the language – and sing in it. He turned me on to it, and I got back into it for a while.

This is a sense I get from U2 – from individual songs and from the unity of the work – of a drawing together of elements, fragments which make some kind of sense which has yet to fully reveal itself. There is a suggestion of an archaeological dig, the watchful sifting through pieces that seem as if they ought to fit together. Pieces of what? The Past? Tradition? Language? Identity? A place? Pieces drawn together from a restless sifting through the music and literature of the world, through the pages of the Bible, through the blur of pop culture. The music rises up apparently out of nowhere, but speaks of something disremembered, like an attempt to memorise the contents of a crumbling vellum manuscript before it vanishes into dust. Like the dust itself returned in a new skin.

The last word for now we will leave to Daniel Corkery:

> How anyone who cares for literature can bear to see a language, any language, die is a thought beyond us. Even an old outworn language digged out of the earth – who can measure its latent power or forecast its influences? Fragments of stone have been picked out of the ground by field labourers: they have so shaken, so disturbed, so inspired, so coerced the whole art-mind of Europe ever since, that one sometimes regrets that ever they were awakened from their dreams!

CHAPTER FIFTEEN

The Uses of the Past

Whisper it: we only *say* that what we are looking for is to be found in the past. We *know* better. But we say what we have to say. There is no virtue in *a* place; the only virtue lies in *place itself*. Neither should we be interested in assertions of proud nationhood for their own sake. 'In the absolute,' writes Franz Fanon in *Black Skin, White Masks*, 'the black is no more to be loved than the Czech, and truly what is to be done is to set man free.'

The natural tendency of peoples whose culture has been denied by colonisation is to assert the value of that buried culture until the hills roar with its worth and wonder. But this, says Fanon, is always the wrong approach. 'It would be easy to prove, or to win the admission, that the black is the equal of the white,' he elaborates. 'But my purpose is quite different: what I want to do is help the black man to free himself of the arsenal of complexes that has been developed by the colonial environment.'

There is therefore nothing to be gained by the colonised man attempting to prove to his former masters that he is not a savage after all. This merely ensures that he remains in some measure colonised, still requiring the approval of an external authority to legitimise his own worth.

'What is often called the black soul,' Franz Fanon cautions, 'is a white man's artefact.' Similarly, Celtic lyricism, the poetic sensibility, is attributed to the Irish by their English colonisers. Because we have been led to believe the clichés, there may very well be a sense in which they have become true; but we must not be bound by them. This is the central paradox of the post-colonial condition. The characteristics which the colonised subject is led to perceive in himself are also those which the coloniser has, for this very reason, repressed in his own character. The Irish are mad poets; therefore the English are sane rationalists. The Irish, to save themselves while at the same time seeming to fall in with the coloniser's arrangements, become sane poets. And their masters go slowly mad from the denial of their own poeticism.

We go back, then, only to allow ourselves to go forward. Our purpose is not sentiment, but self-knowledge. What we are searching for is not relics or heritage, but the spirit that will set us free. What we must find is not the ethos of our ancestors but the makings of an image of our possible selves. A worship of the past, warned Republican leader James Connolly, would serve only to crystallise nationalism into a tradition, 'glorious and heroic indeed, but still only a tradition'. The search we undertake is for what is useful rather than what is beautiful. Of course, what we find is likely to be beautiful as well, but this does not surprise us in the least.

In his introduction to the 1992 Penguin edition of James Joyce's *Ulysses*, Declan Kiberd makes a case for the book as a central text of national liberation. The very idea, in terms of the concepts of nationalism at large in the modern Ireland, seems, on the first contact, absurd. But Kiberd is dealing with a reality far above the prosaic level of conventional nationalist or anti-nationalist rhetoric. Joyce's revisiting of Shakespearian texts, his basing of *Ulysses* on the Greek legend *The Odyssey*, argues Kiberd, is an expression of the colonised man's need to create a new future by *pretending* to undertake a scrutiny of the past. In fact, Joyce, too, was remembering the future.

Kiberd makes a philosophical connection between the writing of *Ulysses* and the Irish revolution with which it more or less coincided. The leaders of the 1916 Rising and the exiled writer scurrying around Europe were tapping into a common source. In crude outline, Kiberd's case is that, just as writers like Yeats and Joyce slip into the part of Shakespeare, in the hope of discovering something new about themselves, so too would the 1916 leaders cast themselves in the role of Celtic heroes or Gaelic chieftains, though their real aims were intimately grounded in the reality of their own time.

> To secure a fair hearing in a conservative country, the exponents of radical innovation had to present their agenda as a return to ancient traditions; and in the process history took on some of the contours of science fiction. Dreaming of a classless society on anarcho-syndicalist principles, James Connolly found himself contending that this would simply be a restoration of the kinship systems of the Gaelic past. Pedantic historians who protested against this misrepresentation of an historical community failed to realize that, for the activist, a subversive new idea is often best gift-wrapped in the forms of the past . . . The ancient analogues – Shakespeare, Cúchulainn, Odysseus – provided the space within which the radicals were free to innovate or improvise. Claiming to be upholders of the past, they were anything but. They knew that they must creatively misinterpret if they were to shape a golden future. Such a future would be less a revival than a birth, a project of self-invention.

During the *Joshua Tree* tour of 1987, my friend and fellow journalist the late Helen O'Connor wrote me a report of a U2 concert in Meadowlands, New Jersey, in which she described one of Bono's early, but since infamous Tricolour-shredding excursions. During 'Sunday Bloody Sunday', he leaned into the audience and pulled a huge tricolour from a willing outstretched hand. He held the national flag of Ireland above his head.

'Do you see green?' he demanded.

'*Green!!*' the crowd answered.

'Do you see gold?'

'*Gold!!*'

'White?'

'*White!!*'

With that he threw the flag back into the crowd.

'All I see', he said, 'is fucking *red*.'

During the summer of 1993, word trickled back from the Zoo TV tour of Europe that Bono was up to his old tricks, but with a new variation. An Irishwoman writing from Germany complained in a letter to *The Irish Times* that, in the course of the concert she had attended in Frankfurt, Bono had torn an Irish flag 'into three separate pieces which he then threw into the audience'. She was astonished by this behaviour, she wrote, as was everyone else she spoke to about it. 'If U2 do not want to proclaim the fact that they are Irish, that is fair enough, but to destroy the Tricolour in front of twenty-five thousand people strikes me as extreme.'

I couldn't say why, but it seemed to me that the reason for Bono's treatment of the flag, far from being an attempt to deny his Irishness, was in fact precisely an attempt to proclaim it.

Let me try to explain. The Cherokee artist Jimmie Durham – I beg your pardon; as I will attempt to make clearer, Mr Durham – which, incidentally, is not his real name, but I am unable to explain that part – is both a Cherokee and an artist, but he is not in fact a 'Cherokee artist'. This artist and Cherokee, who specialises in enigmatic drawings and strange-looking sculptures of wood, stone, animal skulls and scrap metal, has described himself as 'very silly with bursts of seriousness'. His work is focused on issues of authenticity and cultural identity. He mocks both the 'silly pervasiveness of imperialism' and the clichéd images of its victims, of which his own people are just one example. At first sight, his work appears to mock his own culture, but on closer examination we find that what it mocks is the outsider's *perception* of that culture, vested in fossilised images and stereotyped values. He mocks our well-intentioned ethnological enthusiasm for Native American culture by turning its artefacts into black jokes at the outsider's expense. His purpose is to deconstruct the white man's fetish of the Indian soul. 'Don't worry,' he reassures, 'I am a good

Indian. I come from the West, love nature and have a particularly close connection with my environment. I can talk to animals and, whether you believe it or not, I have a great affinity with spiritual matters.'

I read that when Jimmie Durham was thirteen he was given the gift of being able to see anything dead within his field of vision. 'For over thirty years,' he explains in an interview with the *Observer*, 'I have seen every dead bird and animal, every day, wherever I am. It became necessary to see if it was a usable gift or just a dirty trick that would drive me crazy.'

Bono's tearing of the tricolour seems to me to come from the same instinct. Whereas the U2 singer might be more accurately described as 'very serious with bursts of silliness', he is in much the same line of business, turning over the fossils of Irish cultural imagery in its perceived forms and seeing what doesn't crawl out. He too seems to be cursed with the ability to perceive dead things within his field of vision. Like Durham, Bono appears drawn to the question of whether he is who he feels he is or who he is told he must be. 'So here's my new idea,' Durham says about an umpteenth attempt at drawing his own nose. 'If my nose doesn't look like anyone else's and I myself don't recognise it, aren't I free of my nose?'

Bono's tearing up of the flag appears to me to be an attempt at tearing up his tricoloured nose. But needless to say, this is not quite the way he tells it himself.

> Like most things in our stage show, there are accidents, and if they work you repeat them. That's what it was. I can't remember the first time I did it, but it was very much in that character of the song – probably 'Sunday Bloody Sunday'. Whatever mindset I'd be in, it made perfect sense to do that. And then you repeat it, for effect, purely to stir an argument. But the first time would've been genuine – trying to make sense of it at the time. It's important to know, and it's something that's hard for a seated writer to spot – but performing to me is like having a twitch. It just kind of comes on. You're *there*, so you *say* something. You're *there*, so you *do* something. And if you're *on*, that spontaneous thing will come off. And if you're not, it really won't. That's the thing about being spontaneous. There you are in real time, which is slow motion for you. You see a flag thrown up on stage. You're in a state of mind. You look down at it. People are looking at you. You have to do something with it. Pick it up. Are you gonna wrap it round your neck? Are you gonna lift it up? Are you gonna show everyone that you're Irish? No! You *hate* that flag. Why *do* you? You hate the flag because of all the stuff that's gone with it. Because it has betrayed us. Because nationalism has betrayed the nation. So you find

yourself ripping off the orange bit. People are looking at you. You're ripping off the green bit. And you're just about to throw it all away and you're left with the white bit, and then you realise that you've already been in trouble even for that. But it all happens in that kind of way. And then if it works – you go backstage and say, 'That's interesting! I'll do that again.'

There's a syndrome where people are compelled to say what's on their mind. There was a clergyman in Dublin whose wife suffered from this ailment, this mental illness, where she would speak whatever thought came into her head that she wasn't supposed to speak. So she'd be saying goodbye to the parishioners on Sundays standing beside her husband, 'Goodbye Mrs Morris . . . *Fuck off you bitch!*' 'Goodbye Mrs . . . *Hope your car crashes!*' It's Tourette's Syndrome. I have a little bit of it. Just to say *that thing* and see what might be at the end of your tongue! It gets me into a lot of trouble . . . It's like getting into trouble for saying 'Fuck'! *Pathetic. Really, really pathetic.*

The problem with U2 is this problem of scale: you can't be spontaneous, you can't be relaxed. But as that happens to us more and more, I get to care less and less. Now I don't mind when I go out if I'm a bit messy. Now I don't mind letting people down when I meet them in nightclubs. Now I don't stiffen when people stare at me. Now I don't care. The pressure to put a face on for Ireland, or for whatever, is met with an equal and opposite pressure to be a jerk.

CHAPTER SIXTEEN

The Fifth Province

So, there is no Irishness? Well, not exactly. Maybe there is nothing *but* Irishness. Everything, everywhere, *everyone* is as Irish as they want to imagine themselves.

'The Irish thing surfaces, sometimes in spite of itself,' writes Richard Kearney in *Across the Frontiers*, 'when the obsession with an exclusive identity is abandoned.' In the past we could not find it because we were looking too hard, too self-consciously, too fanatically. 'Now, as we are rediscovering ourselves through our encounters with others, reclaiming our voice in our migrations through other cultures and continents – Europe, Britain, North America – we are beginning to realise that the Irish thing was always there. We could not recognise it for as long as we assumed we were at home with ourselves, sufficient unto ourselves, slaves to the illusion that we were masters of a land apart, Robinson Crusoes on our sequestered island. It takes the migrant mind to know that the island is without frontiers . . .'

'The recent revival of an old concept of the Fifth Province,' said the newly elected President of Ireland Mary Robinson in her first address to her people in December 1990, gave her a way of encapsulating the Ireland she would be representing as President. It would be an Ireland of tolerance and empathy. 'The old Irish term for province is *coicead*, meaning a 'fifth'; and yet, as everyone knows, there are only four geographical provinces in Ireland. So where is the fifth? The Fifth Province is not anywhere here or there, north or south, east or west. It is a place within each one of us – that place that is open to the other, that swinging door which allows us to venture out, and others to venture in.' She wanted, she said, to be a symbol of this 'reconciling and healing Fifth Province'.

In a word? 'Imagination,' says Bono. 'That's the opening of *Zooropa*. The opening track is about imagination being the source. That you can go anywhere, do anything. It's not expensive. It isn't about money; it's about imagination. You want to dream up the kind of world you want to live in? And I suppose the people in our country – the mad men, and the smart men as well – who wrote the Constitution . . . this thing of being foolish, of being imaginative, of being political. It's an interesting mix that seems to be

part of what we are. I think we've got to design the kind of Ireland we want
to live in.'

So what might it be like?

> There isn't a sure ending. Becaue we're moving more into a global
> picture. My own stance is that so strong is your line, your gene, your
> root, whatever it is, that you can throw anything at it. I'm really off
> at a tangent at the moment about the Celts being an Indo-European
> race. And that's why in the *In the Name of the Father* thing, rather
> than go, diddley-eye-dil-do, we went for this almost Indian kind of
> feeling. This thing of the pentatonic scale – the ah-haa-aaaaaaaahh-
> aaah-aaah – where's that coming from? That ecstaticism that's on
> that song, that aha-haaa-aaaaaaahaaaah-*aahhaaahh-aaaahhaaahh*.
> That *thing*. When we were talking about a video for that, all I could
> offer was I just wanted tribes: tribes on Wall Street, tribes going to
> Mass, Zulus, Ku-Klux-Klan. Just tribes. I feel strongly this African
> thing, this Mediterranean thing, this Indo-African thing. That journey.
>
> For reasons that I find very hard to explain, I can see that very
> clearly when I'm talking to people. I can feel it from them. Like
> Máire Ní Bhraonáin [of Clannad], for instance – I don't see her as
> Spanish/Irish. I see her as almost Egyptian. And I can see that in
> your face, actually, and in a few people's faces that I know. And I
> know that there's stories of these connections – I'm not maybe
> acquainted with them, but I just feel that. The Dark Irish – '*Oh
> yeah, Spanish Armada* . . .' But way before the Spanish Armada
> there was dark Irish.
>
> If you're talking about Ireland and rock 'n' roll, you have to point
> out the fact that, more than any other culture in Europe, the blue
> note is part of our history. That's the point I make about Africa.
> Rock 'n' roll is Africa and Europe combined in that spastic dance of
> Elvis. That's the moment – one of the defining moments of the
> century. It's what's interesting about America – this collision of
> cultures. The beat from Africa and the melody from Europe – this
> whole thing coming together. We already had that collision, way
> back! And that's a hard thing to prove, but it's there in our music.
> English, German, classical culture – which predominated in
> America, like it did in Europe, before hip jazz, rock 'n' roll, popular
> culture – didn't have any of those notes. We had them. That's got to
> be interesting. Have a look at John Lydon, Elvis Costello, Van
> Morrison, think of John Lennon, George Harrison . . . See it's all
> this thing of *line*. This idea of line is all over the Old Testament.
> There's whole chapters given over to lineage: Malachi the son of

Malachite the son of Milky White . . . You read it and think, what is important about line? And if line is important, that could be a very dangerous idea, because, can you break from your past?

Although the music of U2 has, so to speak, its rootlessness in Ireland, it has its branches in the world. As it grows, it needs the oxygen of the universe, not just to flourish in the world, but to survive the creeping rot from stagnant soil in which it is so flimsily grounded. It is ironic that the band which has explored more than any other Irish artist the connections between Ireland and the Third World return 'home' to find nothing but a sea of white faces, very few of which are their own age. Now, more than ever, Ireland needs that 'swinging door' to open both ways. Is it entirely implausible that the world may need *it* just as much?

Although Ireland continues to produce poets and novelists in abundance, and has recently begun to throw up the occasional film which attempts to come to grips with an aspect of Irish reality, it is arguable that some of the most reliable descriptions of our condition are to be found in what might loosely be called pop music. If you think of Ireland as the Fifth Province, you see the picture begin to widen, its texture become richer. Suddenly, things that you had never thought about in terms of Ireland begin to fit into place.

The greatest British pop band in the 1980s, the Smiths, for example, burst out of the Manchester of 1983. The rock writer Paul Morley, also from Manchester, said that they emerged from 'the solitude of timelessness', which might be another way of saying that they came from the Fifth Province. Seven of the eight parents who begat the four Smiths were Irish people who had emigrated to Manchester in the fifties. Steven Patrick Morrissey, son of Peter Morrissey and Elizabeth Dwyer of Crumlin, was separated from Dublin by less than five years. The slightest quirk of fate would have had the Smiths brought up in much the same environment as the young U2. Instead, they benefited from a Manchester Catholic up-bringing in the 1960s, another vista that remains an unrecognised element of the Irish story.

Mindful of the traps of seeking tradition rather than truth, it is wise to avoid pointing to those aspects of the music of the Smiths which are 'quintessentially Irish' – as against the 'quintessentially English' character-istics which conventional wisdom allows – their swirling tunefulness, their care with words, their hatred of clichés. Better, for the moment, to simply ask: what do you think made the Smiths so different, so unique?

The Smiths gushed forth from their solitude as though fired by a mission to restore the vitality of pop while questioning the meaning of life. They damned by tunefulness and inspiration not just the torpor of post-sixties rock, but the claustrophobia of post-punk Britain in Thatcher's second term. As with U2, the protest of the Smiths was existential rather than political. In essence it was grounded in the knowledge that the unthinkable state of modern life was the result of power being in the hands of people who lacked an ear for a good tune. Their rebellion was more of a shrinking from the world than a wish for confrontation. Their territory was the human heart in all its pain and loneliness, a concern all too easily mistaken for adolescent angst. The Smiths would never have grown up, not because they couldn't, but because they wouldn't want to. What the Smiths were about was 'something quite beyond and more complicated than "adolescence"',' said Morrissey, still innocent after twenty-eight years, 'something that hasn't been thought out yet'. And what was this thing 'Morrissey'? 'Morrissey' was, *is*, that part of each of us that is always alone, no matter what. It is that part which, after all the slog and the heartbreak, the fictions and the furniture, stands suspended against the wind of the world. The Morrissey in us is shy, sensitive, unbalanced, vain yet aware of our ugliness, hurt, vulnerable, alone with the ultimate pointlessness of everything – but ultimately unafraid.

Put on a Smiths record, preferably *Strangeways Here We Come*, and think of Seamus Heaney's line about that capable bat that flits between the light of a practical idiom and the twilight of a remembered previous place.

If you cannot make connections, get hold of the Cranberries' debut album, *Everybody else is doing it, so why not Me?*, and put on track two on side one. The song is called 'Dreams', and on first hearing it sounds like a fine sub-Smiths tribute song, the flinted edge of Noel Hogan's guitar calling up the spectre genius of Johnny Marr, as used to be Maher from County Kildare.

While the Smiths' influence is unmistakable, Dolores O'Riordan's voice allows the song to break open into new ground. It is as though it was written with this purpose in mind. The song begins with purpose and energy, but is broken too soon by a middle eight which pre-empts its expected drift. O'Riordan, in an echo of what is to come, breaks into a wail of pain and longing that reminds you of something but, no, perhaps not. The song begins again, driven by the drums and guitar, building and building. Listen to O'Riordan's vocal dripping from syllable to syllable like a raindrop from a treetop tripping off leaf after leaf on its way to the ground:

> Though my life
> Is changing every day
> In every
> Poss! . . .

> . . . ib . . .
> . . . elle! . . .
> Way

The ending is prefigured by a guitar progression which Johnny Marr would have been happy to stand over. Then O'Riordan returns, in different mode. There are no words to describe what she does.

She goes:

> *Aaaaaaahhhhhhhhhaaahhhhhh-daaaaaaahhhh.*
> *Daaaaaaahhhhhhhhaaaaaaaahhhhhhhaaaaaa-laaahhhh*
> *Laaaaaaahhhhhhhhaaaaaaaahhhhhhhaaaaaa.*

Behind her a male voice, deep and far away, replies:

> *Yaaahahhhahhhh. Yaaaahhaaahaaahaaah*
> *Yaaahaaahaaaahaaaahaaaahaaaaahaaaah*
> *Laaaahaaaahalallllaaahhaahh.*

These are voices from deep in the tribal memory, an echo from the heart of the Indo-European consciousness. Through an incision made by the Smiths, the Cranberries have penetrated deeper into the bank of memory. Put on the soundtrack of *In the Name of the Father*, wait for the opening duet between the bodhrán and the Lambeg, and slide further in.

Neither the Smiths nor the Cranberries, nor for that matter U2, would thank you for drawing similarities between them. Nor is this useful in enjoying the noises they make. The fan does not have a loyalty to a band on the basis of its roots or nationality, but in terms of a relationship suggested by the music. It is not a question of creating connections for the sake of it, nor of reclaiming the Smiths for Old Ireland. It is a matter of acknowledging the possibility of relationships so as to reconstruct parts of the mirror which we lost in fragments to the world.

Then there are The Pogues. Had we been a little less preoccupied, The Pogues might have alerted us to look closer to home for some of those missing fragments. Here was a band clearly rooted in the London punk rock scene of the late seventies but which had something unmistakably Irish. Except that the band wasn't Irish. Apart from Shane MacGowan, their lead singer, The Pogues, to begin with, boasted few Irish connections. They began playing Irish rebel songs as a fuck-off-and-die gesture to the society in which they began, and ended up exposing the smug insecurities of the place where these songs had originated. In the postmodernism of their Irish sensibility, The Pogues reopened the possibilities of Irish music by challenging Irish prejudices and ready-made assumptions about it.

The Pogues fill holes in the Irish consciousness which no one else has even admitted to being aware of. The only entry I have to the world of my aunts and uncles who emigrated to the US in the early years of this century, or to that of the others who went to England later on, is through the songs of The Pogues. There are no novels, no movies, few poems, by which to access the place they inhabited, a place from which I am otherwise only separated by a single generation and an accident of history. The Pogues write songs that become as time capsules from the heart of the diaspora. Songs like 'The Body of an American' give me the scent and colour of a world which existed side-by-side with my own reality but could not be seen.

Other holes are filled in other ways. But mostly through music. For all the wealth of Irish literature, it leaves a great deal unsaid. Like what there is of Irish cinema, it is excessively directed at the territory of Ireland itself. Rock 'n' roll, folk and pop bands like The Pogues, The Cranberries, and dozens of others, like The Saw Doctors, the Sultans of Ping, Elvis Costello, Van Morrison, the Frank and Walters, fill out different parts of the picture of the Fifth Province. They are its wandering bards. U2 fill a different kind of hole, an even less tangible one, perhaps the most hidden hole of all.

If The Pogues give a glimpse of the recent past, U2 attempt to draw sketches of the putative future. The worlds they describe in the landscapes of their songs are the worlds of possibility that lie just in front rather than just behind. They draw pictures of the worlds of the notional future, just as The Pogues fill in the gaps of the probable past.

Because they mostly come from the world of the possible rather than the world we recognise as reality, it is easy to think that U2's songs are simply constructions of sound and sentiment. If you *think* about it, you're halfway to missing the point. With most of U2's music – the best of it – the point is not to write about things but to write the things themselves. The songs are worlds, places, things, people, feelings, which may never have existed or may never do so, but which come into being because they have been imagined by this band and by you too, the listener. U2's best songs are like novels, and their best albums, *The Joshua Tree*, *Achtung Baby* and *Zooropa*, like polyphonic novels, telling different stories as aspects of a single, larger story. They deny the fatalism in the Irish personality which has allowed so much of ourselves that is beautiful and strange to fritter away.

The connections I make with U2 songs are never tangible, rarely more than glimmers and sparks. A letter from my great-aunt Nora made the connection between the music of the Pogues and the buried memory of a lost uncle, a street musician in New York in the early 1960s, found dying beside his accordion. There are no such artefacts, and very few cultural clues, to connect me with U2. But the connections are there. They reveal themselves only in hints and glimpses which often disappear if you focus on them too long. This may be because the music of the Pogues is rooted in a world which, though unexperienced by many of those who are part of it, at least existed in a concrete past reality. The music of U2 is mostly not rooted in any reality, but in a world of possibility which, given the Irish failure to understand ourselves, is as real as anything. Our history is as much a mystery to us as is our future. Our future, then, seems like as good a way as any of coming to understand who we are.

The music of the Pogues is among the most passionate and interested music that has been made by Irish people of my generation. It is interesting because it is interested. It is comprehensible, but what it tells us is not obvious. It tells us things we should have known but didn't. The Smiths open a chink of knowing which makes us dizzy with its possibilities, and the Cranberries widen the chink to let in more light and wonder. The music of U2 tells us things about ourselves that we not only never imagined, but never dreamt might be possible. The music of U2 is ahead of itself and light years ahead of the rest. In terms of what we are conscious of in Irish cultural development, it is like the music of a future generation pulled backwards in time. U2 provide us with a version of ourselves that is just a little unbelievable. They therefore, if we let them, stretch us to the limit of our imaginings, in a way few writers and no painter or film-maker has ever done.

The eight studio albums which U2 has recorded to date may be seen as a journey through both their own experience and through the Irish experience of which they are part. Each album represents a stab at creating a place, a world, a landscape, in which freedom might be attained. There have been frequent complaints that U2 do not 'deal' with the 'reality' of their country or its politics. Well, it depends on which reality you're talking about. The hidden U2 'project' might be described as an attempt to both unearth different realities and create new ones. The first album, *Boy*, for example, if approached from the perspective of an immersion in Irish political realities and ideological battles of the time, seems weirdly disconnected, preoccupied with juvenilia, disengaged. The fact that this is precisely what it was is what makes it relevant to the nature of Irish society of the time. The psychologist Ashis Nandy, in his essay 'Reconstructing Childhood', argues that the ideology of colonialism is rooted in the Western concept of the child. Childhood is a concept which is culturally defined and created. Western culture regards the child as an inferior version of the adult – as a 'lovable, spontaneous, delicate being who is also simultaneously dependent, unreliable and wilful', and who therefore needs to be guided, protected and educated as a ward. This metaphor is what drives the ideology of colonialism and modernity, a presumptuous paternalism which depicts the world of the colonised advancing dynamically towards the model of the coloniser as the human being 'develops' from childhood to adulthood. There is no other way it can achieve 'progress'. In a colonised society, the warped colonial view is transmitted through the warped relationship between parents and children.

If rock 'n' roll has a single definable purpose, it is surely to debunk this notion. What else did Morrissey mean when he said that adolescence was something that had yet to be 'thought out'? Think of this metaphor and look again at the cover of *Boy* – the trusting, open eyes, the defenceless demeanour and then the slight curl of the lip. What is the boy thinking? Maybe that the world could go far if it listened to what he says:

> I see into his eyes, they're closed
> But I see something.
> A teacher told me why I laugh
> When old men cry.
>
> My body grows and grows
> It frightens me you know.
> The old man tried to walk me home
> I thought he should have known

Boy is a plea for recognition and understanding in a society which not merely regards children with condescension or superiority, but actually fears their knowing innocence as an accusation of its own intrinsic nature. 'The ideology of adulthood', writes Ashis Nandy, 'has hidden the fact that children see through our hypocrisy perfectly and respond to our tolerance and respect fully. Our most liberating bonds can be with our under-socialised children. And the final test of our skill to live in a bicultural or multicultural existence may still be our ability to live with our children in mutuality.'

It is at such subterranean levels that the connection of U2's music to Irish society can be observed. That this 'intention' may have been hidden from the creators of the music does nothing to negate it. For Bono, an adult himself long since, with children of his own, it is all a long time ago.

> I wish I could listen to the early albums more than I can. In many ways we didn't think very much about what we were doing. We just made this music because that was what was on our mind. And especially as a lyricist, I think I let the band down by making it up as I went along. I would make up the lyrics minutes before I sang them. I found it hard to write these ideas that I had down. I think I was myself a bit embarrassed by them – I found them easier to sing.

To approach the music head-on will only lead you to the conclusion that U2 were almost completely disconnected from their home place. This analysis perceives songs like 'Sunday Bloody Sunday' and 'Running to Stand Still' as rare instances of U2 writing about Ireland, an assessment based on literal content. Yes and no. 'Sunday Bloody Sunday' is indeed an attempt to grapple with the reality of the conflict going on less than a hundred miles from Dublin, but rather than the conventional political statement which voices on both sides have attempted to appropriate or deny, it might more usefully be seen in the light of these words from the Irish writer Seamus Deane: 'Artists can often be more troubled by the idea that they *should be* troubled by a crisis than they are by the crisis itself.'

From this perspective 'Sunday Bloody Sunday' becomes an articulation of the neurosis which developed in southern Irish society during the late seventies and eighties, a feeling of disgust and disconnection with the Northern conflict:

> I can't believe the news today
> I can't close my eyes and make it go away

When Bono would announce on stage that 'Sunday Bloody Sunday' was 'not a rebel song', the caveat was to most Irish ears superfluous. We knew that! But this was, equally, the way most people in the Republic, if they were honest, had felt about the North of Ireland almost since the Troubles began. A number of Irish bands or songwriters, like Mick Hanly, Christy Moore and Moving Hearts, who attempted to deal with the conflict from a nationalist perspective in the same period were regarded with the utmost suspicion in respectable Irish society.

This isn't to say that U2 were being evasive or cowardly. They were simply being honest and spontaneous about the way the issue bore down upon them. It is in this – elliptical – way that the music informs us about the kind of Ireland they erupted from. To give another example: when the second album, *October*, was released in 1981, my own response would have been typical enough of uncommitted Irish rock fans of the time: Great album; pity about the God stuff. When I heard 'Gloria', I was, as Bono dryly observes, 'hoping she was a waitress'.

But now I know that I wasn't really. I knew what it was about, but also that I didn't have to admit it. I wanted – and had – it both ways. The true meaning carried a necessary camouflage against 1980s cynicism and disenchantment. There was an ambiguity to let you off the hook if you couldn't see your way to owning up to the whole thing. Another neurosis fed and concealed.

In a sense this neurosis was reflected in the continuing conflicts which beset the band itself over the born-again Christianity issue. This confusion was to last, according to Bono, almost into the mid-eighties. 'It's hard for me to remember. I suppose it would have gone through *War*. . . maybe even through *The Unforgettable Fire*. You can tell in a way, because there's not much writing about the self. You're writing about other things, you know? Ideas, or issues, and other people – Martin Luther King. Whereas *The Joshua Tree* was more . . . the self was coming into it.'

War was the album on which U2 went public, in the sense of coming to grips with issues and concerns in the political arena of the time. But for all that *War* was the album with which U2 gained access to a mass audience, it has a strained feel about it that suggests they are less than happy with what sometimes appear as over-literal concerns. Bono's voice lacks conviction, sounding as if it's almost just going through emotions. The Edge seems unsure of what he wants to do with himself. *War* belongs to Adam and Larry. Larry's drumming is furious, like he's crazy from having to hold it together. The music seems, in retrospect, to betray the hidden conflict between faith and medium which threatened to break up the band.

In addition, the overt propagandist demeanour, the white flags and strutting horseback imagery which accompanied the album was, for all its clarity, somehow false, like U2 trying to look like Simple Minds trying to look like U2. It was as if they had forgotten the definition of their own essence which they had earlier seemed so sure of.

Because so much of punk and the music which came after was so very social in its concerns, the ethos which U2 expressed was striking in its deliberate return to personal themes. This gave the band an immediate universality and an edge on, for example, British bands, in the US. But there is a way of seeing the band's development as having caved in with *War*, as becoming strained and distorted by the pressure of the outside world to recognise its reality.

Bono, however, rejects this idea that U2 were simply reacting to accusations that their music was ducking issues, failing to deal with the 'important' things, or that they were pushed by a bad conscience to deal with the nitty gritty of social issues.

> I think along with faith of this kind there clearly has to follow a commitment to social issues and change. They are one and the same. That's part of the love-your-neighbour thing. And I suppose that it is in that way that one *is* attracted, genuinely, to a Martin Luther King. And of course the other reason for him was that it was a great analogy for what was going on in our own country, what was going on up North. And it was hard for people in the south to look at John Hume in the same light – though he probably *was*, had the same courage. It was easier to find that in another culture. But it wasn't *guilt*.

In the late seventies, with punk, you had confrontation. By the mid-eighties, that was anathema. There was no confrontation. In fact, pop music was just celebrating its own surface and then, right at the moment when it was most unhip, if you like, we started back. But it was a different kind of thing, more positive, more universal, more embracing, than confrontational. It was just that generation who were into their Dionysian walk – drinking, going out late at night with girls, sorting out that side of your life; they weren't open to the other part, which is, you know, ahem . . . Apollonian.

Nor does he admit to a sense of confusion on *War*.

It's not confusion that I hear. I think it's quite clear. The graphics of the album are very clear. What I find is the *lack* of confusion, the lack of internal debate, the lack of all that. In a way that's what the flatness is. I don't want to talk in a disparaging way about a record that some people love. I think a song like 'Sunday Bloody Sunday' was an interesting idea, to juxtapose Easter Sunday with this . . . massacre. But it just didn't come across. So I think maybe we had a part in it being misinterpreted. You look at the words and they're not enough, but maybe the music makes it clearer. I just see a lot of unfinished songs, but sometimes maybe that gives more options, maybe they're more open. If you tighten up your songwriting, you can sometimes close down interpretations. But that's, I think, what I would feel – that defensiveness, that uptightness. I think that defensiveness is something we've only shook off recently.

With *Achtung Baby*?

Maybe. Because that's going, 'Let's *go*! *Throw* the shit at us! Let's actually stand in the shitstorm! Let's actually get our hair blown by this.' As opposed to trying to duck it, or thinking that if you only had time to explain it to everybody, they'd *get* it. Which was, I think, one of the dangers. 'They mustn't *understand*! Cause if they *did* . . . !!'

The song to listen to on this album, says Bono, is 'Drowning Man'. It describes what was really going on.

> The storms will pass
> It won't be long now
> The storms will pass
> But my love lasts forever.

He backs away from the thought, mumbles, and deflects. 'I think it's a 6/8 rhythm.' He starts to hum it. 'Do-do-do-dum-do-dum/Do-do-do-dum-do-dum. It's actually the song. I think it's very taut. Tight. And the voice is choked. I don't like the sound of my voice on that album.'

One of the problems with that album: there's no sex in it. That's the feeling that I get. I love the sound of 'New Year's Day', and I think 'Sunday Bloody Sunday' is a beautiful melody and a beautiful thing to attempt. And the violin and the whole thing that begat so much after it. In fact it's what that record seemed to hint at that started so much. There was a kind of positive protest movement of the eighties. It was very different to the Clash's way of placarding. And from it, I feel, we were part of the changing of the climate that brought Live Aid. Because it was incredibly uncool to make this record, and it completely freaked out most people – Geldof being one of them. I remember Geldof saying, 'WHAT ARE YOU AT? I mean this is POP MUSIC we're talking about, and you're taking on these ideas.' All these people – Sting. They were doing the de-do-do-do/de-da-da-das! So this was a break, this was *not* cool – for a band to take this position. But every so often rock 'n' roll is *allowed* to be earnest, and allowed to be forthright, and allowed to be angry and in some sort of righteous way – as opposed to just 'FUCK OFF AND *DIE! ANARCHY* IN THE UK.'

And I was throwing myself into the audience, I was pushing all this. It was echoing a lot of . . . People *did* want their music to approach the world that they lived in, and the things that they were saying on the TV, and having no way to respond to. And that's obviously what happened with that album. And that's why it was successful. 'New Year's Day' was probably a very good song. And 'Two Hearts Beat As One' hinted at it – it was a good soul song or whatever. But the uptightness of that album is something I feel – tight, taut, choked, words choked, not singing them well.

It was as though the band knew what the stances they were taking would mean, and the thanklessness that was bound to follow. 'Take this cup away from me,' it seemed to say.

There was that a bit. But I think we were also breaking ties with some of that – seeking for spiritual truths that were around us. It was an interesting one. It was made under that cloud of, you know, not knowing whether we could continue or not. But I can understand how people who come to rock 'n' roll with a certain point of view – sex, you know, the secularisation that had started in the seventies – would think, you know, *'this does not make sense'.*

200

There may also have been a reaction among people who refused to face up not merely to what this was about, but to what they themselves secretly *wanted* it to be about. This is what we had ordered, in a sense, when we jumped up on hearing 'A Day Without Me'. This is what the deal was, though we told ourselves fibs to allow ourselves to avoid the way our own needs differed from our perceptions of them. This was the gap that cried out to be filled. We heard 'Gloria' and liked it, and told ourselves it was another great song about a girl called Gloria; deep down we knew the truth, and also that the truth was what we needed. In the same way, perhaps, we hoped that the new questioners would be as unchallenging as the old, that they would give us reheated versions of 'No Future' and 'Something Better Change'. We deluded ourselves not just about what U2 were saying but about what we ourselves wanted to hear. In a certain light you might conclude that all the reactions against U2 have been for that reason – a conscious anger against the unconscious truths which they awakened in us, and which we wanted above all to avoid.

I should know about this, because from time to time over the past ten years, I have been the author of the kind of criticism of U2 which, to read it now deprived of its context, makes the steam come out of my ears. One occasion that springs rather readily to mind is the band's participation in the unfortunate Self-Aid Concert for the unemployed in Dublin in 1986, when *In Dublin*, the magazine of which I was editor, carried a cover photo of Bono and the headline 'Rock against the People'. What I imagined I was objecting to on that occasion was the idea of well-heeled pop stars patronising the workless; what I was *really* upset about, I think, was the appropriation of U2's magic to a reactionary project. I'm still glad I threw the brick; I just wish I'd had a better aim. Similarly, while my superficial argument against *War* – that here was U2 manipulating the imagery of war to sell an album which purported to be against it – was a point of view, it was not a particularly interesting one.

Reading Greil Marcus's book, *Mystery Train*, the following sentence makes my hair stand up: 'I knew that when Elvis was drafted I felt a great relief, because he made demands on me.' It reminds me of my own early ambivalence to those aspects of myself which U2 seemed to articulate. Some of the things I wrote or thought about the band not merely make me cringe a little on account of their predictability; the smell of sulphur off them makes me *afraid*. I underestimated U2's intentions and intelligence. More importantly, I had lost the will to *like* U2.

The search for the essence of the Fifth Province took U2 on a journey which was emblematic of the journeys undertaken by their own contemporaries in the renewed waves of emigration in the 1980s. It took them to Europe for

October and *The Unforgettable Fire*, to the US for *The Joshua Tree* and *Rattle and Hum*, and back to Europe with a vengeance for *Achtung Baby*. It was a journey undertaken with knowledge aforethought, with the purpose of drawing together the loose ends of the meaninglessness that lay all around.

'I think that during that period, Bono was educating himself in a literary way, to a very high degree,' Adam Clayton remembers. 'He was immersing himself in a lot of American authors. He was immersing himself in a lot of sophisticated music criticism. While I was going out to clubs, he was reading a lot and trying to figure out these threads of popular culture, relating them back to biblical culture, and probably to Irish culture as well. So I think by *The Joshua Tree*, he kind of had worked out where he was coming from as a writer. And I think that's what his strength has been over the past five, six years of the band.'

With *The Joshua Tree*, U2 came to grips with the metaphor and reality of colonisation in the modern world: America. We Irish, all of us, are haunted by America. Because of our very particular experience of emigration, the meaning of America is for us different from its meaning for others. It is a moving clot at the back of the mind, visible only in moments of great innocence or sadness. Our belief in the American Dream renders us unable to hope other than on its terms. We call it a dream, but we speak, as usual, loosely. Perhaps through no fault of its own, America is a scar on our pasts and a blight on our futures. Because of it, we are only half at home there, and half at home anywhere else. And always, in a sense, away from home.

U2's preoccupation with creating new landscapes out of the world they encountered on their forays out of Dublin have not merely been misunderstood, but sometimes perceived as the diametric opposite of their intended significance. The band's use of the imagery of the desert and the Wild West during the period beginning with *The Joshua Tree* was connected by some critics with the millennial fantasies of Christian fundamentalism. In Ireland, such fears were voiced by, among others, Fintan O'Toole, who in *The Irish Times* coupled the criticism with another complaint: that U2 were indulging in a renewal of worship of the American Dream, which he regarded as unhelpful to a culture still characterised by visa queues outside the US embassy in Dublin.

Fintan O'Toole would have had a good point if he hadn't been seeing things the wrong way up. Bono's explanation puts the matter in a different perspective.

The eighties was a very different time. The eighties, as Bertolucci said, was the most ephemeral era you could ever imagine, and yet he admitted he found himself enjoying the advertising in women's magazines and so on. But, right in the middle of that, our reaction was to completely stare it down. What was happening in music was rock 'n' roll with a wink, and dance music that was almost Broadway, if you think about some of the acts. It was totally worked out, choreographed. And we were just talking about *blight*. We saw things in a very different way. We were talking about America, and for Irish people that had its own meaning. But, in a wider world, America had colonised our unconscious, and it had to be dealt with. If you were an artist living in the eighties, how could you not deal with America? How could you not take it on as a subject in itself? Some people thought we were playing with this imagery like *The Good, the Bad and the Ugly*. They completely missed the whole symbolism. There's a snobbery against rock 'n' roll, where people think that we choose things just because they *look* good – which is *part* of it. But right in the eighties, that statement was the right one for U2 to make. Right in the middle of Greed is Good, 'Material Girl', and all that. Eat, drink, for tomorrow we borrow more. If you look back to the eighties and you want to know what was going on, how many records can you listen to? I know *The Johsua Tree* is one of them. It does paint a picture of the time. And it *is* a mythical America. It's not a real – it's an *imagined* – America that is described. And taking the cowboy hat as an icon, and using it and reversing it, and especially in the light of what was going on in Central America. Because if you go to Nicaragua, and if you've seen those pictures of Sandino [Augusto César Sandino, the national hero of Nicaragua assassinated by forces loyal to the future dictator, Somoza, in 1934], it's the most incredible image. Their hero has this cowboy hat, and yet he's the one they call upon to take on the gringo, to take on the Americanas. And he looks like a cowboy! But none of those resonances, or the imagery of the desert, or the biblical aspects of the desert, were really picked up on, as obvious as they were.

There is a way of seeing U2's albums in pairs: *Boy/October*; *War/The Unforgettable Fire*, and so on. The first opens a new seam and the second probes the depths. Then, a rebirth. *Achtung Baby* can be seen, in this light, as a new beginning in the wake of the exploration of the US that began with *The Joshua Tree* and ended with *Rattle and Hum*. U2 got badly scalded in the wake of *Rattle and Hum*, not just because of its implicit themes, but because of the hype and packaging that preceded it, and the manner in which it appeared to try and place U2, alongside their idols, in a pantheon of greatness. *Achtung Baby*, as a direct result of the backlash to its predecessor, was produced in an atmosphere of pressure. There was a lot at stake. *Rattle and Hum* had seemed to take the band down the dinosaur road, risking the limiting of their options to the role of Pink Floyd for the nineties. The mistake, perhaps, was in making *Rattle and Hum* a double album. There was one album of really great songs which was swamped by inferior material, not to mention by the film and book and the poster and the T-shirt. It was inevitable that people would misunderstand the purpose – the particular leg of the U2 journey which it represented. Perhaps, too, some of the backlash arose out of the fact that U2, having skipped the whole tradition thing, had gone now and visited it, at the end rather than at the beginning, leaving themselves open to the charge of secretly nursing an inferiority complex about the lack of roots which they had previously claimed as a virtue. It retrospectively gave that claim of a proud rootlessness a tinge of sour grapes.

'I think the backlash was towards a Hollywood movie,' says Adam Clayton simply. 'I don't think it was anything to do with music. I would never disparage *Rattle and Hum*, because it's very, very important to see it in the context. We were making a movie, and for reasons of our own input we had to be in LA. One of the reasons for being in LA was to mix a live album, which, if you consider the great live albums, we could've done *Live and Dangerous Part II*. We could've had a great double album, we could've made it *sound* great – *everything*. And it would be the soundtrack of the movie. Stupidly – in terms of *everyone else*, not in terms of *ourselves* – we said, "Look, we've got a few months here in LA, let's try and write some new songs." And the story got caught up with the journey of the film, 'cause we had a couple of roots things in there. And we said, "Look, everyone's gonna appreciate we did this thing really quickly – there's gonna be no pressure on it." And we produced nine new songs, three or four of which are among the best we've done. I think 'Hawk-moon 269' is an awkward motherfucker, but it's an extraordinary song, an extraordinary lyrical development for Bono. I think 'Heartland' has a mood and a musical sophistication that we had tried to capture on *The Joshua Tree* – it was a leftover that we finally finished. 'God Part II' was an indication to me of the way forward – 'God Part II' and *Achtung Baby* are the same thing really. And 'All I Want Is You'. And I think those were four great songs – regardless of one's feelings about the blues and gospel material. I think the blues and gospel songs on that record are still pretty good standards. I think they'll survive.'

Whatever, with *Achtung Baby* there was, he agrees, this sense of everything to play for, of fighting for the band's creative life.

Well, *Achtung Baby* was a very, very destructive record, in terms of its effect on the band. Because it was very, very pressured. And none of us were communicating particularly well. And it took a very long time. The hours that went in . . . Bono and Edge would meet and work on lyrics up until eleven, twelve o'clock midday. Then we would go down and record, and we'd be stuck in the same space for months on end. We would work until between two and four in the morning. And after months of that, your perspective, your paranoia, your disorientation, makes it impossible to deal with anything else other than the recording studio. And even dealing with stuff inside the recording studio is pretty suspect – whether you can make good decisions. All one's relationships, with your family, with your friends, with the members of the band – everything started to disintegrate with that record. And the only thing that really kept it together was the fact that it was a great record at the end of the day. And that we had a new lease of life, to take it out and play it to people. We had a device, which was Zoo TV. And gradually, people did get healed. It was a great tour. But we didn't really have a break – from the recording, to the tour, to *Zooropa*. We were on a three-year roll, and by the end of that I think we really needed to step back from it and grow into our . . . thirty-four-year-old shoes. And make that jump from teenager to manhood.

The way Adam and the others describe it, it sounds like it shouldn't have been a great album. How did it become such in spite of all that?

Force of will. Because everything was against making a great record. I think, no matter how people failed and became isolated, I think they still recognised what was good about it, and still followed what was good about it. I mean, many times the difference between a good record and a great record, or an average record and a great record, is maybe ten per cent. But it's that ten per cent that takes ninety per cent of the work.

Achtung Baby was the album that vindicated everything, that changed the course of U2's reputation from inspired excellence to genius. It came at a moment when we might have understood if U2 had run out of steam. The impossibility of their situation caused them to stumble towards greatness. U2 found themselves facing their own dark centre, their caricatures, their past. They had to confront all these things in themselves. They came out fighting, wearing a mask, deconstructing their previous images and journeys. They hacked into the preoccupations of the time, but also in the minds of those who wished them to fail. They inverted the image of themselves and gave themselves cover to descend further into the ideas that had fuelled them from the start. They were freed to get to the places they couldn't have got to otherwise.

The resolution which U2 achieved with *Achtung Baby* might be seen as a map of the journey which Ireland itself has to make in order to free itself from the limitations of other peoples' opinions of what it is and what it should become. They were expanding their horizons in every conceivable direction – musically, sonically, intellectually, stylistically and artistically. Politically and geographically, also, their focus shifted from the US to Europe, where much of the album was recorded in Berlin after the Wall came down.

'You're drawn to where it's at,' said Bono in the Italian summer of 1992. 'It's as simple and as corny as that. You're drawn to where the heat is. And in the late eighties it was America. Right now it's Europe. Whether you're a painter or a poet, you're gonna see that. Like in the seventies and early eighties it was South America. That's not to say it suddenly goes away. But you sense "That's where I need to be now." When we were in Los Angeles for *Rattle and Hum*, I just knew we were in the right place. And the same thing in Berlin. Berlin was *disappearing by the second*. It was being *bought by the yard*. Every businessman, every hooker as a result, in Europe seemed to be there. It was like goldrush. It was a very interesting energy to be around.'

Achtung Baby has an integrity that will allow it to last after the ancillary aspects of the band's image or the Zoo TV paraphernalia have faded from memory. But it is also the result of U2 being forced to rethink themselves in response to the world bearing down on them, responding to perceptions and caricatures. Some critics welcomed the album as a complete break with the past, seemingly oblivious of the subtler shifts which had happened in the music. U2, they said, had changed everything about themselves, and a good thing too. They had discovered, if you don't mind, irony.

Adam says:

> I think it's so simplistic to say that the band decided to be ironic. In the early days, where we were coming from, which was punk, irony was not something that we understood. We didn't see it, because we were that generation of sixteen-year-olds, listening to twenty-six-year-olds selling us the Punk Idea. And you then looked at the New York bands – at Talking Heads, who were masters of irony – Lou Reed, the Velvet Underground. And gradually as one grew, you started to realise the value of those forms of expression. And that's really all that's happened within the band – just not having that energy to stand up and shout about what's wrong with the world, and the way the world should be, to more realising that you have to accept it, and that it is a certain way. The world *is* broken – it's

probably never gonna be fixed; but there are certain things you *can* change, or certain mental positions that you shouldn't give up in order to be able to survive.

For Bono, the change was not one of either style or substance, but of the relationship between the two. It was a different way of explaining. He told me a few months afer the release of *Achtung Baby*:

> We've been continually remaking the band. This is nothing new. The importance of not being earnest – that's definitely what we're doing. But it's still the heaviest record we've made. There's blood and guts in that record. It pretends to be trash and throwaway. In one sense it is a con calling it *Achtung Baby*. The title is humorous, as was the marketing. But I don't think the album is a lot of laughs.
>
> In one sense some of the mood on the record is plagiarising your own past, your memories of songs rather than those songs. Because you were being formed at sixteen and seventeen, you were hearing music. I remember seeing T-Rex on *Top Of The Pops* and finding myself sexually attracted to Marc Bolan. And I'm not gay. That was just the pure power of the music. And all those awakenings that you have when you're under a soundtrack of Bowie, Roxy Music and then punk, and the aggression of that and the nihilism of that. So I think there's a few of those lying around there in the backroom in the record.
>
> Contradictions. I think there were a lot of contradictions in the early days. Sam Shepard said, 'Right smack in the centre of a contradiction, there's a place to be.' And rock 'n' roll has more contradictions than, I think, any other art form. With the exception of film, maybe, but there's too many people involved in film for it to be a clear comparison. So, between art, commerce, nihilism up against idealism, brutality of electric guitar, a wound-up electric guitar, the voice, drums, bass, flesh and the spirit, the choice that we've always been told that we have to make between flesh and spirit – and great rock 'n' roll is both – all these contradictions, and I think we spent maybe the eighties trying to resolve these contradictions, where now in the nineties we seem to be enjoying watching them fight it out.

I remember once reading a quote from The Edge to the effect that maybe U2 have failed to make music that reflected their personalities. If he said it, he is, I think, correct. If he didn't, he should have. Friedrich Engels once said that the object of British policy in Ireland was to make the Irish feel like strangers in their own land. This sense of strangeness is an overt theme in U2's music, but the feeling they articulate is not so much that of being strangers in their own land as – metaphorically – *everywhere else*, and – literally – *within* their own unfulfilled identity.

Such an exploration could have been undertaken only by a band like U2, containing some elements which were Irish in the normal sense and some which were not. It is a characteristic of the Irish personality that it cannot perceive itself except through the witness of outsiders. In Ireland, nothing is perceived to change except the weather, and Irish people talk about the weather all the time. It is outsiders who come in and point to the landscape and tell us how wondrous it is. When Bono sings of the wind cracking in the winter time, 'a bomb-blast lightning waltz', he is bearing witness to an expression of change which is real to him. The music in which the words are uttered provides a context in which the change can be seen as meaningful in other than an incidental way.

The band feel somewhat uncomfortable about discussing aspects of their music which may have been either wilfully concealed or the expression of a hidden intention. 'It's a tricky one, because at the end of the day it's only rock 'n' roll,' says Adam Clayton. 'And that sounds glib but, really, is it that important an issue? I think we were forced to realise it *was* important, because it was being thrust upon us to define ourselves within the music. And for every misconception that people were latching on to within the music, we then had to try and readjust it somewhere else in the music to try and be true to ourselves. And I'm now beginning to think, "Well that's an awful lot of work to go to. Why should you actually do that?" Just do what you do and get on with it, and it's for everyone else to come up with their theories.'

Zooropa, the most recent incarnation of the U2 journey, almost wipes the slate clean, gives U2 an opportunity to go in almost any direction they want. From the static-submerged keening of the opening of the title track to the sleaze-soul of 'Stay', from the dense-dance, *Saturday Night Fever* pastiche of 'Lemon', to Bono's gospel scream at the close of 'The Wanderer', *Zooropa* is both a soulfood capsule of the essence of rock 'n' roll and a folk music for the modern mind. U2 may have irony on their lips but they still have iron in their souls.

Adam observes:

> It occurred to me . . . look at the history of the band and then the *Zooropa* album . . . and looking at the history of the Beatles, and everything they'd done and learned, and then suddenly . . . *Sergeant Pepper*, which redefined the whole ballgame, and produced a different language, a different sound. And I think *Zooropa* achieves a new language for Bono to use – a language that's more his own, that he feels more comfortable with. I think the late-seventies, early-

eighties choice of language, where if it was American it was West Coast, it was hippie; and if it was British or European it was dole queue. They were not languages which Bono could use. And I think on *Zooropa* he's found a language which allows him to talk about the modern day in the everyday. I hope you can take that language further. And musically, I think, we've defined, or found, a sound that we're entitled to use, that we're competent to use, that says, 'We don't wanna be a grunge band. We don't wanna be looking for that kind of a sound. Using the instruments that we have, which we've now expanded from bass, guitar and drums to samplers and keyboards and drum machines, we wanna keep abusing them, and making them sound different. We don't wanna sound like anything else.' And that's kind of the agenda on that record. Or at least, the agenda was to make that record – now it's a manifesto, and we can take it anywhere. It's a record deep with mystery, for me.

Zooropa takes U2 right into the cyberzone. Everything you knew about them, you find, has been wrong. And yet right, but in a different way. Most of all, anything is possible. But only if it's true. *Achtung Baby* was born out of a spirit of defensiveness, a need to answer back, to deal with certain forces and accusations, to debunk certain clichés, and ultimately to justify the band, but only on its own terms. And yet, out of that, U2 created an album that will last, and which they can stand over. What does this say? Bono, at least, says:

> I think that whole thing of actually drawing out your enemies, this idea of judo, of using the energy that is coming at you to defend yourself, was a real clue. Because the greater the force that was coming at you, the greater it was as a source of energy. The very things that we'd been trying to sort out and resolve, or avoid, were suddenly taken on board; the contradictions of being in a rock 'n' roll band; the contradictions of ephemera and content, of making too much money and painting pictures of a world that was very unlike that. Not specifically that, but, you know, all that stuff that made us so defensive suddenly became energy. I think there's now a great sense of fearlessness in the group – which is very good. It will be artful, it will be limbo dancing. But not that nervous ducking or diving, that's not good. Tiptoeing, actually, is what we call it. And it's *death*.

The question arises: if something is done as a reaction to forces that are a part of a passing moment's anger or misunderstanding, surely they can't really contain the timeless and universal stuff that might qualify them as great art?

Bono intercepts the question:

> I don't agree with that. Because I think that the job of the artist is to see the current in the light of the timeless. I'm saying, 'This moment in time – well, *that's* because of *that* in the past.' And I actually think that all great art has all that in it. All great literature has it. They are both time capsules and completely unfettered by time. That's the great thing about timeless art. And I'm not sure whether a lot of pop music, or a lot of our music, will have that. You just can't tell. But I know the ideas that are in it, and the confusion that is part of it, is definitely vital. Look at Picasso. That's what I love about Picasso: his portrait of, you know, my lover's left breast. Guernica: 'Here's a doll I made.' You know, there's everything! He does what he likes. No fear.

We need to become unafraid to see our own place as the exotic location it appears to outsiders. We must fall in love with it. Community renewal is, as Seamus Heaney said, a creative project, requiring the same kind of creative energy as any work of art. 'Creative work,' he said, 'involves the identification of an origin of energy, then the creation of conditions in which that energy can exercise itself freely in order to transform itself (and the conditions) into something new . . . and not just something new, but something actually renovated.'

'Creative work is a matter is impulse discovering direction, of potential discovering structure, of chance becoming design.' Imagining a national identity is a creative project. To know ourselves we must first of all become conscious of the nature of the place we live in, and be ready to celebrate the full complex reality of it.

Writing about the reality of modern-day Ireland is a tricky business. Part of the reason that nobody has yet made a decent stab at explaining the Ireland of U2 is that nobody, and this includes U2, has the foggiest idea where to begin. To write about this place is to stumble through a maze of ideological constructs masquerading as reality. You approach the future through the past and people can only think of you as wanting to go back. As you proceed, you have to explode each of the ideas that you used to advance your thoughts, and defuse the language you have utilised to map out the target area. As you approach the truth, language becomes useless. More often than not, those of us who try to make sense of Ireland for a living find that, far from making things clearer, what we are able to express merely confirms others in their own prejudices. It is not so much that nothing new is ever *said*, but that nothing new can ever be *heard*. No new insights can be forged because all we will allow ourselves to hear is the grinding of axes.

In no other western country does the past intrude to such an extent on the present. And yet it is not even the past, but different versions of it, that we have to deal with. Because of the shifting nature of the society, we have a greater need to erect certainties at which to glance back for reassurance or resolve. These constructs are almost like the headstones of the people who have left, markers without the sign of life, ciphers for the reality we cannot find. For example, the phrase, 'de Valera's Ireland' continues to have a vital currency in Ireland, despite the fact that Eamon de Valera left active politics in 1959, and has been dead for two decades. The myth of de Valera sustains two views of it – one for and one against – in a way that not even the Kennedy myth has been sustained in the modern mind of America. We cannot – *will* not – see that what we are fighting about is someone else's version of who we are supposed to be. Entire generations have been consumed in a morale-sapping backlash against people dead or dying. Everything that begins as a progressive and radical response to a previous rigidity ends up as neurotic and obsessive as that which it sought to oppose. There seems to be no way of clearing up the clutter.

We have allowed the images of ourselves that sustain us to become fossilised in ideas and ideologies which are, all of them, useless. We are sustained only in terms of the literal past, the 'facts' of history, and cannot find – because we do not seek, because we do not realise that we lack – the language or images that might reshape us. 'Modern' Ireland is fossil. We have allowed Ireland to go out of fashion because we stopped updating our awareness of how it was changing. We allowed ourselves to become trapped by definitions which were mythical, illusory, fake-modern aspirations and caricatures. Meanwhile the real Ireland was allowed to drift as though *it*, and not the myths and shibboleths that were being celebrated, was actually the false consciousness. The failure to deal with this condition rests equally, and in no particular order, with Irish politicians, writers and intellectuals.

Ironically, or perhaps not, the single area in which the gap is least visible is the one most readily dismissed by the voices of Official Ireland. Popular music, the most patronised of art forms, is unequivocally where the stereotype about Irish backwardness is shown to be a lie. In a way, it is not all that surprising that a nation whose language and culture were suppressed through centuries should make the arts of music and writing the vehicles of its spirit, pain and aspiration. Perhaps because of the onslaught from the invader, one another and the weather, we have internalised all our colours, which can therefore emerge only in the intimate arts of poetry and music. In any event, it remains true that in Ireland today, if you wish to know what people really feel, you are better off dropping the needle on Van Morrison than tuning into the national television station, better listening to U2, or Sharon Shannon, or the Cranberries, than reading a newspaper. Only in popular music is the true nature of the modern world being acknowledged or reimagined. U2, contrary to the snobberies which would deny that rock 'n' roll bands can be artists at all, are unquestionably the most important new artistic voice to come out of Ireland in the past twenty years.

The science-fiction writer, Bruce Sterling, has written that sci-fi writers are the court jesters of modern literature, the wise fools who can 'play with Big Ideas because the garish motley of our pulp origins makes us seem harmless'. There is no obligation to take sci-fi seriously, he points out, 'yet our ideas permeate the culture, bubbling along invisibly, like background radiation'. This statement is equally true, both in substance and in texture, of the position of U2 in popular music, in the world and in their country of origin.

U2's music allows us to get in touch again with the meaning of being Irish in the modern world. Is it too much to suggest that what this music contains may be the experience and knowledge of a displaced soul in a technolatrous world? Through it, Irish people catch a glimpse of themselves as they really are. Through it they send signals to a world now experiencing what they have lived with for eight hundred years.

We Irish have long been trotting behind England, the US, Europe, convinced of our innate backwardness. The world, meanwhile, has begun to take an interest in the qualities we offer that we have been unable to see in ourselves. At the moment this is quantified in fairly superficial terms: clean environment, green countryside. But there is a more profound reality, as represented by U2. Outsiders are now coming closer to seeing the totality of what Ireland is, the way all its elements can be integrated in what is capable of being the most modern of settings. True to form, it is outsiders who can see, for example, that organic gardening can be conducted as part of a post-industrial technological economy, that creativity is the key resource of the twenty-first century, and that all these things can be brought together under an Irish sky.

Up until now, it has been our curse to see our best aspects as aberrations. The thought occurs that Ireland's future may actually be the sum of its present aberrations. The array of rock 'n' roll bands now emanating from Ireland gives a sense of what we might become. This need not mean a redefinition of Ireland as a postmodern Coca-Cola culture, which is just another Celtic myth, another glib phrase. There is a truth in it, but it is a clichéd truth. Rather, we should attempt, as Bono says, to become more aware of our reality, to be less afraid of it, and to use it to create pictures that will make sense of our lives as we actually wish to lead them.

The biggest problem, still, is Ireland's human incontinence, which causes us to disperse our greatest resources of imagination and energy to the continents of the world. Those of us who remain get by selling our souls to those who, on the run from the industrial catastrophe, can perceive the qualities which we have rendered invisible to ourselves. The question is: can we find in ourselves the self-confidence to see what we have, and harness it, before somebody else takes it from under our noses? Up until now, we have gone around in a circle holding on to other people's tails, so we never got a proper look at what we've got in our own backpack.

Bono says:

I think that my generation was the last to feel like that. Even just a few years after us, I can see it in the way people walk. I can see it in the way people carry themselves that people are very glad they're Irish right now in the nineties. They feel the freedom that they have in a way they never did before. This idea of being akin to the blacks, but not having the sign of colour, is interesting, because we can blur, we can just disappear into Englishness or being American, very easily. Even the Dublin accent takes on the hues so easily. I personally have the accent of the last person I was talking to. Because I'm a musician and I have a musical ear. And I think that's true of Irish people. Well actually, it's more true of Dublin people than Irish people. Dublin people, because of the influences in Dublin – apart from working-class Dublin – have had their accent chipped away at for years. But that is an interesting idea. Because it's even more alluring, then, to lose yourself in another culture. But I don't think we should – I really think we have something very valuable.

You see, you know exactly what I mean when I talk about Ireland being crap when you were a kid. Crap in the sense that the things it was great at you weren't interested in. But that doesn't happen any more. I look at my cousins, and they're ticking over on a different level. I think that what happens is that they go away and find out that what they have is valuable. And the ones that went away have come back with a reinforced idea of what it is to be Irish. I think Irish people are very strong at the minute, and about to throw off the unwanted baggage of the past, including the Nazi element of the Catholic Church, and of republicanism – these small ideas that have constrained what it is to be Irish for so long. There are things I'm bleak about, but I'm really not bleak about that.

He pauses and smiles. 'Yeah. If your idea of Ireland is the old one, we're an aberration in it. We don't really make sense. But in the new Ireland, we make perfect sense.'

CHAPTER SEVENTEEN

Music Minus Thought

It is unclear how music began, and what relationship it first bore to the sound and rhythm of the world. But all known cultures had some kind of music in them. The earliest forms, unsurprisingly, were vocal, and even the first instruments were based on the imitation of vocal sounds. Music came from inside mankind. Some ethnomusicologists have observed connections between the primary music tones and specific sounds in nature, but this is a limited excursion. Others have referred to the importance of rhythms surrounding the child from the dawn of consciousness in the womb, or have drawn our attention to links with the emotional babytalk between a mother and her offspring in the first months of life. The characteristics of such early communication – that it seeks emotional contact with other humans, hinting at things which human beings need from *one another* rather than the concerns of the individual man – seem to be reproduced in music. 'It is not hunger or thirst, but love, hatred, pity and anger which drew from men their first vocal utterances,' observed the eighteenth-century thinker Jean Jacques Rousseau. Music, in other words, implied communality between people.

The source of music may be a puzzle, but its existence is not the true mystery. Without the suggestions of meaning provided by sound, life would be less bearable: the silence of the grave. Man sought a soundtrack for his existence from the very beginning. With the centuries, music grew away from its vocal roots. The idea that music was an increasingly subtle and displaced refinement of the aural world into a declension of notes and tones, which, once identified and physically defined, could be reproduced and repeated at will, was one that humankind found impossible to resist. The world and Man's existence in it might have suggested music, but they did not provide it. 'I conclude that tonal elements become music by virtue of their being organised,' the composer Stravinsky observed, 'and that organisation presupposes a conscious human act.'

And whether the sounds Man could make with skin and gut and wood and ivory were simply a way of disentangling in his head the chaos with which the world had barraged his soul, or whether they unlocked some secret connection between himself and the external world of which he was part and yet not, Man found that music made him feel better. Perhaps it did *both* – soothing his soul by explaining the chaos in a language he could understand, and opening some channel of meaning between himself and the ostensibly disconnected world which was otherwise closed to the everyday use of the five senses. Perhaps the rhythms of the very body which he found himself inhabiting sought an echo in the sounds of the world. Early music was created for both use and beauty, invariably having a function rather than existing as a thing in itself, whether to provide rhythms for dancing, a context for lovemaking or laments for the dead. Whatever, Man had stumbled on a way of dramatising something which he could only perceive vaguely out of the corner of his eye, and which moved sharply as he turned his head.

Things rested so. Perhaps because the relationship between both the individual tones could not be defined other than mathematically, and that between what was called music and the wider world only be guessed at, the thing began to take on a life of its own. Music became a form, and life went its own way. The two became increasingly casual acquaintances, though maintaining a certain degree of contact. With the development of classical music, whatever connection had existed between the music and the sound of the world became refined almost out of existence. The more complex and chaotic the world became, the more 'serious' music retreated into its aesthetic shell, leaving popular and folk music to make sense of as well as contribute to the din.

The schism between primitive music and the classical form provided a shadow play of the rational and emotional functions residing respectively in the left and right hemispheres of the brain. 'Although there is considerable overlap, as happens with many cerebral functions,' observes English psychiatrist Anthony Storr in *Music and the Mind*, 'language is predominantly processed in the left hemisphere, whilst music is chiefly scanned and appreciated in the right hemisphere. The division of function is not so much between words and music as between logic and emotion.'

Ironically, the more the classical music tradition retreated from both the heart of man and the chaos of the world, the more its proponents affected a sour and high-minded disdain towards the business of grappling with the grubbiness from which it had removed itself. The phrase 'pop music' became a term of abuse.

Brian Eno, who has been producing U2 records for over ten years, is at the vanguard of those who, without making a song and dance about it, insist on believing that popular music, the descendant of primitive cultures, is infinitely capable in ways that classical music is not. Eno, I'm afraid, does not simply suggest that pop music may be, if you don't mind too much, allowed to inhabit the same room as its rich classical uncle; he demands the bridal suite. The modern world, he implies, cannot be served by classical music, because that world is too complex and that form of music too simple, too immature. Classical notation is insufficiently worldly to be of much help in describing modern reality. What is overwhelming in the modern experience does not yield itself into discrete notes and obsessive diction. 'The reason traditional notation works is because classical music is so simple,' he told Tim de Lisle in an interview for the *Independent on Sunday* in August 1992. 'The notes are discrete, and there's not much elision. You tend to go [he sings, like a choirboy] *ah ah ah ah ah*. You don't go *neuurrureeurreeuruhh* like they do in blues or in Arab music. That kind of thing is almost unnotable. And everything else in classical music is discontinuous: a clarinet is a clarinet, a trombone is a trombone. This isn't the case in modern music. There's everything in between as well. You can have a claribone if you want. You can't notate continuous fields.'

The inability of classical music to evolve a language to depict the aural chaos of the world was camouflaged and validated by convenient thinking which defined music as either uplift or escapism, concepts which were themselves awarded different, i.e. opposite, aesthetic values. Classical music was fine because it elevated you to a higher plane; popular music was base because it distracted you from reality.

The opposite of this prejudice may be as close as we can get to the truth: that classical music, because it distils and refines, may be the real escapism; and pop, because of its infinite capacity for chaos, is capable, at least, of opening up a truer avenue by which to pursue both mystery and meaning.

Brian Eno once described to an interviewer how he would sit in the middle of Hyde Park listening to the hum of London, tuning in to the complex layers of sound. 'For me that's as good as going to a concert hall at night.'

At its very best, modern music, at least as much as it is the hereditary product of a genealogical succession or a technological process, is the beating of a human heart, the crying of an anonymous child, the hissing of waterpipes, the yelp of chihuahuas, the accidental harmony of randomly triggered alarm systems, the low hum of overhead jets, the rattle of small change, the howling wind in a disused chimney, the wheezing coughs of starter motors, the tinkle of tea being stirred, the screech of worn brakeshoes, the shouts of boys horsing around, the uncertain murmur of a bass guitar through two concrete walls, the simultaneous revving of thirteen vehicles at traffic lights, the indifferent mumble of a television set in the next room, the tyrannical rattle of pneumatic drills, the vague assertion of a faraway train, the tapping of raindrops on a car roof, the cawing of a delegation of rooks – the aural soup of all these, or the sound of them all except any one, though no one could quite say which, or the sound of them all through a window pane or the sound of them all plus the sound of something you can't quite make out but could be the scratching of fingernails on raw wood, through a window pane with the radio on.

Each listener hears in a different way the sounds which are there in his or her own imagination, and the individual's sense and emotions are decanted by his or her experience of listening. The music contains as many realities as it has listeners. It contains the memories of the cultural context from which it derives, but also acquires the individual associations of the context in which it is first heard by the listener, becoming a magical embalmer of memory and enchantment. From time to time, one sound or strand within a particular song or composition pops above the others to remind you in a most immediate way that the source of this music is not *other music*, but *something else*. Then it occurs to you, for the first time, or certainly for the first time that you remember, that music is not a separate plant from life itself, but a clinging, interwoven creeper that binds us together with our everyday existence.

A window is an opening into the music of human living, observed Franz Kafka. Whoever leads a solitary life, he wrote in *Meditation*, 'and yet now and then wants to attach himself somewhere . . . to see any arm at all to which he might cling', needs a window looking out on to the street. Here, 'looking from his public to heaven and back again', he is drawn into the human harmony. In the time since Kafka wrote those words, the window on to the street has become subject to several new kinds of metaphysical competition. We hear the world through a box on the mantelpiece or the bedside locker, and both see and hear it enacted behind a pane of thick glass in another, larger box in the corner of the room. And yet we continue as though the two might still be separated. This is this and that is that. Art is what we see and hear through the window; the other openings are the source of the something else.

Anybody who is mature enough to listen properly to contemporary pop music will know that it is every bit as capable as Brian Eno suggests, and Bono insists. 'When it started out,' the latter told me in Milan in 1992, 'it was completely not understood. And it was obviously, y'know, music made by idiots, because people couldn't get *this beat*. What was going on in Memphis was one of the most extraordinary moments of the twentieth century – where African rhythm and European melody were married. Two cultures collided in this spastic dance. A guy who wore eyeshadow and a zoot suit. It was an extraordinary thing, but it completely missed the intelligentsia, the people who were going to the opera, or who were listening to what was regarded as the modern music of the time. And here it was happening, in Dogtown, in the back of a shop.'

*

Change, writes Jacques Attali in his 1977 book *Noise: The Political Economy of Music*, 'is inscribed in noise faster than it transforms society'. Music is therefore prophetic because 'its styles and economic organisation are ahead of the rest of society . . . it explores, much faster than material reality can, the entire range of possibilities in a given code. It makes audible the new world that will gradually become visible.' The musician, in this context, has two seemingly contradictory roles: he is both reproducer and prophet, a historian and a subversive. 'He speaks of society and he speaks against it.' Attali's book is essentially a theory of redemption, positing the notion of a profoundly participative role for musical composition in a more democratic future. But for the moment, he is more realistic, identifying three ways in which music is used strategically as a buttress of power. In the first, music is used to make people forget the violence that society does them. In the second, it makes people believe in the harmony of the world. In the third, it serves to silence, 'by mass-producing a deafening, syncretic kind of music, and censoring all other human voices'.

'Make people Forget, make them Believe, Silence them,' Attali summarises.

This process, he argues, has occurred most visibly in popular music, where the commodity-centred thinking of our repetitive society has been given free rein. In repetition, he writes, the entire production process of music is very different from the previous condition of representation, in which the musician was in control. 'Of course, as soon as sound technology started to play an important role in representation, the musician was already no longer alone. But today, under repetition, the sound engineer determines the quality of the recording, and a large number of technicians construct and fashion the product delivered to the public. . . The performer is only one element contributing to the overall quality.' The result, he argues, is a debasement of music, in which error, hesitation, noise and humanity are squeezed out. Musicians are dividing into two categories: authors and interpreters – the anonymous functionaries of the production processes and the performing stars who act out the last vestiges of a previous representational function.

Attali's book was written while punk was still a gleam in Malcolm McLaren's eye, and so its prognostications are more pessimistic than its author's, otherwise naive optimism may have preferred. 'It is not that the song has been debased,' he insists, 'rather, the presence of debased songs in our environment has increased. Popular music and rock have been recuperated, colonized, sanitized.' Attali harbours a dream of a better world, a world characterised by what he calls Composition. 'We are condemned to silence,' he writes, 'unless we create our own relation with the world and try to tie other people into the meaning we thus create. That is what composing is. Doing solely for the sake of doing, without trying artificially to recreate the old codes in order to reinsert communication into them. Inventing new codes, inventing the message at the same time as the language.' Such a concept, he argues, reaches far beyond music 'to the emergence of the free act, self-transcendence, pleasure in being instead of having'.

He is not without optimism. 'We see emerging, piecemeal and with the greatest ambiguity, the seeds of a new noise, one exterior to the institutions and customary sites of political conflict. A noise of Freedom and Festival, it may create the conditions for a major discontinuity extending far beyond its field. It may be the essential element in a strategy for the emergence of a truly new society.' Attali had glimpsed the future, but had yet to hear it. In an Afterword to the 1985 edition of *Noise*, Susan McClary underlines the book's own prophetic nature. Since it was published, she notes, 'extra-ordinary evidence' of its analysis had begun to emerge.

> It was in the mid-1970s that New Wave burst on the scene in England, with precisely the motivation suggested by Attali at his most optimistic . . . Many of the original groups began as garage bands formed by people *not* educated as musicians who intended to defy noisily the slickly marketed 'nonsense' of commercial rock. The music is often aggressively simple syntactically, but at its best it conveys most effectively the raw energy of its social and musical protest . . . The burgeoning of Composition, still somewhat theor-etical in Attali's statement of 1977, has been actualized and is proving quite resilient.

At its best, which is to say its most surprising, rock 'n' roll is capable of restoring, as near as possible, that putative lost connection between Man and his world. It becomes the antithesis of abstraction, a merging of the body and soul of listener with music, and a reintegration of the music with the world of the real. That unit, too, seems to flow naturally from a unity between music and musician. Harry Shapiro and Caesar Glebbeck, a Finnish musicologist, observed in their *Electric Gypsy*, a biography of Jimi Hendrix, that Hendrix's playing was a manifestation of creative energy which liberated the listener because it had firstly freed its creator. 'The whole man vibrates with feeling like a perfectly tuned string.' Many people, they observe, who have seen live performances of Jimi Hendrix have been amazed by this unity of musical content and visual appearance and at the feeling of mastery and freedom that was conveyed just by watching him play. Hendrix knew this well. 'My music, my instrument, my sound, my body – are all one action with my mind.'

The modern world is not merely sound; it is also loud. This poses difficulty for many of those who perceive the sound of music in isolation from its meaning. Even Joachim-Ernst Berendt, who writes without snobbery about the essential nature of music, could not quite deal with the loudness of modern rock 'n' roll. 'Many young people,' he writes in *The Third Ear*, fail to realise that, far from shutting them off from modern society's aggressiveness, 'the "sounds" they think "theirs" correspond exactly to the society (and its noise) they wish to keep at a distance'. But if music is about extrapolating meaning from reality, it is inevitable that the music of an aggressive, raucous and chaotic reality will itself be aggressive, raucous and chaotic. Jimi Hendrix had been a pioneer in the possibilities of the electric guitar, emerging from a folk tradition to confront the challenge of the modern world. He is remembered for, among other things, his hugely creative use of devices like the wah-wah pedal, tremolo arm and fuzzbox. This way of putting it conceals the fact that what he did was create a new aural landscape in music, the invention of which is now almost impossible to comprehend in purely technical terms. And yet the knowledge of it will survive somewhere deep in the sinews and marrow of the music. We see the substance of the act but miss the shadow which was its purpose. Anyone who tries now to follow Hendrix is virtually certain of looking and sounding like a cheap imitator, an amplified ham, precisely because the technology is only part of the medium. The imitators play a form; Hendrix played a language. For all that technology has moved on, nobody has ever succeeded in emulating his degree of connectedness with his instrument. It was as though the technology had been born with him, *for* him, and died in a particular way when he did.

'A musician, if he is a messenger,' Hendrix said in a 1969 interview, 'is like a child who hasn't been handled too many times by man, hasn't had too many fingerprints across his brain. That's why music is so much heavier than anything you ever felt.'

Many of the things Hendrix played, he used to say, the sounds he made, were things he had heard in dreams. 'My own thing is in my head. I hear sounds and if I don't get them together nobody else will.'

Which brings us as close back to music as we're likely to get by chance again. What *is* music? Is it the organisation of sounds from the world or from the possible world in a manner as to make that world or those possibilities more bearable, more understandable, more real? Charlie Parker once said that music was a series of yesses and nos – each one a decision taken in a split second during performance, amounting to thousands in the course of a single concert. Now I play this note, now this one. *Why?* To say who I am? To say where I have come from? To enact the drama of my self-knowledge, or the lack of it?

The novelist Milan Kundera, clearly a man with a problem about rock 'n' roll, has written more than once or twice about 'the idiocy of guitars'.

Whereas the history of music has come to an end, he writes in *The Book of Laughter and Forgetting*, there is now more music than even in its 'most glorious day'. 'Schoenberg is dead, Ellington is dead, but the guitar is eternal. Stereotyped harmonies, hackneyed melodies, and a beat that gets stronger as it gets duller – that is what is left of music . . . No work of Beethoven's has ever elicited greater collective passion than the constant repetitive throb of the guitar . . . Music in our time has returned to its primordial state, the state after the last issue has been raised and the last theme contemplated – a state that follows history.' Kundera's view, however eloquently put, is as misplaced as it is pessimistic. When he speaks of pop music as the return to the primordial form of 'music minus thought', he may be placing more weight on the value of thinking than even he would wish. It was not for the want of either thinking or thoughtful music that, while Elvis Presley was just a boy, mankind descended to the very pit of his basest nature without a three-chord trick in earshot. The problem, such as it is, may be to do with the outsider's incapacity to hear anything but the blur of sound keeping pace and time with the blur of reality.

'That's a classic northern European, classicist attitude to rhythm,' is how Bono begins answering the Kundera charge. 'They just don't *get* the rhythm. Orchestras can't play rhythm. The most brilliant musicians in the world, in the finest orchestras, you can't get them to play rhythm. They don't understand it. It's like a muscle they haven't developed. And rock 'n' roll music is where Africa and Europe collide, there in that moment. And they don't understand *that* half of the equation. So, if you like, it's a bit like if you judged meaning based on verbs and not adjectives, because that's all you spoke. They're not actually *listening*. Rhythm is not articulate to him. He just looks at certain tones and says, "That's very repetitive." And I suppose a lot of rock 'n' roll, that raunchy, cock-rock thing, is pretty base and not very interesting. But what happened to our version of the three chords is that we shared the chord. So Adam held the bottom of it and Edge suspended on top of it. So it wasn't, in fact, the three chords that everyone else was ploughing. There were suspensions. Edge didn't even know the names of the chords; he didn't even know they *had* names. He made them up.'

From this point of disagreement, Bono and Kundera, perhaps to the latter's discomfiture, come to a single mind. Music, writes Kundera just a couple of pages before the aforementioned outburst, is the dramatisation in a wordless language of a hidden action which we comprehend at a level below the conscious.

'This,' he writes, 'is what my father told me when I was five: a key signature is a king's court in miniature. It is ruled by a king (the first step) and his two right-hand men (steps five and four). They have four other dignitaries at their command, each of whom has his own special relation to the king and his right-hand men. The court houses five additional tones as well, which are known as chromatic. They have important parts to play in other keys, but here they are simply guests.

'Since each of the twelve notes has its own job, title, and function, any piece we hear is more than mere sound: it unfolds a certain action before us.'

This is part of what Bono feels about the music he tries to make. 'He's exactly right there. I would actually see that. They play out your past, your memory, and you father's memories. This is what I'm getting to. These melodies – I don't know where they come from, but . . .'

The trouble is, to talk about rock 'n' roll in such terms is to risk ridicule, often from those who claim the greatest love of the medium. The only role they will allow it is to be concerned with minor things. The connections must remain secret, or communicated in self-deprecating codes. This has created a critical culture which apes the music in its approach and style. Most rock criticism is either too serious or too frivolous. The trick is to be neither, and yet both, to care and not to let it show, but yet not to care if you do let it show. The very best rock writing has this ambiguity built into it. The best rock criticism we have is that which survives this permanent condition of ducking and diving, of constantly throwing itself at the point full tilt and sliding away at the last moment. The best critics, or at least the best surviving, are those who can say something without seeming to be saying it, who wait for you to see it for yourself and then pretend to be surprised, who unring their bells in advance but leave behind the echo of the ringing. You are left knowing but not knowing. Everything is deniable. And this deniability itself infects the music, so that it too must say things without seeming to be saying them. Bono calls it limbo dancing. 'That's what we do for a living.'

CHAPTER EIGHTEEN

The Line of Dissent

Men make their own history, said Karl Marx, but not just as they please, under circumstances chosen by themselves; they make it under conditions directly transmitted from the past, the tradition of the dead generations weighing down on them like a nightmare.

We in the self-styled modern world have been, well, conditioned to think of our minds as the product of our environment. We tend to perceive physical attributes as genetic and mental structures as learned. We are the sum of our physical manifestations and what we know we know. Perhaps our assumptions keep us locked into our misapprehensions.

In his theory of language, the great American linguist and philosopher Noam Chomsky holds that language capacity, for all the perceived difference between languages, is an innate, biological feature of the human mind. His findings in the field of linguistics may have profound implications for other aspects of human expression. 'My feeling is that a human being or any complex organism has a system of cognitive structures which develop much in the way the physical organs of the body develop,' he told an interviewer in 1983. Chomsky has observed that language structure follows the same deep-seated principles the world over; there is, in other words, a hidden universal grammar. Because we tend to concentrate on the superficial differences between language, this at first appears faintly absurd. But if we could achieve a distance from our own use of language, Chomsky tells us, we would see that there is a far greater uniformity between languages than there is difference.

'Of course they grow under particular environmental conditions, assuming a specific form that admits of some variation. Much of what is distinctive among human beings is a specific manner in which a variety of shared cognitive structures develop.' The language organ of the child interacts with its early experience and grows into the structure of the language in which the child is raised. But some basic element exists from the beginning. 'Many examples can be found of things that people know about language, things that are standard and simple in their language use and perception, where they have had no relevant experience at all,' Chomsky told another interviewer in 1978. Many of the simple sentence structures which children can put together without assistance, but which follow no logical rules of grammar or structure, are actually unlearnable. 'When we analyse carefully the nature of the knowledge of language a person has, once he has mastered his language, we discover that it simply does not have the properties which are implied by the stimulus-response concept of how learning takes place.' There is, in other words, a creative aspect to language. 'It's a crucial fact about language that a person is quite capable of understanding sentences that have no physical similarity – no point-to-point relationship – to any that he's come across in his linguistic experience or has produced earlier.'

'Normal use of language is not an exercise of any "habit" or "skill". Typically, use of language is "creative", in the sense that it constantly involves the production and interpretation of new forms, new in the experience of the language user or even in the history of language.'

Descartes, Chomsky reminded us, maintained a connection between the creativity which emerges in language and the exercise of free will. The way we use language suggests the existence of a mind within the mind, itself capable of total freedom of will and unencumbered by the mechanical principles that govern the rational mind.

Beyond that, it appears, we know almost nothing. Attempts to adapt Chomsky's theories to music and other cultural expressions have not moved beyond the speculative. In *Music and the Mind*, Anthony Storr makes the following extrapolation from Chomsky's theory of language:

> Language does not emanate from the Earth, but from the human brain. So does music. The universality of music depends upon basic characteristics of the human mind; especially upon the need to impose order upon our experience. Different cultures produce different musical systems just as they produce different languages and different political systems. Languages are ways of ordering words; political systems are ways of ordering society; musical systems are ways of ordering sounds. What is universal is the human propensity to create order out of chaos.

Ethnomusicology has arrived at a similar point of irresolution with regard to the transmission of musical creativity, performance and appreciation, and is unable to get much past the knowledge that musical potential is genetically transmitted and therefore lies dormant in virtually every human mind.

Professor Ivor Browne, Ireland's leading psychiatrist through the second half of the twentieth century, who describes himself as a 'failed musician' and carries a tin whistle about in his inside pocket, believes that while the potential for language and other cultural expression is indeed present in the human mind, there is no memory bank in which a musical culture can be retained intact through generations.

> The genetic potential for language is there, and perhaps for order. But unless it's brought out environmentally through a culture, it won't develop. There's enough examples of humans brought up by animals to know that – they don't actually speak, for example. We're very different from bees, ants, most animals, until you come up to the higher mammals. Their culture, like an antheap, is programmed genetically. You could take two ants, put them out in a field, and they'd set up a whole antheap. Take two humans and they would lose thousands of years of culture. So most of what we have is cultural transmission – allowing for the *potential* we have.

What applies to individual humans applies also to communities, groups, nations. 'In the same way that you have your mental life as an individual, the group also has its mental life: the shared consciousness of the group, which has to be learned by each new generation.' Professor Browne continues:

> Pre-recording, culture is only one generation thick. In other words, it isn't in some sort of genetic memory. There may be certain Jungian archetypes, certain ancient symbols, within us. That's rather unclear. But what we mean ordinarily by culture, say like the Irish harping tradition – once one generation happens that didn't learn that, it was gone. When I first saw Irish music it was happening to the piping. It was as thin as about ten pipers, some of whom I helped to keep alive. And if they hadn't passed that along, there'd be no way you could find that. It's been helped tremendously by recording, but the recording almost didn't come in quickly enough to save it.
>
> I don't think culture can skip generations, except now maybe with computers and recordings – and this never amounts to the same thing. Culture is only one generation thick. There's no evidence for what we are as humans, in terms of our whole richness, being there genetically. The potential for language is there, but the potential is very different from the thing itself.
>
> So it's important to say that, whatever it is that Bono would have in him isn't there genetically some way – other than whatever *is* genetic – it's there by virtue of his participating in a culture that still had in it whatever the elements are, even though he wasn't consciously aware of where it was coming from.

If culture is but one generation thick, is it possible for people who have been deprived of their own culture, to enter into another culture, bringing with them, in some race memory bank or whatever, elements of their own culture which make it come out differently? Yes, says Professor Browne, but not in the genes. Culture is transmitted in all sorts of invisible ways – in language, folklore, humour, sport, gesture, violence, etiquette, painting and a million other forms. But it's not in the blood.

> Although people may be deprived, they are in fact, through speech and a whole lot of ways, picking up remnants of the culture – because they have, after all, been brought up in it. If you take someone who doesn't know Irish, a lot of the English they speak, the phrases, will be in fact translations from the Irish – even though they have no direct connection with Irish at all. They're picking them up from people who *did* translate them from the Irish. So a lot of the richness of Irish vocabulary is still coming from the Irish language, even though people may have no actual knowledge of speaking it. Cultures are carried in lots of invisible ways, but they are still carried by the culture. And if you take Bono, he's been writing a lot of songs. But the very fact that somewhere in him is the *idea* that he can write songs may be coming from that, because there's a whole tradition here of excellence in the use of words, which nobody owns. It's a bit like the excellence of the blacks with jazz. People have to work up to a standard that's there implicitly. So that, in some sense, that's there in the culture saying, 'This is what we do.' He'd have inherited that without ever being aware, just like Roddy Doyle or whoever. So it may not be so much the *music* as the *word* culture. It's at a deeper level; it's something to do with the form of expression.

There is a fallacy abroad in Ireland that sweeping suburban heartlands, such as the area in which Bono grew up, are simply blank, anonymous locations in which life begins again from square one. But, Professor Browne reminds us,

> Those communities didn't come into being with nothing; they brought their culture out with them. Most of them were a mixture of rural people and the indigenous Dubliners going out. You have only to go back a generation or two – even in Ballymun, where those people were brought up, there would have been storytellers. You have this very powerful oral tradition in this country, which didn't die out with Hugh O'Neill. It carried on almost to this generation, in places like Connemara. It's gone now in any direct sense. But in so far as people like Bono are affected, I'd say it's because they grew up as part of that culture.

We're inclined all the time to think of the outside reality as reality. The main reality we deal with all the time is our internal psychic reality, because everything in our outside reality is interpreted through that. So even if you decide Ballymun is urban, the actual psychic realities of the people there may be formed in all sorts of other places, and *that's* what's shared. Some of it might be urban, some of it might be *truly* urban in the sense of the tenements. It has relatively little to do with those particular buildings – okay, it'll be affected by them, and I suppose increasingly so as the next generation grows up. And I suppose there's so many influences now, with television and advertising and so on, that how could anyone make sense of it? But the people who went out there – Bono's parents, say, the culture they had would have nothing to do with Ballymun.

In order to achieve freedom to give expression to our hidden impulses, perhaps we Irish *have to* step outside the parameters of the existing forms. It might well be that, if the conventional entry points into existing forms were barred, the culture would bubble up inside until it found a different way of expressing itself. Music undoubtedly had a much bigger role in Irish society than in other western countries. This may be because the peasant culture lacked conventional cultural carriers, like books, paintings, artefacts, and so the responsibility for the transmission of meaning was invested almost solely in the traditions of storytelling and narrative singing. The external threat to the culture caused the music to take on even greater responsibilities, both as mnemonic device and tribal emblem. There is no reason to doubt that this element of Irish culture has survived longer and to a greater extent than elsewhere, and that Irish people attach a greater importance to the words of songs than peoples with a less traumatised experience. In the modern pop-saturated world, the Irish mind behaves little differently than it always did. 'Part of what we should be grateful to our colonial masters for is that the very fact that they oppressed us taught us how to contain something at a subliminal level,' says Ivor Browne. 'We became experts at serving the explicit culture and yet keeping a whole part of ourselves hidden. We became masters of subversion.'

Most of that school tradition that we had was derived from the British public school. Usually human beings will imitate the aristocracy. We didn't have an aristocracy, so we had this ambivalence all the time: what was respectable was English, and yet we hated it. In one way it helped us to preserve some remnants of our old culture. A lot of it, I think, was preserved unconsciously. If you take the whole verbal tradition, there was an enormous unconscious awareness of the value of what we had. Otherwise, why would they have held on to it so tenaciously? The pipes, the music, the singing, the remnants of the language, and particularly the poetic tradition. Somewhere in the psyche we knew this once had been aristocratic, or valued, that it had its own intrinsic value, and yet we had been told, generation after generation, that it was nothing. So on the surface it was to be derided and made to appear as if it were no longer there. Underneath, remnants of it – and a surprising amount – were kept alive.

The Irish personality can sometimes appear to be mortally wounded. Forget about our seemingly congenital inability to manage our own affairs. Look at the way we walk, the flicker of fear in the corner of an eye, the unspeakable hurt behind a glance or a question. An Englishman in Dublin walks up to a Garda and asks him directions. 'Can you tell me the way to O'Connell Street?' An Irishman in London says, 'You wouldn't know the way to Piccadilly Circus, I suppose,' inviting, as Ivor Browne smilingly avers, the inevitable, 'Yes I most certainly would!' The language is the same, the words are the same, both frame their need in the form of a question, but the difference between them is the difference between master and slave.

'When you go into a shop and say, "You haven't a packet of cigarettes, have you?" it's coming out,' my psychiatrist informs me. 'That's anticipating derision and refusal. So you make it as an apology. And there's all sorts of phrases like that. The "Sorry" count. We're *constantly* apologising. But behind it there's this anger and subversion. There were two dimensions to it: there was the hurt and the oppression diminishing what we might be, and there was the subversive skill of maintaining something below that, which you never let them see. But it survived.'

And, having survived, it trickles and gushes underneath until it finds a way to the surface, like a spring. 'The soul of the enslaved and broken nation,' as Pearse wrote in *The Spiritual Nation*, 'may conceivably be a more splendid thing than the soul of a free nation.' Professor Browne continues:

> Yes, and there seems to be some quality of it, the very fact of it being dammed off seems to increase the pressure and tension. There's this paradox where you have enriched environments which you think should produce creativity and you get this sort of flat Swedish slab. And where you've a miserable environment which got suffering, it's as if it honed the pressures and finally burst out. That's a strange paradox which would mean that, now we are able to be much freer, our creativity will be dissipated. It's almost as if, by virtue of being inhibited, it was building up more and more pressure. There must be some truth in that, because you see it in the various ghetto

cultures, provided there's something there to begin with. The Jews had it in their scholarly tradition, and as soon as they got up a tunnel they burst out. And the same with Irish people who go to America – people who had an inferior school record here – over there you find them racing ahead of Americans. So there's something in that paradox of damming up the expression and actually increasing the expression.

And this is where U2 begin to try to explain themselves. In a certain light, they appear as a kind of cultural advance-party, checking out the terrain of the future for the rest of the tribe to follow on. The questions they ask in their music are sometimes eclipsed by the questions their music asks.

'How do you start with a clean sheet?' Bono frames such a question and then attempts to sketch the place in which the answer may lie.

Nicodemus said, 'Do I have to crawl back into my mother's womb?' And Christ says, 'Yeah!' Because no matter how clean the environment is . . . and the behaviourists have ruled the world for a hundred years – and it's over now, thanks to Chomsky. I mean it really *is*. It's a whole new position in human behaviour and the way we've developed. Environment is shrinking in terms of the perception of its influence.

Look at the Bible and what it says about line. Have you ever tried to *read* one of those books? Such and such begat such and such begat such and such, and it goes on for *weeks*. This area of discussion to me is central to what we have to talk about. How is it that a group that goes so far away from what is called Irish can be so Irish? And I have another theory on this, if you can take this. Fasten your safety belt!

I was sitting on Sunset Strip, having come out of Sunset Sound, where we recorded *Rattle and Hum*, and I was just sitting there on Friday night watching the parade. And it's an extraordinary thing to see. I was watching this Mexican truck-hopping. Have you ever seen that – they can make the trucks jump? And the sounds, *ooooph shihht ptt aatthh, phfpptt phit phfpptt! Wwwgruggggh!! – Chaaaiill!!! Ptt acchh hhauh! Achica-baba-bimp-bah!* And I was going, '*Wow!!*' This *sound*! Like cars *as* stereos! They're putting wheels on their sound systems and climbing inside them and this music is coming across. And this thought came to me in that moment: I've heard this music before – when we were in Africa. This was essentially atonal, call-and-response music, just like the music that you hear out in the bush, where people are banging on cans and going, '*Hyyyyiiiaah puuttcch-chi-puuttch-chi Cuumoonn Babe-baay Cumonaaden.*' And all this. And I thought to myself,

'How is it that kids from the Bronx who had no idea of the structure of the music of their forefathers have, through technology, rediscovered it? How is that? That three hundred years ago, or whatever it was, slave traders brought West Africans to America, and there the slave managers stopped them playing the drums, allowed them to sing, gave them the three chords from the jigs and the reels – eventually it turns into gospel music, as they adopt Christianity. Gospel music has its own reverse side, which is the blues, and the blues and gospel sort of come together in rock 'n' roll, where the beat comes back – they suddenly get their hands on drums – they're not congos, and they're not talking drums, but it's a drum*kit*, that comes through jazz. And suddenly this drumkit that comes through jazz is now back to the very basics. And this mutates through rock 'n' roll, Elvis, it comes back to England. You get the electric – the fuzzbox, the little printed circuits that create the distorted signal in the electric guitar gets you Jimi Hendrix. The blues takes on another mode. It goes back to Europe again, rock 'n' roll as part of popular culture, and Kraftwerk, working with machines. Still it's considered part of music and all the rest. It goes back to America and starts to influence dance music there. The drum machine. Next thing you have people like George Clinton coming out – he starts fiddling with these machines. The sampler is then invented in England, by Sinclair or whoever – where you can snatch sounds. It's usually very arty groups that are snatching, you know, the sound of a cup, or whatever. You start making a symphony with a cup. But it goes back across to the US and George Clinton and people start using it, and then suddenly in the Bronx they discover that they can sample their own records. So there's this journey – this extraordinary journey – through technology, and you get to the state on the streets in the late seventies and early eighties, in New York, in the ghetto – African music has returned to its purest state. So what does that say about line? Because that's a knowledge that . . . That's no 'Here's your heritage – go now and play with the talking drums there Johnny.' This is *people*. They are it. It is in them – that language. That is their language. You couldn't put a bigger obstacle course in front of what it is to be black. It is an extraordinary journey to get back to where you started. It really did blow my mind.

Hold on a mo, Bono, I think Professor Browne is itching to get back in.

This is what I mean about the importance of subversion. Rap music is a subversive language from Harlem. I think the creativity is coming out of it because of that suppression, like a pressure cooker. The ghetto is very important. If you take jazz in New Orleans. If that happened in 1994, and someone as creative as Louis Armstrong appeared, he'd have been taken out of New Orleans in weeks, and jazz would never happened. It needs the oppression and the pressure in order for it to have time to ferment. It's not the Michael Jacksons who create the music, it's the kids on the street. It's to do with some deep spring of creativity that, when shut off in us, given any channel will start to come out.

One of the things you have to realise with Irish music is that it's an old musical language that goes back behind the present classical tradition. And if you impose classical type influences on it, they don't fit well, because it actually has more relationship to Indian or North African music – the use of the natural scale. A natural musician will go back to those natural notes. And that's why you'll find the exact same blue note in Irish music as you do in jazz, which is derived from Indian music, and particularly in blues. But of course other musics too don't just go in half-tones. There's a lot of little tones in between. The Arabs do it, the Indians do it, and the *sean-nós* singers do it. Part of it is the modes, and a lot of Irish music would be on the modal scale; in other words it doesn't use many black notes. And there's also the use of quarter-tones. On the instruments you won't hear them playing much in the way of quarter-tones, but the singers do. And that's why you get a much older link back to Indian music.

Only our rivers, the song would have it, run free. But what if these were to include the rivers of words and sounds within ourselves? Bono smiles his 'what-if?' smile and says:

We Irish have developed a new form of the English language, more ornate, more like our native language. Even Joyce – his revenge on the English language by distorting it, mangling it, and twisting it. And Beckett the same. Fucking up the language, bending it, boxing it, as if to spit it out, or maybe to make it our own. And if you go further along this line, what else do we have? What else has come up out of the past? It's obvious to me that it's not just going to be poor eyesight that's handed down, or strength, or a particular bent, but that other stuff is going to be coming down the line as well. And if that's happening on the positive, it's going to be happening on the negative side as well. It means there's baggage that comes down. It might explain the kind of hatred that goes beyond logic in our island – that isn't explainable by one generation. A friend of mine, a painter, who's from the North and married a Catholic, was saying when he hears rebel songs the hairs go up on the back of his neck. He becomes full of hate. And he can't explain it. And he was saying, 'It's like it's in my genes.' And I was thinking, 'Well, maybe it is!' And is that what Christ was all about – you have to be born again? And the guy says, 'Wha? You mean crawl back into your mother's belly?' And I love that idea! You have to literally start again. To be free of the baggage of your forefathers, as well as your own. So this is a century based on your own baggage – psychoanalysis, your relationship with your dad, environmentalism, behaviourism . . . But maybe the line goes deeper. I'm so freaked out by this idea – that we have baggage personally, but we also have it as nations. And I am truly convinced that, both personally and on a grand scale, you have to deal with this idea of line, and the past. This Catholic thing is amazing, the Catholic idea of repentance. It's an incredible thing. And one can confess to a priest, to a friend, to whatever one sees as God; or, you can write songs. Talk shows are where Americans go to confession. But it's the *getting out* – this thing of confession. They are all the ways which, through music and through movies, a nation looks at itself. For instance, in America, the Vietnam movies – that is the way America faced up to what it had done in Vietnam. *The Deerhunter, Apocalypse Now* – here it was, facing itself – something the politicians couldn't admit was coming out through the movies. And to me, without sounding too pretentious, there's a kind of healing in that. The truth of it is that, through those movies, some may have repented about what they did to America and the American Dream; they still haven't repented about what they did to Vietnam.

And I suppose what I'm sensing as a musician is, 'I'm Irish – I can explode what it is to be Irish, because I'm *still* Irish. You can cut it up in as many pieces as you like, but it's *still* Irish. Smash it with a hammer, but it's still Irish.'

CHAPTER NINETEEN

The Hazel Rod

The bystanders would ask to have a try.
He handed them the rod without a word.
It lay dead in their grasp till nonchalantly
He gripped expectant wrists. The hazel stirred.
Seamus Heaney, 'The Diviner'

The music of U2, taken either in its entirety or separate parts, is still much more than the sum of obvious ingredients. If you attempt to understand it in terms of conventional rock 'n' roll genealogy, it doesn't make a lot of sense. There is much in the music that appears mysterious, that seems to have emanated from some place which cannot be located by means of the known archaeology of pop.

The music is not something the band 'thinks up'. In a sense its meaning and source are beyond the comprehension of the individual members of U2. Bono once said that one time in the studio he tried to play the guitar like The Edge. He plugged the guitar in like The Edge did, set up the machines the way he did, got the same plectrum and played the same chords. What came out was 'a pitiful noise'.

The Edge plays the guitar like a divining rod, the forked hazel stick of Heaney's poem. The pluck comes sharp as a sting and the music is summoned from God knows where – 'Spring water suddenly broadcasting/ Through a green aerial its secret stations'.

U2 did not grow out of any tradition. They had no roots in blues, rhythm 'n' blues, soul, gospel or rock 'n' roll. Neither did they appear to have any overt connection with the ancient tradition of Irish music, or even with its more modern expressions. They stood alone, more or less, an immaculate conception. It was as if the pearl of U2 had formed around the soul of a grain of sand, but the grain itself was absent. They began with their roots 'in space somewhere'.

Or did they? The question of ancestry in culture, Greil Marcus writes simply and definitively in *Lipstick Traces*, 'is spurious'. Why? Because 'every new manifestation in culture rewrites the past, changes old maudits

234

into new heroes, old heroes into those who should have never been born. New actors scavenge the past for ancestors, because ancestry is legitimacy and novelty is doubt – but in all times forgotten actors emerge from the past not as ancestors but as familiars.' This happened, as Marcus notes, in the rock 'n' roll of the 1960s, with the rediscovery and veneration of the 1930 bluesman Robert Johnson; it happened, too, in Ireland in the 1960s when the folk revival rehabilitated a whole generation of ignored traditional and folk musicians. Ancestry is in the eye of the inheritor.

U2 never had any problems with their irrefutable novelty. From time to time they may have fretted about their lack of obvious roots. But it should not be forgotten that this, in the beginning, was an advantage. Most of their contemporaries had roots that were only too obvious. The lightness of U2's baggage allowed them to step deftly through the minefields of cliché and prejudice.

The ways in which culture is transmitted are manifold and mostly invisible to the cognitive eye. Even in a primitive setting there is enough confusion to advise caution against straight, sweeping connections. Recording, and the ceaseless flow of radio and television, have given us infinite cause for both confusion and wariness. There are certain things we can say, certain elements we can record, to sketch in the parameters this side of an infinity of possibilities. In keeping with our virtual unknowingness, it is necessary to adopt a demeanour of boundless humility.

We can observe, for instance, that Paul Hewson's father, Bobby, a post office worker, had dabbled, as a young man, in oil painting, that he also loved opera and that, before he was married, he used to sing in musical societies around the Dublin of the 1940s, but that thereafter he confined himself to the odd piece of light opera while performing his morning ablutions. Or we note, for the sake of noting it, that Bobby's father was a sometime stand-up comedian in the Dublin of his time. Or we observe that The Edge's father, Garvin Evans, was a founder member of the Dublin Welsh Male Voice Choir, and that his mother, Gwenda, was a member of the Malahide Musical Society. We observe such things and write them lightly on the page.

The list of pop references to be found in early accounts of U2 is at one level eclectic and in another sense confined: Led Zeppelin, Peter Frampton, Deep Purple, Fleetwood Mac, the Bay City Rollers, the Sweet, David Bowie, David Essex, Rory Gallagher, the Rolling Stones; later on we pick up dropped names like the Clash, the Sex Pistols, Television and Patti Smith. All four members of U2 will list somewhat differing sets of formative musical experiences, but, by and large, the mix is pretty much what you'd find in any random group of four teenage boys of their time who had grown up listening to Radio Luxemburg and their older siblings' record collections.

The general U2 experience, as Adam remembers it, was most interesting because, although it was unexceptional, it seems in retrospect to contain shapes of a different way of relating to a normal pop experience, but which emerge transformed in the U2 story. 'I can remember pre-punk and post-punk,' Adam recalls. 'I can remember pre-punk listening to Led Zeppelin, Black Sabbath, Ted Nugent – and not *connecting* but knowing that there was *something* there that I liked and that it brought me into contact with other people. I think Larry's association with music was probably much more chart-orientated; the local disco. Edge was probably more of a technical musician because of his background, with his father and the choir, and playing the piano – that kind of musicality. So he would have studied music, but not identified in a lifestyle way perhaps. And Bono, again, the fantasy of David Bowie, the glam years, Lou Reed, the lyrical dimension, the lifestyle connection, Bob Dylan.'

Norman Hewson is almost eight years older than his brother Paul. His record collection included the standard mix of Rolling Stones, Who, Bowie, Hendrix. These were the first records the young Bono began paying attention to. He remembers:

> I was about twelve when I heard this duo. I thought it was like Simon and Garfunkel: David Bowie and Hunky Dory! I thought their album was very good! I was really into them. I remember being into metal music as one would be into motorbikes, having much more to do with hormones than anything else. And actually then realising that it wasn't really where I was at. And old Stones records. About 1975, I got into the Stones, the Beach Boys. The *Beach Boys*! I was really interested in them. I remember in 1976, taking the Beach Boys into the band and saying, 'This kind of rock 'n' roll, this three-chord thing, this is where we're at. This is the future. And the Stones. We should stop playing all these horrible cover versions of Rory Gallagher – or, *trying* to play them – because we *can't*. Edge can, but *we* can't.' And knowing this, and then when punk happened and Adam came back from working in London, this is what we talked about. And we said, 'This is *it*! This is what we talked about! It's happening *now*! And it's called *punk*!

'When punk came along,' says Adam, 'suddenly all the things that we were *feeling* about being able to express ourselves and be understood, were naively expressed within punk in a very manufactured way. And we went with that. And punk kind of freed us up to just get on with the job of exploring what it was – what it could be. Because all those other bands were studied, they were *formed*. They weren't organic. Somebody was the songwriter and the singer, and they collected some guy who played guitar quite well, and a drummer, and they were forced to stick together and work together. Whereas, we really just said, "This is where we're at. These are the tools that we have available to us. And let's use them." '

Eamon Dunphy records in *Unforgettable Fire* that one of the pieces The Edge played at the first get-together of the nascent U2 precursor, Feedback, was the guitar piece from 'Blister on the Moon', by Taste, then at the height of their popularity in Britain, with the Irishman Rory Gallagher on guitar. 'It was one of the songs that, as a budding guitar-player, I wanted to figure out,' said The Edge in 1993.

> I couldn't play it now. I think it was just a riff. I don't think I could actually play the *song*. The Irish guitar players were obviously Rory and the guys from Thin Lizzy. They were the guys that were doing it, so there was obviously a connection there. They represented, I suppose, the success-stories of Irish guitar playing. Looking back now, I think my approach to guitar and both Rory Gallagher's and the guys from Thin Lizzy would be very different. At that stage, the furthest thing from my mind was to join a group. They seemed to be happy to work within the form, to accept its principles and groundrules – of the blues in Rory's case and straight rock in Thin Lizzy's case. So I don't know if I would still find what they were doing as interesting as I did then, when I was a fifteen-year-old picking up a guitar for the first time and not knowing what to do with it. But I suppose that you are what you eat. Even the stuff I ate back then is still coming through!

The young U2 were experimenting, but what they were looking for was something off the beaten track. They may have heard the same music as others of their generation, but what they heard *in it* does not seem to be what others heard. Most aspiring musicians spoke about music as a technical competency; The Edge seemed to want to pass through the technique phase as quickly as possible, to get to a place no one else seemed to know about. Listening to him play, it is possible to see that he filleted much of what constituted his formative influences, taking from them the things that others missed often just the smallest splinter of style or sound. While most young guitarists looked to Rory Gallagher for speed and technique, The Edge seems to have taken merely the idea of an energy seething just this side of violence. He then moved on, oblivious of fashion or calculation, to seek what he was looking for in every available crevice. The Edge has never shown the slightest disposition towards gunslinger guitar-playing. He seemed, from as far back as we can see, to feel that the point was about something else altogether. Before long he had picked up on the most recent wave of US punk, the New York scene of Television and Patti Smith.

> I had friends at school who were in garage bands and they were into John McLaughlin and the Mahavishnu Orchestra and all this kind of thing, and it really did used to leave me cold. I mean, you could appreciate it, but it did not connect in any way. And albums like *Horses* and *Marquee Moon*, and seeing the Jam on *Top of the Pops*, and the first singles from Tom Petty. It just seemed that around that time there was so much happening. And that music was just, by comparison, so potent, and connected so strongly. Listening to Tom Verlaine and Television proved to me that it was about using your judgement and your brain, rather than your fingers. That's where the important work would happen. It wasn't about the ability to squeeze as many notes into the bar as possible – it was really just about approach, and I suppose, *ideas*. And, yeah, I suppose I just rejected that white blues thing, which I still don't get.

The skill factor, or the lack of it, was not the issue. If punk did nothing else for the embryonic U2 – and it possibly didn't – it liberated them from the tyranny of competence which had ruled the Dublin rock scene. Adam Clayton remembers that, 'In the world out there, people played in bar bands and could play very fast riffs. They were still crap. In the pub-rock circuit of Dublin in the seventies, I don't think those players were really as good as everyone gave them credit for. They would learn a set of covers, and because we were all so badly educated, we thought it was really good and really exciting. I wonder, if we went back now and saw the Jimi Slevin band, if we would really go "Oh *Yeahh*!"'

The Edge remembers even the earliest U2 perspective as being focused on ends rather than means.

> I think we have a very open-minded approach to influences. They can come to us from anywhere, and any time in music. It's not that we see ourselves as part of a tradition we're following, particularly. I think because we're trying to define something that is our own, it's by definition *without* a tradition. And maybe that's been the ethos of the band from the beginning. Coming out of punk was our interpretation of that. What we saw it as being about was describing the past and trying to find the essence of the overall spirit in music. The generation of Irish musicians before us were most definitely part of a tradition. You could see where they were coming from, and trace it back. And we did go through a period when we

tried that out, but it didn't ultimately ring true for us. I suppose we've never had an obvious tradition, and we found that trying to plug into one ended up sounding false for us.

I think that need to define ourselves in some way has been with the group from pretty much the beginning. It's hard to say why it turned out the way it did the last few records, why we suddenly ended up where we ended up. It's a combination of following the music – and, as corny as that sounds, a lot of the time that's what it is – but also that you have programmed yourself to some extent. And maybe because you don't have a tradition to be able to relax into, we are as a band a lot more aware of what's happening, what's going on. Because everything, for us, creatively, has always been in that state of flux anyway. You kind of need to find new answers to the same questions every time you go and make a record. And I suppose, the world that's out there led us to get into this Zoo TV thing.

The Edge is a sort of Samuel Beckett in rock 'n' roll guitar playing. He plays the guitar as though to *uninvent* it. He performs the miracle of loaves and fishes in reverse, spiriting the plenitude back into the basket until it has been reduced to the strictly necessary. There is no waste, no excess. As Beckett seemed to regard each word he had to write as an imposition to be weighed carefully before it was lumbered on the page, so The Edge seems to seek a logic that avoids the superfluous or the showy. His is a minimalism which seems to arise not from an inability to play, but from a desire to play as little as is meaningful. 'I think of notes as being expensive,' he says. 'You don't just throw them around.' He scrambles across the devastated territory of guitar idiocy and excess, conscious of the precise value of everything that has been done up until now. He must know the clichés in order to avoid them. He must know how to avoid them and how to hide the fact that he is avoiding them. The Edge is either the Last Guitar Hero or the First Guitar Anti-Hero, but because he comes at the end of rock 'n' roll history, he must avoid heroics. He must be original, yet knowing; conservative, yet subversive; cautious, yet explosive. He searches for unexplored territory, or perhaps for a new way of *seeing* the ground that has been trampled to crap. He says:

> From the beginning, I guess that's one of the things that we took out of the post-punk era – the sense that finding your own voice within a well-established form was the most important thing. Whether it was guitar, or drums-bass, or as a singer and lyricist – to *avoid the clichés*. We didn't see it as a 'craft' in that sense of getting closer to perfection within an already established form. We saw it as some-

thing very personal, and something that spoke about *us* in our specific situation. We had no interest in retreading the ground other bands had already been over. That's not to say we weren't prepared to borrow the ideas or sound, sounds, whatever, and reapply them in our own way. We always, from the very beginning, felt that the band should have its own unique identity musically. So that really formed our approach to songwriting and recording, and playing live as well.

Bono once said that he started out seeing his voice as an instrument. He was as interested as much in the sound of the words as he was in their sense: 'the way they bumped against each other'. On the other hand, somebody – it may have been Bono – said that The Edge played the guitar like a singer who didn't sing. He seemed to reach beyond the sonic content of the music, to be in touch with some underlying quality. As in no other band that I'm aware of it, the music of U2 is a *unity* of all its parts. There is no sense that the music can be divided into its constituent elements – into voice, guitar, rhythm section, backing, accompaniment. It comes to you whole, maybe because that is the way it is imagined. The Edge plays the guitar, as Bono sings, Larry hits the drums or Adam plays the bass, not as an end in itself, but in order to serve the song. Voice and instruments are united in a single purpose: they *tell the story*. The guitar doesn't *make sounds*; it *says things*. You can see the difference between The Edge and other guitar players from the way he holds the instrument, the way he prowls the stage. Sometimes it's like the guitar is dragging him along, sometimes as if it's fighting him. Other guitar players – with the exception of a small handful, including Jimi Hendrix – wield the instrument as though it were a bodily member, and provide an auto-erotic performance. Hendrix played as though the guitar was an instrument for receiving sounds from the air, as though by holding it a certain way he could pick up things that nobody had ever found until that moment. The Edge, similarly, doesn't so much play U2's music to the crowd as play their *version* of it for them. He seems to follow the guitar around, trying to find a position in which it will receive a clear signal. It is as though the music is being received by the audience through him, and the process is making him sweat and run and stretch for every stray note of it. It's as though the instrument and the musician have reversed roles. It's not like The Edge playing the guitar at all; more like the guitar playing The Edge.

I think that was probably born out of the music that we were listening to at the very beginning. It was during the era of 'Shoot Led Zeppelin', 'Death to Hippies'. And guitar solos, if they happened at all, were generally very short and abrasive. It was not guitar players showing off, it was more a blurting out of some sort of expression of feeling. It was much more expressive than it was about technique or whatever. So I suppose, as we carried on, we took that on board as a band. I was much more comfortable playing songs than playing the guitar. We thought in terms of *songs*. It just seemed that to be a band meant playing *together*, working towards the same *thing*. We didn't really think that out either; it just seemed natural. It seemed the obvious way to go.

The Edge serves the music, always. He plays as though in a field of energy created by the band; where he stands, where he walks, how he attacks the instrument, appears to be dictated by the presence and position of the other three members of U2. His instrument, too, picks up things that nobody else can do other than hear, but it's as though he can do it only within the aura and field of energy which U2 creates.

I suppose I'm trying to really connect, in an emotional sense. That's, I suppose, where what I do would cross over into what a singer does. I've always had this thing where I'm drawn to those notes and those phrases that seem to take a piece of music into another place, emotionally. I just guess that's my thing. I don't think that came from other groups, except I guess maybe from Patti Smith – but not her guitar playing – her music, more. Television were not an emotional group. I suppose the group, or the artist, that had that, in a completely different way, was Bruce Springsteen. Again, not in his guitar-playing, but like in the saxophone playing of Clarence Clemmons or in the piano or whatever. Wherever it was, he had that thing, that connection. And I was only looking for that, as a guitar player.

Those who look, then, for the genealogy of The Edge's guitar style in the pantheon of rock guitarists are searching in the wrong place.

'Yeah, maybe,' he thinks about this. 'Yeah. Because I'm not a great technical player. I don't draw on techniques loaned from other people. I'm much, much more instinctive, and therefore there really isn't any technical heritage or genealogy that I'm part of. I guess we just started out making it up as we went along, and found that it worked for us. It's hard sometimes, because we don't really have a craft to rely on. You are, in a lot of cases, as we describe it sometimes, "songwriting by accident". You're relying on inspiration to arrive in the middle of improvisations when you're half-asleep in the middle of soundchecks, and you do something and suddenly it sparks you. You can't really formularise it.'

If pushed to give three reasons for U2's success, I would list the following: the fact that they couldn't play properly, the fact that they were friends and thought of that friendship as an important aspect of what they were doing, and the fact that everything they did subsequently was centred on supporting the community of inexperience which they comprised. Some attempts to explain the band seek to focus on the logical consequences of this implicit manifesto: their choice of the right manager, the right record company, the right roadcrew, the right producer. Make no mistake about it: all these are vital elements of the U2 success story. In a medium like rock 'n' roll, and especially the level at which U2 operate, the processes of the form are almost impossible to separate into neat categories like 'creative', 'production', 'management', etc. Paul McGuinness's role, for example, has clearly been central to the U2 success story. McGuinness brought a number of key ideas to the band from the beginning which streamlined their partnership in a way that freed it up in creative terms. It was he who created the organisation which protects and supports the creative dimension of the band. It was McGuinness, too, who in the early days pushed the band towards the US rather than Britain, recognising the cultural bias against Irish music – indeed things Irish in general – in the UK. He it was who encouraged them to publish on a cooperative basis, which meant that writing credits and royalties were divided evenly between the four. This provided a strong cohesive force in the band, eliminating the kind of internal squabbling which has riven many bands at critical moments in their careers. Paul McGuinness later fought successfully to get back ownership of the band's publishing, making them virtually unique in rock 'n' roll in terms of control over their own material. All of these things, as well as innumerable contributions by hundreds of others, have their place in the U2 story. But ultimately they are, every one, incidental. The essence of U2 is now the same as it was at the beginning. It comes down to four men and the nature of their friendships with one another. Above all other considerations, these friendships have been the cornerstones of their achievement.

'The organism,' says Bono, 'the artform for U2 is the organisation. It's our ability to cooperate and move together. To be creative. It's not as simple as the music, or the videos or whatever. The business to me is as much a part of that as the music. It's all a thing. It's all about negotiation, and people from very different backgrounds working together. That's the thing that Brian Eno goes on about. The thing of cooperation, the way we work with each other, around each other. He says, "That's the thing."'

The Edge agrees:

We are a band probably like no other band that I've ever heard of, certainly that's been successful, in that the friendships are still intact, and in the whole respect that's still there, and in that the love's still there, and friendship, whatever. We've survived through the difficult times, and been successful, or whatever, with everything still working. And definitely I think the reason is that it's a healthy cooperative. We all realise how we benefit from interaction with the other members of the band. I think we all need one another. So that creates a kind of stability. And I think we all realise we wouldn't be having half as much fun if we were doing something else. We try and focus everything back into, in terms of music and stage production, back to the idea of the group of four people. Obviously Bono is the point of focus, but it's all centred back on the group. So I guess that we're all aware that ultimately *that* is the most unique thing about what we're doing – the fact that it's the four guys that are doing it, and it's their personality coming through, and the combinations of Adam-Larry, Larry-Edge, Adam-Edge, Bono-Adam – all those interactive relationships make what U2 does what it is.

The determination of the four to come together, stay together and stick together is something that is inextricable from the reputation for integrity they have earned with their music. The history of rock 'n' roll – and Irish rock 'n' roll more than elsewhere – is littered with the corpses of bands that broke up before they rightly began. Musical differences, personality incompatibility, personal rivalries, have attacked the creative capacities of the best bands in the world. U2's determination not to let that happen to them allowed them to overcome shortcomings which would have left other bands dead in the water. Once these four young men had found each other, the all-or-nothing instinct seemed to both protect and nurture them.

Adam Clayton says:

I think it was within all the individuals. I think it's probably within everyone at that age. A certain amount of it, I suppose, could be called Christian principles: not wishing to compromise and not wishing to sell your brother down the river, believing in your own viewpoint, your own vision of what it was that you are and what was to be achieved. In the beginning it was just, 'We can do this without compromising and through our own effort. We can learn what this is about and make music that transcends the everyday situation, which is what we consider successful and great music to be.' And also there was a certain amount of trepidation; we didn't want to have to sleep with the managing director of a record company to get a record deal. And we knew Larry wouldn't agree to it anyway! We didn't want to be marketed as a pop band, because we were very young. That was an easy route to go down. We didn't want to alienate anyone, we didn't want to fire anyone in the band. Initially record company people would come along and say

[Cockney accent], 'The band's alright. Songs are okay. But the drummer can't play. Think about getting a new drummer?' All that kind of shit, you know. 'Your image is wrong.' And we said, 'No, that's not what we're about. We're not a one-hit wonder. We'll get there eventually. Thanks for your comments, but we're not signing a deal under those circumstances.'

I think very much that that is an Irish thing. And although I'm not born and bred Irish – having lived here for long enough for it to be my natural state now, I think it's very much, when you come from this island, there is a natural instinct to stick together outside of it or whatever. And knowing that although they can silver-tongue you to death out there, you do know where you're from and what your abilities are, and you kind of keep it within that particular family.

This solidarity carries through into the core of the music. In other bands, with the possible exception of the Beatles, everyone seemed to fill in a particular part of what was created. With U2, the music goes beyond the normal arithmetic to acquire a geometric dimension – there is a multiplier at work; the whole is greater than the sum of each member's input.

The cliché has it that U2's music developed out of their musical limitations. This is literally true. Another way of putting it is to say that it grew out of the internal sets of loyalties in the band. What makes the music function as a unit is both its vigilance against cliché and the codes it developed to serve this instinct. This was not wholly deliberate, a large part of it arising from the initial musical weaknesses of the individual band members. It was usual in the early days for contemporaries to dismiss U2 because they couldn't play. The most generous assessment held that, okay, maybe The Edge could play a bit. Maybe if he got himself a decent rhythm section . . . And as for that *eejit* of a singer . . . Adam Clayton got into the band by pretending he could play the bass. He then bluffed through until he had established his indispensability in other respects. The early U2 developed a distinctive sound by compensating for one another's deficiencies.

The Edge says:

First of all, you've got to be *interested* in doing something new, and not rehashing old ideas. And then your limitations actually start to help you to define what it is that you're gonna do. We were really, I suppose, quite limited musically, and therefore our options were not huge. But then options just complicate your life, sometimes, musically speaking. So I do see it as a strength. It's hard to remember back to the early discussions about what way we were going to go, but in terms of our approach and in terms of our choices musically, the overall sound of the band at that point was really a direct result of a single approach to playing, and just a highly developed sense of what was good, without necessarily a good technical ability to back it up. We just kept working till we found something we knew was the real thing. And I think, had we been more versatile, we would probably have made our *first* idea sound right, rather than pushing on and on until we found something that was really great without needing to be given, in a technical sense, that high-gloss finish.

It was, for example, Adam's idiosyncratic bass playing which pulled The Edge up from the bottom end of the sound spectrum and required him to fill in the spaces with filigree chopping rhythms. The bass and guitar in U2 are complementary of one another much more than in other bands, as though, in a certain way, they are a single instrument. And yet another aspect of the band is that nothing is true except in the most general way. Sometimes Adam follows the melody while the guitar goes *dhigga-dhigga-dhigga*, filling in the space. Then again, Adam provides a rhythm, or goes around the back of the melody like a real bassist. There are almost no rules, and only the broadest general patterns. Both Adam and The Edge carry out several roles, but often in the wrong places, depending on who's there in the right place at the right time, and who happens to be at a loose end right at that moment. The Edge agrees:

> Yeah. Sometimes in the wrong places. In a lot of cases, Larry and me are almost the rhythm section. And Adam is providing the driving force, and in some cases underpinning Bono's melody. So he's taking on a very important role musically. And again, that was not really a plan; that was just the way Adam played, and the way I compensated in order to keep the sound, I suppose. I think in those early days, Adam and Larry formed a powerful, solid base. But what I discovered was that the echo, in a lot of cases, gave me, and gave the band, more polyrhythmic aspects, which in other groups might have been provided by the rhythm section, or by another rhythm guitar player, or a percussionist, or whatever. So those roles, as you've said, were almost reversed. There's a lot of examples of how the guitar had a much more rhythmic role than in most other groups. That just happened, I suppose.
>
> At that time, all we were interested in was melody and getting the idea across in as energetic a way as possible – or as *vital* a way as possible. So it was a real stripped-down sound. In an obvious sense, we weren't interested in brass sections or lots of overdubs. And rhythm wasn't high on our priority list. We weren't trying to make any statements in rhythm. So it really did come down to what Adam

and I together could do to support the melody that Bono was singing. We used to jam together a lot, as a four piece, but essentially, once the backbeat was established, it was really only Adam and myself, trying our different things.

Listening back to our early albums, the arrangements between bass and guitar are a lot more intricate probably than the arrangements of the more recent songs. And I suppose that's because that's where our energy was at that time – this marriage between the two guitars and finding out what you could do with two guitar voices. And we discovered that there was *a lot* you could do. A few reviews of our first record, *Boy*, started to examine it in a very analytical way. I remember some review in, I think it was the *Village Voice* in New York, approached the album from a music-theory critical standpoint, and I couldn't understand what he was talking about. He was going on about the 'fifth interval' and it being part of a well-drawn tradition in Irish music. To us it was an instinctive thing – certain sounds and certain modes that one gravitated to. The use of the drone as a thread through a lot of those early songs. These things came through instinctively without us having to think about it. And after – *after* – as we started to know what we were doing – we started to realise what it was. *Now* I can see *to some extent* what it was. But to some extent I'm also still in the same position as I was then, which is a kind of naive appreciator – a naive writer. In terms of the music, for me it *works* or it *doesn't work*. I don't analyse things too much. I think that instinct, in musical terms, is a much stronger force than pure analysis of what you're doing. I'm still blown away by some of the things on those early records, just in terms of their sophistication – and yet their simplicity. That was the thing which, in those early records, we seemed to at times hit on – this combination, that minimalism, which is something that I still value, and even early on, the intricacy of the structures of songs, which is pretty interesting.

Adam Clayton may never be a great bass player. What he is great at is being Adam. What others perceive as his weaknesses are, in the context of U2, the very resources he makes most use of. There is a technical limitation, he maintains, that he wouldn't want to get beyond.

I prefer as a player to mine my own self. And with each record I do grow. But my interest in growing moves around the culture. Sometimes I want to play better as a blues player. Or I want to understand the construction of country music. At the same time I could listen to Nirvana, and say, 'Yeah, I remember when that was what excited me about bass playing', and I can use everything that I've learned since to go back to that. When I want something simpler, that stands out and says 'Listen to me!' I've got a loud, aggressive, nasty sound there. So I've found that the influences and anchors by which you come to a bass part are taken from all different reference points now, and your interest changes.

Adam maintains that, even in the grip of the most advanced technology the medium can offer, U2 continue to play to their limitations.

It's interesting when people say, 'Well, now you're using sequencers and stuff' – but it's the same methodology. Our limitations on our primary instruments have taken us as far as we can go with those limitations. And our openness to new ways of using those limitations is what has progressed the band. We've said, 'Oh yeah, that's relevant to us to use a sequencer, because we ain't never gonna learn how to play, you know "Stairway to Heaven", so we might as well steal it.' So it's the same thing being progressed forward as technology is there to help us.

I can hear now in bands when people aren't playing together, in a way that I never could before. I think Larry and myself are an essential backdrop to what Edge does. I think Larry and myself are so strong now that Edge has a lot of freedom. But I think his influences always come back to what we're doing. And it's quite interesting when we're writing a song – somebody will have . . . call it a riff, but there will be a bit of melody in whatever part somebody is doing . . . and you'll hear that melody go to different instruments in the course of the development of that song. Bono will take a melody that maybe started on the guitar, that I took to the bass while Edge moved on and developed his parts more, and I kept the essential parts of that melody, Bono will then pick up on a tiny section of that and that'll become part of his melody for the vocal. So it does move around. And the influences are very internal to the band.

In a sense every instrument get its moment at the microphone. In the development of a song, everyone's a singer.

'Yeah,' says Adam. 'And in ways it does catalogue the development of the song, because then you get into the overdubs, and an overdub that you don't use in the final mix again becomes the root for another melody. I don't know if there are other bands that have achieved that closeness, long-term, because I think a lot of bands tend to separate, move to LA. It's more of a day job. Somebody writes a song and passes the tape around. But to us it's a very integral way in which we work. And it's very important to us that we have a relationship between us that works.'

The complex nature of the internal sets of relationships in the band, as expressed in the music, provides one explanation for why, until recently, so few U2 songs were successfully covered by other artists. 'They're codified,' explains Bono. 'They're actually quite difficult to do. It was almost part of the point of doing them, because nobody else could do them. The lyric depended on the guitar line which depended on the bass. They were all kind of interdependent. They weren't existing as songs.'

The music, in fact, exists as a conversation which emerges from the internal friendships of the band. And these, says Adam, are even stronger now than when they began.

> We understand it better now. In the earlier years there was a lot more fighting and resentment and jealousy. But it was good. I mean, that was energy. That made people talk, that made people row. It made people need to communicate with one another. I think in one sense that energy has been downplayed for just straight loyalty and respect and support. We have less friction. But I think that's just the nature of people's lives at the moment. Its strengths come and go at different times. There are times when people do need to separate from it a bit. I think people do have a lot of balls in the air that they're trying to deal with. But I think the underlying knowledge is that this is our future, that it is a future that is together, that nobody wants to break up or separate from it. And in a sense it becomes more honest as people reveal their vulnerabilities. The judgemental mentality that I think you have as a young idealist in your early twenties – I think you become a lot more tolerant of how people live their lives, and how they deal with things. So, yeah, that is maturing.

The Edge confirms this:

> They've always been tensions. Positive tensions, about everything – from the way the group should sound to much bigger issues like where the album should go – where you end up in a compromise situation, which actually in ways is a positive place to be. It's not a compromise of quality; it's just a compromise where more than one set of ideas is accommodated at the one time. You get a much more broad set of attitudes and personality, rather than just one. I think if we were all perfectly in sync, it would definitely be a less interesting group.

In the band we all instinctively protect each other. And in the way that Bono will critique my guitar playing, and parts that I might come up with, I would also look over his shoulder and make sure he's got some sort of objective opinion to bounce off. I play devil's advocate a lot of the time when he's working on words. I suppose I can stand back and see where he's exposing himself to the slings and arrows, where he's just opening himself up unnecessarily. And I would constantly – well, certainly on the last record – be that voice: 'No, don't do that . . . It's too on the nose . . . You're not doing yourself any favours.' But I think it's very hard sometimes for Bono to hold back, because he's a very emotional and intense individual. It means that he's not cool in any sense as a performer or a singer – in the original sense of the word 'cool' – as in non-committed, laid back, expending no energy. He's the opposite of all of that. And for a lot of people, especially people who are not necessarily fans of ours, that is such an assault. It's tough to withstand.

'It seems to be very elastic,' the singer himself elaborates. 'People are allowed to get to various different extremes. It changes shape. It's this amorphous thing. But out of it, at moments, come these songs and these performances that are very special. But it's not as simple as those things. I'd love to be able to say, 'Listen, that's all that's important. Deal with the song. And I'll go off and I'm Paul Simon. But it's *not* that. It's *something else.*'

CHAPTER TWENTY

The Shape of an Angel

A 'random' story from the U2 homeland

My grandmother had died. I was about five or six. And my father told me that he was going to get a gravestone made, or a 'monument' as he called it. And we went to a place on the Old Road in Tuam, to a stonecutter there. He was in my view an artist, craftsman, creator, in the great historical sense. And his knowledge of that had been handed from one generation to another. His father and *his* father before him had all been in that trade. And they had absorbed a sense of shape and size and form and appropriateness and use of materials. This is the kind of thing which defines our civilisation. When we have visitors from other countries, these are the kinds of things we show: the great statues, the great paintings and so on. But a lot of this was what I would call unselfconscious craftsmanship. And when we arrived my father said that he wanted a monument.

And the stonemason said, 'Do you want a cross?'

Now, had my father said he wanted a cross, he would have then described all the different kinds of crosses he could have had. But my father said, 'Well, no. I was thinking of a figure.'

So he said, 'Well, what about Christ with a crown of thorns?' And my father looked a bit shocked by that, because some of these figures were quite grotesque. And he said, 'Well, *nooo*, no, not exactly that.'

And he said, 'Well, what about the Mother and Child?'

'Not really.'

And then he said, 'An angel!'

And my father said, 'Oh, well, *yes*, an *angel*!'

And he said, 'Well, would you like the angel looking sad down on the grave?' And he held his hands in a very deferential way and looked down towards the ground.

And my father said, 'Well . . . *mmm* . . . *noooo*.'

And he said, 'Well, what about looking up to heaven?' And he held his hands together, now higher than before, almost at his face level, and looked up towards the sky.

And my father said, 'Yes. Yes. *Yes*. Something like that.'

And he said, 'Would you like the wings outstretched?' And he spread his arms out behind him.

My father said yes he would.

That was the total description that was given. The only quantification, the only attempt to give a sense of scale, was when we were leaving. The stonemason said, 'I'll make it about as big as meself.' And sure enough the figure was about the same size. He was able to call up a whole set of images in my father's mind. They were communicating at the level of language and image, with a very, very shared perception of what they were talking about, which can only come when you are deeply merged in a community and in a culture.

And the stonemason could see that I was fascinated by it all, and I was putting my hands on the different pieces of marble and stone. And he said to me, 'We'll have the *shlab* in in two or three weeks and I'll show you about it.' And when I came by, he showed me the nature of this slab of stone, and pointed out that the weak point of the figure would be the neck. And that another weak point would be where the hands protruded outwards. And he showed me that he'd have to use one part of the stone for that, where the grain was at its most dense. And he then set it upright and started to work on it. And he said, 'If you come back in two or three days the head will be out.' And it was as though the head was actually emerging from the stone, as though it were being born out of the stone. And I came back and I was amazed by the beauty of it. The head was just kind of escaping out of the stone. And he said, 'If you come back in a week's time the hands will be coming out.' And sure enough, the hands were emerging from the stone, these beautiful feminine hands, the fingers delicately folded together, with sleeves that hung down from them that you'd almost expect to see moving in the wind.

And when we designed this very complicated interface for this advanced manufacturing system, we used that conceptual framework, and we displayed on screen the blank piece of material, and the skilled person programmed the machine by drawing around on the screen the component that was still imprisoned within the material.

Without the culture, the solid-state physicist would describe exactly and in incredibly precise details the molecular structure of the piece of stone, but that wouldn't allow him to see the beautiful potential of that stone. He could only see it in this narrow reductionist universal way. Whereas someone in, say, an African culture could see the potential of the stone in a different way – the images are created differently there. The different local cultures mean that what you can see in the stone, or in the material, or in life itself, is a reflection of that possibility. So that instead of the stone having a one best use, whatever that might be, if it's located in the diversity of regional cultures, each part of it can be seen as something different. This gives us enormous potential as we face ecological and other disasters.

A stone is a stone. But it's only if you have absorbed that culture through generations of work that you can actually see the angel in it. We used to play a game when we were children of passing around a piece of wood and we'd sit round in a circle and pass the piece of wood around and ask everybody to say what they saw in it. And everybody would see something different. Some would see the head of a dog because they was a knot that looked like an eye. Others would see the knot as being like the stone in a piece of fruit. Others would see it like a clenched fist.

(Professor Mike Cooley, in a conversation with the author. Professor Cooley is an engineer and one of the world's leading technological philosophers. His home-town, Tuam, Co. Galway, was also the birthplace of Johnny Rotten's father.)

CHAPTER TWENTY-ONE

Composing the New Noise

Music is a bit like laughter and libido – if you think about what it is, it disintegrates in front of your eyes. As the source of the attraction begins to deconstruct itself into, as the case may be, narrative expectations, double meanings, puns and punchlines, or organs, limbs, squelchy bits and damp patches, the magic evaporates. Those who talk about it most do it least; those who talk about it least don't do it at all. Boom-boom. Or, if you prefer: bang-bang.

Music, too, has cause, almost by definition, to be suspicious of words. This is not because there is nothing to talk about, but because talk is nothing by comparison. To listen to a piece of music to which you can connect is to achieve a state of knowing that makes words seem superfluous. All discussion must take place in the acceptance that it seeks to *suggest* rather than *contain* – that the music remains floating just beyond the field of rational cognisance, and that the best words can do is point in the general direction of the sound. Still there are few things as interesting as hearing a musician, who knows and understands the nature of the limitation, attempting to put flesh on the mystery and meaning on the process of it, in Seamus Heaney's words, 'advancing by the unpredictable path of intuition rather than by the direct and earnest path of logic'.

The poet was talking 'about a psychic event in which impulse discovers direction, potential discovers structure, and chance becomes intention'.

The Edge says:

> I think you can talk about the ideas that start to form *behind* the instinct. But it's very hard to explain why you chose one chord over another, why you went for one sound and not the other. That's just the instinct of writing, of creating music. It's impossible to explain, although it *is* the *key*, I suppose. As Keith Richards said, it's all about making decisions. When you're in the studio, can you differentiate between the 'right' thing to do and the 'wrong' thing to do? If you can, then you're a songwriter, and if you can't, then you're not.

I think it's not the same as writing words. Words are symbols for something, therefore you have to be very specific. You're dealing with tangible meaning. But in terms of the music, it's much more subconscious, much more instinctive. It's like a completely different part of your brain. So the intelligence or the sophistication is not, in my case, conscious. It's instinctive. It's an attempt to grab on to something that is in my head, but purely in my imagination. It's not an *idea* that can be *expressed*. I'm drawing from somewhere and trying to express on my guitar these bits that I hear in my imagination.

A lot of our songs start out as a strong mood, a strong feeling, a strong emotional thing. And the rest of the song is almost extrapolated from that – from eight bars, or maybe *two* bars. 'Where the streets have no name' started out on a four-track cassette player in my house in Monkstown. I just had this guitar idea, the transition into the song, with keyboards behind it. The process of writing was the process of writing the main body of the song and making the arrangements work. And obviously a huge part of that was Bono working on melodies, but the actual essence, the location of the song, was in that opening part. And that's pretty much *all* I had. And we worked from that little clue, that beginning, to the song that it eventually became. But the mood, the emotion, the place it brought you to was all in that sixteen bars.

From such a starting point, is it possible to go to *many* or *a few* different places, or is there just *one* destination which you must identify and find?

In a lot of cases, there's actually one conclusion that you're working towards. Sometimes you arrive there, or get very close, and you realise that it's actually not all that interesting. Or something else might happen along the way that might send you off in a different direction. We tend to follow those moments right down to the end.

But sometimes it's an awful lot of perspiration and hard slog. The irony is that often the most sophisticated, complicated, intricate things just come out of the sky. Sometimes it's the simplest thing that you have to work on. It took us ages to hone down the melody of 'Mysterious Ways', and it's almost a nursery rhyme in style. Bono and I were there for two days, just trying different ideas, listening to tapes. This one, that one, we'll try this, we'll try that. And we kind of just slowly but surely came, by a process of elimination, to this melody. And we said, '*That's* the one.' And it's the *simplest* thing.

From the beginning, writing songs was for Bono the most natural thing in the world.

I was amazed that I could hear a chord and hear the next one. And when I'd play the next one I'd hear another one. It seemed to be so easy, to me. And even when we were rehearsing, I'd hear a chord and I could hear a melody. And they'd kind of look at me and I'd say, 'Listen.' So we could start writing our own songs very early on.

When I was sixteen and kind of hitting a wall, songwriting became a real liberator. Because it's so easy for me. It's like discovering you can fly. *You* can; you think *everybody else* can. But you didn't even know that you could, really, until you jumped off the building and there it is. It's not something I have to work at, although I've heard about other people who sit down and work out melodies. I wake up with melodies in my head. I wake up with words in my head. But disjointed words. Occasionally I'll get a verse, or something like that. And I write it down. And occasionally I'll write a song very quickly. And in that sense the melody is so easy. And if you ask anyone who's in the studio with me, I'll constantly write *new* songs, because I love starting and I hate finishing. Because finishing means coming into the finite, into the facts, into the words, into the resolve, into the completeness. Whereas what I love is that pure melody. And if it's a great melody, it feels like it always existed. We call them eternal melodies. They're just *there*. A lot of Van Morrison's melodies are eternal melodies; you just can't imagine that melody not existing. So in that sense the creative thing is spontaneous. But in order to get better, rather than just relying on that spontaneous thing, I have to match it with some kind of craft. And craft and laziness do battle in me. Because I'm very lazy. I'm capable of *doing* an awful lot, but I'm not capable of *finishing* an awful lot. I get bored very quickly. So I start things – it could be a house, it could be a . . . *night club*! It could be anything. Off I go and I'm just totally driven by it. And I imagine that I will always be this excited by this project. But I'm not. And that's a real problem. So I'd start writing loads of songs. This was a vein that you'd cut into that you think is never-ending, but it *is*. So a lot of the songs when I listen to them they sound unfinished. And that is for a very good reason – they *weren't* finished.

'Sunday Bloody Sunday' was a great idea for a song. And it *hints* at a great song. This idea of Easter Sunday, contrasting it – the whole thing. The rat-a-tat-tat of this Onward Christian Soldiers aspect of the beat. The melody is there. But finally, to me, it's just a demo. And that's very hard for me to say because there are people to whom that song means so much. My line was, 'I'll get back to that!' But I didn't.

Sometimes you get the sense that what U2 do goes beyond the normal urge of songwriters to write songs that are epic, definitive, great. Others seek always the big statement, the perfect structure, the ideal marriage of couplet and tune, of verse and middle eight. Other writers seem to be going always for the Best Song Ever Written. Sometimes you think that what U2 are searching for, and what they have tended mostly to find, are the fragments that others have ignored, little chips of metal which they shine and shine until they gleam. Bono says:

> It's very curious, and it's very important for people to realise that what the music hints at, particularly in the early days, is what is striking about it. It's the same with the language: it's what the language *hints at*. Language and words – they weren't my skill. I wasn't coming from the point of view of a writer into music. I didn't come in from the point of view of anything. We didn't get *time* to have a point of view. It wasn't like Lou Reed who was at Syracuse University studying English language, who then gets into rock. I joined this before I finished school, before I had words. I had things to *say*. There's an incredible phrase of Hubert Selby's . . . 'a scream looking for a mouth', and I really understand that. The music is *catching up* with what it has to put across. The words are catching up with what they have to say. It's not like the words are there to show themselves off. They're there to try and *put across* stuff, and you can see that in the songs that are unfinished. You can see songs where you think, 'I could get a better phrase than that.' And that should ask the next question: *were they not looking for a better phrase? And why not? That's* interesting. Because isn't that what this is about? So if it's *not* what it's about, what *was* it about?

Isn't it about the limits of language? That the best writers are those who understand that you really can't succeed in saying *anything* – that the best you can hope for is to be able to hint at something, to nod in the direction of the rock under which the secret lies. That it's not even in the music, but maybe *outlined* by the music?

> It's *around* the music. It's *around* the words. Get that across and I'm very happy, because I know that . . . particularly a lot of journalists . . . they listen to song lyrics and they're actually thinking, 'How good is that couplet?' Because that's their language. Words. Recently I've gotten interested in couplets, so I've written a few

good ones. But, like, *so what?* That was the furthest thing from our minds when we got together.

So in a sense, the 'better' you get in a certain way, the greater the danger of getting further away from what you want to get at?

Well, what I think is that, hopefully when you know what you're at, you can afford to be a bit more expert. But it would've been very dangerous early on. I think it's okay now. It's okay now to, every so often, write a lyric or something. But the backbone of this is like trying to catch lightning. It's trying to capture a feeling. It's like, 'Was the feeling there?' *Yeah.* 'That's *it!*' And you'll have Eno and Edge saying – 'That's it!' And I'd say, 'Can't I fix that? Can't I just *finish* that?' 'NO! Why do you *want* to? If it's *there?*' And I would have to say that, every so often, that has depressed me – because of ego. And the best example is the opening verse of 'Where the Streets Have No Name' – which is so *banal* – as a couplet. And yet, what it suggests is one of the most extraordinary ideas. And particularly said in front of twenty thousand or fifty thousand people. You know, this idea of 'I want to run, I want to hide/I want to tear down the walls that hold me inside.' A bit ABC. But if you say 'Reach out, touch the flame . . .' If you put this in front of people and say, 'I want to go to this *other* place. There *is* another place. It is *accessible* – now – in this moment. And I want to go there *with you*. Do *you* want to go? Do *you* think that's possible? A step of faith?' That is . . . *Phew!* . . . That is *amazing!* And you can *feel* that. That was the most incredible opening, ever. You didn't see the band. They walked on stage and that's what they said. First thing. 'Let's go somewhere else.' This other place. And yet the couplet that expresses it, the language, is so *simplistic* . . . That I could have written that – my vanity goes [snorts]. But it was just a quick sketch to get the feeling across. Then they'll go, 'That's *it*. You've sketched it. You've *got* the thing. What do you want to make it *smarter* for?' We're not in the business here of smart, are we? We're trying to be higher than smart.

The way U2 write songs, and Bono's early lyric-writing, in particular, has about it more of the qualities of archaeology than sculpture. It's as though they are seeking to unearth things that already exist, in a fragmented state, rather than assert their own novelty. Bono's 'laziness', then, could be an expression of impatience and restlessness once he feels he has established the *shape* of the object which has been glimpsed. Completion is, in a sense, superfluous. He admits:

That has a horrible ring of truth about it. Intellectually I might know. And you see I'm getting vainer now. Now I'm starting to think more about what other people think. I'm thinking, 'Better not rhyme that couplet. I'll leave it.' That's one of the things that the English couldn't get about the early U2 – the lack of vanity. The lack of self-consciousness. Now we're very self-conscious. Or, actually, maybe not self-conscious – just *conscious*. Up until *Joshua Tree* it wasn't about lyrics. There were always lyrics in there, but there were almost *accidental* lyrics. They were the things that you'd write quickly. It wasn't about lyrics, it was about feelings. It was about mood. It was about shapes. *And* ideas.

It works in painting. In one sense I should stop explaining it. Because it's like saying, 'Where's the fucken *arm*? You've left her arm off! *That* can't be a woman!' Because I like those impressionistic things, and that's probably what I am.

It's also an aspect of the U2 sensibility which might be missed if it were to disappear into a murk of competence, confronting as it does the reductionism of all communication to clinical thought, the insistence on not merely trying to pin things down but on the idea that there *is* nothing except what *can* be pinned down. To fight that, you must go towards the shapes and shadows.

Yeah, cause if you *describe* it, you've limited it. It's generous not to spell things out. Because it gives people their own freedom of access. When you pin things down – that's meanness. That's why some songs are a bit meaner than others, because they're only about *one* thing, and that's *it*. You're not giving away much. Language can be reductive, that's what it is. You can reduce the experience by pinning it down. And I suppose what I've tried to do is to get out of the way of the feeling that the music we're making suggests. And then again isn't it that knowledge is about exclusion – like computer language? Binarys. The way people have their own language to exclude everyone else. And what is a very simple concept, their language makes complex. Speaking in tongues is an experience that makes complete sense to me. To break the code requires the step of faith.

But the listener also has to believe in, even to *like*, U2.

It's like, 'I'm on this journey, and I have to believe that they know where they're goin'.' But isn't that true of so many things? This is an interesting starting point for a good row – that in fact *all* painting, *all* books, *all* of what we call works of art, need a surrender of the will. That's a scary idea, isn't it? And that, in fact, one of the problems of pop culture now is a crisis of faith – people can't believe in it any more. And in not being able to believe in it, they can't make it right. So, if you like, there's no faith in it. Most of the people who are writing about it have lost their faith.

Sometimes, in interviews, Bono or The Edge will talk about pursuing colours in searching out the shapes of songs. The Edge says:

There are times when certain things conjure up very definite colours, but not always. Some pieces, for me, just bring you to a certain place in your life, a certain time in your life. It's like smell. It conjures up not necessarily a very specific concrete thing, but almost an era or a moment which you've experienced at different times in your life. A recurring moment. And that's sort of the way with a lot of the songs – they bring you to a place in yourself. And I would say that's more what I pick up on. That's the imagination for me. Almost like scenes in a movie. They're universal. You may mould them into something quite special and specific, but there's certain universal things that you're really aware of.

The way we write, sometimes we feel that the song is written, the song is already there, if you could just put it into words, put it into notes. We *have* it, but it's not realised yet. It's not formed. We very rarely lose a song to some kind of limit. If you saw us in the studio working sometimes, you'd be scratching your head trying to figure out what we were doing. Mostly, if we get the feeling that we're on to something good, we eventually do get there. And 'Where the Streets have no Name' is a great example, because that took weeks of work to arrive at. Brian Eno wanted to erase the multi-track at one point, and almost did. We weren't in the studio at the time and he asked the assistant editor to leave the room, because he wanted to erase the multi-track, because he was at that stage so frustrated at the amount of time going into this song. And the assistant engineer wouldn't leave the room and sort of stood in front of the tape machine, arms outstretched like, saying, 'Brian, you can't do this!' And he didn't. This was when the song was definitely right before our eyes, but we hadn't performed it well enough. Sometimes a song might be a pretty good song, but until it's actually performed well, you can't really see that. And at this point in time it still sounded like a wonderful idea that just wasn't right. And sometimes you can chase them for weeks and weeks – and waste a lot of time. So Brian's problem was the amount of time we were putting into this piece. He just thought that other songs were being neglected as a result. But he was wrong! [Laughs.] And it took the band so long to find a way of playing it in the studio, and in the end, having tried various band arrangements, we reverted to just building it up layer by layer. And eventually, after Brian tried to erase the multi-track, we eventually pushed it through. And it's funny, but the essence of the piece had never really changed, but we lost it somewhere along the line. We lost sight of it in amongst the work that we put into it. I think that the point is that the song itself is there, but getting it down on tape, and mixed the way you want it, was a real struggle.

Is there an actual place in which a song happens? Yes, says The Edge.

You start off with more a feeling, but by the time you're finished, most songs are definitely some sort of location. Not all songs, I think, have that. 'Where the Streets Have No Name' obviously is. I think it's very cinematic. *Zooropa* also conjures up for me a certain kind of a cityscape – as an album, and particularly the title track. But some of the other songs just conjure up this weird mood. 'Some Days are Better than Others' is very claustrophobic, it's some-where inside, some strange little room somewhere. And then somesome songs are just wide open spaces.

How is this discussed within the band? Is there a shared location which is explicit in the discussions about an evolving song?

I don't know. We speak about the location, but not so much while we're working. It's funny. We tend to agree most of the time when something is in keeping. I think that's what being a songwriter is – it's recognising, even from a two-bar section of a piece, whether you've got something of interest. A songwriter will recognise that and immediately focus in on what it is, and then you start to develop that, and you create a whole piece. But it might only be a few bars long.

We could differ about this, I'm sure, but it is arguable that The Edge is the first guitarist since Jimi Hendrix to seek out a new purpose for the guitar, to stretch the instrument beyond its obvious capabilities. And yet, he seems the most casual of guitarists in not appearing to have any sentimental attachment to the instrument. On *Zooropa*, he propped up the guitar in the corner of the studio and spent most of his energies at the mixing desk. He seems to see the guitar as a tool rather than as a showpiece, a means to an end rather than an end in itself. He reflects:

I used to be more like that. I'm getting much more sentimentally attached to the instrument now. I used to go through torture trying to find something that hadn't already been used up and made redundant. So that as soon as I figured it out and found something that I was happy with, the last thing I wanted to do was pick up the guitar again. It was a constant struggle and a real risk. It was very humbling a lot of the time, as you found it very hard to get something that you were happy with. I think that few people really know how much we had to fight against the inertia of our early musical limitations. I'm sure this is not unique to us, that it happens to a lot of groups, but it's so easy for things to turn out average. It's so easy for ideas to ossify. To get a great idea from the very moment of inspiration to the finished song, and for it to be carried through all the different stages and retain the spirit and whatever that thing is that makes it unique and interesting – that's *so hard* to do. And every step of the way it seems that everything conspires to push it into moulds. And you have to constantly check yourself. The pure knowledge is what's interesting. As soon as you start to mess with it, we all seem to have this knack of pushing things into conventional moulds. I don't know what it is. Maybe it's the difference between the conscious and the unconscious mind. The conscious mind seems to be completely wrapped up in structures that are already known. And a lot of the time, the unconscious mind is so free that the ideas that come out are much more interesting.

Therefore, with the guitar, I used to try and do as few takes as possible, because I knew that if I got something good, most likely if I kept working on it I would ruin it. So I had this almost superstitious approach to guitar playing, where I'd constantly try to find that moment of unconscious creativity, and once I'd achieved it, leave it and not mess. Because I know how hard it is. I know, because I know I've been working on songs and I've wiped over take number two, and taken twenty takes more to get something else: 'Actually, that take wasn't bad, but I think I can get it better.' So you wipe over it and you're instantly into *average*. And then you lose it.

Sometimes you'll lose a song for a while. Sometimes it just goes. And you have to just put it to one side, forget about it. And then you listen back and you rediscover what it was you liked. Things can get old for you even before they're finished. But the great pieces tend to write themselves almost, because the strength of their identity is so *there* when you first start working on it that you're rushing to get the ideas down they're coming so fast. You can't record it fast enough. And there's other songs that you struggle over every part because nothing's connecting, nothing's adding up. But sometimes you get through that and then something comes out the other end.

While there is a sense in which U2's lack of orthodox virtuosity has allowed them to develop a relative immunity to clichés, isn't there a limit to this in that when they hit their technical wall they are closed off from a whole range of possibilities which require particular forms of competence?

> Early on, that used to sometimes happen. But we rarely lose an idea. We're very protective and very conscious of those moments that happen. And they do, they really *do*. It's almost like a spirit descending on the session, and suddenly something is cooking, and there's a vibe in the air. And everybody knows it instantly. That can sometimes happen when you're working alone. But that's the moment you're trying to capture, to capitalise on, and relive. Sometimes all you get is a recording on a little tape recorder – just ten bars of the band playing together. Once that is down, once that's established, and whether it's on a Walkman, whether it's on multi-track – however we manage to capture that moment – it's amazing how you will always be able to use that as a reference, and get back to that place. It's like, it's *there*.

Brian Eno has been heard to describe U2 as a band that will spend four hours talking about something and five minutes playing it.

> Yeah. That used to happen sometimes. We'd really be weighing up and comparing different possible approaches. It happens quite a lot that, in the studio, we start out with a rough idea for a song, and we'll try out various different approaches. I'll try various different guitar approaches and sounds and parts, ideas – most half-formed rather than fully-formed. And it's in this kind of murk of poss-ibilities that you start to try and home in on the direction that you want. It's in that sort of murky situation that most of the discussions take place. It's not like you are trying to *talk* the song into existence, but it's as if through the various choices that are open you try to steer the song in the direction that we all think it should go. Sometimes there's disagreements about it. And some of the songs have had so many different incarnations. I could play you mixes of some of the songs which you would never, ever recognise as the final song. 'Who's Gonna Ride Your Wild Horses?' – that song had so many different incarnations, so many different mix approaches, that it just took weeks of sifting through the ideas, and trying to figure out the best approach. Sometimes it's like catching quick-silver, because you sense that you have something there, but

actually homing in on exactly what it is that's giving you that feeling – in other words, to find the essence of the piece and bring it out – can be so, *so* difficult. And that's where we end up talking – about *this* guitar approach, *this* drum approach, 'It's too heavy-handed,' 'This one is naive but it has certain qualities that if we pushed it further over in this direction, it would do this,' and, 'I think this acoustic guitar part is the important element' . . . So it's about debating the pros and cons of the different possible directions of the songs.

The only rule is that there's no rules. I mean, there are certain ways that we have written down through the years. The first way we ever wrote was through improvisation, where we'd just be playing together, and we'd just take interesting sections – playing around with them, finding other sections to go with them, and we'd end up with a song. But you can get into a rut very easily doing that all the time. So I started writing ideas by myself and bringing them to the band. And that's been useful over the last few records.

Soundchecks are where we mostly continue to do improvisation. But once we actually get a start on a piece, the actual studio technique varies so much. For example, 'Until the End of the World' – we demoed that and it wasn't really as we wanted it. But we knew there was a big song in there. So I reworked the chords and the music around the thing we all knew was good, which was the guitar hook. And we recorded that as a backing track on, like, the first day we were in the studio. I don't even think that Bono was there that morning. We then went on for another week to improvise different versions, to see if we could improve it. But we went back to the very original way. So that was very straightforward. It was, 'Here are the new chords; here is the new structure.' And everybody learned this thing. And we went in and we re-recorded it as a backing track, and it took probably half a day – to get the sounds and then a performance.

The best example of the other thing that can happen is probably 'Who's Gonna Ride Your Wild Horses?' That song started out as a very simple piece, which we had problems with. We took that song in every conceivable direction, to try to arrive at a satisfactory arrangement. We recorded it a few times, and . . . so many different guitar overdubs and approaches, changing bass parts, changing chords, to the point that, when we eventually finished mixing the song, the only thing that was original to that multi-track was the hi-hat cymbal! Everything had been replaced at one point or another. So . . . sometimes you're fumbling in the dark, and sometimes you really know that there's one problem that you just have to solve and the whole thing will be right. And then sometimes a song is there and we just don't know it. A typical example of that would be 'One', which started out in Berlin. We captured a very special moment in Berlin, which became a song. It was just acoustic guitar, bass, drums, and Bono. And piano; I put a piano in it. Then we laid all this stuff on it in dubbing, to try to, I suppose, give it some foreground, because everything else we'd been working on supported the melody but didn't really provide foreground. Danny [Lanois, co-producer on several U2 albums] put some guitar down, I put some guitar down. And we put percussion down, and did all kinds of things to try to make this thing work. And we never could really come up with a mix that we were happy with. We knew the song was finished, we knew the lyric was great. We knew everything was fine. It's just we couldn't get a mix that we were happy with. And Brian arrived in, as he does, often when we're working together, after a couple of weeks away, flew in . . . And we said, 'Brian, would you take this and just see what you can do.' And he just sat down in a studio and started putting up individual faders, and saying, 'Well, I like *that*,' 'Like *that*,' '*Don't* like *that*,' 'Don't like *that*,' '*This* guitar stays,' 'This keyboard *goes*,' '*This* stays,' 'This *goes*.' He just really decided in a very subjective way what he liked, and brought us back this mix. And it really worked. It wasn't the final mix – we remixed it later – but that was the breakthrough for that one piece. It was just getting over the difficulty of what is the arrangement going to be. What are the elements in this vast array of possibilities that are actually going to prevail in the balance? So there is no real rule, except that you don't give up until it's right. That's the rule.

That's the thing about Brian, how his style matches our own. He is quite cerebral, but not where it matters. He is, like ourselves, a kind of naive appreciator of music. And that's an example. He was not using his analytical mind to decide what was right. He was literally just going, 'I like *that*,' '*That's* got the shit I like in it,' 'And *that* does too,' 'But that *doesn't*.' It's a completely subjective way of looking at music. I think afterwards, when the dust has settled, it's often the right time to start sitting back and trying to figure out the hidden logic which in our music is often present.

Is technology your friend or a jealous god?

Well, the only way we use technology in the band is as a tool to aid our work from inspiration to the final song. We never use technology for its own sake. It's always a means by which we can create. A more efficient, a more free way. We start out, in most cases, in that kind of creative play, and we just hit on something and go, 'Wow! Do that again!' And it's afterwards that you're able to take a step back and say, 'Why is that so cool?' And then you go, 'Ah, that's what it is!' So it's not necessarily that you are arriving in this place by thinking yourself into it. It's much more that you've programmed your subconscious in this phase of experimentation, and then you recognise when you've got something good going.

One of the things about the medium which may become more problematic as it becomes more technologised and complex is the danger of being distanced from the integrity of the original unit and its basic impulse. As the sound and identity develops, it becomes more and more dependent on relationships between the band and outside agencies – technology, producers, and so on. There is, for example, some currency among U2-sceptics for the idea that Brian Eno is the Man in the U2 creative engine, as Paul McGuinness is said to be the manipulator who has engineered the U2 success story. Does it worry the band at all? Yes, says The Edge, and no.

Generally not, but it's something I'm aware of. You have to make sure you don't undervalue the essence of the group, which is ultimately the four members playing together. In that respect, the group is a wonderful leveller and discipliner of ideas, because no matter how much store you put on an idea you might have, it ultimately has to go through the process of the band, and that's when it starts to take on its essential identity. A song is never finished until it's been played by the band. And that's why it is what it is.

Do the band look for something they already see using the technologies, or experiment with the technologies in order to come upon something new?

I would say both, but I would say the best things, or some really good things anyway, have come out of a search. Like the guitar part for 'Pride (in the Name of Love)' came out of a search. We had an idea. It was really a successful piece rhythmically, so we had to tie down the rhythm, and this idea then came through. It was like, '*There* it is!' *Bang!* I think actually it was Bono and myself working together in his tower in Bray. The basic chord pattern came from a soundcheck jam, but it wasn't really *there* yet. The two of us were trying different things to get an arrangement out of it. It happened, and we *knew*. 'There it is!' 'That's one!' *Done!* Job done! But a lot of the best things come out of when you start by picking up the guitar, messing with sounds. And suddenly you find yourself inspired and creating some sort of a world of suggested ideas, a location, an emotion, or whatever. And it goes from there. Sometimes it's quite hard, because of the way I approach everything, to just turn it on – which is why, sometimes, our more traditional songs, like 'When Love Comes to Town' or 'Angel of Harlem' – are actually the most difficult for me, because it's really not what I do. So to find my way around a song like that is very hard.

For example, all the basic pieces for *Rattle and Hum* started out as recordings I made on Walkman cassettes during the *Joshua Tree* tour. 'Angel of Harlem', 'Hawkmoon', 'All I Want is You', 'Desire' – they were all just me with acoustic guitar. Starting with some kind of riff, but then taking that, which was really, again, just a clue . . . Some of them were fairly well developed before we started recording them. I did some four-track demos. But then I had to put on another hat to say: this is no longer just an acoustic guitar thing, this is now a U2 thing. This is a song – where am I gonna fit into this? And I discovered I had painted myself into a corner, and that finding an electric guitar part that fitted in to those songs was really, really hard. So I learned that writing on acoustic guitar sometimes, although you can do some great things, for me as a guitar player it's not really the best thing to do. Sometimes if I write on keyboard, I then find it easier to find a place for electric guitar in those arrangements.

Having bypassed the tradition up until then, U2, with *Rattle and Hum*, doubled back to fill in their own gaps.

Yeah. We wanted to – we needed to – develop more ways of writing songs. So I pretty much said, 'Well, I'll learn!' Because we were relying too much on improvisations, which just weren't coming as easily as they had done. So I just had a lot of ideas and we waded through them. We just chose the ones that seemed to be the best. And Bono was also working on some stuff, and he came through with 'Love Rescue Me' and 'When Love Comes to Town', and I think a couple of songs came from improvisations. So it was in the spirit of attempting to develop our songwriting resources, and having just spent a long time in America, we kind of developed into this journey to find a source, I suppose. And it kind of evolved – that record, the film – around the various different decisions that we made, mostly instinctively, in terms of deciding to write in a different way.

Each U2 album has been a phase in itself, and yet there have been these longer phases, or 'eras', in which over the course of two or three albums, the band goes through a phase of reinvention. The actual change of musical direction is the end rather than the beginning of these shifts in stance and perspective, which, as Adam Clayton explains, are grounded in an organic relationship with the world.

> At the beginning of an album project, or at any stage throughout a year, Bono will say, 'These are the things I'm gettin' interested in. This is what I've been reading. This is the way I'm thinking. What are you thinking?' So we'll all immerse ourselves in those things in our own particular way. Pick up the same books, check out the same documentaries – whatever it is. So then we can argue about making that more pointed, or less pointed, or what's right or what isn't right. And then when it comes to the actual music, you know what are the creative and sonic constraints on it, and it's down to making it work. So it's not just a playing thing – it's a whole supportive role within the commune. And it's always redefining itself.

What defines a song as a U2 song, and what excludes some and not others? It isn't as if the band have a very narrowly defined style – even from 'Lemon' to 'The Wanderer' is quite a journey, but both are on the same album. How can the two be U2? How, for example, does 'Lemon' pass the U2 entrance exam?

The Edge laughs.

> I had my doubts about that one until it was finished. That one to me is the balance between two or three complete extremes, which come together by the slimmest connection imaginable. Somehow, when all considered simultaneously, they add up to a U2 song, for me. If you *just* had Bono singing the way he sings. If you *just* had the rhythm section. If you *just* had my guitar, keyboard and effects. Or if you *just* had the block vocals – in isolation those elements would not be U2 at all. But somehow, when they're together, it is. And I can't actually tell you why! I suppose because it doesn't sound like anything else; it has characteristics of other things, but it's an original of some sort, and as such we're quite happy to put it out.

This gives currency to the idea that U2 were developing in the way we could perceive, and yet there were all the time these other parts, which the band touched on, delved into, dallied with, which they would then decide to leave alone because they weren't, for the time being at least, what U2 were 'about'. It's as if the U2 we know is the tip of the iceberg, that other parts have been hidden from view because they didn't suit at the time. And yet, as the band have progressed, what U2 are perceived to be 'about' has expanded in all kinds of directions, to the point where there is almost nothing which the band does not now feel able to attempt, or which their audience couldn't accept. It's as if the rest of the iceberg is slowly being revealed. Do we conclude that 'what U2 have been about' has been two separate ideas – one, the reality, which was that anything was possible, and two, the public perception that the band meant something specific, and which limited the way the band could grow and build on its music publicly?

Yes, The Edge agrees, there has always been a lot of material which has not been able to get in, because, at the time anyway, it wasn't 'U2' enough. There are also, he says, examples of songs which did not fit when they were first written but which subsequently became absorbed by the expanding U2 organism.

> I guess 'Love is Blindness' is an example of that. Bono wrote that while we were working on *Rattle and Hum*, and it came out on the subsequent record. 'Even Better than the Real Thing' – again, we couldn't really make sense of it around the time of *Rattle and Hum*, but the new direction that we were taking around the time of *Achtung Baby* made sense of that song.

Certain songs, as Bono says, are like scouts – 'advance parties into terrain you will later discover'. But there is always the danger of the changes in direction being not purely creative developments, but the result of steering a course through the commercial environment and the critical response. Or is it that they arise out of the feeling that the music has hit a brick wall in creative terms? The Edge responds:

> I think that we do rely on being inspired to get the best out of the band, and that makes us move into new territory. That's the way we work – by being in a new environment musically, in a new place, and finding our feet one way or another. We never had a problem in changing, because there's nothing really to change *in* us. Because there's no rulebook for us, there's no craft in what we do – I mean there is, but it's the craft of instinct and of intelligence, rather than the craft of a pattern of work, a pattern of songwriting. I suppose it's an instinctive craft as opposed to a methodology – and because of the lack of methodology, we've never had any problem in moving into new territory. In fact, I feel confident that we can do almost anything, and still make it sound like us. Because that's kind of the way it's been from the beginning. And the limitations and the strengths, and the original perspective, all end up coming to bear on

any idea, forming it into something that ends up being us. We're quite strict with ourselves about what we will and will not release. Some songs that, for one reason or another, don't become us, we will leave to one side, or we will rearrange until we feel we have imparted our own special touch to them.

The growth in the music occurs first of all out of the relationships within the band, and after that out of the band's relationship with the audience. 'After the dialogue with yourself', says Bono, 'comes the conversation with your imagined audience. Their context is important and is unconsciously, if not consciously, borne in mind.' But the process must guard against responding to the prejudiced perceptions of those who are determined to dislike U2 anyway. The Edge concedes:

> It's a difficult balance because inevitably you start to second-guess yourself all the time. More on the grounds of 'Is it good?' rather than 'Is it valid?' From time to time, obviously as you're making judgements about current work that you're developing, it's very easy to nudge it in a particular direction because of the influence of what people are saying – just knowing you're going to end up getting into trouble for certain things. So I think that *Zooropa* was probably, in that respect, quite a free record, because we had no expectations and we had no agenda *per se*. Or even an idea going in of what we were gonna end up with. We really just let it happen in a very natural way. I've always felt that our best work came quickly and seemingly effortlessly – though it's never effortless, and it only seems quick relative to other work; in fact, it's the other songs that you were trying to write and failed to write that probably gave you the opportunity to write the one very quickly. But on *Zooropa*, a lot of that material seemed to come through without much struggle, and that was interesting.

Zooropa represents a kind of musical crystallisation of the U2 condition as of the mid-1990s. In its stance and demeanour, it is, as Bono says, eclectic and postmodern. And yet, as he also observes, it is unified by its building materials (plastic, chrome) and texture, rather than its mood or style, which varies from track to track. The title track, for example, sounds like two pieces, both of which might have existed on their own, but which, put together, seem to have been made for one another. In a certain light, it's possible only to see the cut-up ethic of modern pop music as an expression of a fascination with the random and fragmented. What if it's the opposite – bringing together things which belong together, which come from the same place, but were born disconnected?

The way The Edge describes the creation of the title track suggests something which was broken up in the process of excavation, but which emerged as something which passed for spontaneity. So, in a sense, what appears to be mere technical dilettantism is the conscious reconstruction of the spontaneous idea which had temporarily concealed its interconnectedness.

> Yeah, I like what they do to one another, but I know what you mean. They were part of the same improvisation, but probably about fifteen minutes apart. I just found these bits, and said, 'There, that's one bit,' and then, 'That's another bit,' and then stuck them together. That track came out of an improvisation somewhere in America. The backing track was recorded by Joe [O'Herlihy] at a soundcheck. I just took the best bits, fed them into a digital editor, and stuck it together into a structure, and then laid acoustic guitar and stuff on top, and played it through the editor and I liked that. And then everything else just went on top. But the essence of that piece just came out of the air.

One of the things which hits you for six about *Zooropa* is the relative absence of guitars. The music seems to occur somewhere behind a murk of sound that summons up the murk of the world, but has managed to transcend instrumentation to some degree. It's as though the Last Guitar Hero/First Guitar Anti-Hero has begun to see the end of his instrument's history. He admits:

> It's an increasing struggle to find new ways to play the guitar and new things to say with the guitar. It's been the centrepiece of rock 'n' roll since the beginning, and a lot of the potential has already been used up. So from time to time you go through periods – well, certainly I do – where I find that I'm reaching for keyboards or whatever. The guitar seems sort of dried up. It's like a cycle thing. At the time we were doing *Zooropa*, there were a few other guitar songs, but in the final few weeks before we finished the record we kind of felt that they were the odd pieces in the collection that we had, so we decided to leave them off. We felt that the other pieces coming together seemed to have some kind of continuity of sonics and aspiration that meant that they belonged together. And one or two of the pieces that we left off sounded as if they were from a different record. They were much more guitar-orientated pieces.

Is this a phase, or is it to do with the point the music has reached in whatever kind of tunnel it's in?

We keep jumping ship because it's a constant struggle to find new things. And part of that process was the exploration of finding other styles of release for inspiration, freshness. And it's almost necessary to challenge yourself in order to provoke that. I wouldn't say it's a product of the music's development; I would say that it was really a part of a particular moment in time rather than being indicative of an overall curve, an overall turning away from the guitar.

In their search for new sounds to clothe the music in, U2 may be reflecting a deeper and increasingly urgent difficulty. Several of the songs on *Zooropa* seem to exist in the middle of this other sonic landscape, speaking from behind a veil of sound of the tenuous grasp of the individual on his own reality. Listening to some of the tracks you hear things which, for a passing moment, you're not quite sure come from the record or the outside world. It could be your fridge on the blink, or it could be Brian Eno's idea of a joke. It seems to speak about the world and fulfil another function inside that. It's as though the hard core of U2 has become more and more difficult to smuggle through the world. But it's still in there, the soul at the core of the pearl of sound.

'The core being just the spirit of the band?' the Edge enquires.

Yeah. That's never changed, and I hope it never does. You can use craft to do certain things, but whatever that is, that core that makes U2 what it is as a group, that's not something that we have ever been able to figure out. And it comes and goes within recording sessions, and even within shows. It's there or it's not. When it is there we recognise it, and when it's not we recognise it. It's a consistent thing in all our best work – hopefully in all our work. But the precise form with which it's clothed, the sounds that we're using, the structures, the craft – *that* varies. At the moment, I suppose we've got through a point where we were very disenchanted with rock 'n' roll sounds, with guitars and snare-drums and the regular-sounding thing. And so in *Zooropa*, I suppose, we were attempting to reinvent or redefine the sound of those primary colours. We used a lot of distortion to give things a new identity, and I guess a lot of influences would've been non-musical ones. But some of them were coming from the dance music movement that's happening now, that kind of industrial hardcore dance movement. And, yes, sometimes, it's just an unconscious thing that starts to flow and there's this sonic agenda starting to develop, some kind of sense of a possible vocabulary. And then, as we start to experiment, to try different things, those imaginary sounds start to become real. There's a lot of experimentation and fumbling around, but it's always in a very pointed direction. It's never aimless. It's never throwing mud against a wall to see what will stick. But by using the studio as an instrument, you start to home in on precisely what it is that is still only in your imagination and has yet to be made real in sound on magnetic tape.

'There was this feeling,' Bono told me about the recording of *Achtung Baby* shortly after its release. 'There's a point where you're standing around in a studio and somebody comes up with something, and we're saying, "Nah, that sounds like U2. That sounds like The Edge." And he goes, you know, "But I *am* The Edge!" We started with one point of view, the point of view being that if you stripped the surface or the face of U2 away, it would still be U2 because that's a *spirit*. So we could gouge away. And we did kind of deface U2 in doing so. And yet the spirit is there. It's as though there's something in the spirit of what we do that isn't copyable.'

With *Zooropa*, the band appears to have located a language which has allowed that spirit to exist in almost any form. Adam Clayton agrees:

> Yeah. I think that somehow we have achieved that. I'm not sure whether it has anything to do with what we've done, or whether it's the strength of our character by association. I listen to the stuff we did with Robbie Robertson and Daniel Lanois, and Bono and Edge's work with Roy Orbison, and they all have a validity within the U2 camp. And I just don't know if that's because of our input into that material or because, once you know it's us, suddenly you can't get beyond that. I'll tell you what I think – that whatever we now do, there's an identity for us in it. Although we may never have achieved the musical sophistication that the musoes achieved – I think in the way you can always tell the way Keith Richards plays a riff – I think each of us, as players and performers, has got to that essence . . . there's an honesty in whatever we do that is *us*.

One thing must be said about U2. What they are they did not become, but always were. Deep down they knew, and it showed. It is the incidentals that have changed over the years. Talk to those who were there at the start and are not too cool to say, and they will tell you that there is nothing there now that was not foreseeable at the time. The foursome seemed to contain the image of their greatness. It sounds like hype or bluff or cockiness, but it was none of these.

'I wish', says Bono, 'I could say that it was a bluff. It would be *so* much better. But it was just an absolute fact. It's like, all the work was nothing, because you caught a glimpse. We *knew*! It was like we'd been in a room and seen what happened. It was like something walked through the room.'

CHAPTER TWENTY-TWO

Laughable Angels

U2 are not funny. I hate to spring this on you at the last moment like that, but it had to be said. Forget all this talk about irony and humour, or at least try to see it for what it is: a jokescreen to hide a deep and solemn purpose.

There are two kinds of laughter, writes Milan Kundera in *The Book of Laughter and Forgetting*, 'and we lack the words to distinguish them'. True laughter, he maintains, is the province of the Devil, a laughter tinged with both malice and relief. Malice at the refusal of the world to behave in accordance with the Divine plan, and a certain relief on account of the release from responsibility which this allows us. The other kind of laughter, the laughter of angels, is not real, but an attempt to turn the Devil's tactics against himself, to drown out his laughter and reassert the meaning of God's plan. The angel's laughter is subversive and tactical, but also itself open to ridicule. 'Seeing the laughing angel,' Kundera writes, 'the Devil laughed all the louder, all the more openly, because the laughing angel was infinitely laughable.'

So the jokes which U2 perpetrate are jokes about jokes, double negatives seeking a positive, an attempt to restore a balance to the cabaret of life. World domination, as everyone knows, may be divided between demons and angels. But, as Kundera observes, the good of the world does not require the latter to win – 'all it needs is a certain equilibrium of power'.

This is the meaning of the apparent changes in U2 over the years. When they were younger, they too thought that the angels always needed to win. Now they know that this is neither desirable nor possible. This knowledge has led them closer to, rather than further from, the heart of the territory at which their music is aimed. The journey has been made within themselves, within individual souls and a collective heart.

The Fly, the character which Bono began to portray in the wake of *Achtung Baby*, is a good illustration of this solemn purpose. The Fly is not Bono, and yet is a part of him not visible before. The Fly is both mask and confession. But he speaks of me and you, too. We all share his confusion, his cunning, his ugliness, his style, his contradictions. He is me turned inside out, just as he is you turned inside out. Perhaps it is only in such inverted images that we can deal with a world in which bad is good and good is bad.

The human race is an accidental by-product of insect activity. Our poetic notion of battling dinosaurs and great apes is largely a Hollywood fiction based on what was a minor sideshow on the evolutionary stage. It was the behaviour of flying insects which led to the evolution of flowering plants, which in turn resulted in the first primates. The Fly begat the flower, the flower begat the tree, the tree begat the hairy mammal from which our humanity evolved. Within us all is the aspiration of the Fly. But we cannot find it in ourselves to love him, because he reminds us of our own dark centres.

At stake is more than the issue of evolutionary justice. It is a question of being able to see straight. Our tendency to develop a prefabricated version of our own world – in which inconvenient connections are separated and obscured from one another – has led us down the path of delusion and hubris. Not only have we managed to separate ourselves from the consciousness of our own flyness, we have succeeded also in dividing off every element of our apparatus for dealing with the world – the acts of consumption and production, the cause of pollution from its effect, the First World from the Third, tradition from modern, human from technological, high art from low art, and on and on. As the world heads towards self-destruction, carried forward on a thrust towards growth, development, wealth, progress, we manage to conceal from ourselves the truth that the earth cannot sustain this process for much longer, and that the bustle which moves us is not merely unnatural, but possibly fatal. As the danger grows, our capacity to describe it is reduced by the day. Everyday language has become so contaminated that it is useless as a means of describing what we feel and know. Words become increasingly crude instruments, allowing us to give but vague hints of what we feel. Like ourselves, they have been colonised in the service of utilitarianism, allowing us to no more than scrape the surface of our own meaning.

All the things we talk publicly about, as well as the way we talk in public about them, give the impression that we have no idea whatever of how much faster things are occurring, how time is being devalued, how quickly our values and beliefs are being consumed and burned out by the forces of change. This unknowingness does not occur for the want of talk. But our ceaseless debates assume always that the extent and rate of change is still within our control. In a world dominated by technological communication – where, at any given moment, human voices are being conveyed simultaneously by several million impulses through the cyberzone, a technology that is also capable of the remote-control zapping of a cityful of human collateral – human beings are dwarfed and rendered less and less in touch with themselves and one another. The more communication, the less.

Everything is technology and commodity – especially ourselves. We have arrived at the most perfect form of colonialism the world has ever seen.

In this postmodern world, beliefs can be expressed only as uncertainties, permanence as movement, identity as flux and truth as irony. And yet, the more unpredictable the world grows, the more simplistic, dogmatic and polarised public discussions seem to become. As the world's man-made systems career out of control, the only permitted dissent is that expressed in the babytalk language of our fossilised collective intellect and the dynamics of its impotent discussion. Words like 'progress' and 'modernity' have been so infected by ideology and propaganda that we can see, hear or use them only as virtuous concepts, without a downside. Only the inevitability of our demise, it appears, will cause us to see where our delusions have landed us.

And so it may be that the prospect of crisis becomes not something to be feared but a thing to be welcomed; not as an embrace of the apocalypse, but as the only way of correcting our crazy impulse towards self-destruction. Only in sight of the road's end will our fear reach the pitch of provoking a rethink. So, whoever lures us to that point, by flattery, threats or gifts, is our friend disguised as our enemy, an angel in a devil's coat. What is bad becomes good. To perceive our true nature we must climb into the belly of the beast that is ourselves. To fight it is merely to delay the inevitable. Each of us must be our own Judas, must sell his soul for thirty pieces of silver, must kiss the man who gave us the warning, both to betray him and allow him to say, 'I told you so.' To refuse to do so is not merely naive, but is the response of the meddling enemy of understanding and renewal.

My good friend Professor Mike Cooley is an engineer and computer designer who specialises in the development of human-centred technologies. He comes from Tuam, Co Galway, in the west of Ireland. Although he is not the least familiar with the music of U2, his view of the drift of progress and technological development is singularly germane to the area of cultural expression in which I perceive their importance. Professor Cooley is one of the world's leading experts in his field, and in 1981 won the Alternative Nobel Prize for his work. His book *Architect or Bee? The Human Price of Technology* which has been translated into more than twenty languages since it was first published in 1980, addresses the need to perceive the present drift of technological progress as just one of a range of possible options. A narrowly defined view of the machine, he maintains, is causing us to create technology which will not merely usurp the creative impulses of human beings but actually truncate our potential for further progress. He argues for the development of an approach to technology, systems and language which will enhance rather than limit the imaginative input of human beings.

We should be in no doubt, he says, about the gravity of the crisis facing us. Our own cleverness as a species has led us to fashion technologies which liberate us from onerous physical tasks, but so successful have we become at conferring activities to machines that we have diminished ourselves to the point where we may not much longer be capable of invention at all. Part of what his analysis suggests is that the dynamic underlying technological progress may not be what it appears. The most fundamental hubris of which the human race has been guilty may be the belief that knowledge and competence are historically cumulative. In fact, as Cooley says, each new layer of knowledge supplants a previous one, pulling the ladder up on our awareness of how we got to that point.

One way of putting it is to observe that mankind has followed a pattern of creating technologies in the likeness of himself, and then proceeded to see in such creations a precise mirror image of the human condition. There have been three broad stages in this evolution: machines that walk, machines that feed and machines that think. The first machines worked by clockwork: Man, by winding up a spring, gave life to something outside of himself. Art and culture began to mirror this, depicting human beings as machines, all sinews and cables and joints. The second stage was machines requiring an energy form like coal or wood. The steam engine, for instance, became active and independent once 'fed'. We again began to see ourselves as such a machine. The third, perhaps final, stage is the 'thinking' machine. 'You get the computer scientists,' observes Mike Cooley, 'saying things like, "The human brain is the only computer made by amateurs", and, "Humans will have to accept their true place in the evolutionary hierarchy: animals, human beings and intelligent machines." '

There is a high price to be paid for this technological narcissism. 'Once you begin to perceive machines as being capable of thinking, you begin to reflect on the human mind as a machine, and things like imagination and intuition go by the board. There's a kind of metamorphosis going on in which the created, the machine, is becoming more real, and the creators are becoming more artificial.'

Machine-centred thinking has spread like bushfire to other aspects of human thought. We have reached a stage, maintains Cooley, 'where we can accept something as rational and scientific only if it displays three predominant characteristics: predictability, repeatability and mathematical quantifiability. And, by definition, this precludes intuition, subjective judgement, passive knowledge, dreams, imagination and purpose. And that, it seems to me, is going to be very damaging in the long term.'

276

This is the point of the concern to create human-centred systems: technologies which will preserve and enhance human nature as the core of progress. The kind of computer and other systems we tend to create are fast, reliable, but non-creative. The human being, on the other hand is, in systems terms, slow, inconsistent and unreliable. The fact that it is also highly creative is undervalued. What we have been doing is perceiving our own path of development as a species purely in terms of the One Best Way dictated by the developing machine.

That technological trend is reflected also in political, geographical and cultural patterns. As we have come to believe in the One Best Way of organising our activities, so we have come to believe in the One Best Place (the West), the One Best Tongue (Anglo-American), the One Best Way of Seeing (the rational world-view). The cultural aspect of our condition is characterised by a vacuous restlessness, a void within our souls that we mistake for boredom. Life, we are convinced, is elsewhere. Reality always disappoints us. Where we stand or sit, in this moment, is fixed and ordinary, where we are not is steeped in a seductive exoticism. We need more and more diversion, but somewhere else – around the corner, across the ocean, at the other side of the globe. Our disbelief in the virtue of a place has led us to a placeless unease. The original colonisers simply told their victims that they were worthless, and would have to live with it. The modern form of mass-media colonisation tells us that we are only worthless if we remain where we are; it bombards us with images which devalue our own place, diminish our psychic gravity, and lure us away. We are all angels now, rootless, restless, horizonless, homeless.

Pop is part of the problem: a common language for the race of angels who inhabit the Universal City. In this sense, it encapsulates perfectly the seemingly contradictory elements of oppression, victimhood and collaboration which characterise our colonised condition. But the possibility arises: can it also be part of the solution? If there is no future in admonishing the tide, perhaps the answer lies in getting our feet wet.

This, I think, is what U2 are on about. But I'm not sure, for reasons which I hope to make clear, and then perhaps unclear again. So when I ask Bono if I am right, I give him a choice. This is what you are *on about*, I say. Or perhaps what you are *up against*?

'Up against,' he stresses, and pauses long and silently. 'We're *on about* it in a much more . . . Yeah, we're *on about* it.'

What you notice in talking to U2 is the extent to which questions, which on the face of it appear unconnected to the business of making music, are almost invariably greeted without surprise. The questions scientists like Mike Cooley have to grapple with are also the material of the kind of creative work which the band regard as their business.

'That kind of mentality of control, dominate, synthesise into some sort of structured format, is where so much of the world's culture is going,' agrees The Edge when I ask for his perceptions of the dialectics of the technological trap as observed through the U2 experience. 'And ultimately it's not culture, but anti-culture. Anti-difference, anti-individuality. It's going to a very dangerous end. We talked about totalitarianism of the fascists and the communists, and I think in a weird way, as we get closer and closer to a single world order, where technology gives governments power to locate any individual instantly – which is where we're headed – that's a very dangerous place to be.'

Is there, then, any hopeful way of seeing it?

I think the key to it is freedom within the constraints of technology. What we find liberating about technology is when you are free to be truly creative with it. And that means to discover it for yourself and to approach it almost like play, to approach technology as a toy. The problem is, almost as soon as some new idea gets developed, there's an adult set of instructions which you're given which destroys the chance to be creative within it. We describe is as 'abuse of technology' – the creative approach. I think sampling, for example, as a technology, has all the hallmarks of real creative play about it. People have ended up using samplers in a way that nobody envisaged they would be used when they were first developed. And the second, third, fourth generations of samplers are now being designed with this use in mind. Fairlight was the first generation, and everybody was making recordings of jamjars being hit. Sampling was going into the area of sonics and unusual instrument sounds, almost helping people to capture nature, capture natural sounds and bring them to the realm of conventional recording. No one imagined that people would be sampling recording itself, and collaging previously recorded works, and making new pieces out of old pieces – which, in fact, was absolutely in sync with what was going on in literature and a few years behind fine art. That was really hip, but none of the technical people had thought about it.

It seems to me that what U2, and all the best modern artists, are engaged in is an attempt to bring to the surface things which we know but have lost the means of saying. We need to discover old languages and apply them to the latest things. The struggle is against the One Best Way, against seeing the world in terms only of what is codified and written down, rather than understanding it by what is known to us in a much more instinctive and passive way.

Mike Cooley says that the dichotomy between right and wrong approaches can be seen as an undefined shape in the difference between analogic and digitalised views of the world – the capacity to see angels in a slab of stone or to see only the figures and measurements which describe its physical characteristics. Again, that dichotomy is one with which U2 must constantly grapple. Bono agrees:

> We talk in those two terms all the time in the band. Neil Young has spoken about the way sound has been ironed out by the digital process. That is, the kinks of the sound, which is what we're attracted to, are removed. We've known this for years. We tried working digitally, and my description was that it had the personality of ice. So that there's this kind of evening-out of responses. But I'm not sure that it is the gagging of a culture. One of the things we're also learning is that maybe music isn't best suited to the new media. Maybe there are better media for digital. And that often happens, and there's an awkward moment when the old ideas can't be expressed in the new way. Like the best way to use sampling wasn't rock 'n' roll, but a new format: rap. So you create new media. And that's what our music is. We have to stop thinking in terms of the rock 'n' roll group thing. We have to break with our peers and our past and our idols.

As a species we seem to be coming to a cultural wall. Under the pressure of technology and convergence, the Tower of Babel collapses into a single heap of words, but coherence brings a shrinkage, rather than an expansion, of understanding. And we are all both perpetrators and victims. We lead ourselves to believe we are exercising choice and freedom, but the freedoms we choose are destroying more fundamental ones. So compromised are we by the consequences of accommodating ourselves to our own comforts that we no longer have the consoling luxury of someone to blame. Caught in our own web, we make ourselves comfortable.

'There's been a new movement away from conspiracy theory,' says Bono. 'Conspiracy theory comes out of the idea that there was someone in control. It also suited the drug of the time. I think that ganja is great for conspiracy theories because it's a kind of paranoid thing. And cocaine. But we're more into amnesia now. The drugs are more amnesia-type drugs. And into the void comes the much scarier notion that no one is in charge. The idea that there were a few people sitting around deciding to assassinate J.F.K., that is much less scary. That there is this right-wing vein running right through society, controlling everything. It finds George Bush when he is six and plants him in the White House. All those theories aren't half as scary as the idea that *there is no one in charge*.'

'If you *were* a conspiracy theorist,' observes The Edge drily, 'you might start to get worried about the way things are being refined and pasteurised – every avenue of culture. Differences are disappearing so fast. There was a time when being connected to the Continent was a wonderful idea – it was a place of unbelievable variety and cultural richness. And now it's not the Continent anymore, it's the European Union. How long before we'll all be drinking the same coffees? The bread, the cheese will all be the same. We'll all be speaking some kind of pidgin French-English and using the same currency. The things that made it so attractive are being slowly eradicated.'

Language is at the centre of the battlefield. We cannot fight, only answer back. Our language mutates to match our mechanised view of the world, locking us into our potentially fatal condition. Public language, as utilised in politics, economics and other areas of civic discourse, is disintegrating, narrowing in its capacity to express what we really feel. But while the rhetoric of progress as irrefutably virtuous may have built itself into our language and thinking, there is a paradox that we cannot escape: as we hand over our skills, memories, narrative abilities, we actually abort the possibility of further progress. Far from progressively embracing the future, we paint ourselves permanently into the present. By mortgaging our own cultures, creativity and imagination, we are running the risk of obliterating our capacity to progress.

What is happening is indistinguishable from an advanced and most perfect form of colonisation. But Mike Cooley, for one, believes it is in the nature of the species to fight back.

> The notion of colonisation is something that is rooted in power relationships and historical senses of how it takes place. But you can never succeed in fully colonising something, unless ultimately you destroy it. Because there will always be part of it that will remain outside your control. The American Indians could not understand how we Europeans thought we could buy the land. In the great letter from Chief Seattle to the President he said, 'How can you buy the ripple on a stream? How can you buy the whisper of the wind in the trees?' What he was saying was that there is always a part of any process or activity which is outside our colonising abilities. And I see that in a cultural sense. You see, they cannot quite get at the gold in people's minds. They cannot get at the imagination and the consciousness that is unique to every human being. They will be able to get to part of it, which is the codified written part. But they can't get to the other part, and since they can't get control of it, they tend to organise things, consciously or

unconsciously, to destroy it. It's a kind of cultural scorched-earth policy.

Since the rational mind cannot reduce everything to rule, it has had to persuade itself that what it cannot quantify is no longer relevant. Only what can be objectified counts. Facts matter, feelings don't. Maybe the fact that I am unable to properly articulate my fear that I am losing the capacity to articulate certain fears means that such fears are not only unimportant but possibly non-existent?

'As a scientist and an engineer, I've always found', the Professor reassures me, 'that the things you can state explicitly constitute only a tiny part of that which is the human experience. How do you state explicitly: love? How do you state explicitly: fear? How do you state explicitly: affinity? Such things are processes as well as definitions. And therefore they are things which we have to possess. To really describe love for something or somebody, we must demonstrate it rather than simply define it, and they haven't found any way of doing that. So what they tend to say is that if you can't state something explicitly, it isn't real knowledge in the modern sense.'

It may well be just a phase we're going through. Out of the depths of our colonial condition there may emerge, from time to time, the sudden flash of the real. In the throes of the disease, we may seek a cure within the reserves of the human soul. Our thought processes, though squeezed into a shrinking space, may just become more capable as the threat of extinction increases. 'If you think of knowledge as consisting of a core of fact,' outlines the Professor, 'around which are the fuzzy reasoning, the imagination, the intentionality: one person sees a sunset and that sparks a certain thing: another sees a little skeletal spiderlike child on a television set that hasn't even got the strength to take a fly from its eyes. And these things move us, in spite of everything. I am not pessimistic. My view is that it requires imaginative dialectical turnarounds. I sometimes talk about centring on the periphery, refocusing on the edge, beginning to valorise diversity. We need a renewed recognition of cultural, regional diversity.'

Here lies the importance of discrete and individual tongues and cultures: to tell of the way the world tastes to us, from inside of ourselves, not through the mediated languages of the marketplace or the global village. If the twenty-first century heralds a renewed interest in minority languages, it will not be for sentimental or racialist reasons, but because of a flipping over of our thinking from One Big Tongue to all the little tongues. The virtue of language or ethnicity is not to do with maintaining an attachment to one place, one nation, one landscape, one tongue, but with the capacity to have a metaphysical relationship with any place, any landscape, any language, so as to be able to live in the world at all.

'I think,' says Mike Cooley, 'the reason the idea of the One Best Way is so rooted in our psyche goes back to the Tower of Babel. People had the arrogance to believe that they could build something right up into heaven. And, as a way of punishing them, all this diversity was imposed on them. So they began to speak with diverse tongues. And this was seen as an awesome thing to do to people. Whereas, in fact, in nature and in biology it is this tremendous diversity which is so important. Yet, right from our species' origins we have been intimidated by the idea that this is a terrible disability.'

It is in the diversity of our languages that we carry different ways of understanding things. We cannot trust the translation to say what we really feel. In the absence of words and specific meanings, we lose not merely the distinctive emblem the language affords but also the consciousness that it contains. We need our diverse tongues not just to communicate with others, but to gain access to the knowledge within ourselves. Instead of looking to the external model, which is agreed and defined and fixed and codified, we must go back into the bank of knowledge which has been passed to us by the culture of which we are part.

We come, then, to the $64,000 question: can a people, when their culture is under severest threat, go into their innermost resources to try and save it and themselves? Is there an instinct that will enable, perhaps compel, us to fight back? This is, for me, the meaning of the U2 story. It is to do with the extent to which, in infiltrating the mass medium of rock 'n' roll, they have succeeded in sneaking past the gates of the One Best Way the values and impulses of their peripheral beginnings, their marginal place, their eccentric conditioning, all contained inside the Trojan Horse of their implicit understanding of the nature of seduction in the pop marketplace. Professor Cooley acknowledges this:

> I'm sure that's a possibility. I don't think that most of these things happen in a very conscious way. If things are not done consciously, we don't regard them as being significant, because we're obsessed now with planning. It may just be that it's a natural part of our efforts that if something is suppressed it surfaces in some other form in some other way. Just as in some cultures you have trigger words that resonate things in the unconscious and bring up whole pyramids of knowledge, it may be that with groups like U2 they consciously or unconsciously use words or metaphors or descriptions or forms of music that call up these things within us, and that we feel an affinity for this kind of thing; that it somehow speaks to some part of our suppressed consciousness in a significant way.

There are basic movements and body rhythms and images that are deeply rooted in our psyche. When a particular rhythm is played by people from a particular culture, that will call up that kind of morphic resonance in a particular culture.

Or perhaps something is so deeply rooted in our species that, even when we don't hear it, we feel a deep need to somehow try and recreate it. And if we come across it even accidentally, once we've heard it it begins to fit in with some pattern that we've absorbed from our past. All biological species build in all kinds of capabilities through their own evolution. I marvel at the capacity of salmon to navigate from Lough Corrib to Nova Scotia. They don't *consciously* do it, but they *can* do it.

We are essentially an analogic species, and I think there is great damage when we move to a digital way of knowing things. It is terribly difficult sometimes to cope with information, whereas often an analogy will make the whole thing clear. And I think a lot of music draws analogies with things, the words of songs and all that. They don't quantify things, they just fit in with the way one sees things. I notice that sense in a lot of pop songs, which I think is incredibly powerful. So I see it as supporting and reinforcing that part of us that is analogical rather than digital.

A new self-awareness is only just beginning to surface in Ireland, the merest chink of a belief that perhaps there is something we are useful for after all, that perhaps our past has not been entirely an expense of spirit in a waste of shame. Put simply, it is the growing awareness that, in a world being swept to its ruin by centrifugal forces, hopes of a better future may lie in a return to a view from the fringe, a view which, by virtue of its marginality is less contaminated by the forces of convergence. In other words, the extent to which Irish forms of thought remain 'primitive' may be increasingly useful in the coming years.

In his essay, 'Dreaming of the Middle Ages', Umberto Eco asserts that the Middle Ages are the root of all western society's contemporary 'hot' problems. Most of the systems and technologies we now use, including modern languages, capitalist economy, banking and trade unions, he points out, have their beginnings in the Middle Ages. To look back to the Middle Ages is to look to the infancy of what we call 'modern' society.

For this reason, Eco asserts, what we now call 'modern' societies have been hankering to revisit the Middle Ages almost from the moment that era ended. Mostly this has taken the form of nostalgia, a continuous return in search of lost romanticism. By dreaming of the Middle Ages, writes Eco, we have created a New Middle Age in which to live. Drawing an analogy between the fall of the Roman Empire and the present disintegration of the American Dream, he observes that what is required to make a good Middle Ages is the collapse of both a great peace and a great international power that has unified the world in language, customs, ideologies, religions, art and technology. These conditions, which ushered in the 'previous' Middle Ages with the collapse of the Roman Empire, are replicated in the collapsing certainties of western society. Eco observes that a study of the two ages reveals a 'perfect correspondence' in the way in which both attempted to camouflage their paternalistic efforts to control the minds of their people. Both used visual communication to disperse images of ideologies which they had developed in written form, thereby seeking to bridge the gap between learned and popular cultures. The Middle Ages Eco describes as 'the civilisation of vision, where the cathedral is the great book in stone'; today, the same function is fulfilled by television and pop culture.

The filthy modern tide, then, the modern and the postmodern, the surreal and the absurd, the science fiction and rock 'n' roll, are all expressions of our hankering after our lost spirit of Byzantium, arising from the need to 'dismantle and reconsider the flotsam of a previous world, harmonious perhaps, but by now obsolete'. What we face, then, is a period of permanent transition, requiring what Eco calls new hypotheses for the exploitation of disorder, 'entering into the logic of conflictuality'. There will be born, he begins to conclude, 'a culture of constant readjustment, fed on utopia'. The possibility insinuates itself: what we call postmodernism may not be about chaos at all, but a kind of instinctive response to deal with the detritus of the Industrial Revolution.

The postmodern mind is a post-colonial condition. The best versed are therefore likely to be the most practised in the post-colonial limbo dance, the tip of the cap that conceals the sly turn of the mouth, the laughable laughter of angels. As we approach the doorway in the wall that guards the end of the millennium, the confusion we are now obliged to channel through the narrowest of forms may open like an umbrella on the other side. We in Ireland may be sitting on the secret of taking the lighted flame safely through.

The early part of the 'original' Middle Ages was characterised by a wave of intellectual activity sweeping through Europe, with the 'saints and scholars' to the fore – Irish monks who, as Eco reminds us, crossed Europe 'spreading ideas, encouraging reading, promoting foolishness of every description' among the barbarian civilisations. Here, in the chaos of disintegration, massacres and plague, western man achieved the maturity to go on.

One of Eco's books, *Chaosmos*, deals with the dialectic between medievalism and modernism in the work of James Joyce. The title is a word borrowed from Joyce. 'Obviously,' Eco remarked in a 1992 television interview with Richard Kearney, 'an author who has invented the word chaosmos was a little obsessed by this possibility of creative opposition.' The only flourishing civilisation during the medieval period, Eco acknowledged, existed in Ireland, and this civilisation already contained the seeds of the Joycean moment. 'What happened with the Irish medieval culture was that Marginalia became Centralia. The *Book of Kells* is made only of Marginalia, and that is the way in which Irish culture was already Joycean at that medieval moment, trying to introduce extraneous elements, to disturb the order of things, to find a different order.'

The thrust of the argument is obvious: we can do it again. What it hints at it that there may be something in the Irish mind, a consequence of its unique historical experience, which, being for whatever reasons more attuned to chaos, is therefore more qualified for the present quest for a different order. In the 'first' Middle Ages, Irish monks and poets contributed significantly to the development of new forms of thought; in the New Middle Ages, beset by the same quandary of transition, does the Irish mind have the presence to do the same again?

What might the vital characteristics be? Richard Kearney, in his introduction to *The Irish Mind*, observes that this mind does not reveal itself as a single, fixed and homogeneous entity. It could nevertheless be seen to have remained largely free of the linear, centralising logic of the Graeco-Roman culture which dominated most of Western Europe, which insisted that order and logic could come only from the separation of such 'contradictory' concepts as reason and imagination, soul and body, and so on. But, observes Kearney, 'in contradistinction to the orthodox dualist logic of either/or, the Irish mind may be seen to favour a more dialectical logic of both/and: an intellectual ability to hold the traditional oppositions of classical reason together in creative confluence'. This non-dualistic 'tolerance of opposites,' Professor Ivor Browne has observed, 'is characteristic of much of Eastern thought, both in the ancient Taoist tradition in China and in the Vedantic traditions of India . . . and may well derive from the early Indo-European culture, the origins of which are now lost in the mists of time'.

One of the paradoxes of the Renaissance may have been that, in uniting the European mind, it began a deep division in the human psyche which, consolidated by the Enlightenment, possibly helped provoke the most appalling nightmares of this century. In the separating of classical and popular culture, of 'high' and 'low' artforms, it separated also thoughts and feelings, senses and soul, mind and heart. It was only a short waltz to Auschwitz. Having read lots of books, as writer and critic George Steiner observed to Richard Kearney in the *Visions of Europe* TV-interview series, does not prevent people becoming barbarous. 'It did not prevent the collapse of European civilisation into ultimate barbarity: it did not prevent savagery. Instead, it may even have abetted it.'

The reducibility of the world is a classical idea. The attempt to force life into behaving as though the divisions we ourselves had created were natural and sensible is the root of the crises – ecological, political, economic – which now threaten us. To remind us otherwise must be the purpose of all art: to tell us that we carry within us all the possibilities of our flyness. To venture out at all in the acid rain of modernity, the human soul must clothe itself in garments appropriate to the blur. Perhaps rather than the fascination of the damned, postmodernism is just a rummage for the right coat. Maybe our present confusion is an inchoate beginning to a new kind of response, which will mutate to bring all this chaos into the light of . . . God? Bono responds:

> That's a positive thought. If you take on the idea of modernism as having a spiritual root, that it begins in the Reformation, and is in one sense a German/Anglo-Saxon movement to get back to the essence. In that sense it is anti-Catholic. That situation has not reached its end. We have straight lines and blank walls, but we don't have essence. We haven't got back to the purity of . . . like Rothko. There was something going on in that painter's head that was, to me, modern. But it was also spiritual. So where modernism meets the spirit: that's where we're at now. If you take away the spiritual aspect from all this, then I imagine that all you're left with is postmodernism. But there's two tracks you can take here; one is away from postmodernism, towards essence and simplicity, and still on that same journey, the same trajectory. And the other is postmodernism.
>
> What we were praising, or attempting to praise, on *Zooropa* was uncertainty as a good first step. That was the annoying thing about modernism; it was so certain. It was so sure of itself. That's why you could have revolutions where people could be discounted. Like Stalinism. Like America in its own way. It was so certain of this new future that it became a dangerous place to be. When you start to see individuals as of less value than ideas, you're in trouble.

George Steiner is a man who has given thought to the problem of what he calls 'the Americanisation of the planet'. His is not the old, predictable gripe; the situation is not for him without its ambivalent aspects. The elite notion of culture, he concedes, is now coming under threat, but this is not unmitigatedly bad. There is an understandable anger, he concedes, felt by those who have been left out of the club of recognised culture, which he hopes may lead to some self-questioning by those on the inside about the price to be paid for their elitism. Steiner is alive to the possibility that, somewhere between the apocalyptic and the blasé, there may be an avenue of progress. The question is, as he has so correctly observed: are we going to find something better than Disneyland? He, like Umberto Eco and Bono, believes that the way forward might be through a revisitation of the distant past. 'I think we should be studying more about what is wrongly called the Dark Ages,' he told Richard Kearney on the *Visions of Europe* series, 'when small groups, particularly Irish monks, scholars, wanderers, lovers of poetry and scripture and of the classics, began copying them by hand again, began founding libraries. We've been through difficult stages like this. I'm not at all pessimistic. I see a pendulum motion between a certain elitist rapture of excellence and the ordinary passion for having a better day and night of it.'

There is a curious resonance between the statements on this subject from George Steiner and Umberto Eco, not merely in their tentative pointing to the same point of possible resolution, but in their sketchy knowledge of the place where the answer may lie. While Eco has some knowledge of popular culture, Steiner has only a mannerly, if patronising, tolerance. But both assume that, for example, pop music is always synonymous only with entertainment. Both men seem vaguely aware that the direction in which they are pointing is the right one, but they seem unconvinced that there is anything there. Steiner looks on Disneyland 'in despair', as though having examined it he has found it falling short of his expectations. Because he does not understand popular culture, he writes off everything else as well. 'And yet,' he muses, 'you may ask me, do I have something better to offer? What am I going to do for human beings who don't think that reading Kant, or Joyce, or Goethe, is the be-all and end-all of their lives, and who, nevertheless, want more leisure, want more elbow-room for sensibility? That is probably the most difficult question of all, and in a funny way, people like us, privileged intellectuals, have almost disqualified ourselves from answering it.'

Everything Steiner says makes sense. But he is missing some vital pieces of his jigsaw. He bemoans the Americanisation of the planet, and also the fact that what the outside world receives of US culture is actually its worst bits: 'McDonalds, Kentucky Fried Chicken, the comic book, and all the dreadful soap operas.' The American language, he protests, has taken over Europe. 'With the exception of the Beatles, there has not been a major counter-statement with any kind of comparable explosive dynamic, in the English language.'

Well, no, actually. It is arguable that, mind for mind, heart for heart, the impact of U2 in both the US and the rest of the western world is now at the very least comparable to that of the Beatles. George Steiner has possibly never heard of U2, and might be puzzled at the idea that he should know anything about them. And yet, when he gesticulates vaguely at the merest speck he perceives on the horizon, he may be pointing directly at U2.

U2 may not thank me for associating them with a putative return to the Middle Ages, but when you trace the stream of thought from Eco's dream of the Middle Ages, through Steiner's prognostications, to the Irish mind as defined by Richard Kearney and Ivor Browne, the possibility surfaces that an Irish band with sight of its soul, working in a medium which makes a virtue of fragmentation and brevity may be best placed to make sense in a world disintegrating at the edges. In a colonised world, the only reliable vaccine is the hair of the coloniser or the heir of the slave. And perhaps we can dare to go a step further. If our narrative capacity has been permanently impaired by television, to the point where our memory is incapable of absorbing anything longer than three minutes, mightn't a three-minute pop song be the ideal communication of the future, the ultimate Marginalia in which to scribble the secrets of the soul? And who better to write and sing those songs than the descendants of the saints and scholars who colonised the mind of medieval Europe, using foolishness of every description? I merely ask.

In the face of the pace of modern life, conventional art forms surrender and vegetate. There are no great modern Irish painters or composers, and many of our writers seem content to lean upon the past glories of the tradition they claim. Irish cinema, for all its recent strides, is still in its infancy. In the possibilities of pop music there seems to be something.

Everything you know is wrong. The slogan means exactly what it says. Bad is good. Old is new. The centre is the edge. A laugh is a cry in disguise. In the twenty-first century, the sight of the end of the road will bring us to the realisation that we have been on the wrong road for some time. This will move Ireland from the periphery of things, to the heart of the matter. The periphery will be transformed into the core, not as a return to simpler values, but as a different way of seeing how modernity can be shaped and formed. If the sight of the Gate of Hell does anything at all, it may alert us that progress must become the servant of human beings, rather than the other way around.

We will, if we're clever and lucky enough, unscramble the knots of flawed and dangerous thinking which have brought us to the brink of destruction. The periphery will become the core. Life will cease to be something that occurs only elsewhere. As the absurdities of industrialism become more clear, we will look to the losers and the wronged for the undoing of the destruction which the winners have wrought. Those people and places which opted or were pushed out of the madness will show us the way forward. The victims of greed, imperialism, power and limitless growth will be the ones with the best grasp of how to go on. As the suction of economic centrification eases, the sense of place will renew itself. As we rumble the way in which the benefits for our own evolution have been commandeered by the most poweful forces in the marketplace, we will need to relearn, or perhaps learn for the first time, to make relationships between the most modern technology and the cultural heritage from which we emerge, to understand both with equal profundity. We will begin again to respect diversity, to understand that good does not reside in being alike, homogeneous, but in being different and yet in touch with what unites us.

Because Ireland is still among the most 'backward' societies in the western world, because we have escaped the most ruthless effects of capitalist development, we still have a chance of learning from the mistakes of others. The most 'primitive' and unspoilt might lead the way back from the brink.

'There's something about coming from this island,' The Edge agrees. 'It makes you view the rest of the world somewhat differently. You feel like you're standing slightly outside of the mainstream anyway. Although that's changing. It's astonishing to see how Ireland, at incredible speed, is falling into sync with the rest of the world. And I wonder where that will bring us in years to come. The thing, I suppose, that every eighteen-year-old gets so frustrated with is that it has been so out of sync with other parts of the world. But in some ways it's what makes it more interesting. And if we start to fall in step, how will that affect things? I don't know.'

We have a problem. The Edge is not Irish, at least not in the conventional sense. He was born, of Welsh parents, in London. I wonder if it is useful to ask if he feels Irish, English or Welsh? 'I feel culturally Irish. Most definitely,' he says. 'I don't feel particularly Welsh culturally. I've spent a lot of time abroad, but I feel most at home in Ireland. Although I've always felt something of an outsider in Ireland. Growing up as a kid, I always felt that I didn't quite belong here, for one reason or another. Nor do I belong anywhere else. I guess I've grown accustomed to being just slightly displaced – not in any heavy way, but I have this sense of being just slightly different. And in a weird way, that's why I got into music, maybe in an attempt to resolve that to some extent.'

That instinct might yet serve us all. The essence lies not so much in the music which it provokes, but in the possibilities which that music suggests. Music, as Jacques Attali observed, has the capacity to destroy or renew. Or rather, it embodies in sound our own capacity to do either or both to ourselves. It can silence us or allow us to speak from the depths of our souls.

Totalitarian theory, as he noted, perceives 'noise' as dangerously subversive, because it articulates demands for cultural autonomy and support for marginality and difference.

Pop music is therefore at the heart of the modern paradox: it is product, palliative and prophetic subversion. If it fails to fulfil any one of these functions, it either doesn't survive or becomes part of the problem. To have any currency at all in the postmodern world, art must not simply observe or recreate, but must participate with and feed into the everyday world. This should not be confused with simply conveying the condition of chaos and disorder. There is a line between communicating chaos and abetting it, and the best artists are those who can get in closest without breaching that line. Art must run the risk of seeming to be something else. The materials of the truly modern artist are not simply canvas and paint or pen and ink, but his body, soul, self and imagination clothed in the mud of the everyday murk. He is both actor and activist, creator and catalyst, form and theme, medium and message.

The communications media refuse to perceive celebrity, for example, as anything other than a by-product of an industry called entertainment, at best a function of a parallel creativity. But at the hands of an intelligent artist, celebrity becomes an instrument of illustration and illumination. Virtual reality works both ways: the world becomes more technocratic, commodified, absurd, surreal, unbelievable; but art, instead of holding up a mirror or wagging a finger, runs to embrace the clamour. At the moment of contact it is impossible to tell what is real and what is not. The closer to truth, the harder it is to tell whether life or art is the most unreal. The true may be a moment of the false, but the 'real' truth, of course, is that, in the modern world, nothing is more than virtually real. Everything is ambiguous. U2, their music, their identity, their performances, and the sum total of these which comprises their art, are among the best examples of this modern artistic phenomenon.

U2 show the signs of a people well versed in the psychology of colonialism from both perspectives – of both the didactic instinct and the inner knowledge of a people in whom what was worthwhile and inspired was stifled and buried. Perhaps we are arriving at a time when this may be able to emerge into a light which will make its confusion seem normal. The world U2 evoke in their music is the world as it is and might increasingly become. What they seek to suggest is what we might do about living in it, and to this purpose they remain fixed on a place within themselves. They are *of* that world and yet maintain a primitive but timeless integrity which both transcends and embraces the filthy modern tide. Most of their contemporaries sought to run away from the gore and mystery of the past and also somehow to avoid the whirr and rattle of the future. U2 sought a way of bringing the two together to help them live in the present. Like the 'Cherokee artist' Jimmie Durham, though in a vastly more complex form, they are postmodern primitives, cutting up the past to make a better future. Theirs is a moral art without being moralistic. It carries a health warning for the human soul, but one that presents neither ultimatum nor advice. U2 have a 'view', but it is an ambiguous one, one that crystallises rather than bemoans the modern dilemma. They are neither nihilists, nor reactionaries, nor apocalyptics. They represent, as far as is possible, the condition of being alive at the end of the twentieth century. They offer no 'but's, no 'if's, no 'unless'es. This is the way the world is, they say, and it won't stop. But this doesn't mean that we have to become as hard and passionless as the world we inhabit.

After fifteen years, U2 remain as much an aberration within the rock business as in their home territory. They're still not 'cool'. Perhaps it is this very factor that has allowed them to tap into a longing which runs deep in the mind of western society – the desire for a more true means of expression, for what Umberto Eco described as 'the injection of genuine elements', a return to soulfulness, a reconnection of thought and feeling in the soluble capsule of a three-minute song.

'There's a warmth and humanity in Irish music that I don't see in the big city music of London or New York,' Bono told Richard Kearney in 1988. The kind of music people would be 'holding under their arms like holy books or treasures' in the 1990s would, he anticipated, be much more traditional, whether Irish, American, soul, reggae, cajun or whatever. 'These musics may be reinterpreted by the new technology, but as we are more dehumanised, urbanised, corralled into confusion, surely we will turn to simplicity, to "the pure drop" of Seamus Ennis, the voice of Van Morrison.'

Bono's view has changed only as much as it has needed to in the meantime. Four years on he says:

Even in music and art there's a changing of the guard. It's the end of the 'cold wave' and hopefully of the hardness associated with modernism, where chaos is not challenged, just reflected – like a mirror. I don't want to get into Anglo-Saxon bashing, because there are such great attributes to that culture, but emotionally, I think, as well as intellectually, we Irish have a lot to offer. It's a less empirical view, if you like, that Irish people have. It's more into magic. And that's the future, even the future of science. The future of physics is in the area of metaphysics. The next century could be full of all kinds of baloney, but it'll be a very interesting time. Because there are two ideas that dominated this century, and one of them was, I suppose, that there is no God, and the other was communism, which is itself a materialist point of view, which saw things very logically – that you can, in a controlled environment – 'evolve' people to a point where they're not greedy. But that doesn't work. People start to realise that greed and avarice are problems of the human *spirit* more than they are political or social. And so the things of the spirit are very interesting, more important, now. People in medicine are starting to realise that our minds and our bodies are linked much more closely than we imagined. And ideas which were laughed at – like repentance, for instance – are centre-stage in psychotherapy now, and that the simple act of confession turns out to be *years* ahead of its time. It's like the idea of speaking to somebody about something that you've done, and leaving it with them, and leaving that little box without it, hopefully – that, actually, from a point of view of physical wellbeing, makes you well. So, even Catholicism, which at times had its hands on the throat of Ireland, and maybe oppressed us more than England – there's even value *there*. I can't take a lot of the dogma, but there are worthwhile things. I'm just saying, in a roundabout way, that we have something to offer, we have a point of view, we have a *bent* that's worth something as we go into the next century. It's not the *whole* of the story. It's a *piece* of the story. But it's a piece of the story that's *more* important rather than *less* important than it was.

U2 did what they did by being hot when everyone else was not, by being warm when everyone else was cool, and by being cold and calculating when the rest of us were getting cosy in the web we had fashioned for ourselves. They detached themselves in their semi-detacheds. They watched and waited. They worked, dogged and deliberately, like the parable of the talents. They pulled themselves clear of the mediocrity in which they were mired and changed, as a wise rock critic said, from gauche to gods. Slowly, but knowingly, they contrived a noise which might fill the aching hole in the belly of their times. They succeeded in this because they saw holes where no one else saw them. Because the possibilities of the sixties had been so great, and the disappointment so total, most of us thought of the thing as a failed project or at best a nice try for an unattainable ideal. Hope was not ours, but belonged, with a bit of luck, to those who would come of age in a decade in the next century sufficiently separated from the last rays of hope that a new seed could be planted in a spirit of naiveté and forgetfulness. The rest of us saw in the recent dawn either a vindicating failure or an accusing heroism. U2 saw the unfinished business. In so far as we made a connection between the music and the ideas of the sixties, most of us heard the music of the Beatles, Elvis, the Rolling Stones, and thought of it as an end in itself, as a closed book with a sort of ending. U2 saw it as a first volume. Most of us saw punk as a rude reprise, a sequel, a retreading of the old noise for a new generation. U2 recognised it as the flawed first sentence in a new story. They were smart enough to see that a new generation wouldn't be satisfied with a slightly louder version of the same idea just because they liked the noise that it made. The rest was easy, because hardly anyone else was bothered enough to begin the enquiry. Some of us laughed a lot. But when we heard the new noise, we were forced to ask, 'Why didn't *I* think of that?' It was a good question, but what worried us even more was the vague awareness that we had thought about it but had dismissed it out of hand.

One of the problems U2 were to suffer from was a crippling knowingness. Unlike Elvis, or even the Beatles, they couldn't do what they did without appearing to think about it. There were too many ghosts walking through the room. John Lennon had queered the pitch by talking too much sense, by thinking too hard, and by being right most of the time. There could never be another Elvis or another Beatles, any more than there could be another J.F.K. or Martin Luther King. Those who didn't want to believe only had to point to where the bodies were buried.

Could U2 really betray their times? No rock 'n' roll band can. The medium itself demands, above all, godlike presence and egotism. Innocence and virtue, though interesting attributes, can be applied only in diluted form. This is partly why some people wish to attribute so much of the U2 magic to Brian Eno. He has the appearance of virtue, which rock bands, by reason of being rock bands, appear to lack. Being mere gods, they lack the luxury of purity, but have to slip and slide within the arena that is provided for the main business of selling the new noise in the high street. But while it is possible to acknowledge the breathtaking scope of Brian Eno's genius, and even to predict the discovery of his own music by the commercial market in the next century, there is no point in declaring Eno a superior artist simply on account of his purity of spirit, his air of thoughtful asceticism. Without the mud of the arena, the dust of the street market, he would neither exist nor have a reason to. His purity is only possible through the existence of the excesses which he so sensibly avoids.

If the tentative knowledge we have of our situation has only become possible through a vision of hell, the full truth will be driven home not by the pious warnings of the righteous, but by the Devil who drives us harder to the edge. For this reason it is necessary for the angels to don the horns and imitate the Devil's laugh. This is why it was as useful as it was necessary for the folk music of the twentieth century to become itself a product of industrial capitalism, so that the seed of the human spirit might be carried as far as possible along the road, so that the gates of hell might be recognised when they came into view. The music of angels must be as indistinguishable

293

as possible from the music of the Devil, so that the Devil will be made envious of its textures, rhythms and poise. Only then will it appeal to both the light and the dark in us, and leave a chink of hope that the light will carry the day.

The seemingly problematic status of contemporary music as both commodity and art form, or both global demagogue and intimate confidante, can perhaps be seen as a necessary contradiction in terms. 'I think it's one of those wonderful tensions, creative tensions,' said Bono to me in the summer of 1992, 'that you're making very private and personal statements on a public address system. The scale seems to deride the personal nature. One of the most extraordinary things about rock 'n' roll is that, by definition, it is not a private party. I think that, almost by definition, this artform is a public one. It seems to get more interesting the more it draws on its contradictions, and the bigger it gets. I just don't think the Beatles would have made the music they made were it not for the fact that they were a phenomenon. I don't think, if it was just a Liverpool thing, that you'd have got past, maybe, *Rubber Soul.* And I suppose that, also, it reflects what's going on anyway, which is this kind of breakdown of personal cultures and country dividing lines, and that whole blur. It seems to draw on the blur.'

'It's a music right now that feeds on bullshit,' he told me in that summer. 'And there's plenty of that about. If you're lookin' for inspiration, just turn on the TV, go to a glass church, open *Hello!* magazine. It's just everywhere. Yes, it's these contradictions. I feel like I've got one hand on a positive terminal, one hand on the minus, and I'm just letting this stuff just go through us. And that is the very energy of rock 'n' roll, actually.'

Contained within the concept we know loosely as rock 'n' roll in its modern state are all the signs and clues which can inform us of both the dangers and the possibilities of a future life. The music is poised on the tightrope between human weakness and the endless possibilities of the technologies which man is capable of developing. No other artistic medium utilises technology in the same way. No other medium has the same capacity to engage the human spirit using the possibilities of the most inhuman products of that spirit. No medium is therefore more capable of articulating the contradiction of what it will mean, in the future, to be human. As Brian Eno said once, 'Rock music has always been teetering on two borderlines. One is the borderline of a very advanced technology, and the other is a borderline of people using it who don't have a clue of what to do with it.'

U2 are a perfect example of this. What the best modern rock 'n' roll artists show us is that it is possible not merely to preserve the spirit of humanness through the process of technology, but that there is nothing in the technology which can threaten that spirit if the human beings continue to know who they are and what they should desire.

The contempt of the outside world has led the medium to sell itself short of its own promise. The 'philosophy' of cool has served to divide those elements of life which are aesthetically or politically pleasing from those which are 'merely' everyday, human and necessary. But this lie, too, has been rumbled in the U2 story. There is no point in saying that it's *only* rock 'n' roll. Far from being a radical or even cool position, this is merely stupid. It is to say that there is a state of human existence which is about nothing other than believing the myths of the prefabricated universe. Whether we admit, or even know, the reasons we do things at all are, however tangentially, however perversely, to do with surviving, with making the time pass in a more bearable way. The irony is that it is people who most *like* rock 'n' roll who say that it is 'only rock 'n' roll', and in doing so betray the promise of the music they claim to love by damning it with low expectations. Play the guitar! they say, and keep your opinions to yourself! Boogie on down! and don't be annoying me with your angst and ideas. But we know that they are not telling the full truth. Their superficiality is a disguise to hide their need to pretend the drug they're addicted to is more harmless than their appetite for it suggests. We know that the real reason for their irritated insouciance is that they do not want us to know how important it is, and how much it reflects of their own private griefs and desires. Their superficiality signals the need for a new form. Perhaps from now on we should refer to two forms of modern music: 'rock 'n' roll' and 'only rock 'n' roll'.

'There are some very dull minds out there,' says Bono with a sigh. 'It's actually like saying, "What's wrong with being a painter?" Well, *be* a painter then. And if you're a really, really amazing painter, it transcends the problem. But there *is* a problem. There really *is*. Because painting just isn't what it was in the seventeenth century. But by all means. What I find a bit embarrassing is . . . [he lifts a phantom brush] "Look! I'm a painter!" Because there was a time when there was an excitement in that explosion. Wow! But just because it's the first time you've plugged in a guitar and turned it up to eleven, don't expect the rest of the world to get excited about it. If, however, you create something with this rather archaic thing, then we will all get out of your way. The annoying thing is when postmodernism allows us to repeat, without reinvention, a moment. That's what I can't cope with. And that's what I find so hilariously funny about some of the groups that are out there now. We like them because they remind us of something that was great.'

The response of the only rock 'n' rollers to the reinvention of U2 that occurred around the time of *Achtung Baby* was broadly positive. At last, they said, U2 are beginning to loosen up and behave like a real rock band should. Weeeee-ha! Rock 'n' roll! Yeahh! In a sense, of course, the change was effected precisely to invite such a response, not so much for its own sake but for the measurement it conveyed of the success of the manoeuvre. This, of course, opened up two possibilities: the 'reinvention' might be an attempt to update the camouflage while focusing more precisely on the same targets, or it could be an exercise in pissing about. Actually there's a third: it could be both.

'Well,' says Bono, 'it's definitely the third.'

Isn't that dangerously ambiguous, ambivalent almost?

> Even talking about it is betraying it to some degree. You see, to have an agenda is in one sense very restrictive. That's why you have to be loose with all this stuff. Because if you try to tie it down and get serious and reach conclusions, you're leaving your own medium behind and entering into another one. Part of what we do, part of what any artist does, is illusion: you suggest rather than spell out. I think it's very important to keep that flirtatiousness, to write trashy pop songs set in these worlds. This was the great thing about William Gibson. He realised that science fiction as a genre was in a very interesting place: nobody was taking it seriously. Wonderful! Now we can really get the work done. He writes almost Chandler-esque sci-fi novels – street sci-fi, whatever you want to call it – that also keep their feet in the mud. He doesn't allow it to move into theory too much. But it's set in theory. And I think the same is true about rock 'n' roll – it's great that nobody expects too much out of it, and part of you wants to keep up that perception, whereas the other half of you is taking it seriously. It's like John Lydon saying, nearly twenty years on, that he based Johnny Rotten on Richard III. I laughed my head off. But I'm sure it's accurate. I'm sure he thought very seriously about it. But he could never have said that. He can't even say it *now*! This is the thing about the mystery and the mischief again. So we say things, and then dance back from them and run like hell.

This flirtatiousness characterises both the music U2 make and the packaging in which it is enwrapped. The flame that burns at the heart of the music is enclosed in a sound that makes it resemble the world which it attempts to subvert. It appeals to both the devil and the angel in the listener. Similarly, as The Edge explains, with an elaborate project like Zoo TV, which appears to be removed from and at odds with the music, and yet enables its strength to come through.

Television is no longer just the medium of visuals, moving pictures – it's the whole culture of television, which is itself a medium almost. Since TV has now gone global, and stopped being just regional, I think that there's been a massive shift in its influence. So I'd say that the questions it raises are the big questions of the moment. Whether or not we're able to illuminate what we're doing or whether it ends up just being a wonderful kind of postmodern mess and diversion, I don't know. We're certainly trying to expose and to illuminate through what we're doing. But is that enough? I don't know. People from time to time criticise us for being politically too simplistic, politically forthright, politically active. On the other hand we've got a lot of criticism for being non-political, for being too standoffish and not getting stuck in. In this instance I think we're being a bit more subtle about how we're putting ideas across, and what we're trying to say with our songs. It's not quite as open a book.

The only reaction to madness it to laugh at it. And chaos, I suppose, is somewhat the same. To try and create sense out of it is impossible. And I suppose when everything else is stripped away, all you're left with is a certain kind of humour and irony. I guess that's our best defence ultimately – to be able to laugh at what's going on, and at the tragedy in our confusion. And in some ways it's a triumph. Our interest in irony and our decision to get away from being earnest and hitting topics head-on is an attempt, I suppose, to allow ourselves to be more human in our work, and also to give ourselves the release of that approach of not necessarily taking things too seriously whilst at the same time hopefully covering some important ground. The problem is that people, if given the opportunity to mock a strongly expressed opinion, will often do that rather than taking the slightly more difficult route of engaging with the idea. There's so much trust involved in that, implicitly, that sometimes it seems like it's asking too much. You're asking people to go along with the emotion of a song and to follow it through, and in doing that you're really exposing yourself. It's too much for a lot of people. We've decided to go underground, I suppose!

Nobody could seriously suggest that the strong moral sense with which U2 developed, however much to do with the hidden desires of their times, was simply a branded product, a unique selling point. But the problem arises that, as they get better at imitating the Devil's laughter, they will become more and more indistinguishable from what the Devil would try to sound like if he was even half as clever as we have been led to believe. The both/and mentality, however adaptable, has to know its own limits. You cannot really be both angel *and* Devil. And while U2's desire to escape their reputation for excessive earnestness is entirely understandable, there is still a planet to be saved. Deep down, I like to think, they are still serious, with short bursts of silliness. If they go the other way, there is the danger of becoming indistinguishable from what people who completely misunderstand every-thing will see as a logical progression from where, they wrongly imagine, they are now. After a short burst of serious thought, Bono says:

> You see, what our point with the whole thing was: we are still serious. *Painfully* serious. Obsessively, boringly serious about all the questions that we were so earnest about in the eighties. It's just that we've gotten better at disguising that, at packaging that, at knowing how it works. But I don't think for a second that we were ever that far away from that place. So the people who say, 'Well, thank Christ U2 have relaxed!' – I don't think they could be further from the truth. I think we got really heavy. When we were in Berlin doing *Achtung Baby*, it was definitely the most serious sessions we've ever had. Terribly tormented. And, yeah, there's probably some people saying, 'Lighten up!' . . . 'For what?!' Get me a reason to lighten up, I'll lighten up.
>
> But, I mean, that shift collided with lots of things. We refer to that whole thing as 'Glasnost'. We refer to ourselves as the Gang of Four and the Politburo – and this is how people refer to us in the organisation. And on another level that change was as banal as wanting to join the rest of the planet in getting *out of it*. But even there I am just a pain in the arse, because I'm thinking . . . 'Out of it'??? *That's* interesting! What are you getting out of? And why? So in one sense you are experimenting on yourself.

'I think that primarily we've used our music to change us, rather than trying to change people or places,' is how he explained the same idea to me a couple of years before. 'I think our music will become *more* personal, and in doing so maybe much more political in the real sense. But I'm not going to say that I think rock 'n' roll should be kept in its little box, like as if politics is something that mere mortals cannot understand or grapple with. I really object to that. And I'm not going to deride the ideas of cooperation that work within U2 as just part of youth culture, or what they call in Ireland "The Youth".' He laughs. 'And The U2!'

As to where the present phase might lead musically, all there is to go on is the occasional clue, perhaps in the things that didn't quite fit into *Zooropa*. Bono says:

There was one song called 'Wake up Dead Man'. I've been trying my hand at writing these, like, psalms – off the wall, shouting at God. Funny and irreverent and all this. This one goes: 'Jesus help me/I'm all alone in this world/And a fucked-up world it is too/Tell me/Tell me the story/The one about Eternity/And the way it's gonna be/Your Father/Who made the world in seven/He's in charge of Heaven/Would he put a word in for me?' And then the last verse goes: 'Jesus/I'm waiting here boss/I know you're looking out for us/ But maybe our hands aren't free.' That didn't make it to the last record, and that's interesting. Maybe it's that we had to go out to there to come back to where we're at. But it's all part of the same stretch in my head. What I'd like now is to go back to that three-stranded chord again. I want to be able to move, rather than in albums, and maybe even rather than in songs, to move in phrases in between these lines. Rather than work in broader strokes: 'This album is about that' – these last two albums were very clear in terms of their identities – what I'd like to do on our next record is to move in and out of modes, to turn on a sixpence. I want to be able to shift through those extremes. Rather than going *out there* with one album and going *in there* with another, I'd like to do it on one record. See I don't mind there just being ordinary songs written on an acoustic guitar. If they're great ones, they're fine. But that's not where it's at. We will definitely do them, but it's to be able to be that and not to be it. We're still trying to make that perfect album – in our heads it would be like our *White Album*, I suppose. Where the songs are very clear on one level, but on another the music is completely out there. At the moment, I'm looking at it from a thematic point of view. What songs do I want to sing and can I get away with singing next to each other? That's a fairly tangible ambition for the next project.

Some people would say, 'That's over.' But I don't think it is. I think you can have that on the one hand, and something else on the other. That's what I'm saying. I think that we can be putting out videos that are not records, that are pure visual media – at the same time as we have a song on the radio, at the same time as we're playing concerts. Different formats. Imagine we have a record and we remix it as a dance record, so that U2 is playing in that format. In every city there are clubs with sound systems that these particular set-ups work on. You have to play to it. So you work within that framework, and enjoy it. But that's a different framework to the song that's on the radio. Or maybe you don't even have that song on the radio. So you're further pushing out that idea that you don't have to be one thing or the other.

It is, after all, 'only' rock 'n' roll. That too. Both/and. It is ephemeral and throwaway, and yet, for that very reason, perhaps the only artform capable of dealing with the fragmented reality of the modern world. But how does the artist convey this to people who, because they are outside, don't know the codes?

What I've come up with is that it's not a problem, that there is a code, and if you can't break it, you're not invited in. And that maybe rock 'n' roll should stop explaining itself. People like me should stop talking about it. Rock 'n' roll is about mystery and mischief. And in a way, the eighties was about airbrushing it and trying to explain it so that everybody could get into it. Now I'm starting to think that, without throwing a ring around it, you can allow the people who don't understand it to stay where they are.

But if you stand in that arena, with this show happening, you realise that in one sense it's a form in its infancy. There's so much energy there, especially if you go into the big shows, the big outdoor events, seventy thousand people, a hundred thousand people. This incredible energy that can go right or wrong. I get the feeling that it's becoming even more vital.

I think it's a lack of imagination that leaves us with the music that we've got at the moment. I think the form itself is more exciting than ever. There's a lack of vision, I think, and also a small-mindedness in the media. There is an environment that music grows out of, there's no question about it. Jimi Hendrix, the Beatles, there were people around them, translators, writers, who were actually understanding what they were doing in a bigger picture, feeding them back this information, recreating and making it bigger, and larger, and passing it on. This amazing whirlpool of activity that threw out great records like *Blonde on Blonde* or the *White Album*, or whatever. And I think part of the reason that's not there is environment. I think that writing about rock 'n' roll has become so banal. I grew up reading Tony Parsons and Charles Shaar Murray, and later Gavin Martin. These people inspired us to be in bands in the first place. And I think one of the reasons the music was coming out of there, and also one of the reasons it hasn't got further than there, is because they've tied ropes around the feet of bands, they won't let them leave ground. I think that rock 'n' roll, by definition, is *about* leaving the ground, heading to . . . wherever, the Planet Narcissus! Up there! Out there!

This is what it comes down to: you sit in a bar after a long day. You have crawled through the streets on fire. You have looked out at the world from a body missing on two cylinders. You have breathed in the smell of stone and tar and oil and urine until they are as one in the soul of your skull. You have been invisible because the people you meet have refused to see you. You have sought in vain your own image on the signposts of other faces in the monotone of motion. You sit to escape the spite of the town without light. The bar is crowded with people as empty as yourself. A television set blares from a shelf in the corner. In the din you can make out two other strains, both of them vaguely musical. You think you recognise one of them but have forgotten what it is. You take out a newspaper; it contains nothing but pithy bites of knowing nonsense.

This is as much as we can hope for: That out of the din there may arise from time to time a song that will lift your heart a little. A voice comes to you out of the sonic blackness. A guitar that embraces the murk and cuts through it. For three minutes the song diverts you from the bedlam all around. It has, you fancy, something in it of the quality of water. Its sweetness seems to melt on the tongue of your soul. 'You don't know if it's fear or desire/Danger the drug that takes you higher/Head of Heaven/Fingers in the mire.' The sound of the guitar makes your body move in a different way. It has in it the life of the building, the laughter of angels, the spit of the Devil, the ripple of the Fionn Glas, the voice of the Goddess Echo, a little mystery, a little mischief, and the merest promise of the future. In this three minutes is contained the only self-recognition you have felt all day. You wash your face in the sound and finish your drink.

You walk back into the street, a little less afraid to die, but curiously, or perhaps not, a little more determined to go on living. You catch an eye and smile a greeting: 'He have a roundy head!'

CHAPTER TWENTY-THREE

The Horse with the Long Neck

It is to be our last meeting about the book. We have covered all the ground that we have been able to see and are having what policemen like to describe as a general conversation. The interrogation is over, the confession completed. The dark spark at the heart of U2 leans over and whispers conspiratorially, 'D'ya want to know what my biggest fear about the group is?' I look around. You talkin' to me? He's talking to me.

> Okay. I don't believe in evolution particularly. I know it exists and everything, but I don't pay as much heed to it as some people. You've heard of the horse with the long neck? Everyone thought they would find the horse with the long neck. But they never did. A hundred years now looking for the horse with the long neck. They have the giraffe, they have the horse. But they don't have the horse with the long neck. What they say is that there are efficient stops along the way of evolution. Basically that there is a horse out there with a long neck; but there wasn't enough of them for the chances of leaving behind a fossil.
>
> And that's what I'd be worried about. We don't want to be that horse with the long neck.
>
> So, you have the Beatles, the Stones, punk, and so on, and then you have some new thing. And we're in between there, but we're neither. That's the biggest fear. Because, ahem . . . there's a great freedom you get when you're a giraffe. It's all there for ya. It's great. You get all the food at the top of the tree. And your mates, the horses, are all down there in the Curragh involved in the horseracing. But *you* are the freak. *You* are this fucking horse with a long neck and small ears, and everyone's pointing at you. Beating you with a stick. You can't run the race and you can't get the food at the top of the tree.
>
> I'm happy with everything except that.

302

Acknowledgements

The author would like to extend heartfelt thanks to the following people who provided assistance of every conceivable kind in the writing of this book: Bono, Jackie Bennett, Sharon Blankson, Ivor Browne, Candida Bottacci, Dermot Bolger, Noel Barber, Billy Brown, Adam Clayton, Eamon Carr, Mike Cooley, Liam Carson, Jane Carr, Anne Cassin, A. Doody, Suzanne Doyle, Tim de Lisle, Kevin Davis, Marie Donnelly, Derek Dean, The Edge, Brian Eno, Gavin Friday, A. Gannon, Luke Gibbons, Kathy Gilfillan, Jackie Hayden, Seamus Heaney, Anne-Louise Kelly, Nick Kelly, Patrick Lynch, Greil Marcus, Larry Mullen, Paul McGuinness, John McHugh, Fintan O'Toole, Caroline Van Oosten de Boer, Smita Patel, Eileen Pearson, Bob Powell, M. Rocca, Sheila Roche, Niall Stokes, O. Tracey, Colm Tóibín, Anne Tannahill, Gwyneth Williams, Jonathan Williams.

The author and publisher gratefully acknowledge the following for the use of extracts from works quoted in this book: William Heinemann Ltd, Michelin House, 81 Fulham Road, London SWB 6BB, publishers of Neil Postman's *Amusing Ourselves to Death*; Random House UK Ltd, 20 Vauxhall Bridge Road, London SW1V 2SA, publishers of Don DeLillo's *Mao II*; Penguin Books, 27 Wrights Lane, London W8 5TZ, publishers of Greil Marcus's *Lipstick Traces – A Secret History of the 20th Century* and of his *Mystery Train*; Viking Books, 27 Wrights Lane, London W8 5TZ, publishers of Greil Marcus's *In the Fascist Bathroom*; Von B Press, PO Box 85336, 3508 AH Utrecht, The Netherlands, publishers of Caroline Van Oosten de Boer's *Gavin Friday: The Light and Dark*; Gill and Macmillan, Goldenbridge, Dublin 8, publishers of Tom Inglis's *The Moral Monopoly*; Pluto Press, 345 Archway Road, London N6 5AA, publishers of Franz Fanon's *Black Skin, White Masks*; Gill and Macmillan, Goldenbridge, Dublin 8, publishers of Luke Gibbons's essay, 'From Megalith to Megastore' in *Irish Studies, A General Introduction*; Penguin Books, 27 Wrights Lane, London W8 5TZ, publishers of Greil Marcus's *Dead Elvis*; *Studies*, 35 Lower Leeson St, Dublin 2, for permission to quote from Richard Kearney's essay on Seamus Heaney in *Studies 300th*; Wolfhound Press, 68 Mountjoy Square, Dublin 1, publishers of Seamus Heaney's essay in *Migrations*; Veritas Publications, 7–8 Lower Abbey St. Dublin 1, for permission to quote from Fr Martin Tierney's *The Church and New Religious Groups*; Hummingbird Productions, The Barracks, 76 Irishtown Road, Dublin 4, for permission to quote from Philip King's television series 'Bringing it all Back Home'; Gill and Macmillan, for permission to quote from *The Hidden Ireland* by Daniel Corkery; Penguin Books, 27 Wrights Lane, London W8 5TZ, publishers of the Penguin *Ulysses*, Introduction by Declan Kiberd; Polygram International Music Publishing for permission to quote from the lyric of The Cranberries' song, 'Dreams'; Harper Collins, 77–85 Fulham Palace Road, Hammersmith, London W6 8JB, publishers of *Music and the Mind*, by Anthony Storr; Tim de Lisle for permission to quote from his *Independent on Sunday* interview with Brian Eno; Manchester University Press, Oxford Road, Manchester, publishers of Jacques Attali's *Noises: The Political Economy of Music*; Black Rose Books, 340 Nagel Drive, Cheektowaga, New York 14225, USA, publishers of Noam Chomsky's *Language and Politics*; Faber and Faber, publishers of Seamus Heaney's poem 'The Diviner'; Wolfhound Press, 68 Mountjoy Square, Dublin 1, publishers of *The Irish Mind* (ed. Richard Kearney) and *Visions of Europe* (ed. Richard Kearney).

Special thanks to Dermot Bolger for permission to quote from his novel *The Journey Home* and also from an essay by June Considine published in *Invisible Dublin*, Raven Arts Press, PO Box 1430, Finglas, Dublin 11; also to *Hot Press*, 13 Trinity Street, Dublin 2 for permission to quote from Virgin Prunes interview by Peter Owens and *October* review by Neil McCormick; to Patrick Lynch, editor of U2 fanzine *Cyberspace*, for general assistance and advice. Thanks to Debbie Williams and David Carroll at Polygram International Music Publishing for permission to quote from lyrics of U2 songs.

Every effort has been made to locate the copyright holders of material used in this book and to obtain permissions for same.

Lyrics Permissions

'The Wanderer' (Hewson/Evans/Clayton/Mullen)
© 1993 Blue Mountain Music Ltd for the United Kingdom
  PolyGram International Music Publishing BV for the World
  excluding UK/Eire/Japan

'One Tree Hill' (Hewson/Evans/Clayton/Mullen)
© 1987 Blue Mountain Music Ltd for the United Kingdom
  PolyGram International Music Publishing BV for the World
  excluding UK/Eire/Japan

Acknowledgements

'A Day Without Me' (Hewson/Evans/Clayton/Mullen)
© 1981 Blue Mountain Music Ltd for the United Kingdom
PolyGram International Music Publishing BV for the World
excluding UK/Eire/Japan

'Twilight' (Hewson/Evans/Clayton/Mullen)
© 1981 Blue Mountain Music Ltd for the United Kingdom
PolyGram International Music Publishing BV for the World
excluding UK/Eire/Japan

'Gloria' (Hewson/Evans/Clayton/Mullen)
© 1981 Blue Mountain Music Ltd for the United Kingdom
PolyGram International Music Publishing BV for the World
excluding UK/Eire/Japan

'In The Name Of The Father' (Hewson/Friday/Roycroft)
© 1993 Blue Mountain Music Ltd for the United Kingdom
PolyGram International Music Publishing BV for the World
excluding UK/Eire/Japan

'Bullet The Blue Sky' (Hewson/Evans/Clayton/Mullen)
© 1987 Blue Mountain Music Ltd for the United Kingdom
PolyGram International Music Publishing BV for the World
excluding UK/Eire/Japan

'A Sort of Homecoming' (Hewson/Evans/Clayton/Mullen)
© 1984 Blue Mountain Music Ltd for the United Kingdom
PolyGram International Music Publishing BV for the World
excluding UK/Eire/Japan

'Sunday Bloody Sunday' (Hewson/Evans/Clayton/Mullen)
© 1983 Blue Mountain Music Ltd for the United Kingdom
PolyGram International Music Publishing BV for the World
excluding UK/Eire/Japan

'Drowning Man' (Hewson/Evans/Clayton/Mullen)
© 1983 Blue Mountain Music Ltd for the United Kingdom
PolyGram International Music Publishing BV for the World
excluding UK/Eire/Japan